Me & My Brothers

Volume 1

Hari Tokeino

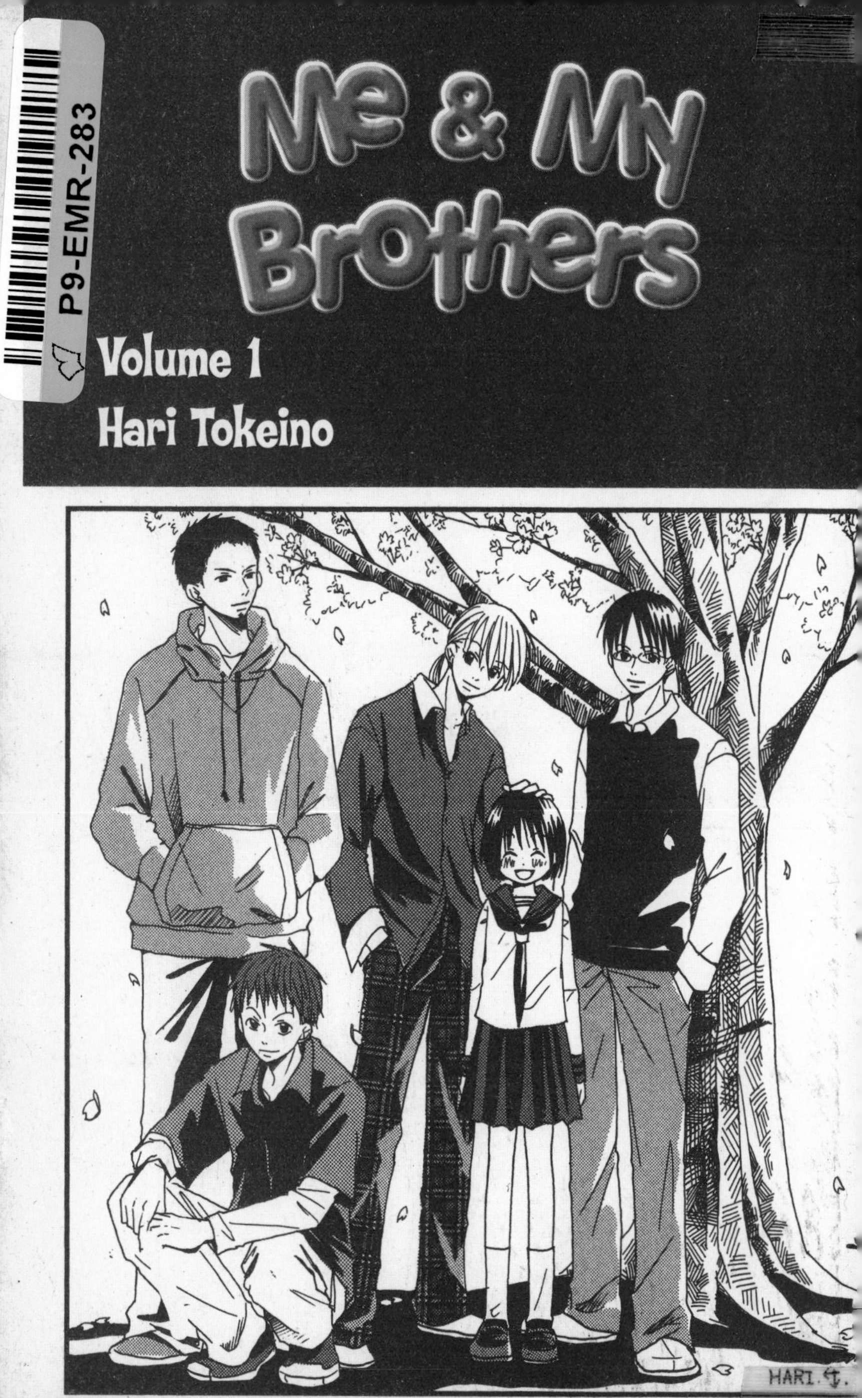

Me & My Brothers Volume 1
Created by Hari Tokeino

Translation - Haruko Furukawa
English Adaptation - Jeffrey Reeves
Retouch and Lettering - Star Print Brokers
Production Artist - Michael Paolilli
Graphic Designer - Christopher Tjalsma

Editor - Hyun Joo Kim
Digital Imaging Manager - Chris Buford
Pre-Production Supervisor - Erika Terriquez
Art Director - Anne Marie Horne
Production Manager - Elisabeth Brizzi
Managing Editor - Vy Nguyen
VP of Production - Ron Klamert
Editor-in-Chief - Rob Tokar
Publisher - Mike Kiley
President and C.O.O. - John Parker
C.E.O. and Chief Creative Officer - Stuart Levy

A **TOKYOPOP** Manga

TOKYOPOP and 　 are trademarks or registered trademarks of TOKYOPOP Inc.

TOKYOPOP Inc.
5900 Wilshire Blvd. Suite 2000
Los Angeles, CA 90036

E-mail: info@TOKYOPOP.com
Come visit us online at www.TOKYOPOP.com

ISBN: 978-1-4278-0071-8

First TOKYOPOP printing: July 2007
10 9 8 7 6 5 4 3 2 1
Printed in the USA

Me & My Brothers

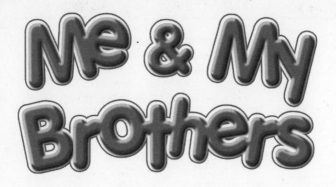

Volume 1

Hari Tokeino

TOKYOPOP®

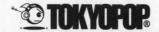

HAMBURG // LONDON // LOS ANGELES // TOKYO

Contents

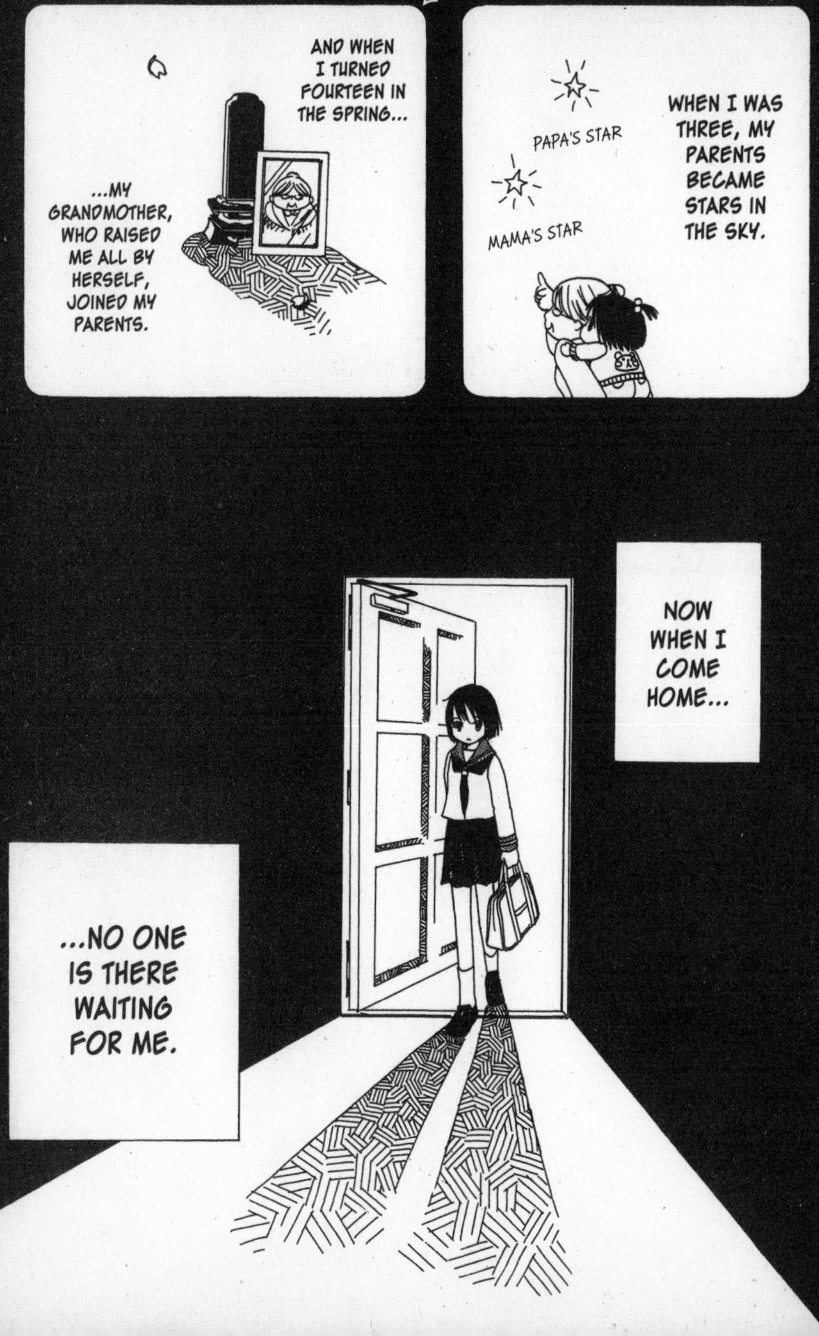
WHEN I WAS THREE, MY PARENTS BECAME STARS IN THE SKY.
PAPA'S STAR
MAMA'S STAR
AND WHEN I TURNED FOURTEEN IN THE SPRING...
...MY GRANDMOTHER, WHO RAISED ME ALL BY HERSELF, JOINED MY PARENTS.
NOW WHEN I COME HOME...
...NO ONE IS THERE WAITING FOR ME.

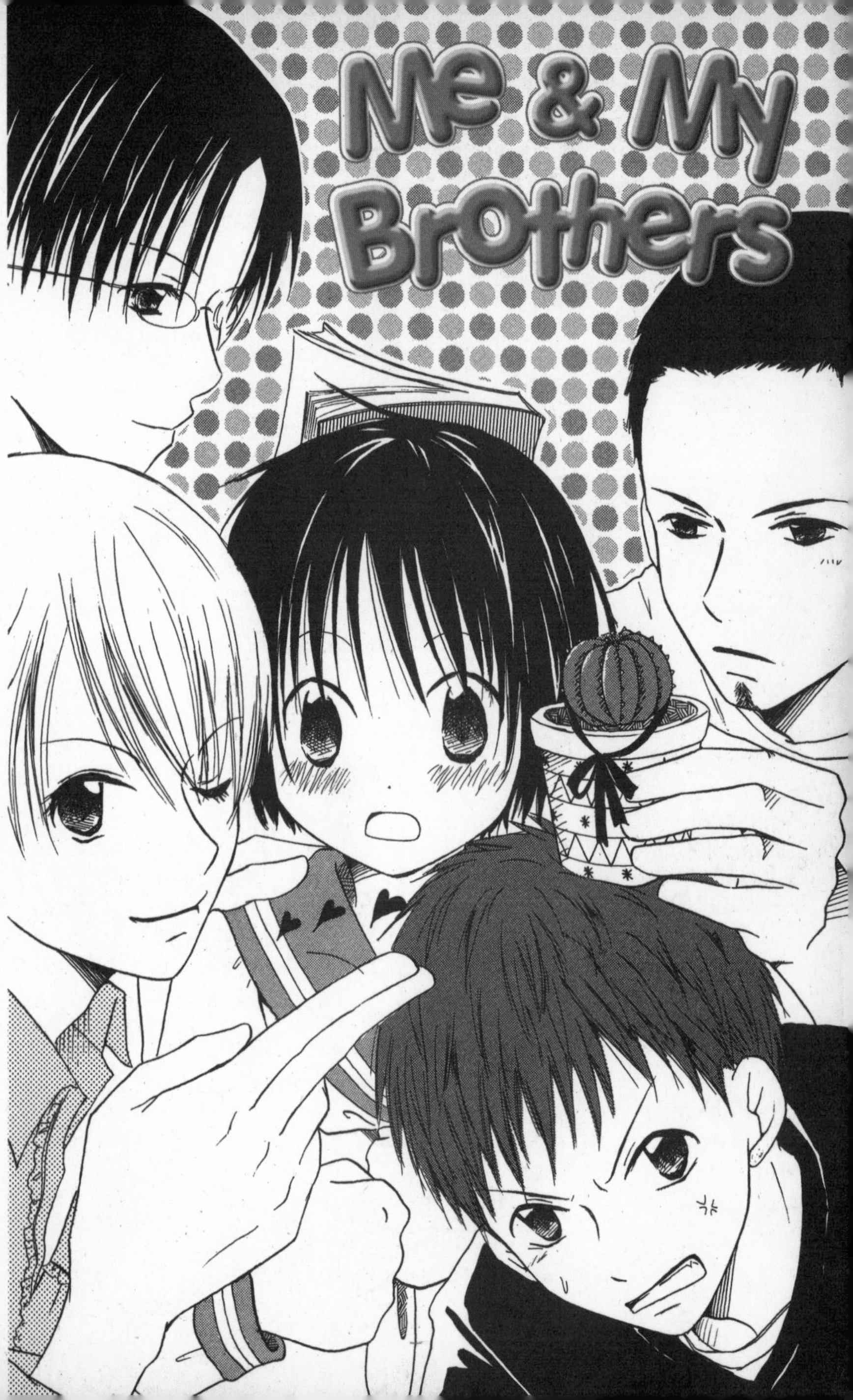
Me & My Brothers

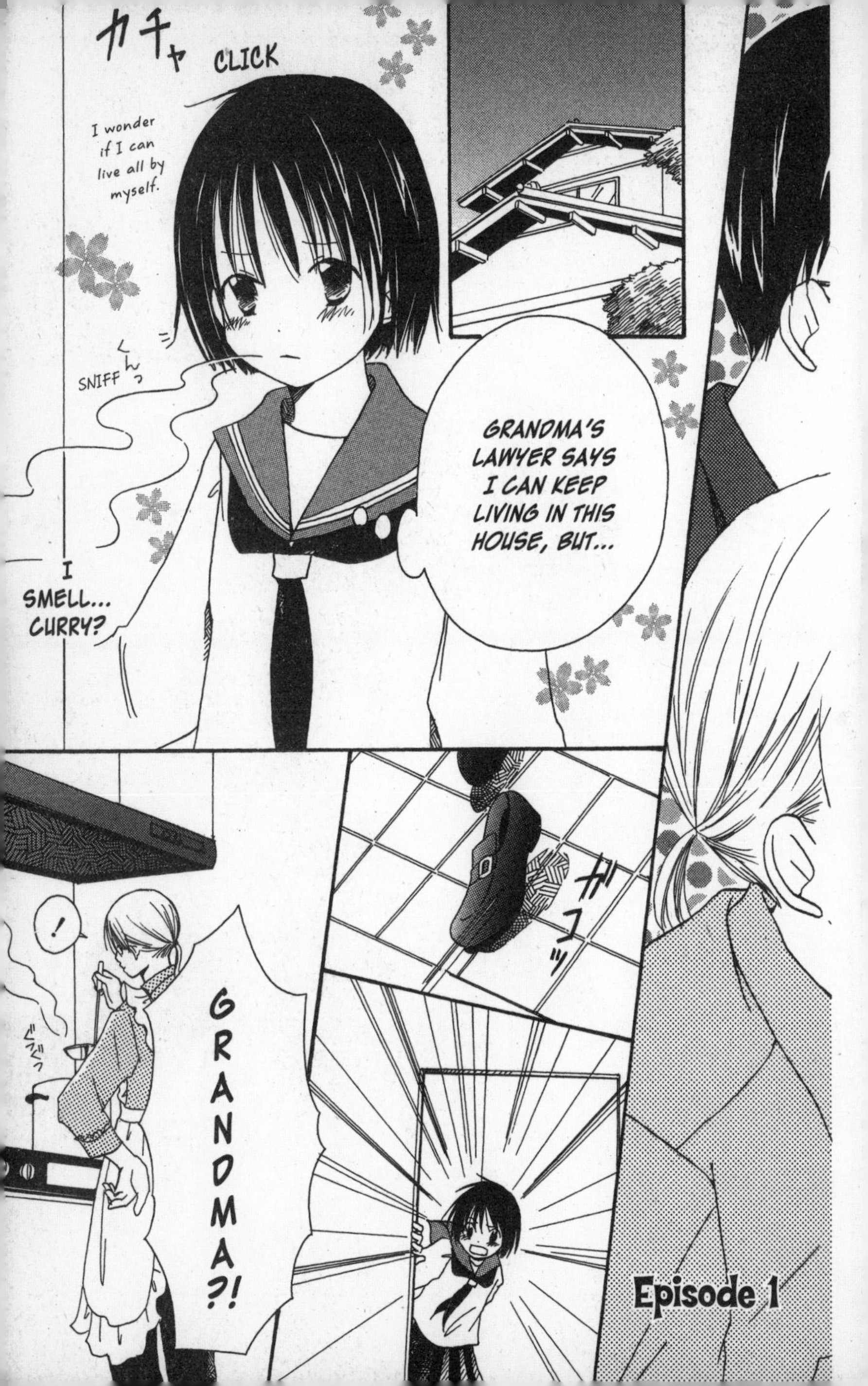
Episode 1
カチャ
CLICK
GRANDMA'S LAWYER SAYS I CAN KEEP LIVING IN THIS HOUSE, BUT...
I wonder if I can live all by myself.
くんっ
SNIFF
I SMELL... CURRY?
ガコッ
!
GRANDMA?!
ぐつぐつ

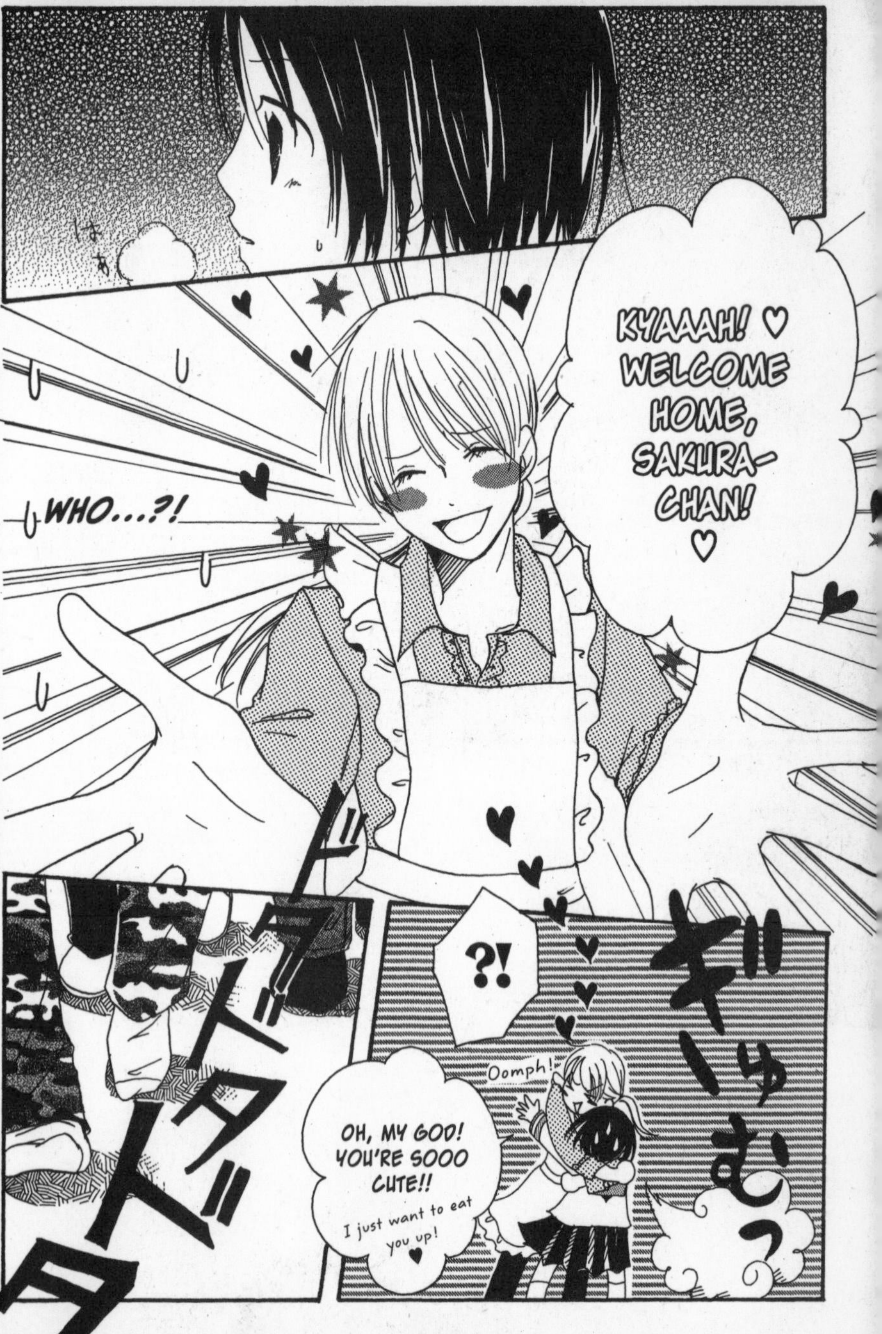
はあ
KYAAAH! ♥ WELCOME HOME, SAKURA-CHAN! ♥
WHO...?!
?!
ぎゅむっ
Oomph!
OH, MY GOD! YOU'RE SOOO CUTE!!
I just want to eat you up! ♥
ドタドタドタ

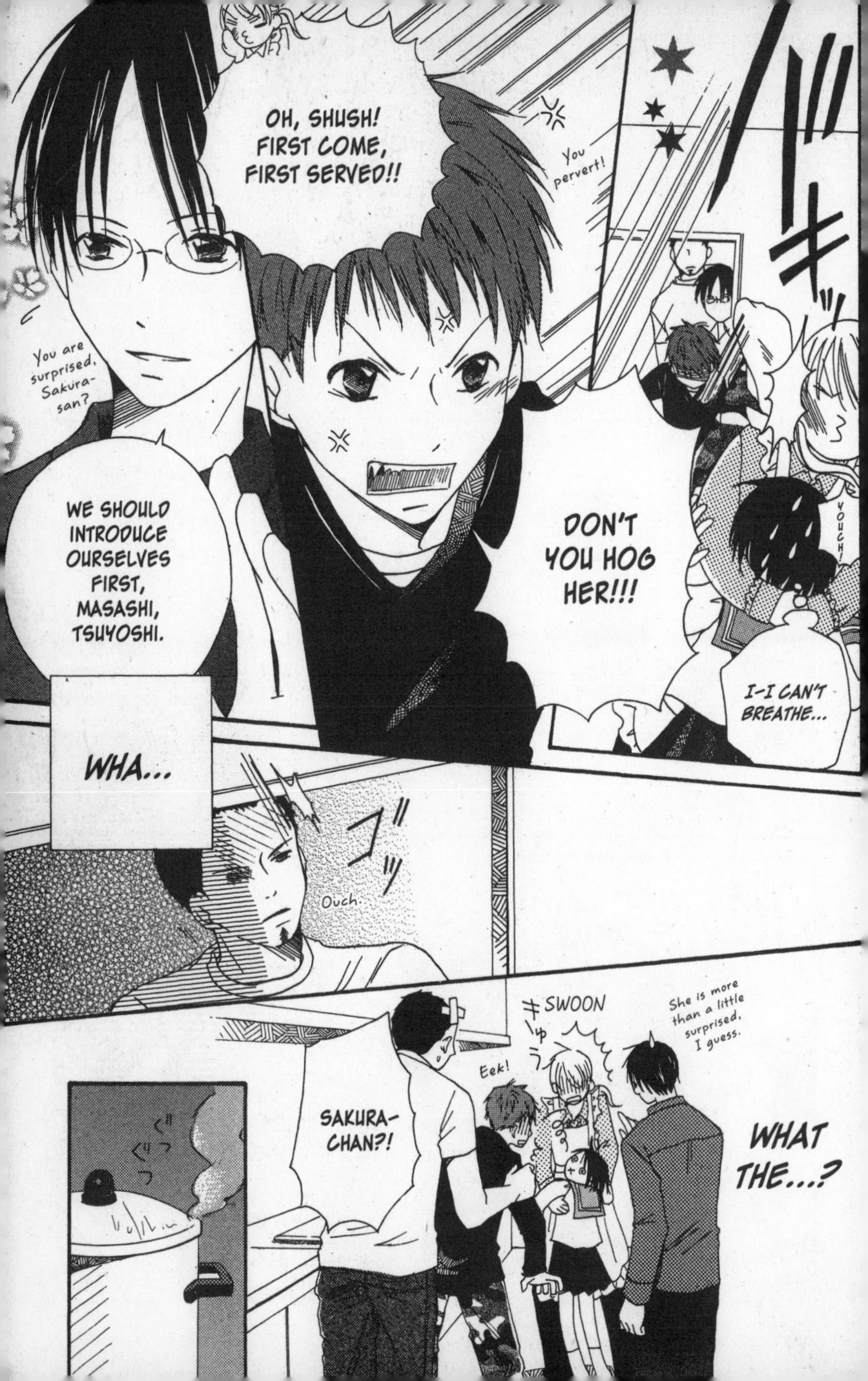
You pervert!
DON'T YOU HOG HER!!!
YOUCH!
I-I CAN'T BREATHE...
OH, SHUSH! FIRST COME, FIRST SERVED!!
You are surprised, Sakura-san?
WE SHOULD INTRODUCE OURSELVES FIRST, MASASHI, TSUYOSHI.
WHA...
Ouch.
She is more than a little surprised, I guess.
WHAT THE...?
SWOON
Eek!
SAKURA-CHAN?!

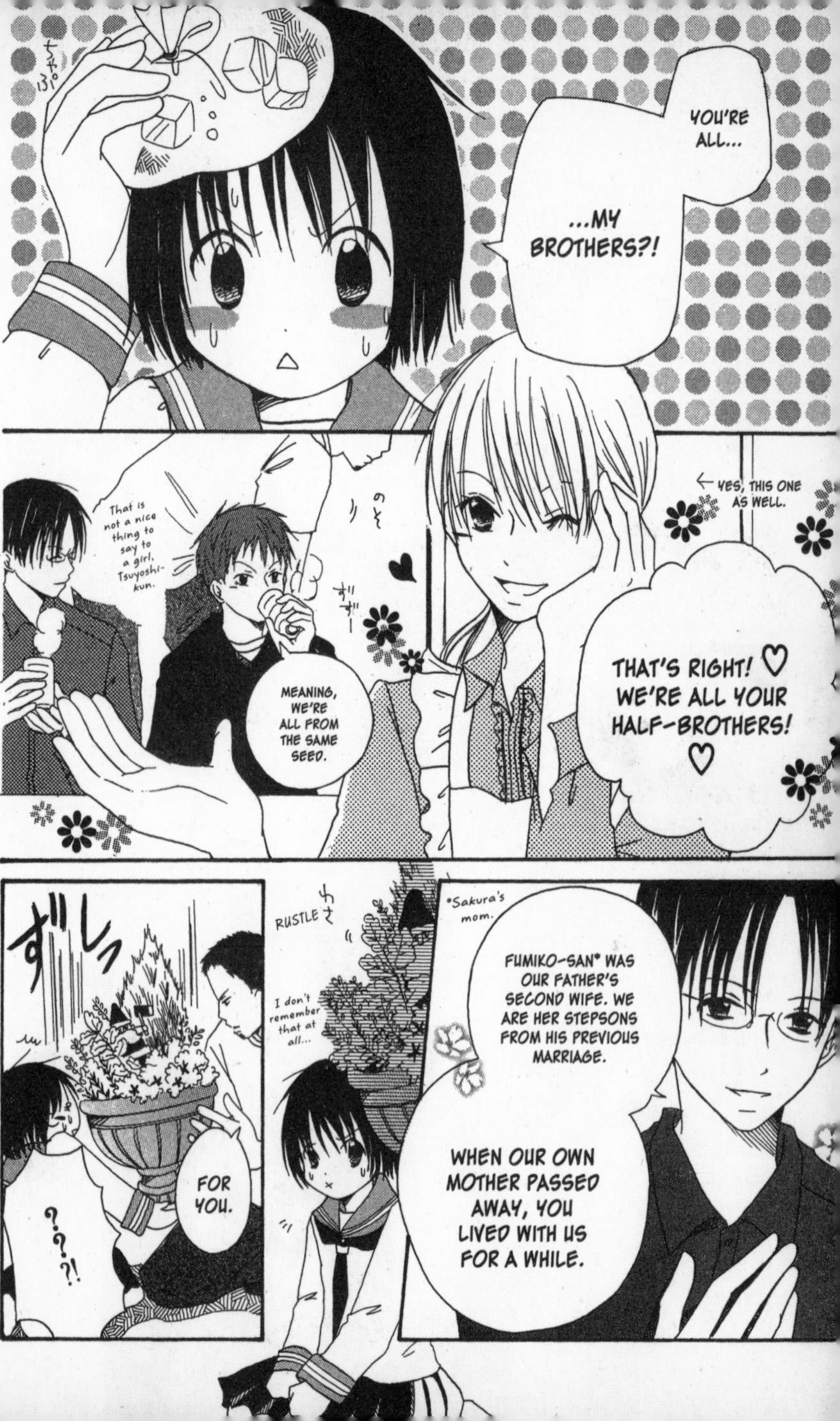
YOU'RE ALL...
...MY BROTHERS?!
← YES, THIS ONE AS WELL.
THAT'S RIGHT! ♡ WE'RE ALL YOUR HALF-BROTHERS! ♡
MEANING, WE'RE ALL FROM THE SAME SEED.
That is not a nice thing to say to a girl, Tsuyoshi-kun.
*Sakura's mom.
FUMIKO-SAN* WAS OUR FATHER'S SECOND WIFE. WE ARE HER STEPSONS FROM HIS PREVIOUS MARRIAGE.
WHEN OUR OWN MOTHER PASSED AWAY, YOU LIVED WITH US FOR A WHILE.
RUSTLE
I don't remember that at all...
FOR YOU.
?.?.?!

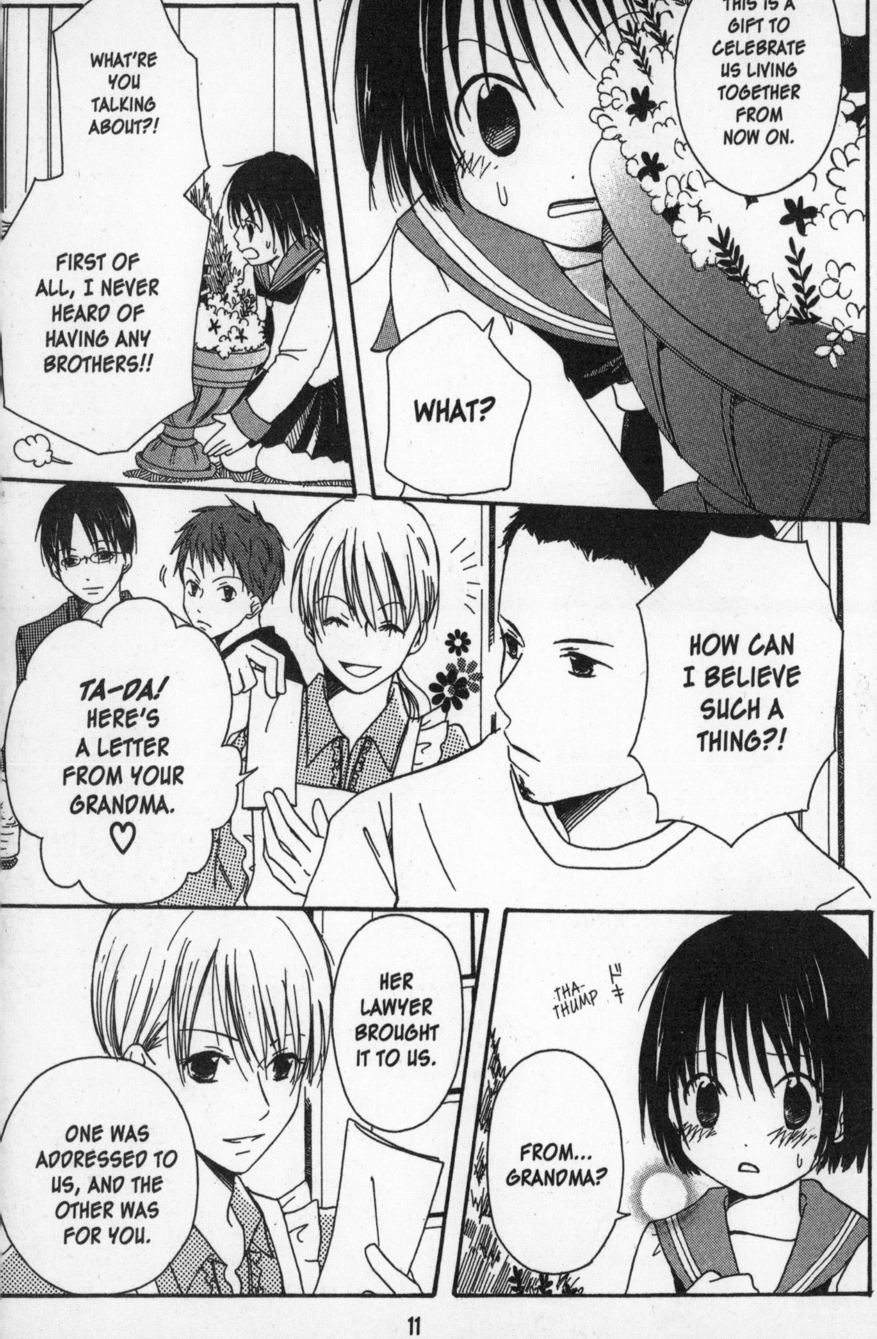
THIS IS A GIFT TO CELEBRATE US LIVING TOGETHER FROM NOW ON.
WHAT?
WHAT'RE YOU TALKING ABOUT?!
FIRST OF ALL, I NEVER HEARD OF HAVING ANY BROTHERS!!
HOW CAN I BELIEVE SUCH A THING?!
TA-DA! HERE'S A LETTER FROM YOUR GRANDMA. ♡
THA-THUMP
ドキ
FROM... GRANDMA?
HER LAWYER BROUGHT IT TO US.
ONE WAS ADDRESSED TO US, AND THE OTHER WAS FOR YOU.

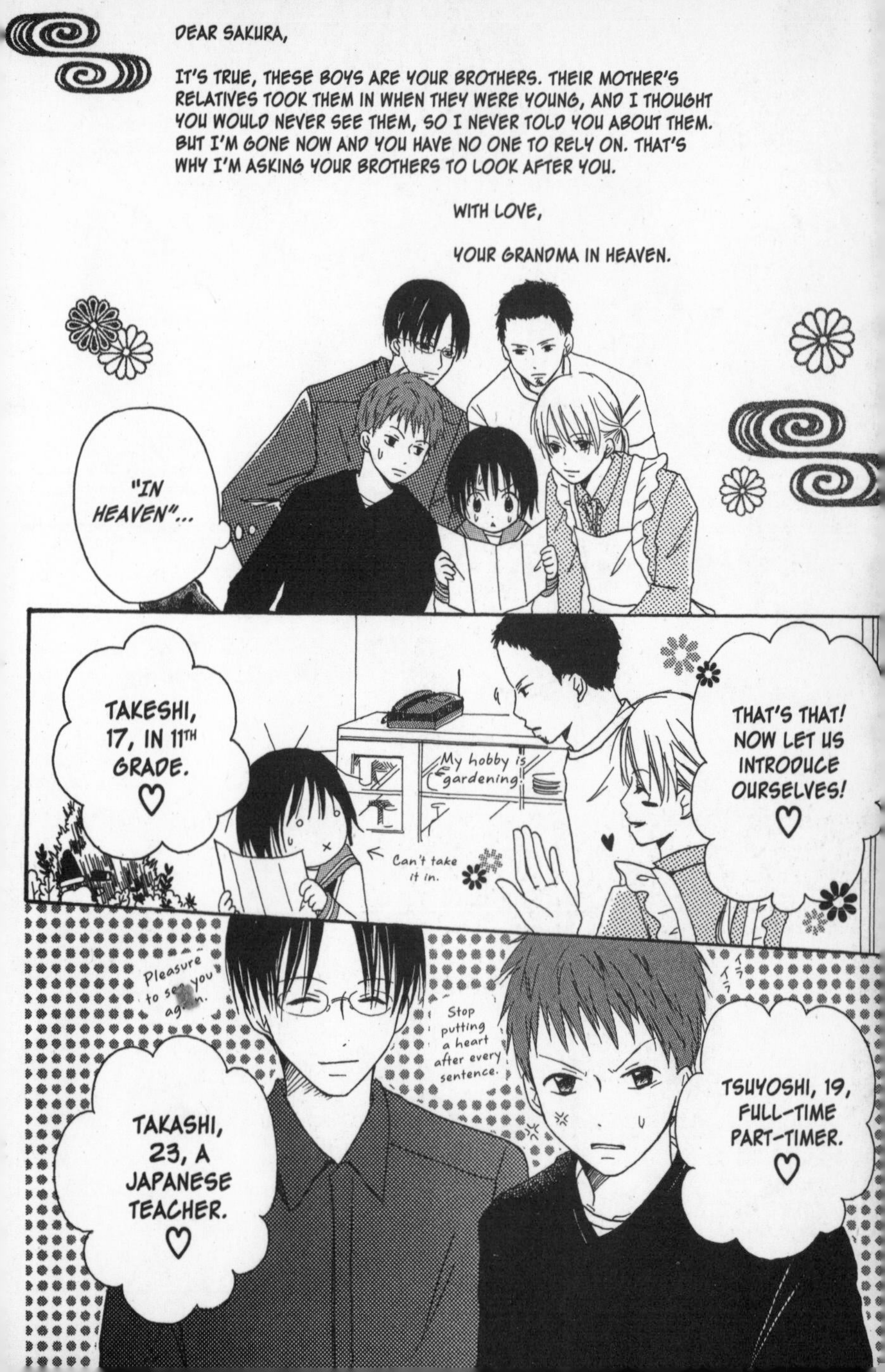
DEAR SAKURA,
IT'S TRUE, THESE BOYS ARE YOUR BROTHERS. THEIR MOTHER'S RELATIVES TOOK THEM IN WHEN THEY WERE YOUNG, AND I THOUGHT YOU WOULD NEVER SEE THEM, SO I NEVER TOLD YOU ABOUT THEM. BUT I'M GONE NOW AND YOU HAVE NO ONE TO RELY ON. THAT'S WHY I'M ASKING YOUR BROTHERS TO LOOK AFTER YOU.
WITH LOVE,
YOUR GRANDMA IN HEAVEN.
"IN HEAVEN"...
THAT'S THAT! NOW LET US INTRODUCE OURSELVES! ♡
My hobby is gardening.
Can't take it in.
TAKESHI, 17, IN 11TH GRADE. ♡
TSUYOSHI, 19, FULL-TIME PART-TIMER. ♡
Stop putting a heart after every sentence.
Pleasure to see you again.
TAKASHI, 23, A JAPANESE TEACHER. ♡

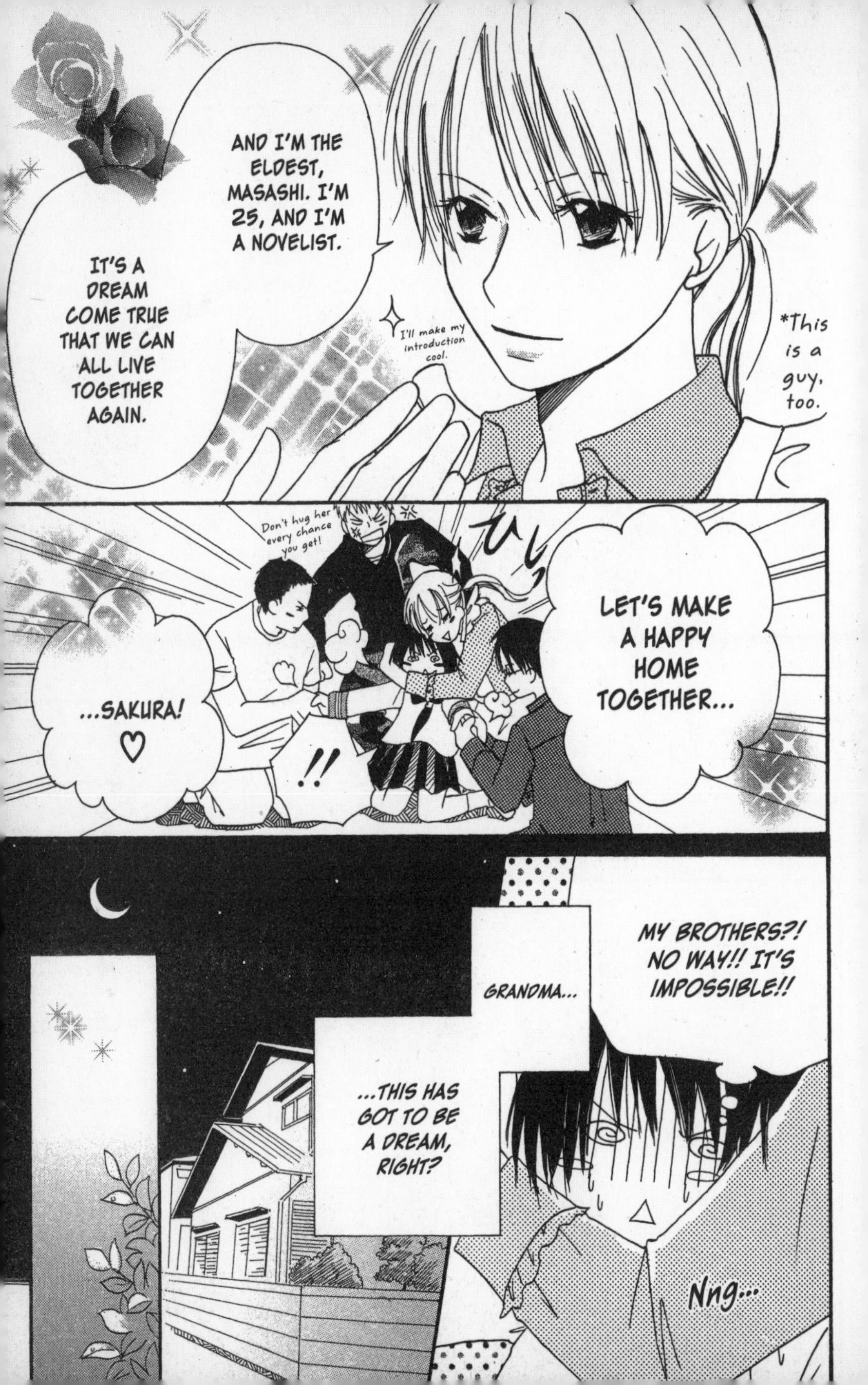
AND I'M THE ELDEST, MASASHI. I'M 25, AND I'M A NOVELIST.
I'll make my introduction cool.
*This is a guy, too.
IT'S A DREAM COME TRUE THAT WE CAN ALL LIVE TOGETHER AGAIN.
LET'S MAKE A HAPPY HOME TOGETHER...
Don't hug her every chance you get!
...SAKURA! ♡
!!
MY BROTHERS?! NO WAY!! IT'S IMPOSSIBLE!!
GRANDMA...
...THIS HAS GOT TO BE A DREAM, RIGHT?
Nng...

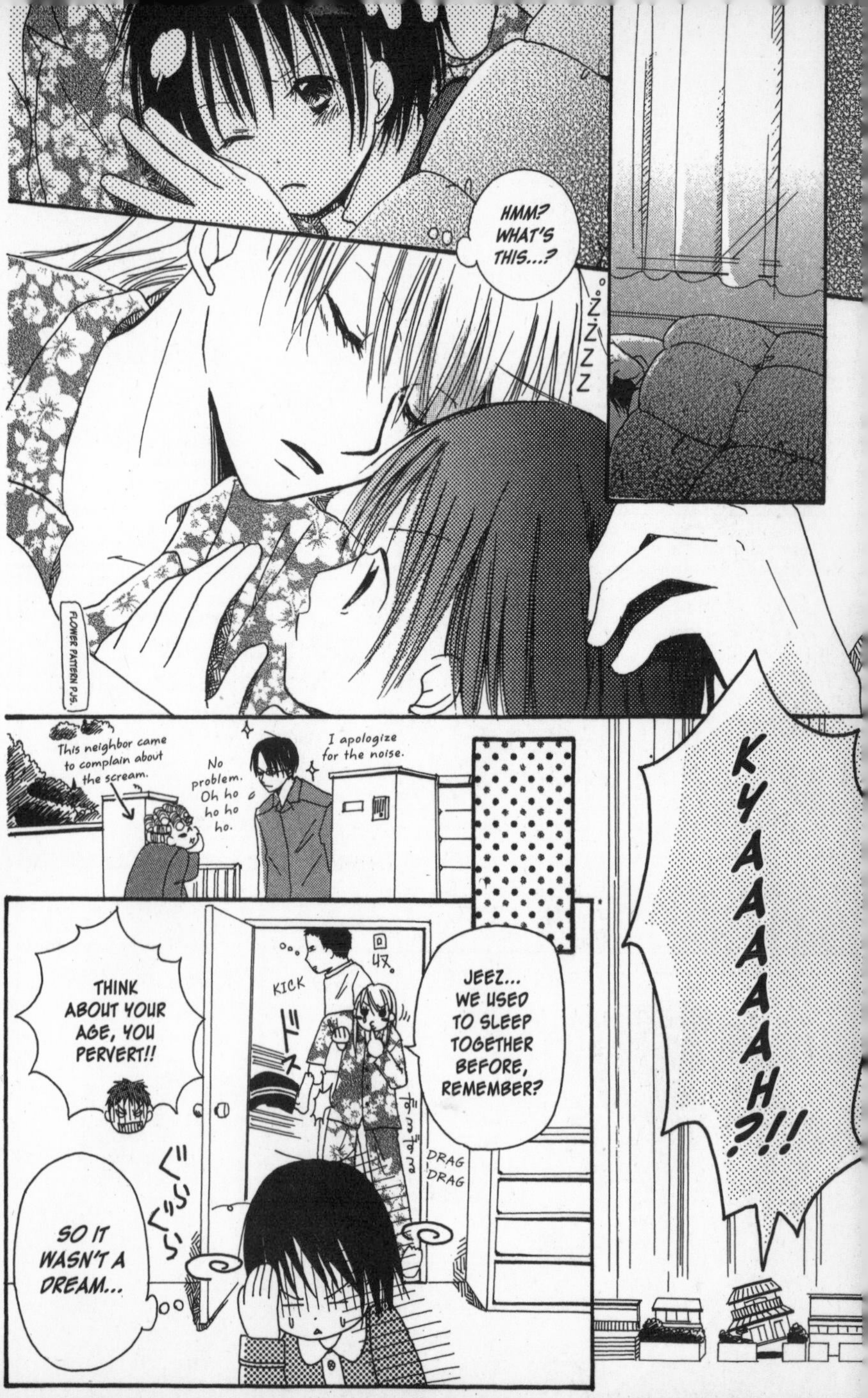
ZZZ
HMM? WHAT'S THIS...?
FLOWER PATTERN PJS.
KYAAAAAAH?!!
I apologize for the noise.
No problem. Oh ho ho ho ho.
This neighbor came to complain about the scream.
JEEZ... WE USED TO SLEEP TOGETHER BEFORE, REMEMBER?
KICK
DRAG DRAG
THINK ABOUT YOUR AGE, YOU PERVERT!!
SO IT WASN'T A DREAM...

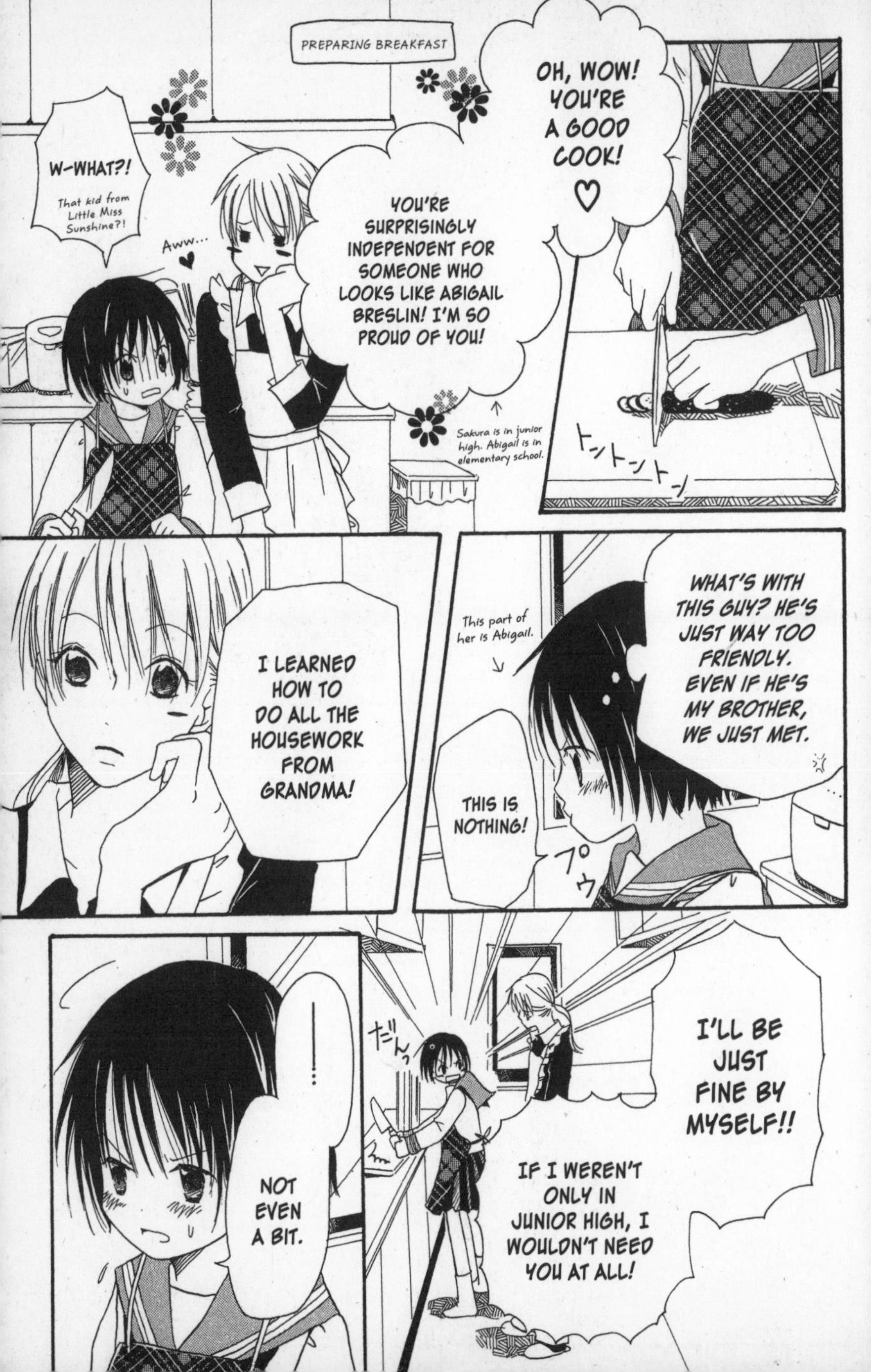
OH, WOW! YOU'RE A GOOD COOK! ♥
トントントン
PREPARING BREAKFAST
YOU'RE SURPRISINGLY INDEPENDENT FOR SOMEONE WHO LOOKS LIKE ABIGAIL BRESLIN! I'M SO PROUD OF YOU!
Sakura is in junior high. Abigail is in elementary school.
W-WHAT?!
That kid from Little Miss Sunshine?!
Aww... ♥
WHAT'S WITH THIS GUY? HE'S JUST WAY TOO FRIENDLY. EVEN IF HE'S MY BROTHER, WE JUST MET.
This part of her is Abigail.
THIS IS NOTHING!
プゥ
I LEARNED HOW TO DO ALL THE HOUSEWORK FROM GRANDMA!
I'LL BE JUST FINE BY MYSELF!!
だんっ
IF I WEREN'T ONLY IN JUNIOR HIGH, I WOULDN'T NEED YOU AT ALL!
……
NOT EVEN A BIT.

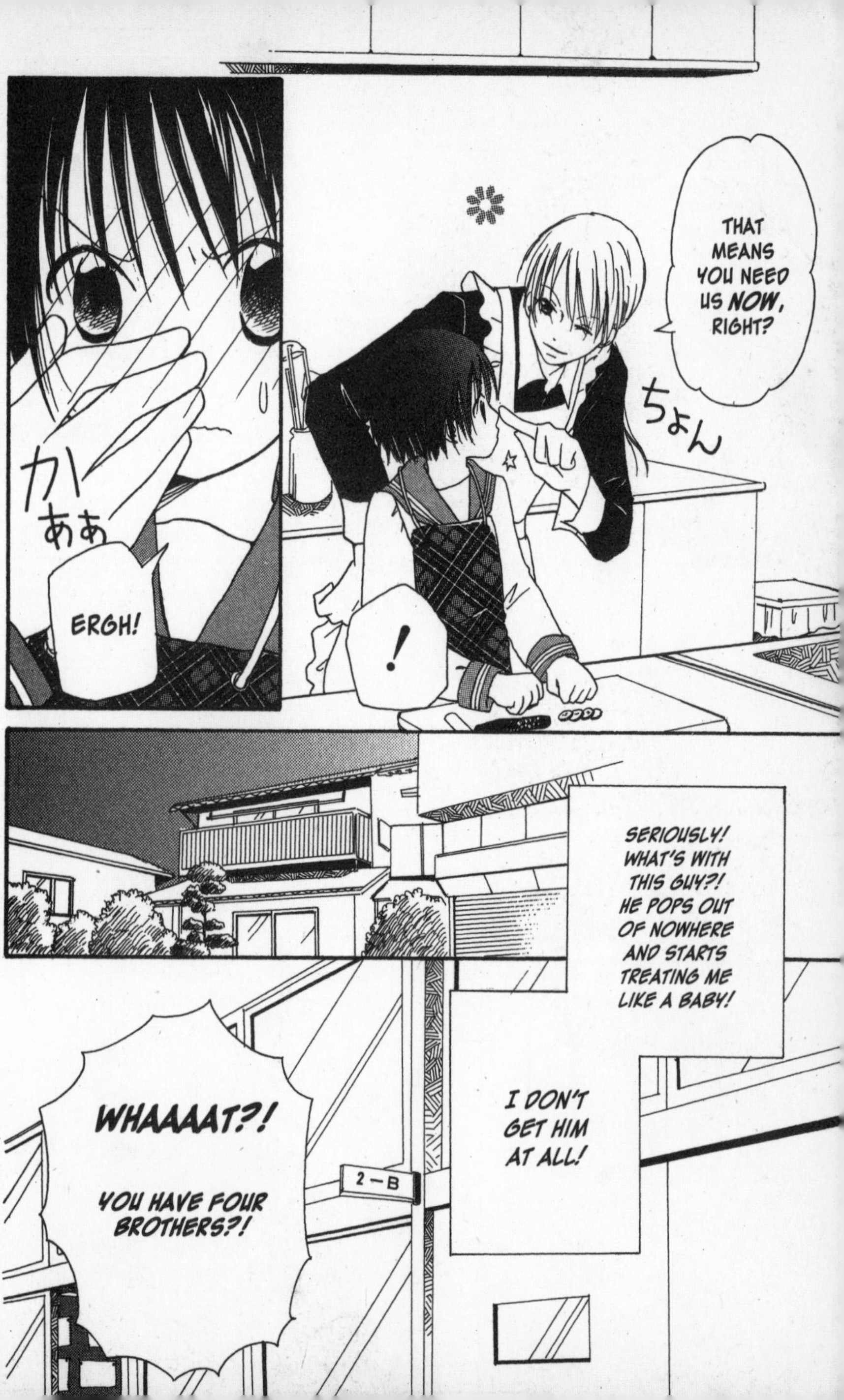
THAT MEANS YOU NEED US NOW, RIGHT?
ちょん
!
カああ
ERGH!
SERIOUSLY! WHAT'S WITH THIS GUY?! HE POPS OUT OF NOWHERE AND STARTS TREATING ME LIKE A BABY!
I DON'T GET HIM AT ALL!
2—B
WHAAAAT?!
YOU HAVE FOUR BROTHERS?!

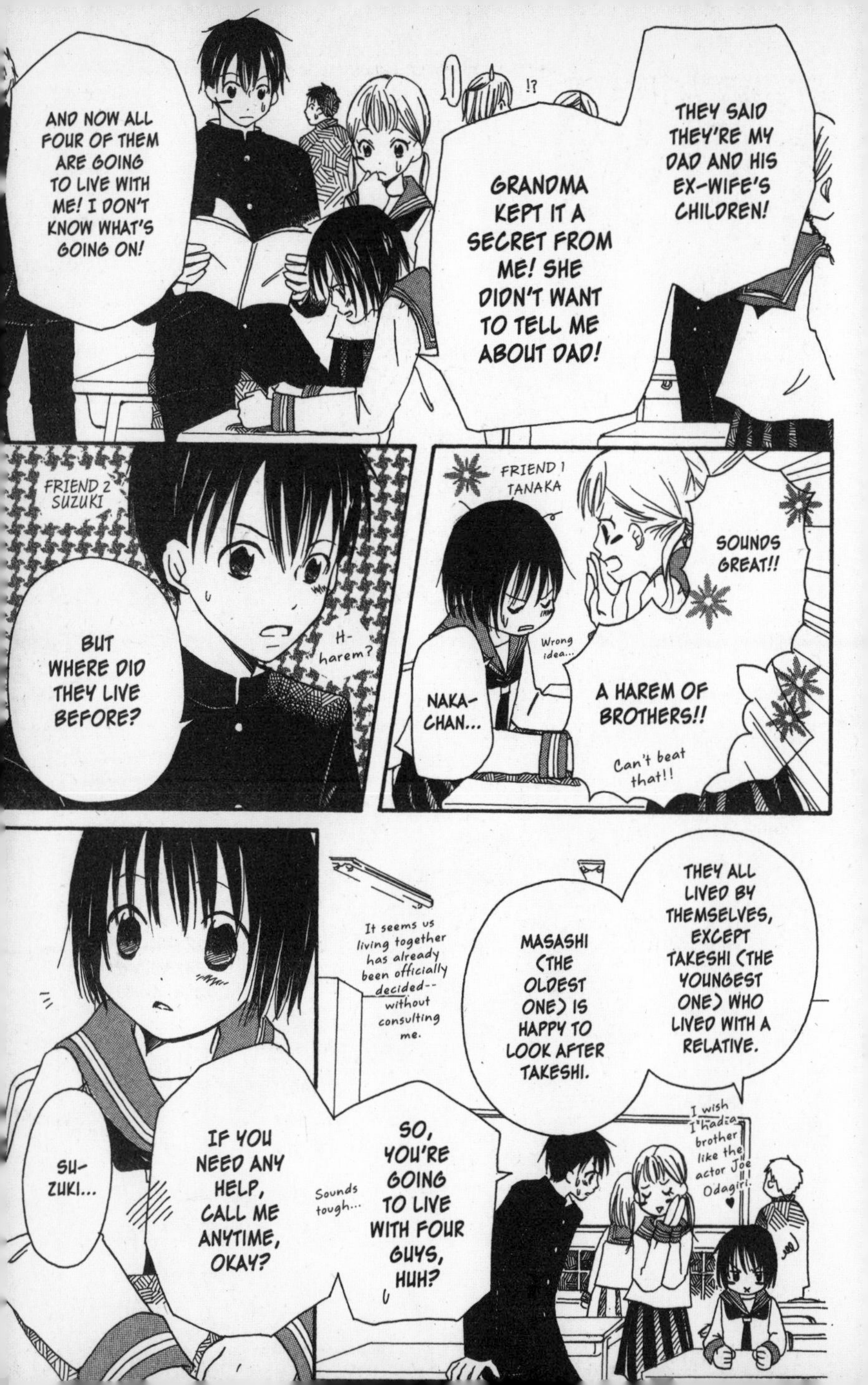
!
!?
THEY SAID THEY'RE MY DAD AND HIS EX-WIFE'S CHILDREN!
GRANDMA KEPT IT A SECRET FROM ME! SHE DIDN'T WANT TO TELL ME ABOUT DAD!
AND NOW ALL FOUR OF THEM ARE GOING TO LIVE WITH ME! I DON'T KNOW WHAT'S GOING ON!
FRIEND 1 TANAKA
SOUNDS GREAT!!
A HAREM OF BROTHERS!!
Can't beat that!!
Wrong idea...
NAKA-CHAN...
FRIEND 2 SUZUKI
H-harem?
BUT WHERE DID THEY LIVE BEFORE?
THEY ALL LIVED BY THEMSELVES, EXCEPT TAKESHI (THE YOUNGEST ONE) WHO LIVED WITH A RELATIVE.
MASASHI (THE OLDEST ONE) IS HAPPY TO LOOK AFTER TAKESHI.
I wish I had a brother like the actor Joe Odagiri!♥
It seems us living together has already been officially decided--without consulting me.
SO, YOU'RE GOING TO LIVE WITH FOUR GUYS, HUH?
Sounds tough...
IF YOU NEED ANY HELP, CALL ME ANYTIME, OKAY?
SU-ZUKI...

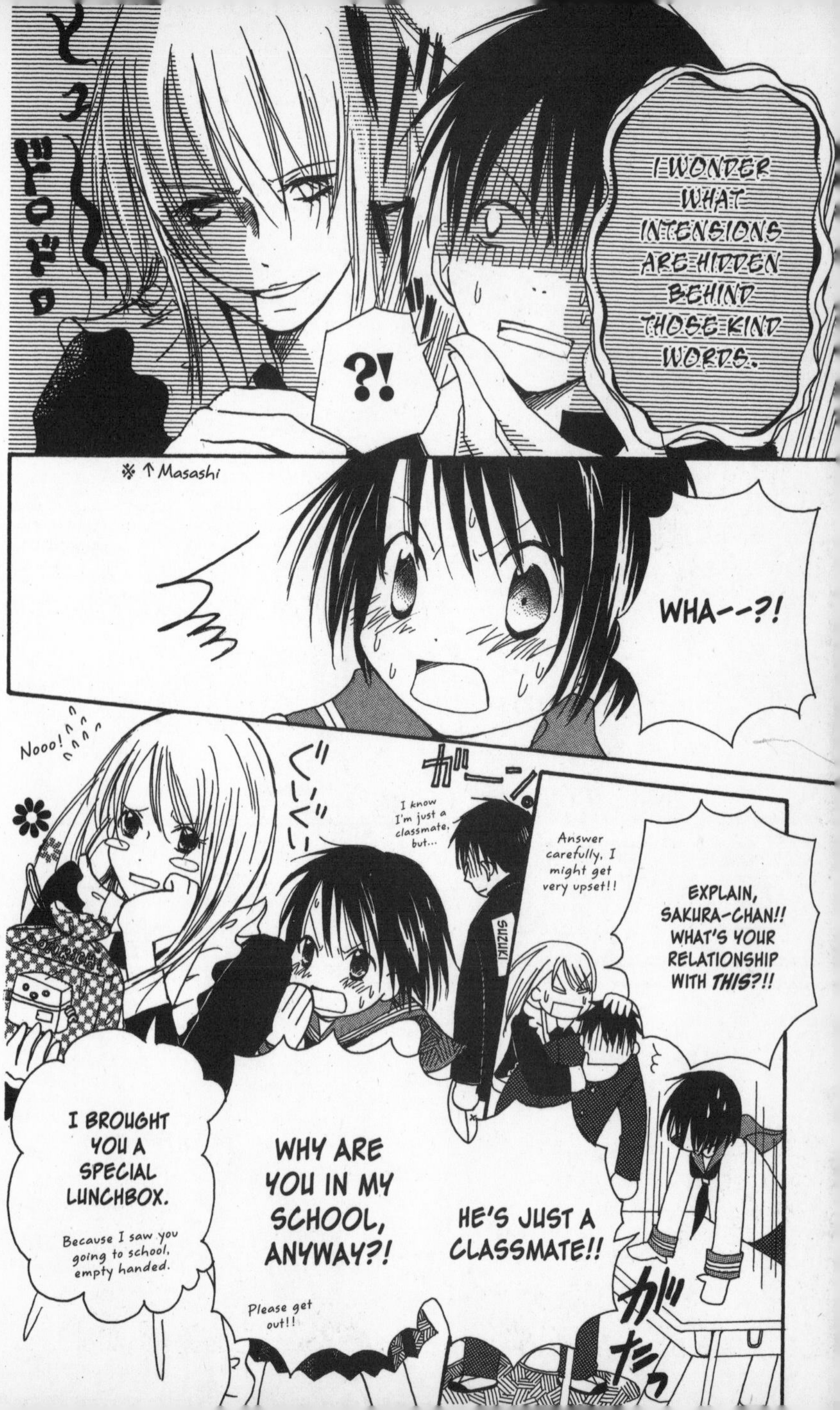
I WONDER WHAT INTENSIONS ARE HIDDEN BEHIND THOSE KIND WORDS.
?!
WHA--?!
※↑Masashi
EXPLAIN, SAKURA-CHAN!! WHAT'S YOUR RELATIONSHIP WITH *THIS?!!*
Answer carefully, I might get very upset!!
I know I'm just a classmate, but...
SUZUKI
HE'S JUST A CLASSMATE!!
WHY ARE YOU IN MY SCHOOL, ANYWAY?!
Please get out!!
I BROUGHT YOU A SPECIAL LUNCHBOX.
Because I saw you going to school, empty handed.
Nooo!

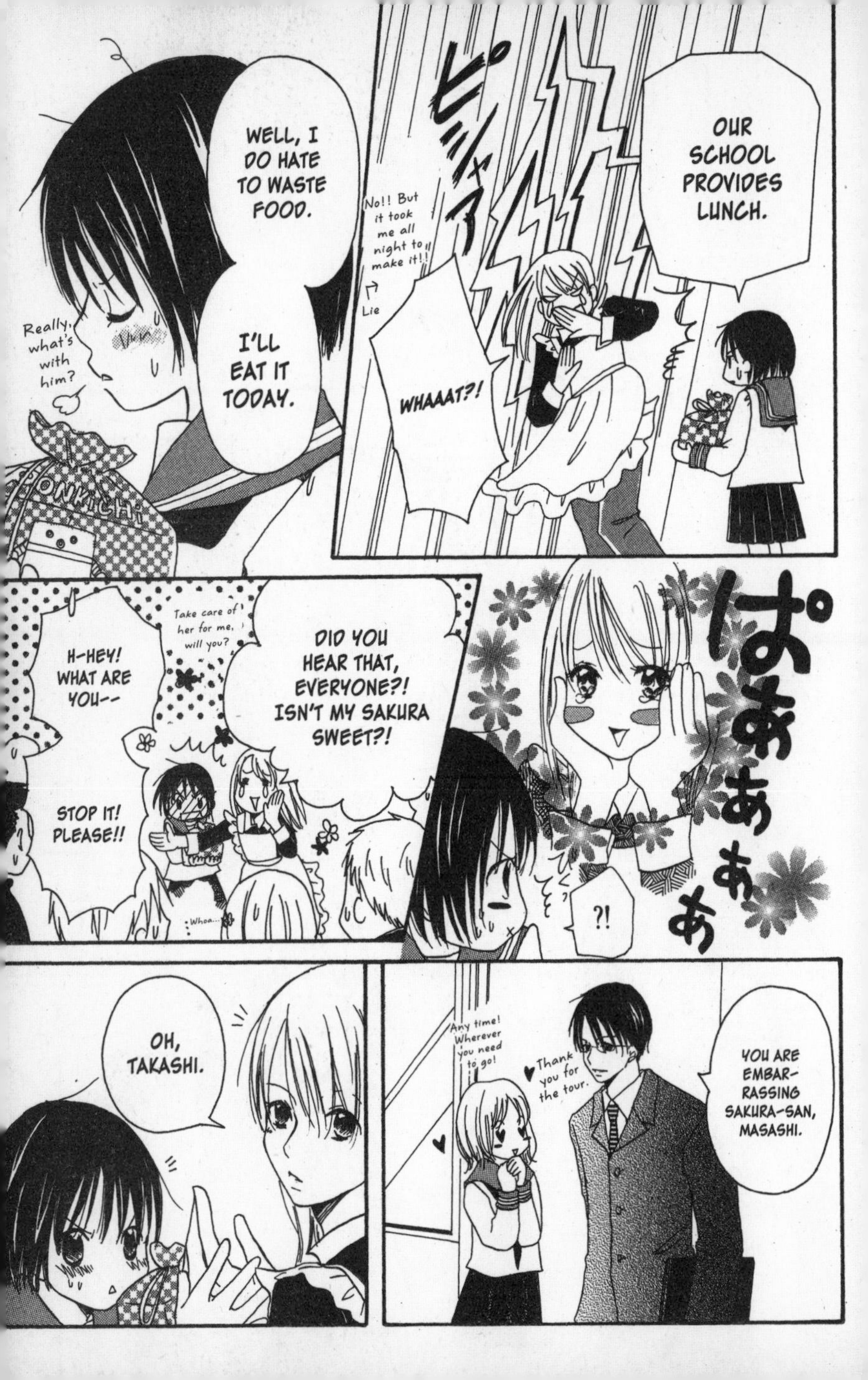
OUR SCHOOL PROVIDES LUNCH.
ピシャア
WHAAAT?!
No!! But it took me all night to make it!!
Lie
WELL, I DO HATE TO WASTE FOOD.
I'LL EAT IT TODAY.
Really, what's with him?
ONKiCHi
ぱあああ
?!
DID YOU HEAR THAT, EVERYONE?! ISN'T MY SAKURA SWEET?!
Take care of her for me, will you?
H-HEY! WHAT ARE YOU--
STOP IT! PLEASE!!
Whoa...
YOU ARE EMBARRASSING SAKURA-SAN, MASASHI.
Thank you for the tour.
Any time! Wherever you need to go!
OH, TAKASHI.

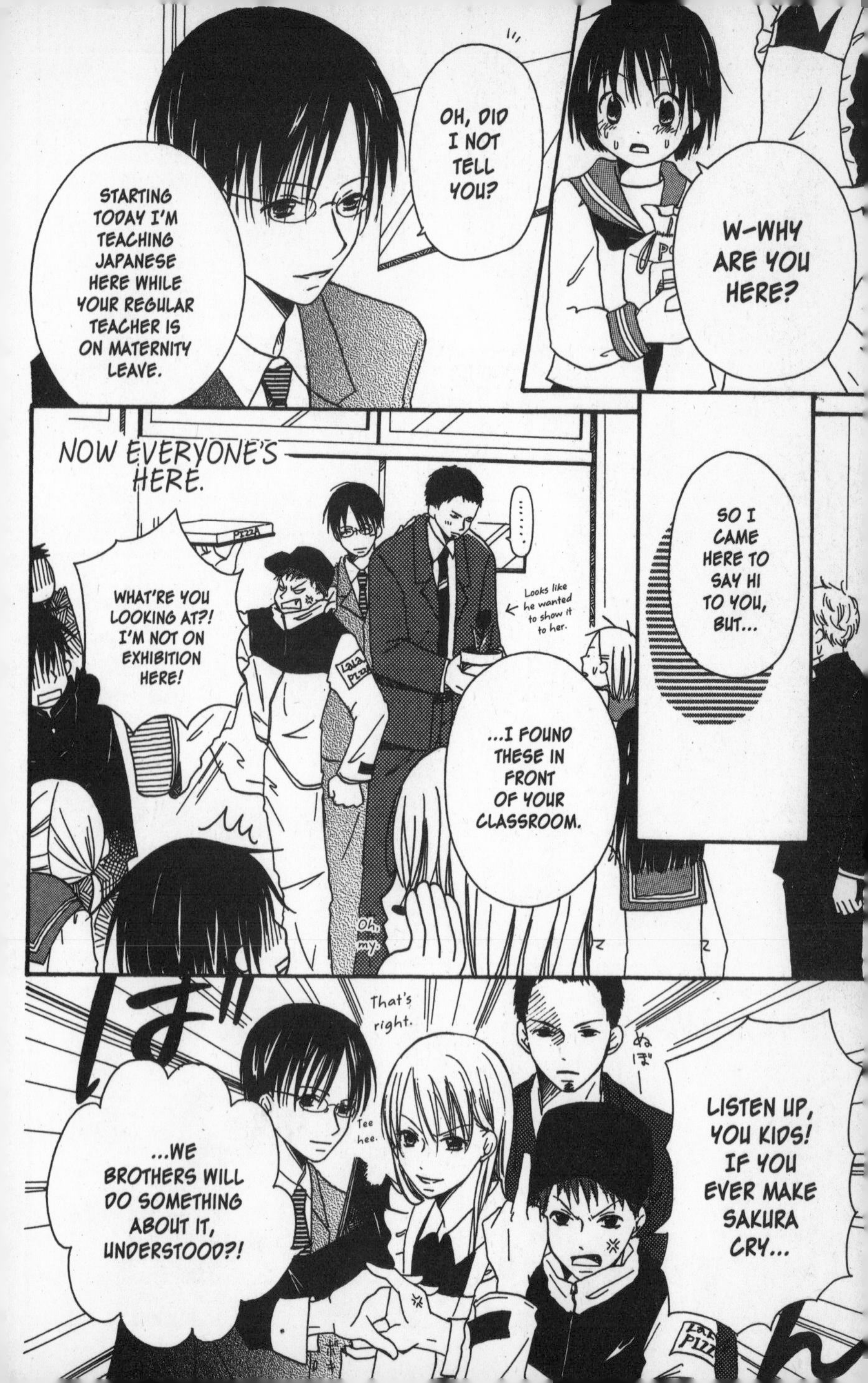
W-WHY ARE YOU HERE?
OH, DID I NOT TELL YOU?
STARTING TODAY I'M TEACHING JAPANESE HERE WHILE YOUR REGULAR TEACHER IS ON MATERNITY LEAVE.
SO I CAME HERE TO SAY HI TO YOU, BUT...
......
Looks like he wanted to show it to her.
...I FOUND THESE IN FRONT OF YOUR CLASSROOM.
NOW EVERYONE'S HERE.
PIZZA
WHAT'RE YOU LOOKING AT?! I'M NOT ON EXHIBITION HERE!
Oh, my.
LISTEN UP, YOU KIDS! IF YOU EVER MAKE SAKURA CRY...
ぬぼ
That's right.
Tee hee.
...WE BROTHERS WILL DO SOMETHING ABOUT IT, UNDERSTOOD?!

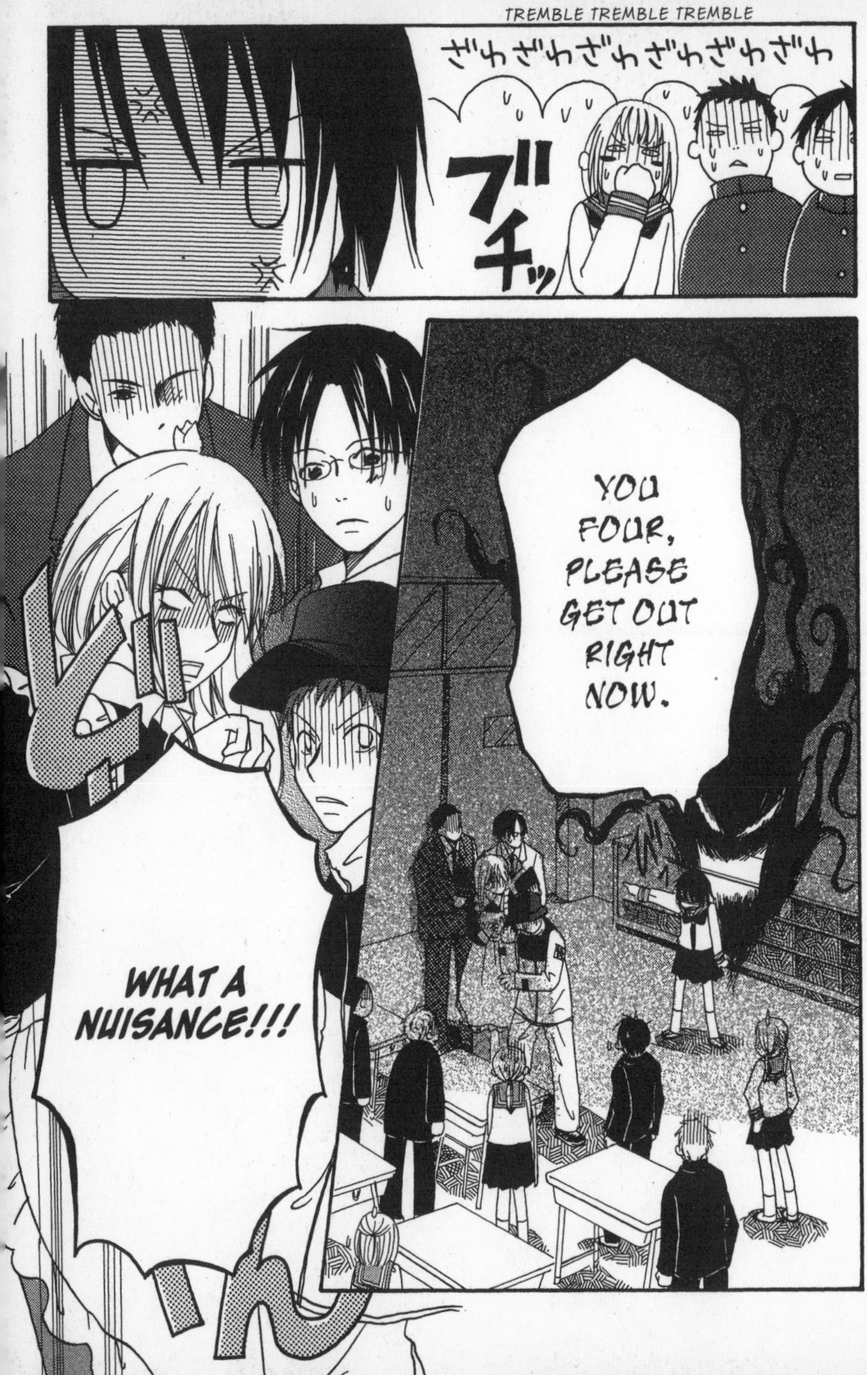
TREMBLE TREMBLE TREMBLE
ざわざわざわざわざわざわ
ブチッ
YOU FOUR, PLEASE GET OUT RIGHT NOW.
WHAT A NUISANCE!!!

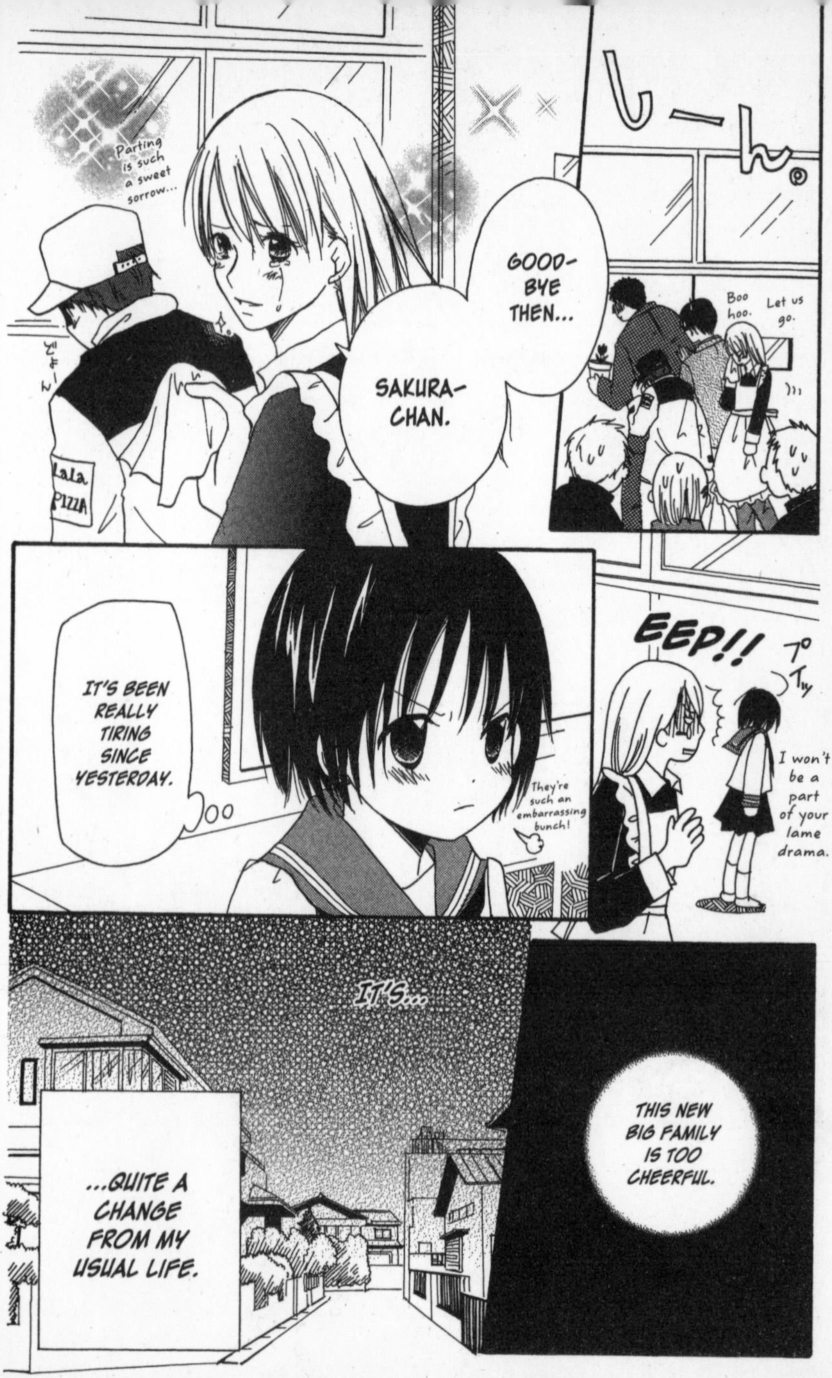
しーん。
Boo hoo.
Let us go.
GOOD-BYE THEN...
SAKURA-CHAN.
Parting is such a sweet sorrow...
LaLa PIZZA
EEP!!
I won't be a part of your lame drama.
IT'S BEEN REALLY TIRING SINCE YESTERDAY.
They're such an embarrassing bunch!
THIS NEW BIG FAMILY IS TOO CHEERFUL.
IT'S...
...QUITE A CHANGE FROM MY USUAL LIFE.

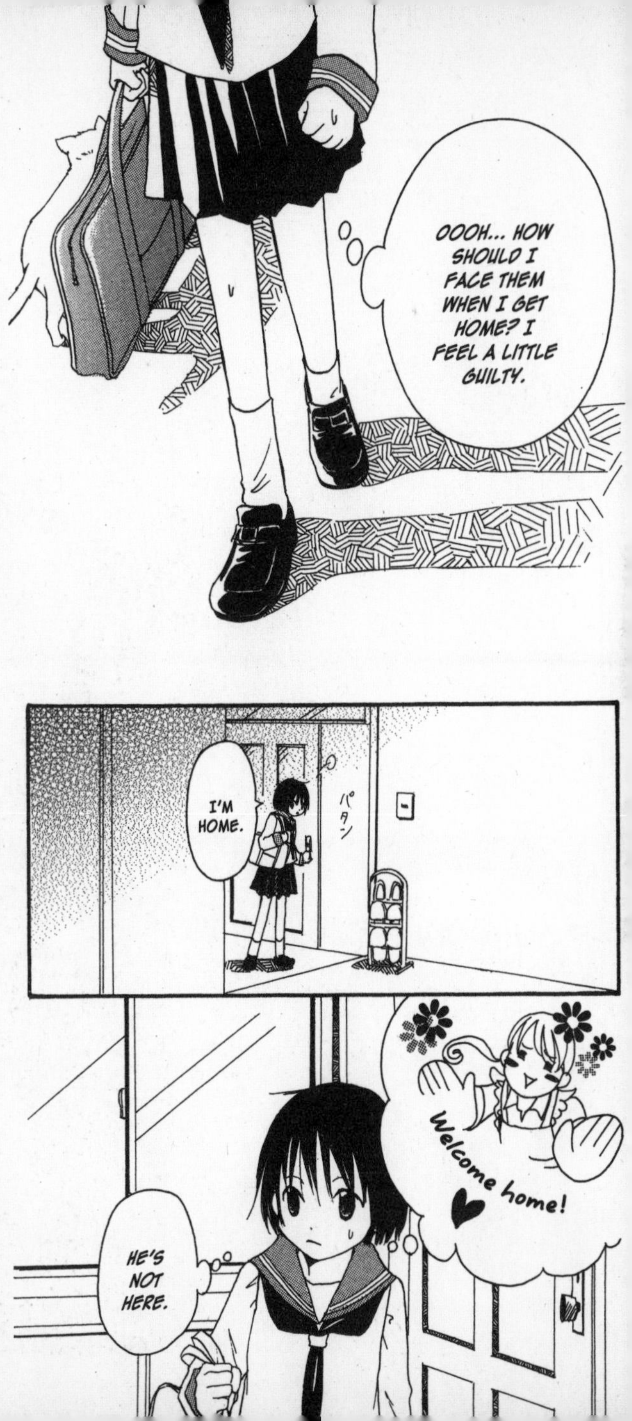
OOOH... HOW SHOULD I FACE THEM WHEN I GET HOME? I FEEL A LITTLE GUILTY.
パタン
I'M HOME.
Welcome home!
HE'S NOT HERE.

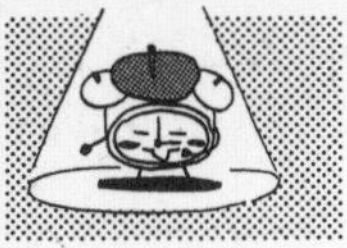

☆ 1 ☆

How do you do? I'm Hari Tokeino. Weird name, yes? And this is my **first comic!!** You are reading this right now...you're a nice person! Thank you very much!!!

☆☆☆

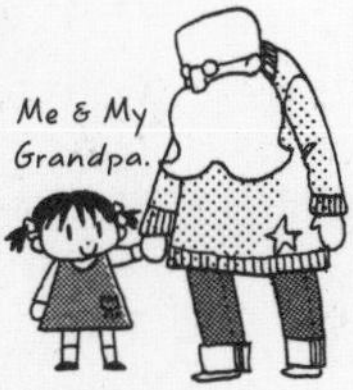
Me & My Grandpa.

☆☆☆

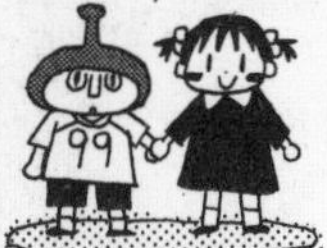
Me & My Alien.
99

☆☆☆

IT'S ME & MY BROTHERS. HOPE YOU ENJOY IT.

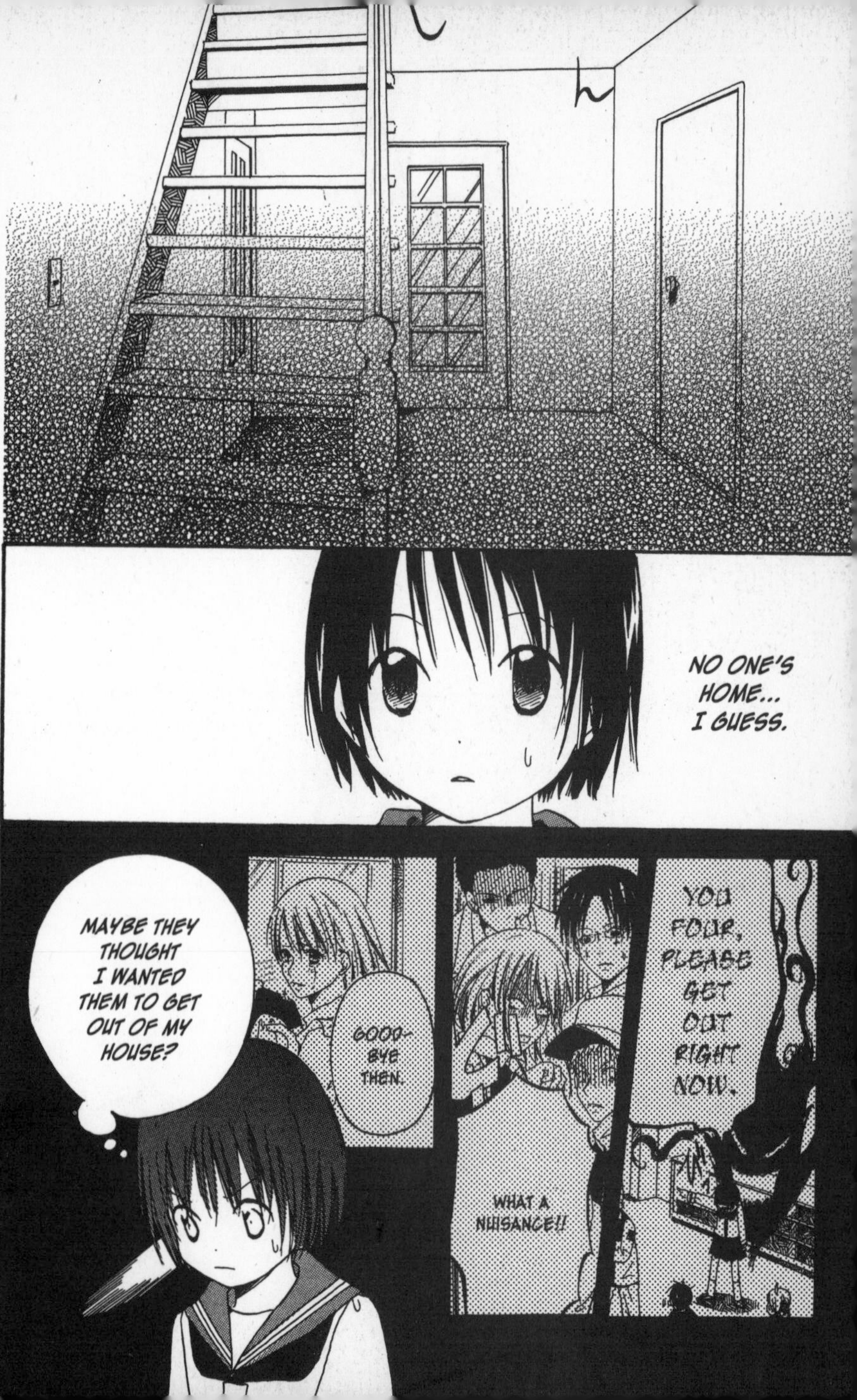

NO ONE'S HOME... I GUESS.
YOU FOUR, PLEASE GET OUT RIGHT NOW.
WHAT A NUISANCE!!
GOOD-BYE THEN.
MAYBE THEY THOUGHT I WANTED THEM TO GET OUT OF MY HOUSE?

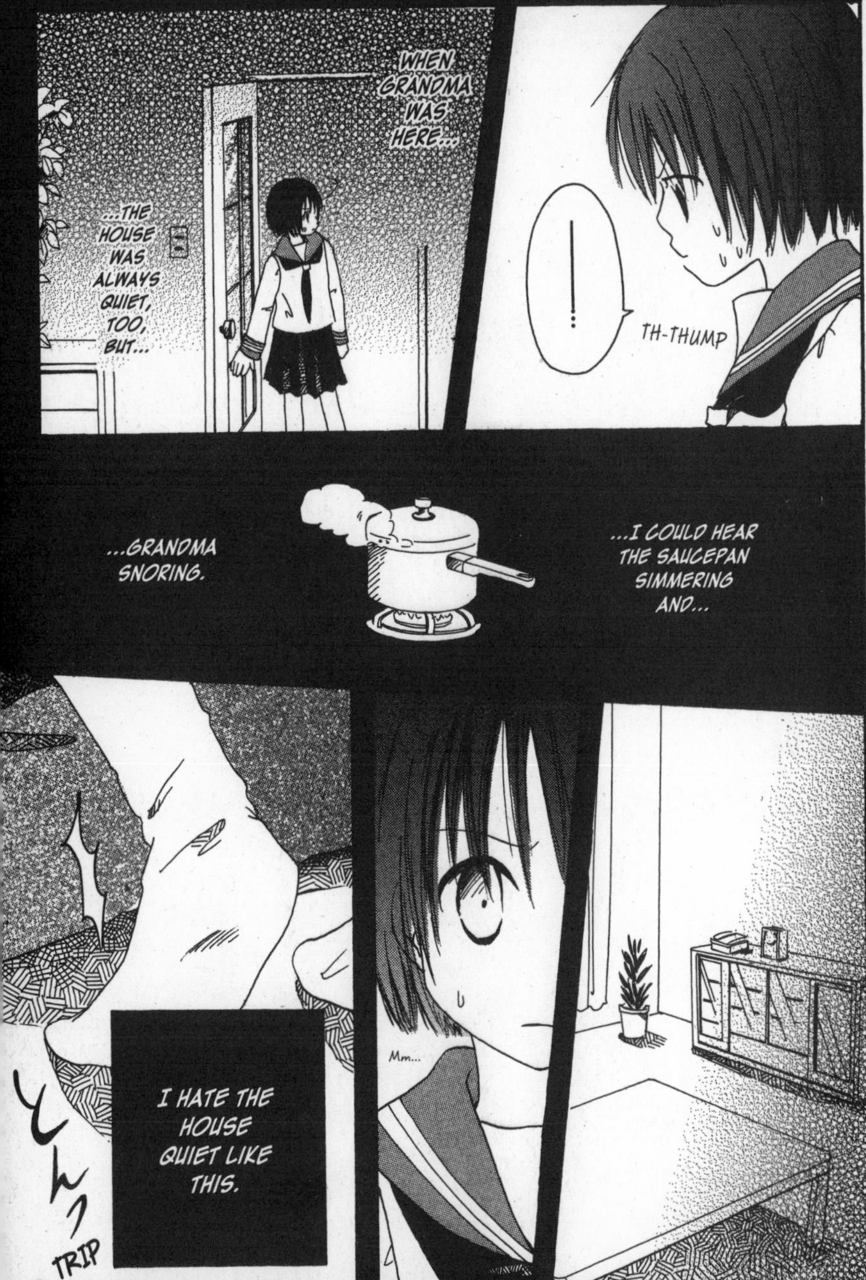
TH-THUMP
WHEN GRANDMA WAS HERE...
...THE HOUSE WAS ALWAYS QUIET, TOO, BUT...
...I COULD HEAR THE SAUCEPAN SIMMERING AND...
...GRANDMA SNORING.
Mm...
I HATE THE HOUSE QUIET LIKE THIS.
TRIP

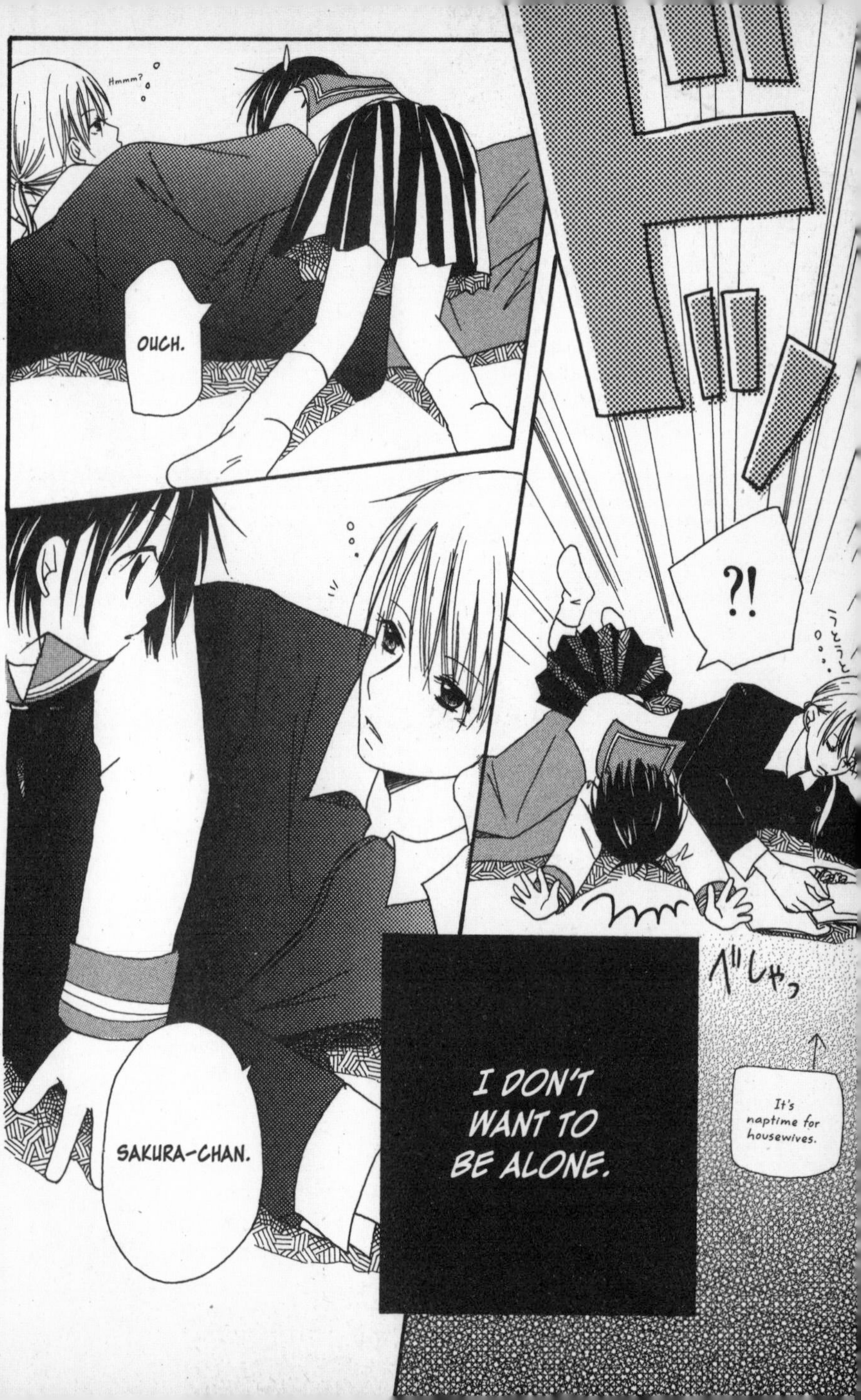
ドッ
?!
うとうと
べしゃっ
It's naptime for housewives.
Hmmm?
OUCH.
I DON'T WANT TO BE ALONE.
SAKURA-CHAN.

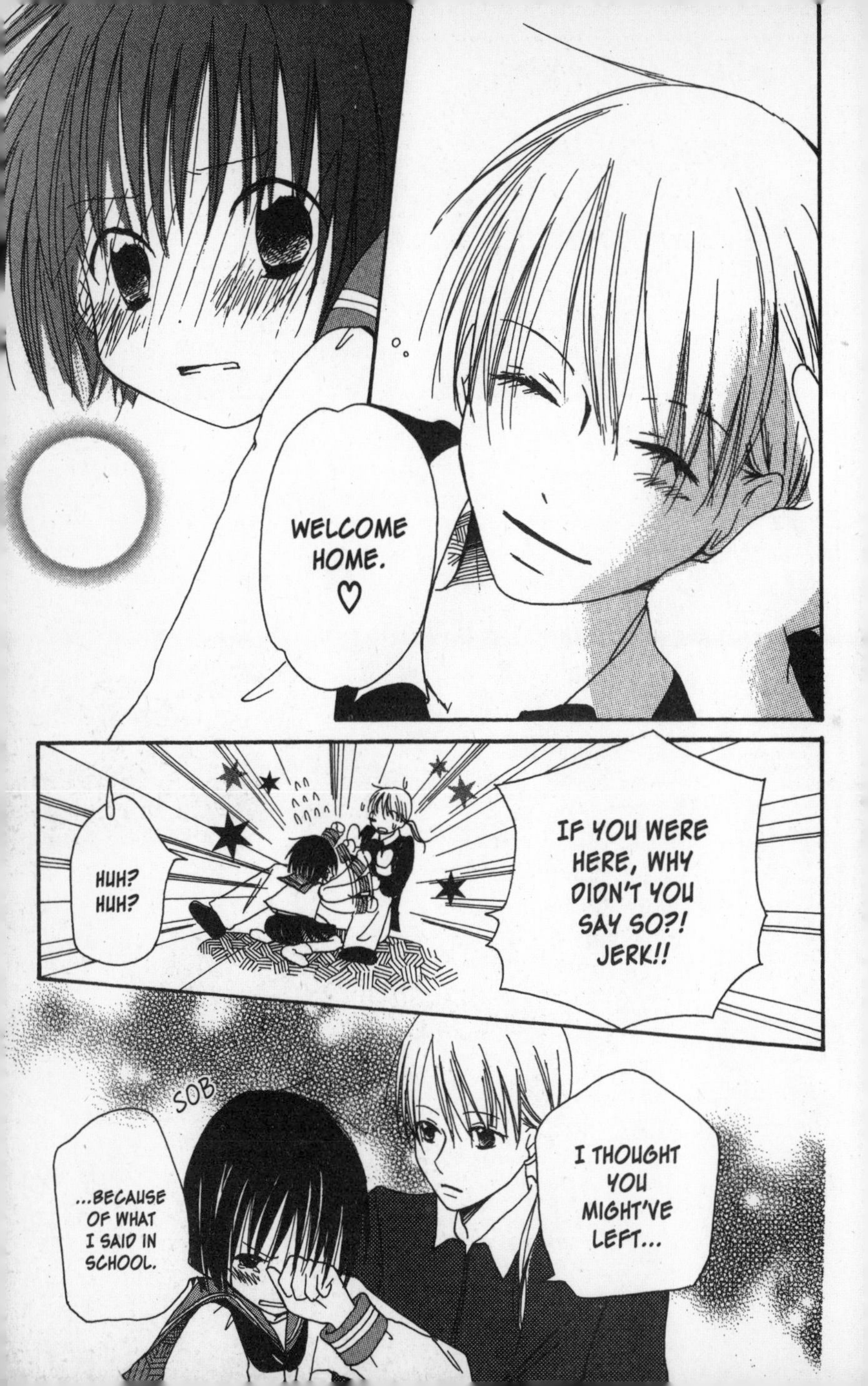
WELCOME HOME. ♡
IF YOU WERE HERE, WHY DIDN'T YOU SAY SO?! JERK!!
HUH? HUH?
I THOUGHT YOU MIGHT'VE LEFT...
SOB
...BECAUSE OF WHAT I SAID IN SCHOOL.

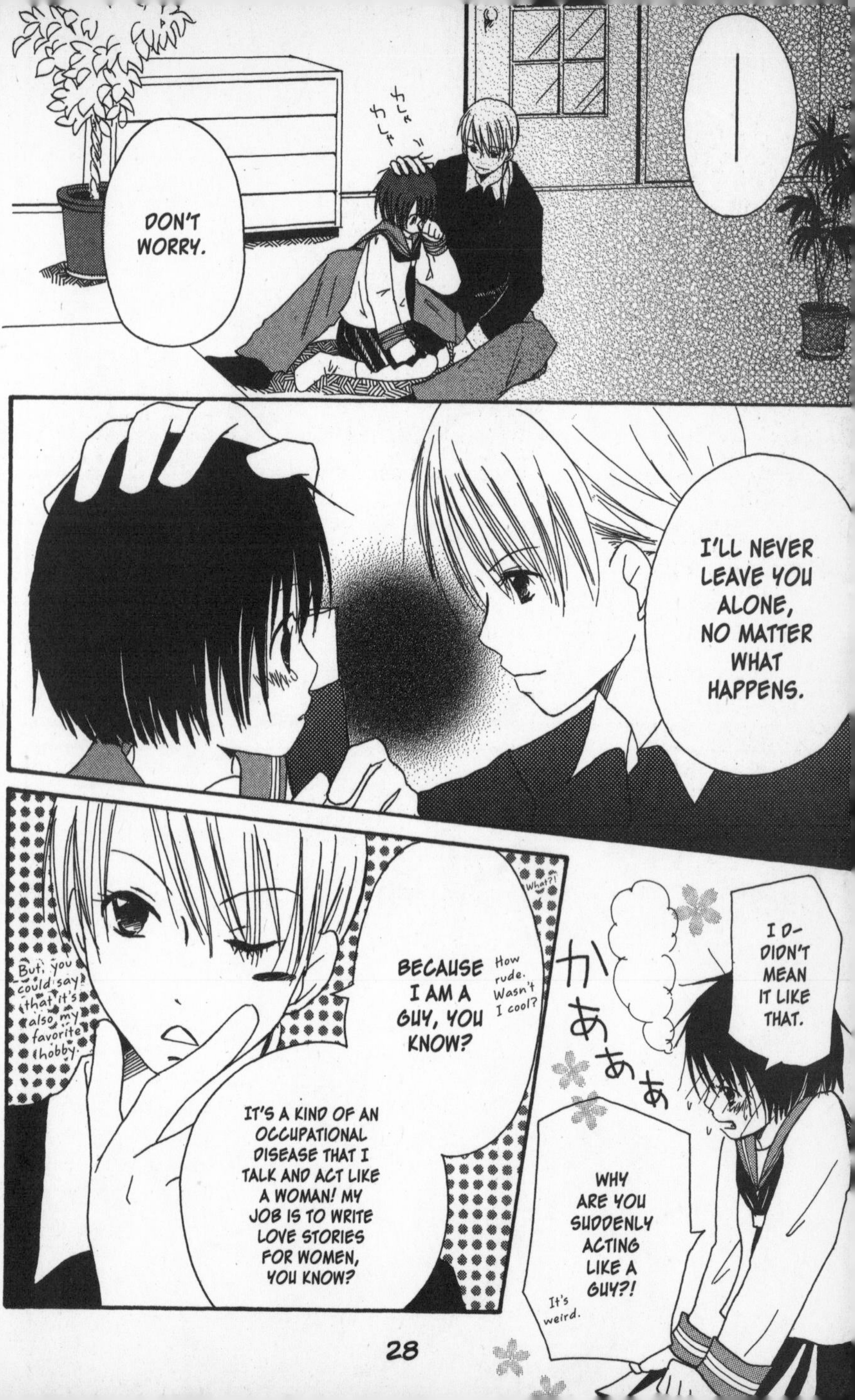

—
カしゃ カしゃ
DON'T WORRY.
I'LL NEVER LEAVE YOU ALONE, NO MATTER WHAT HAPPENS.
I D-DIDN'T MEAN IT LIKE THAT.
かあぁぁ
WHY ARE YOU SUDDENLY ACTING LIKE A GUY?!
It's weird.
What?!
BECAUSE I AM A GUY, YOU KNOW?
How rude. Wasn't I cool?
IT'S A KIND OF AN OCCUPATIONAL DISEASE THAT I TALK AND ACT LIKE A WOMAN! MY JOB IS TO WRITE LOVE STORIES FOR WOMEN, YOU KNOW?
But, you could say that it's also my favorite hobby.

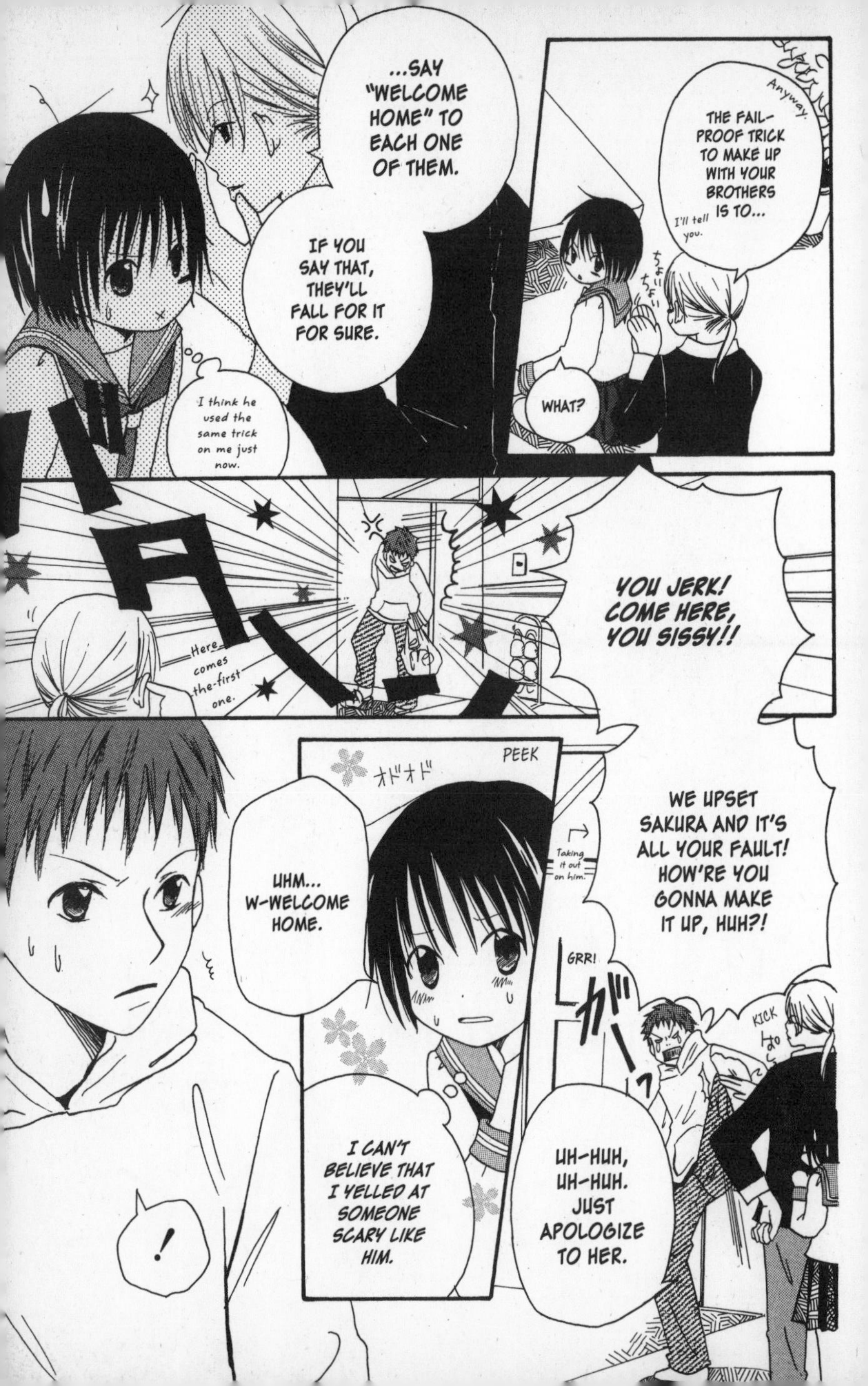

Anyway.
THE FAIL-PROOF TRICK TO MAKE UP WITH YOUR BROTHERS IS TO...
I'll tell you.
ちょいちょい
WHAT?
...SAY "WELCOME HOME" TO EACH ONE OF THEM.
IF YOU SAY THAT, THEY'LL FALL FOR IT FOR SURE.
I think he used the same trick on me just now.
YOU JERK! COME HERE, YOU SISSY!!
Here comes the first one.
WE UPSET SAKURA AND IT'S ALL YOUR FAULT! HOW'RE YOU GONNA MAKE IT UP, HUH?!
Taking it out on him.
GRR!
KICK
UH-HUH, UH-HUH. JUST APOLOGIZE TO HER.
PEEK
オドオド
UHM... W-WELCOME HOME.
I CAN'T BELIEVE THAT I YELLED AT SOMEONE SCARY LIKE HIM.
!

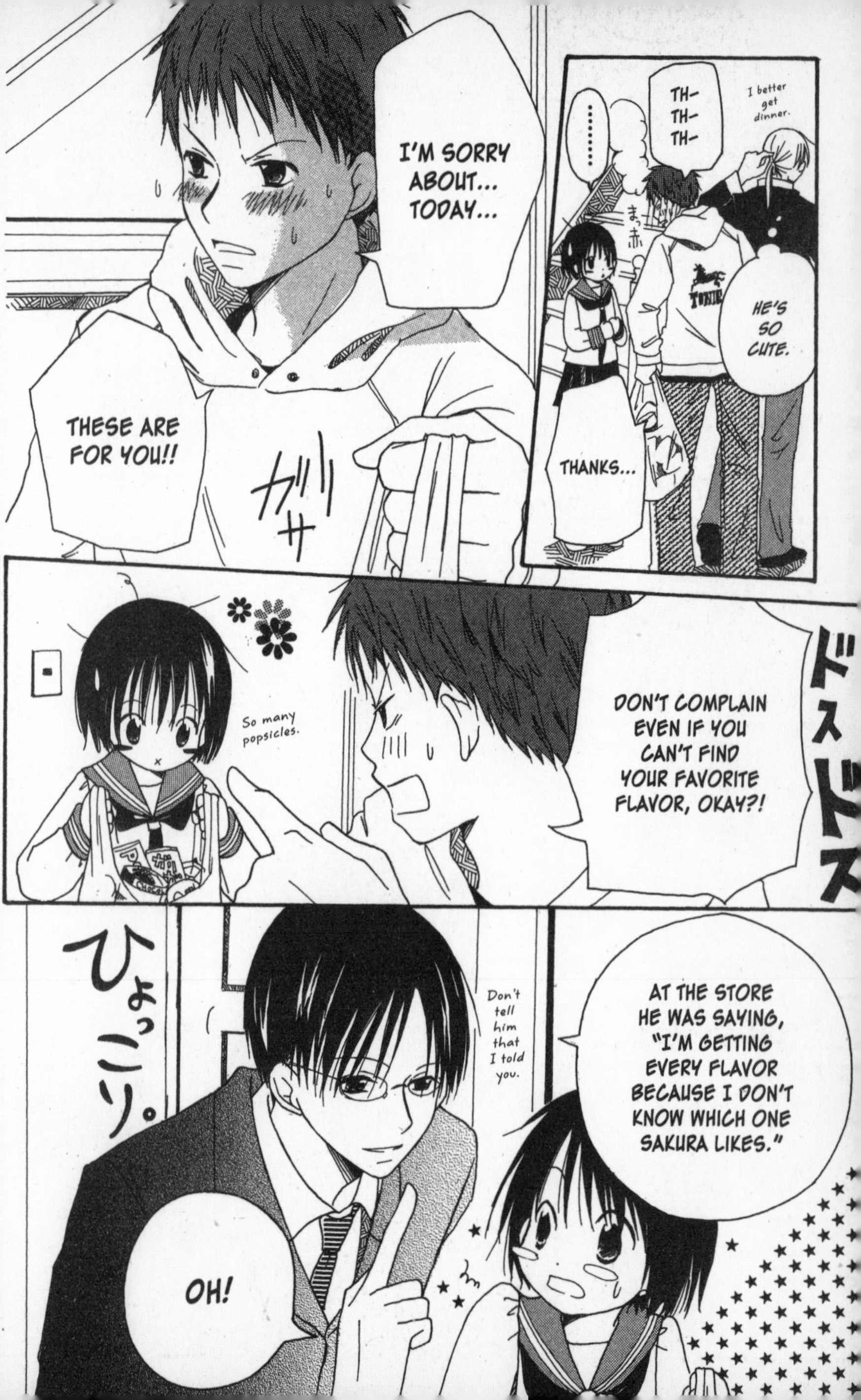
I better get dinner.
TH- TH- TH-
......
まっ赤
HE'S SO CUTE.
THANKS...
I'M SORRY ABOUT... TODAY...
THESE ARE FOR YOU!!
ガサ
ドスドス
DON'T COMPLAIN EVEN IF YOU CAN'T FIND YOUR FAVORITE FLAVOR, OKAY?!
So many popsicles.
AT THE STORE HE WAS SAYING, "I'M GETTING EVERY FLAVOR BECAUSE I DON'T KNOW WHICH ONE SAKURA LIKES."
Don't tell him that I told you.
ひょっこり。
OH!

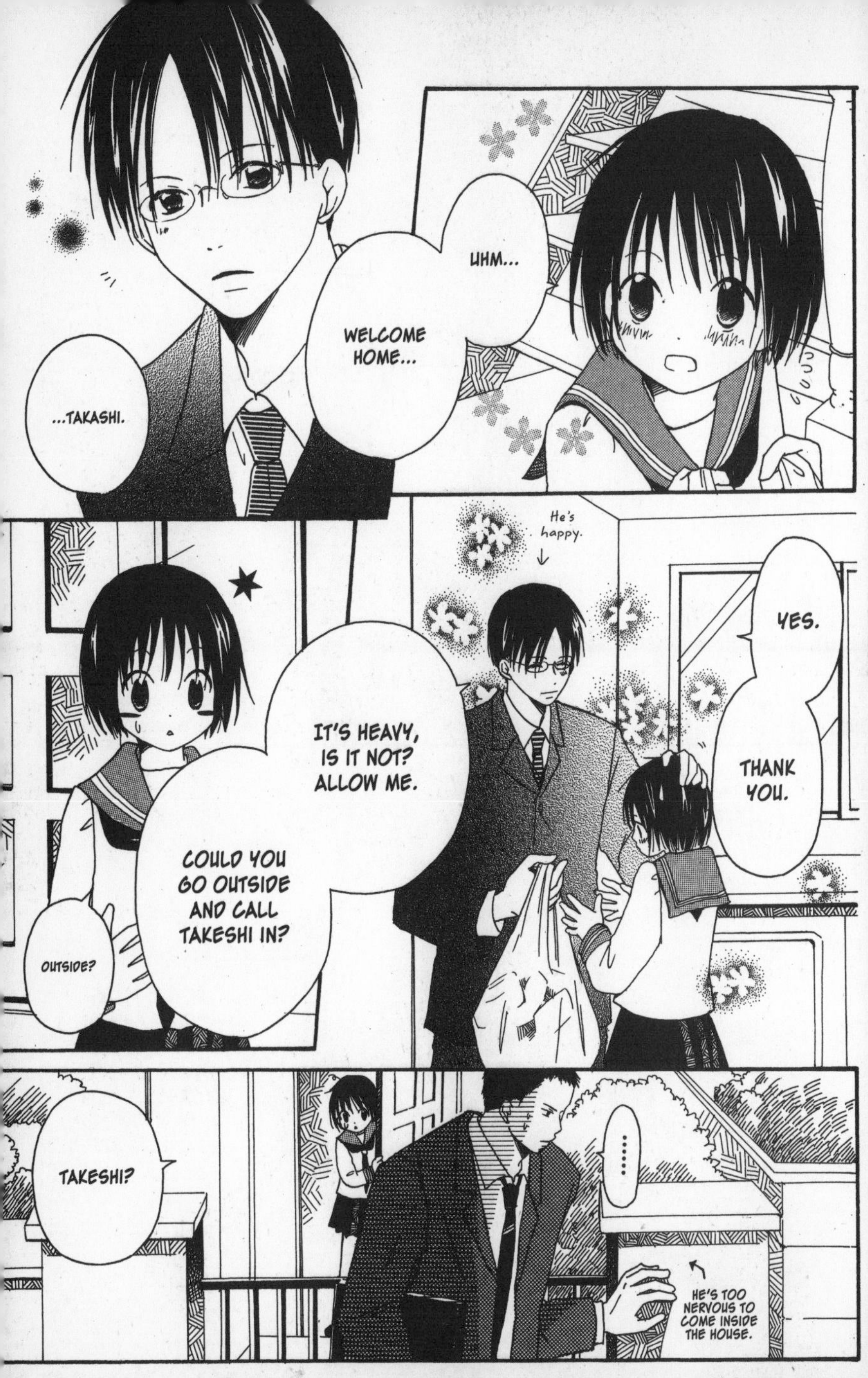
UHM...
WELCOME HOME...
...TAKASHI.
He's happy.
IT'S HEAVY, IS IT NOT? ALLOW ME.
YES.
THANK YOU.
COULD YOU GO OUTSIDE AND CALL TAKESHI IN?
OUTSIDE?
......
HE'S TOO NERVOUS TO COME INSIDE THE HOUSE.
TAKESHI?

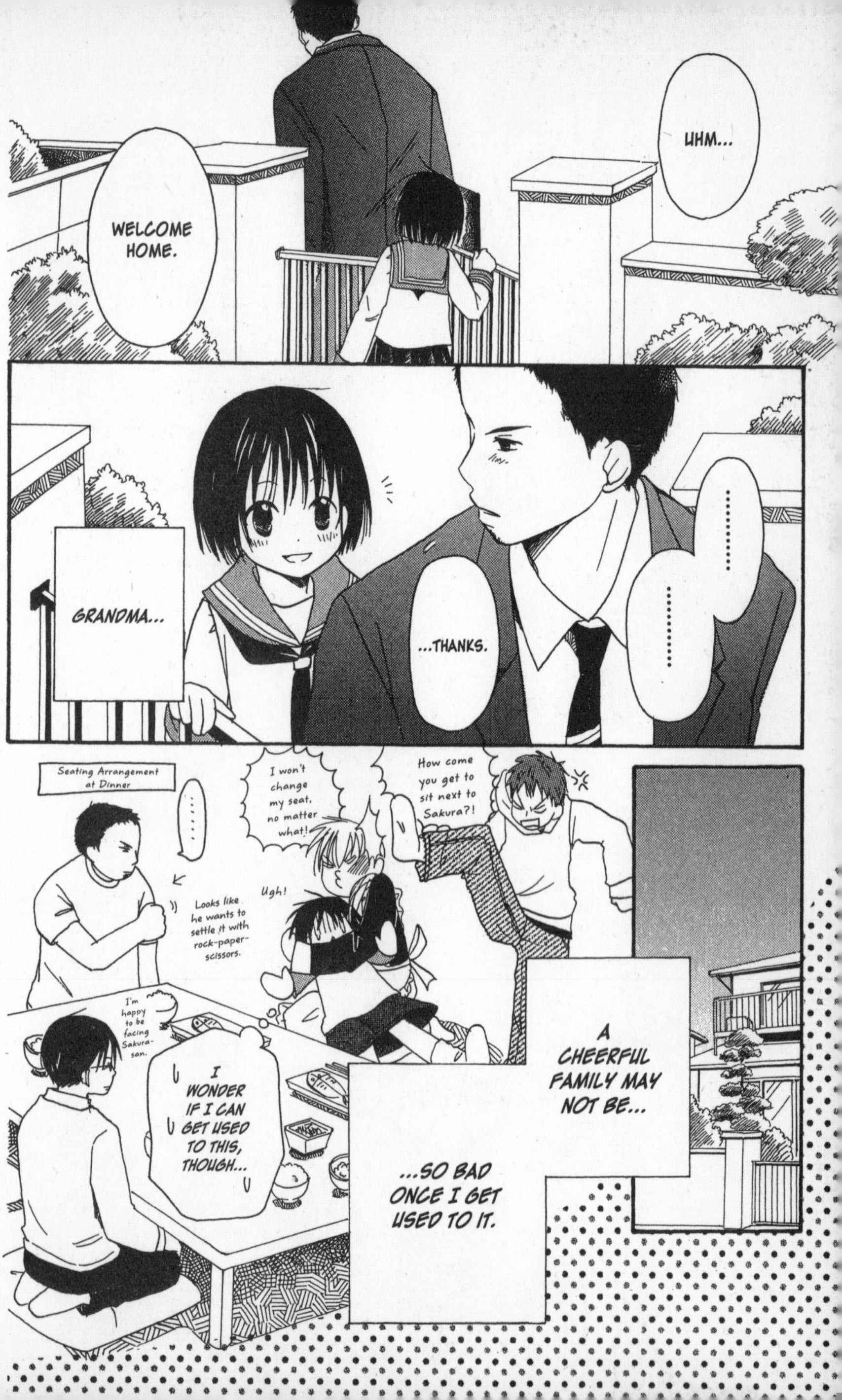
UHM...
WELCOME HOME.
......
......
...THANKS.
GRANDMA...
A CHEERFUL FAMILY MAY NOT BE...
...SO BAD ONCE I GET USED TO IT.
Seating Arrangement at Dinner
How come you get to sit next to Sakura?!
I won't change my seat, no matter what!
......
Looks like he wants to settle it with rock-paper-scissors.
Ugh!
I'm happy to be facing Sakura-san.
I WONDER IF I CAN GET USED TO THIS, THOUGH...

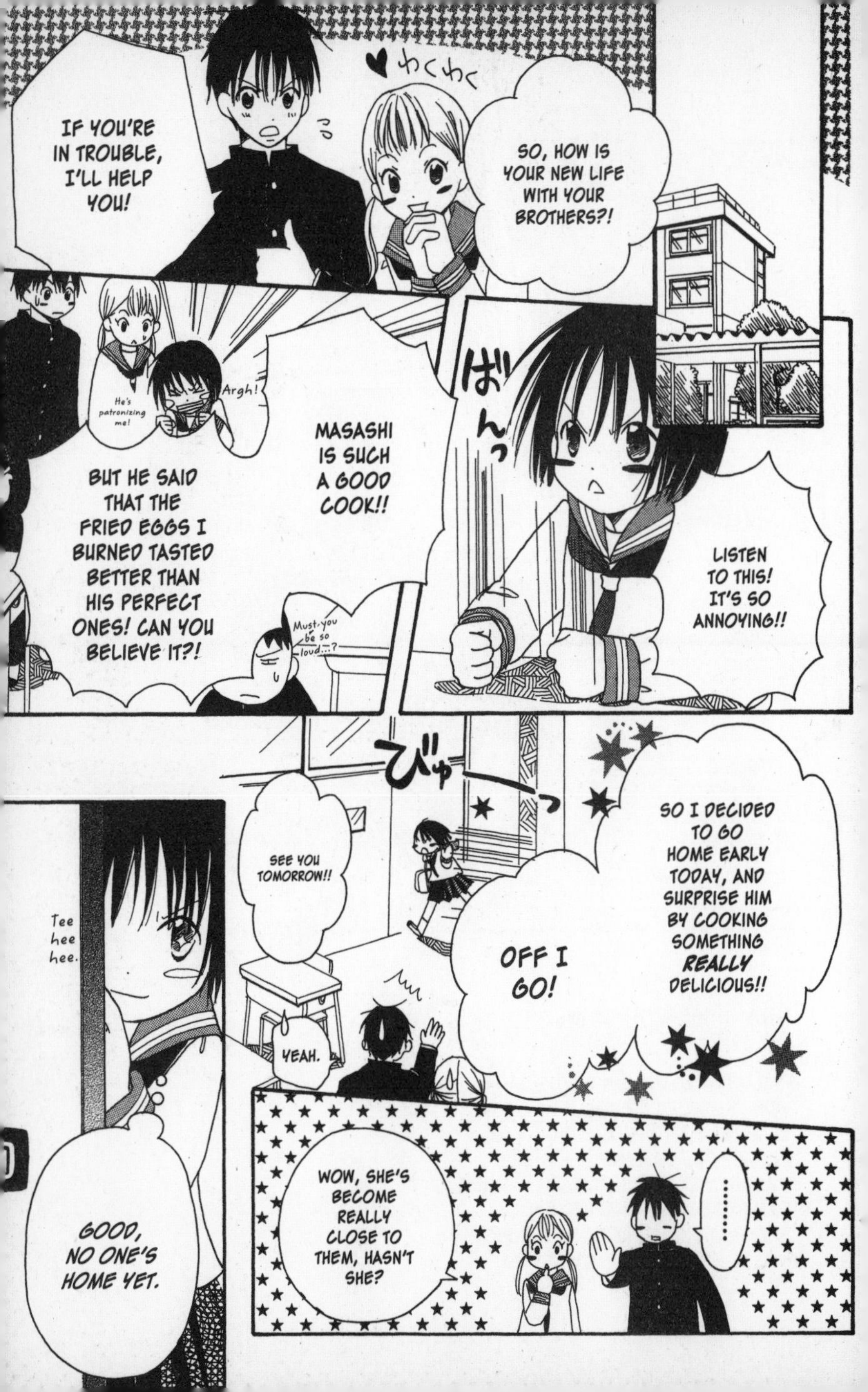
わくわく
SO, HOW IS YOUR NEW LIFE WITH YOUR BROTHERS?!
IF YOU'RE IN TROUBLE, I'LL HELP YOU!
ばんっ
LISTEN TO THIS! IT'S SO ANNOYING!!
MASASHI IS SUCH A GOOD COOK!!
BUT HE SAID THAT THE FRIED EGGS I BURNED TASTED BETTER THAN HIS PERFECT ONES! CAN YOU BELIEVE IT?!
Must you be so loud...?
Argh!
He's patronizing me!
SO I DECIDED TO GO HOME EARLY TODAY, AND SURPRISE HIM BY COOKING SOMETHING REALLY DELICIOUS!!
OFF I GO!
びゅーっ
SEE YOU TOMORROW!!
YEAH.
......
WOW, SHE'S BECOME REALLY CLOSE TO THEM, HASN'T SHE?
Tee hee hee.
GOOD, NO ONE'S HOME YET.

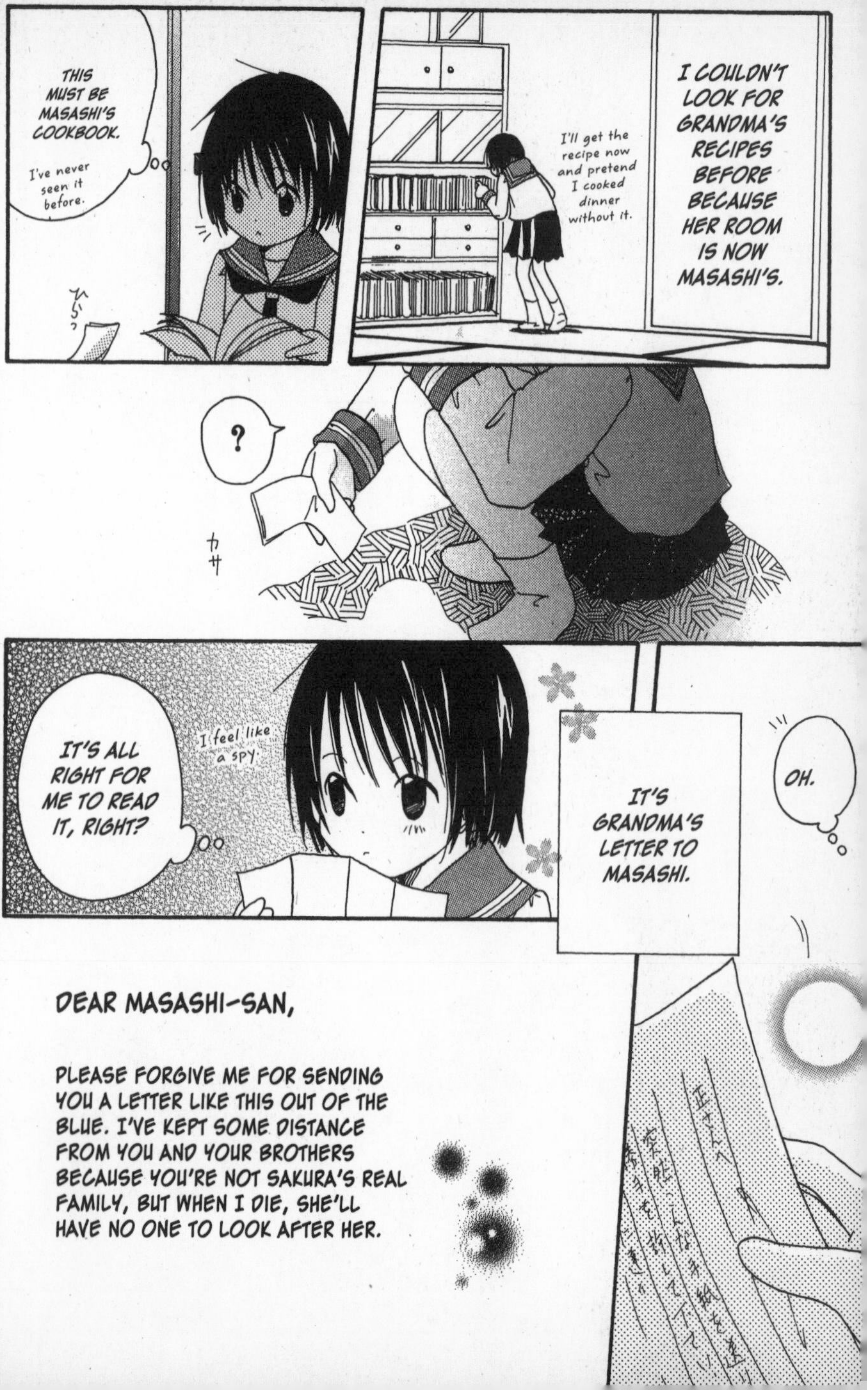
I COULDN'T LOOK FOR GRANDMA'S RECIPES BEFORE BECAUSE HER ROOM IS NOW MASASHI'S.
I'll get the recipe now and pretend I cooked dinner without it.
THIS MUST BE MASASHI'S COOKBOOK.
I've never seen it before.
ひらっ
?
カサ
OH.
IT'S GRANDMA'S LETTER TO MASASHI.
I feel like a spy.
IT'S ALL RIGHT FOR ME TO READ IT, RIGHT?
DEAR MASASHI-SAN,
PLEASE FORGIVE ME FOR SENDING YOU A LETTER LIKE THIS OUT OF THE BLUE. I'VE KEPT SOME DISTANCE FROM YOU AND YOUR BROTHERS BECAUSE YOU'RE NOT SAKURA'S REAL FAMILY, BUT WHEN I DIE, SHE'LL HAVE NO ONE TO LOOK AFTER HER.

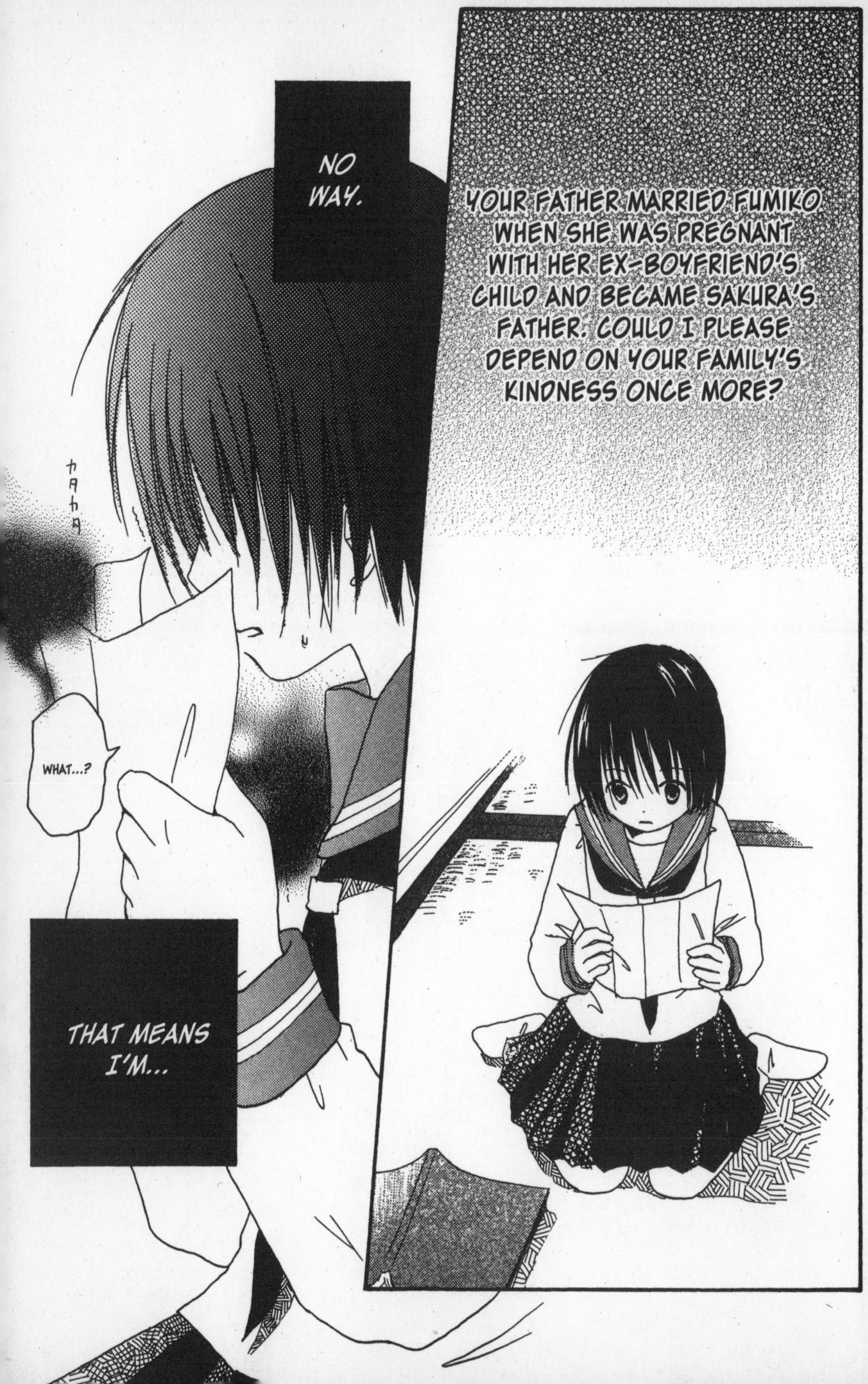
YOUR FATHER MARRIED FUMIKO WHEN SHE WAS PREGNANT WITH HER EX-BOYFRIEND'S CHILD AND BECAME SAKURA'S FATHER. COULD I PLEASE DEPEND ON YOUR FAMILY'S KINDNESS ONCE MORE?
NO WAY.
カタカタ
WHAT...?
THAT MEANS I'M...

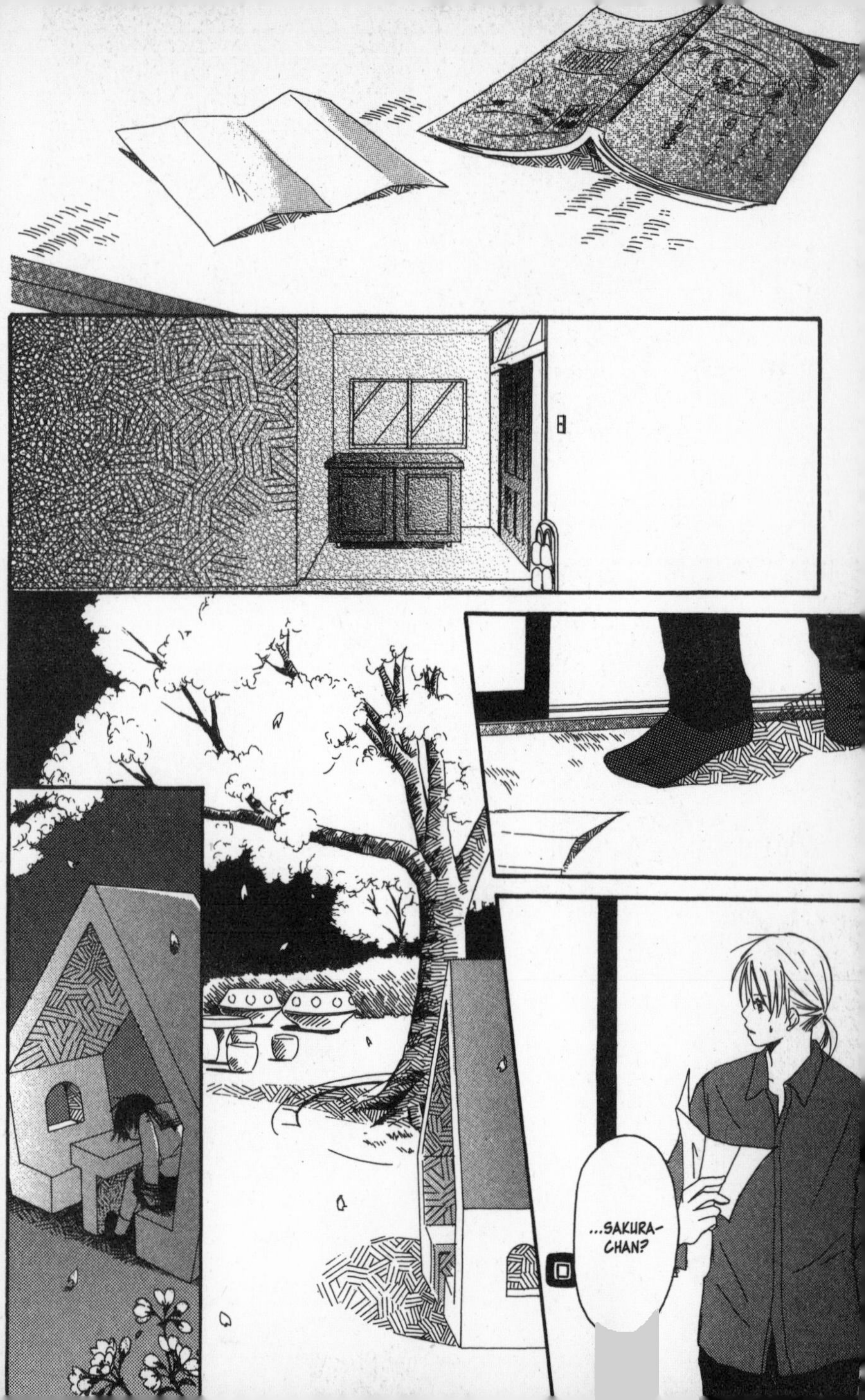
...SAKURA-CHAN?

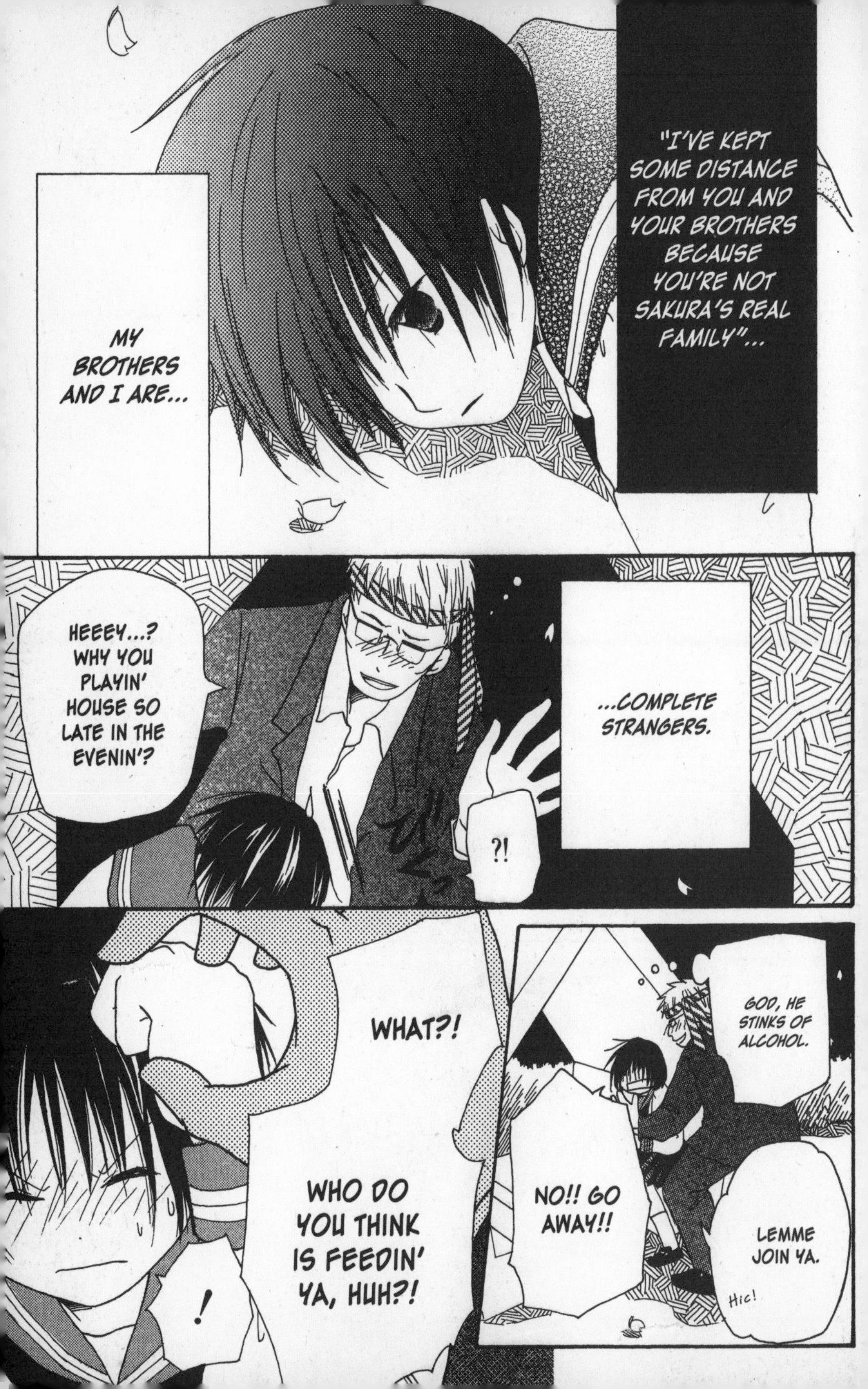
"I'VE KEPT SOME DISTANCE FROM YOU AND YOUR BROTHERS BECAUSE YOU'RE NOT SAKURA'S REAL FAMILY"...
MY BROTHERS AND I ARE...
...COMPLETE STRANGERS.
?!
HEEEY...? WHY YOU PLAYIN' HOUSE SO LATE IN THE EVENIN'?
GOD, HE STINKS OF ALCOHOL.
LEMME JOIN YA.
Hic!
NO!! GO AWAY!!
WHAT?!
WHO DO YOU THINK IS FEEDIN' YA, HUH?!
!

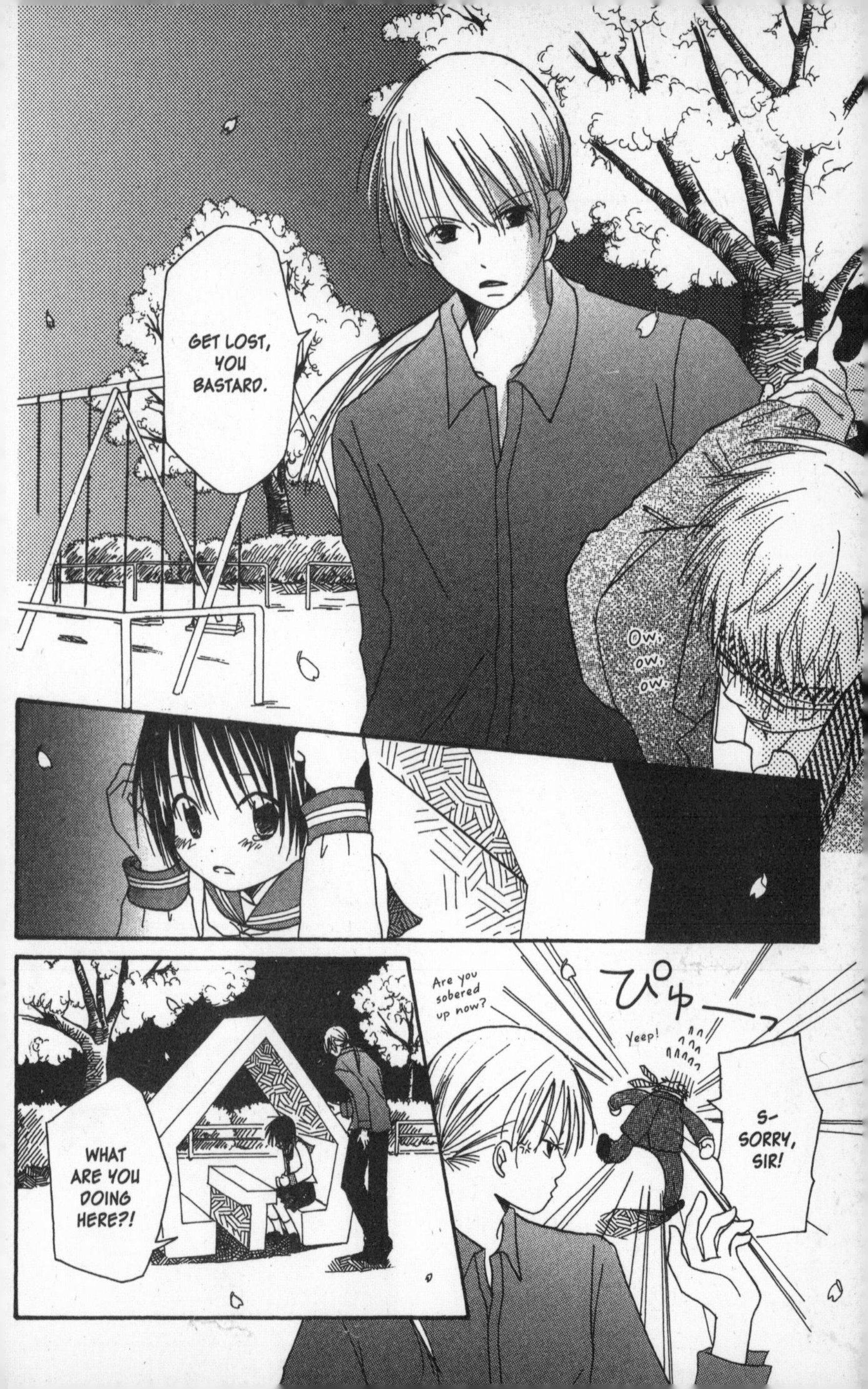
GET LOST, YOU BASTARD.
Ow, ow, ow.
ぴゅーー
S-SORRY, SIR!
Yeep!
Are you sobered up now?
WHAT ARE YOU DOING HERE?!

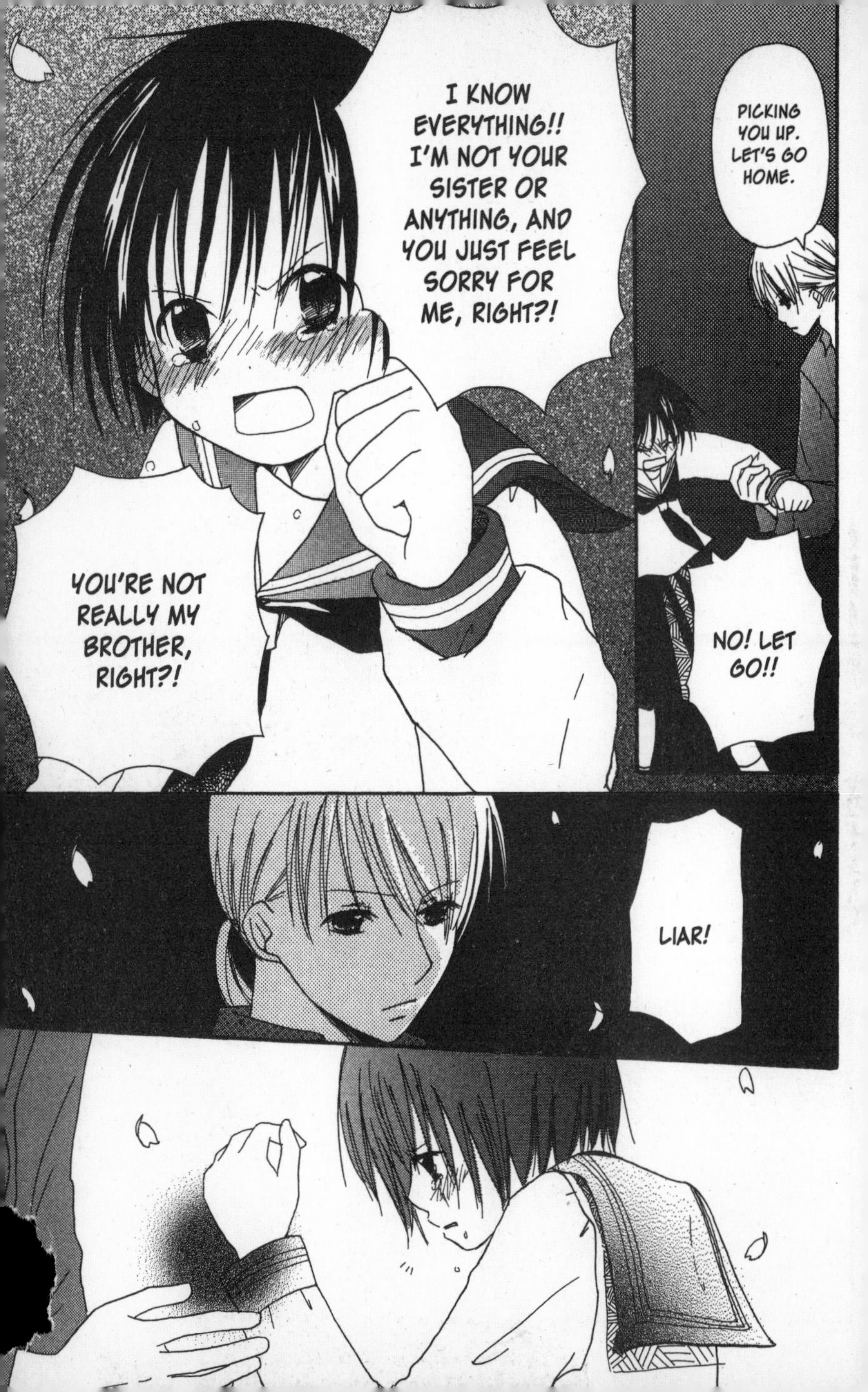
PICKING YOU UP. LET'S GO HOME.
NO! LET GO!!
I KNOW EVERYTHING!! I'M NOT YOUR SISTER OR ANYTHING, AND YOU JUST FEEL SORRY FOR ME, RIGHT?!
YOU'RE NOT REALLY MY BROTHER, RIGHT?!
LIAR!

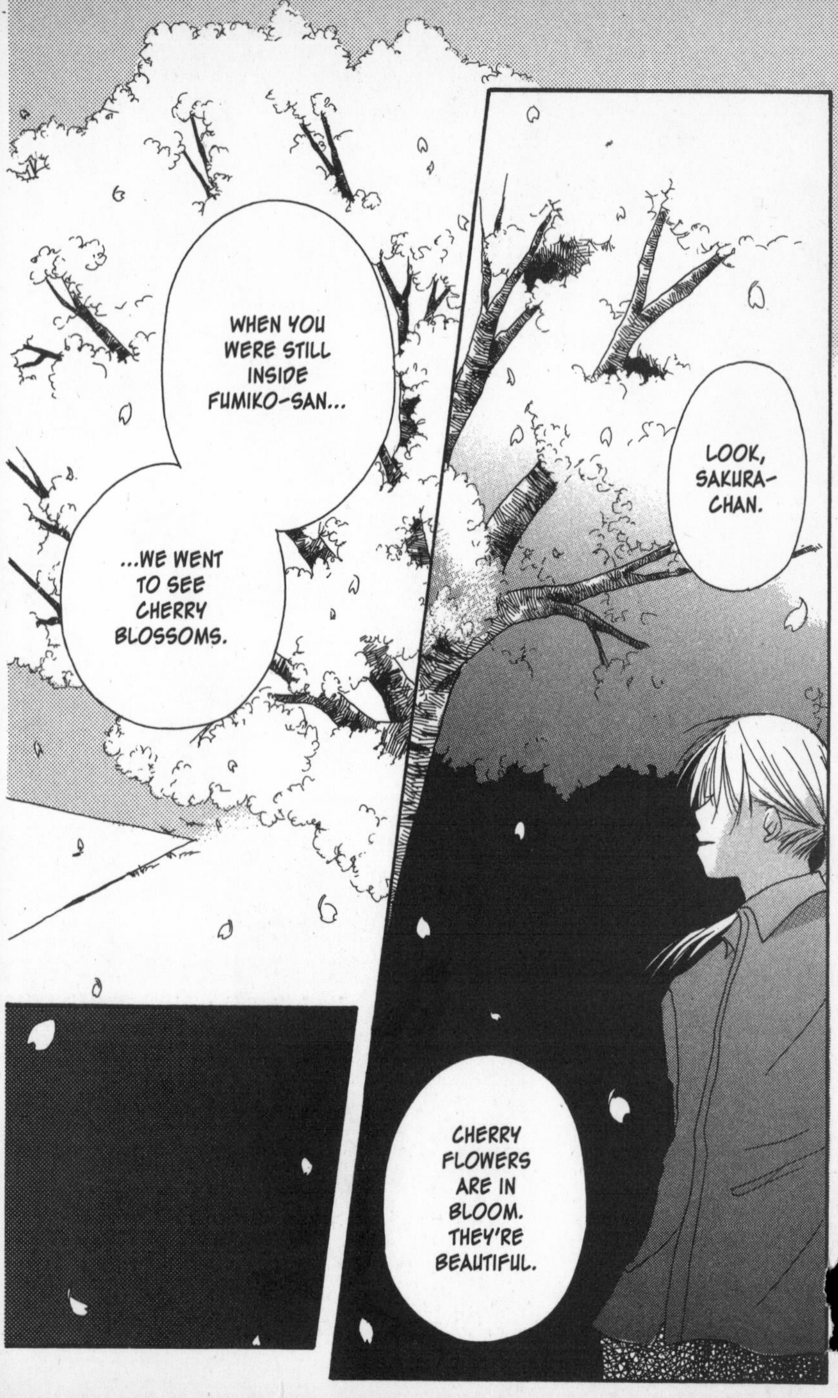
LOOK, SAKURA-CHAN.
CHERRY FLOWERS ARE IN BLOOM. THEY'RE BEAUTIFUL.
WHEN YOU WERE STILL INSIDE FUMIKO-SAN...
...WE WENT TO SEE CHERRY BLOSSOMS.

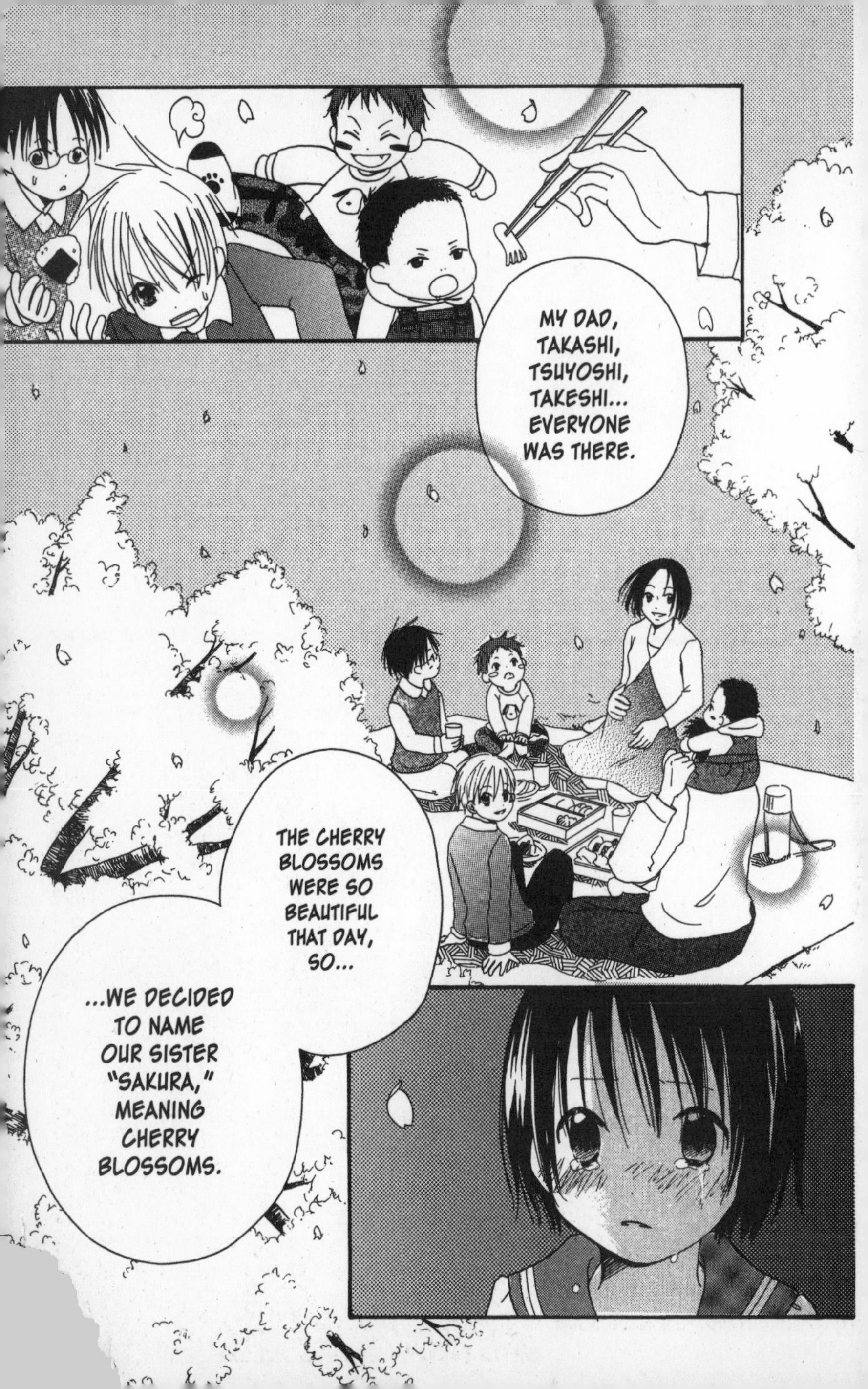
MY DAD, TAKASHI, TSUYOSHI, TAKESHI... EVERYONE WAS THERE.
THE CHERRY BLOSSOMS WERE SO BEAUTIFUL THAT DAY, SO...
...WE DECIDED TO NAME OUR SISTER "SAKURA," MEANING CHERRY BLOSSOMS.

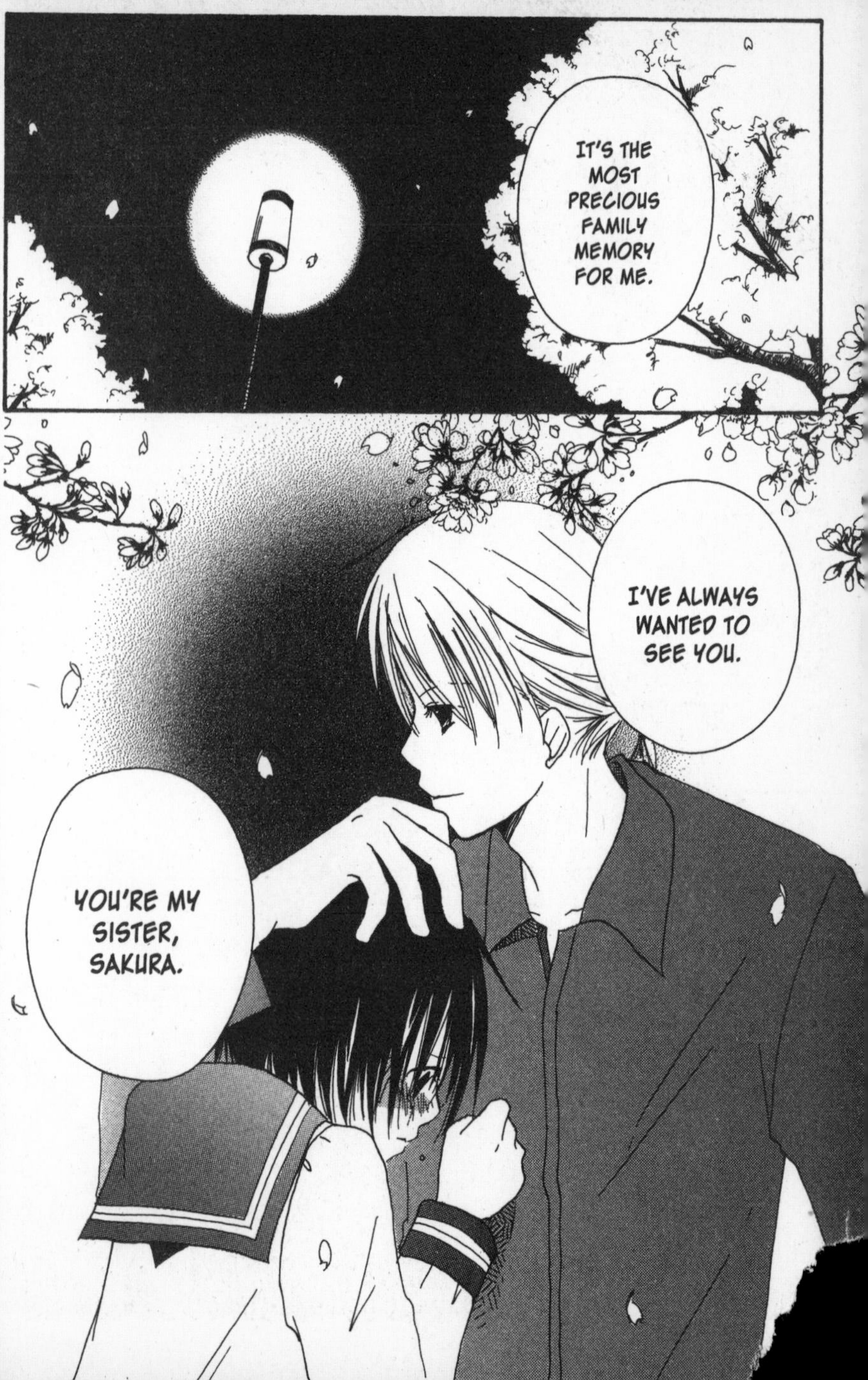
IT'S THE MOST PRECIOUS FAMILY MEMORY FOR ME.
I'VE ALWAYS WANTED TO SEE YOU.
YOU'RE MY SISTER, SAKURA.

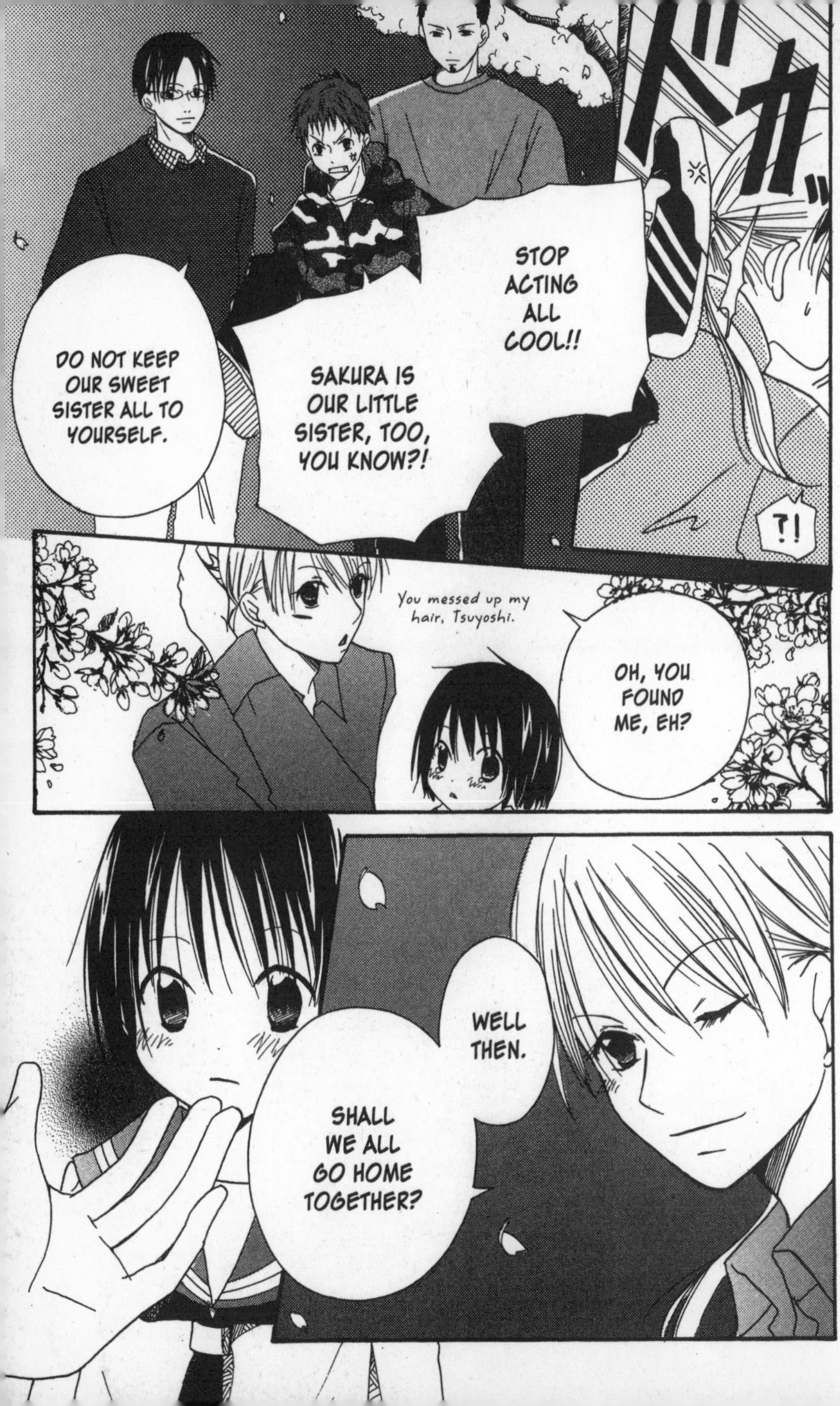
ドカ
?!
STOP ACTING ALL COOL!!
SAKURA IS OUR LITTLE SISTER, TOO, YOU KNOW?!
DO NOT KEEP OUR SWEET SISTER ALL TO YOURSELF.
OH, YOU FOUND ME, EH?
You messed up my hair, Tsuyoshi.
WELL THEN.
SHALL WE ALL GO HOME TOGETHER?

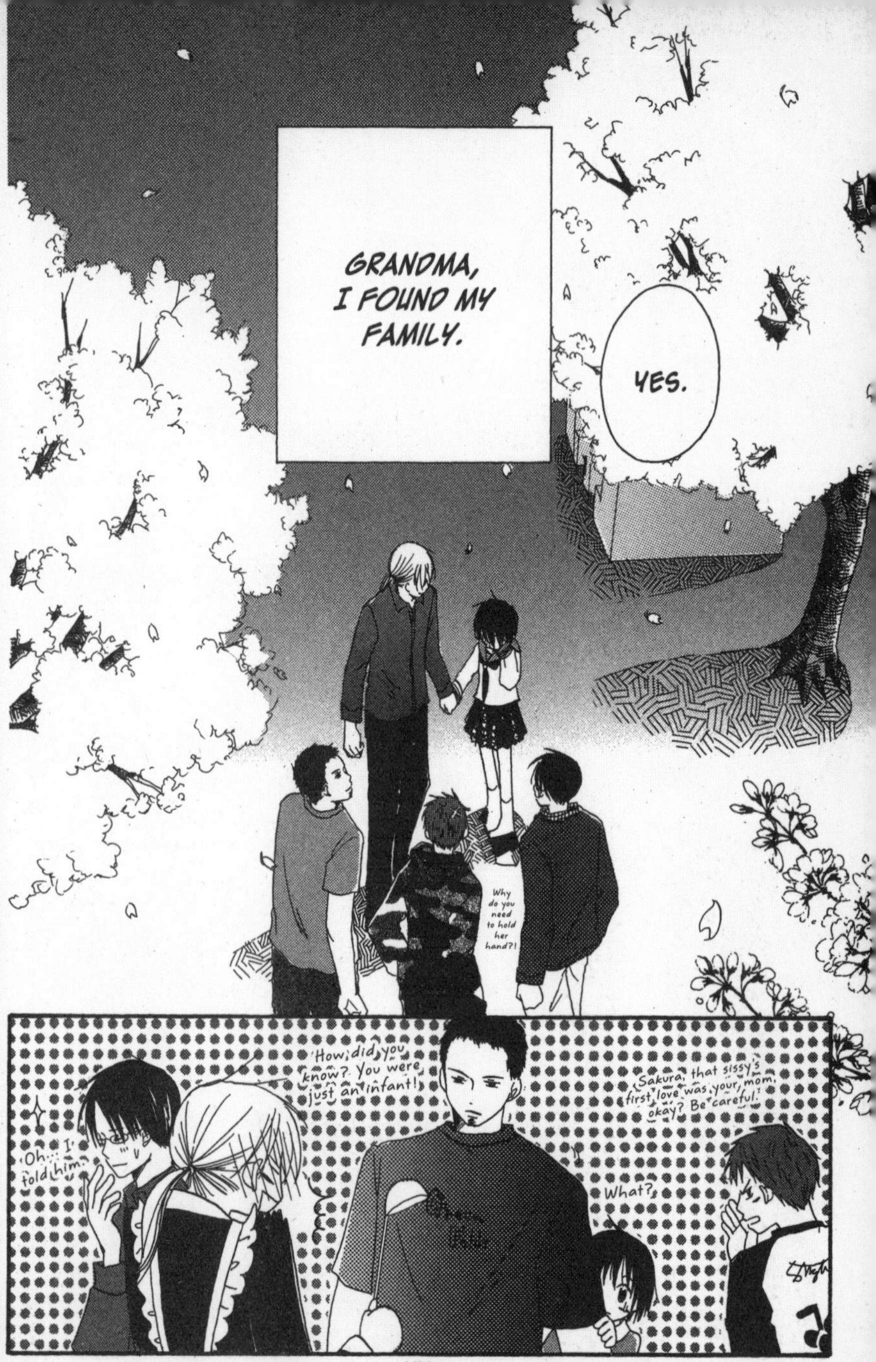
GRANDMA, I FOUND MY FAMILY.
YES.
Why do you need to hold her hand?!
Sakura, that sissy's first love was your mom, okay? Be careful.
What?
How did you know? You were just an infant!
Oh... I told him.

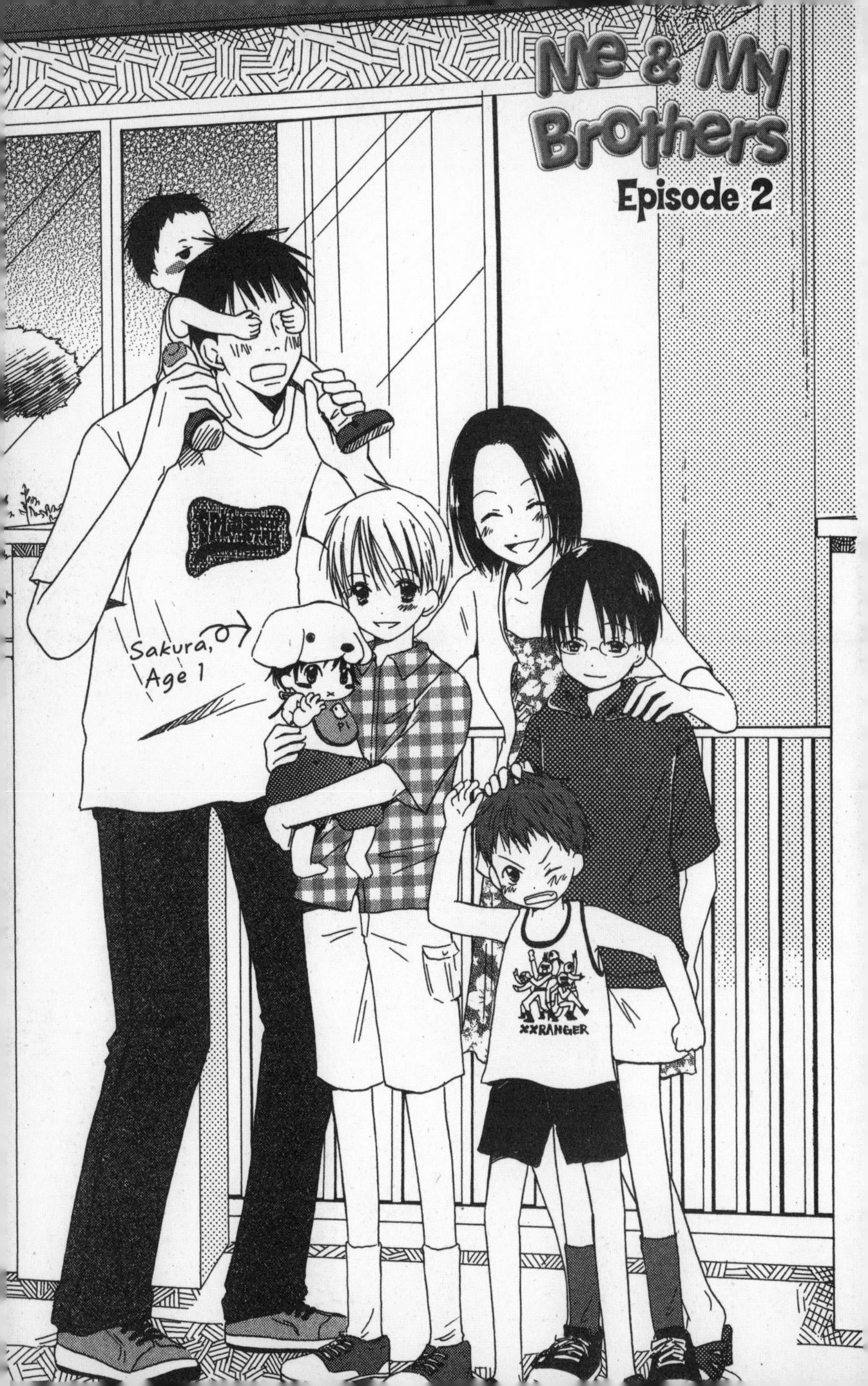
Me & My Brothers
Episode 2
Sakura, Age 1
xxRANGER

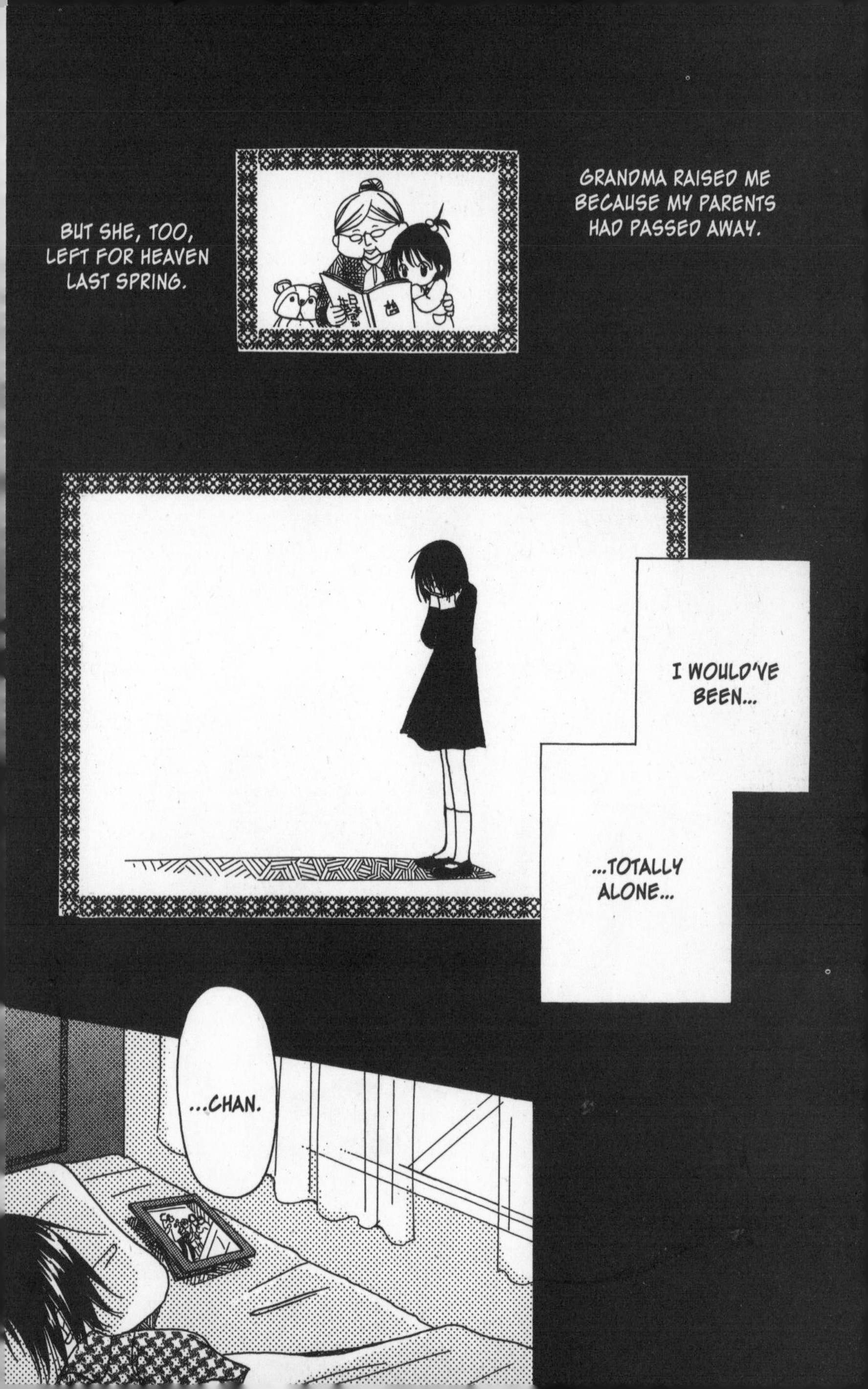
GRANDMA RAISED ME BECAUSE MY PARENTS HAD PASSED AWAY.
BUT SHE, TOO, LEFT FOR HEAVEN LAST SPRING.
I WOULD'VE BEEN...
...TOTALLY ALONE...
...CHAN.

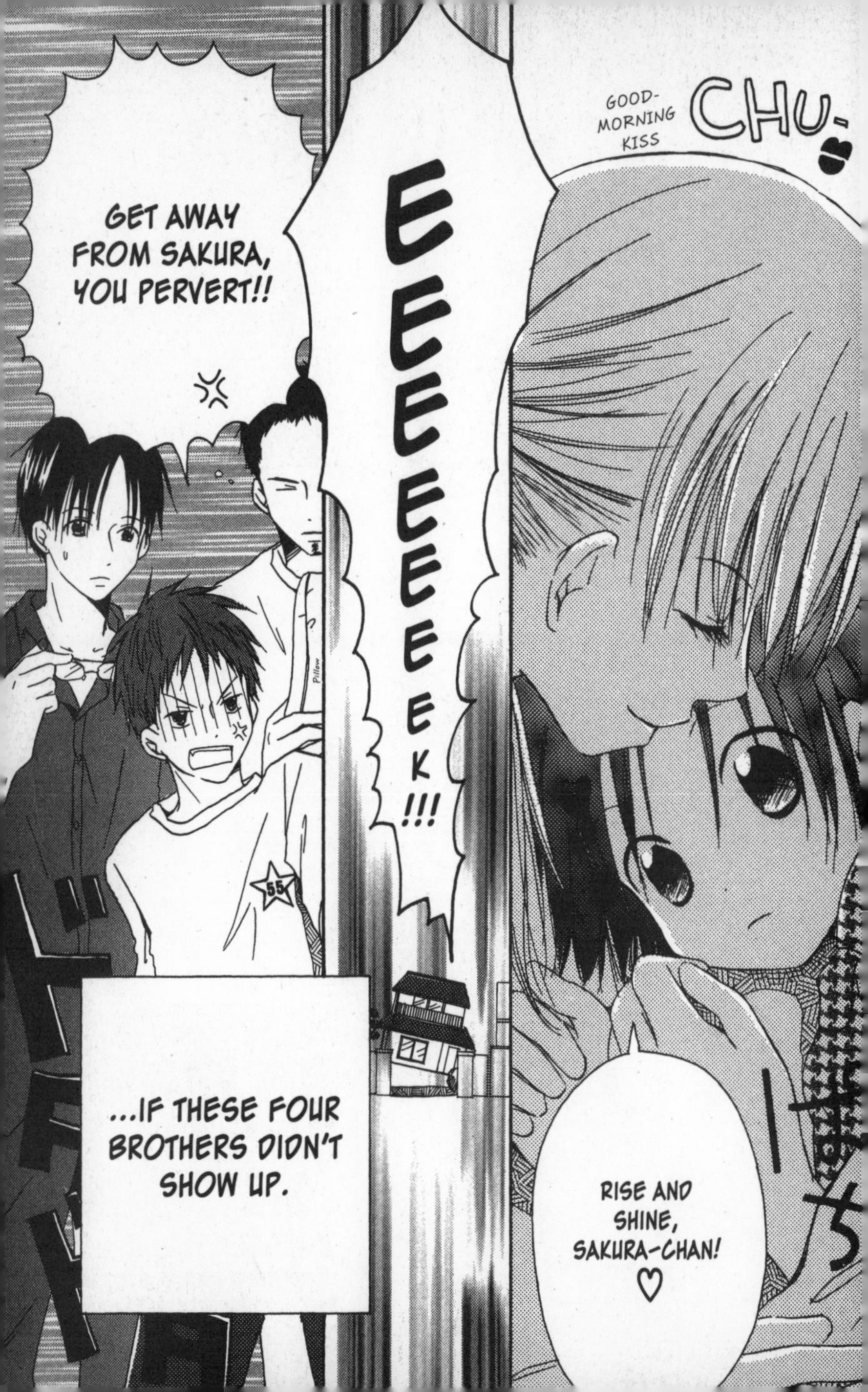
GOOD-MORNING KISS
CHU-
RISE AND SHINE, SAKURA-CHAN! ♡
EEEEEEEK!!!
GET AWAY FROM SAKURA, YOU PERVERT!!
Pillow
55
...IF THESE FOUR BROTHERS DIDN'T SHOW UP.

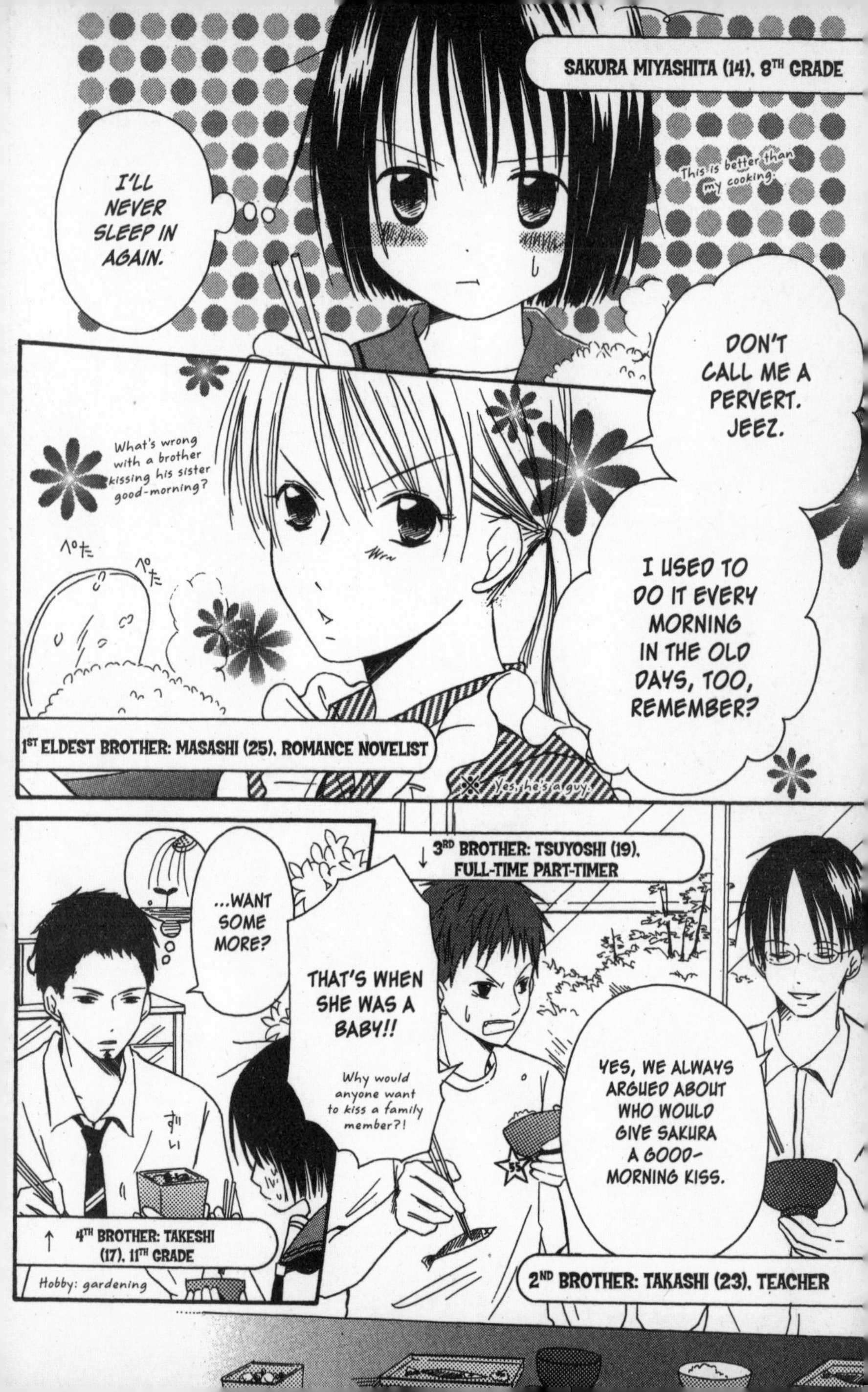
SAKURA MIYASHITA (14), 8TH GRADE
This is better than my cooking.
I'LL NEVER SLEEP IN AGAIN.
DON'T CALL ME A PERVERT. JEEZ.
I USED TO DO IT EVERY MORNING IN THE OLD DAYS, TOO, REMEMBER?
What's wrong with a brother kissing his sister good-morning?
ぺた
ぺた
1ST ELDEST BROTHER: MASASHI (25), ROMANCE NOVELIST
※ Yes, he's a guy.
YES, WE ALWAYS ARGUED ABOUT WHO WOULD GIVE SAKURA A GOOD-MORNING KISS.
2ND BROTHER: TAKASHI (23), TEACHER
↓ 3RD BROTHER: TSUYOSHI (19), FULL-TIME PART-TIMER
THAT'S WHEN SHE WAS A BABY!!
Why would anyone want to kiss a family member?!
...WANT SOME MORE?
↑ 4TH BROTHER: TAKESHI (17), 11TH GRADE
Hobby: gardening

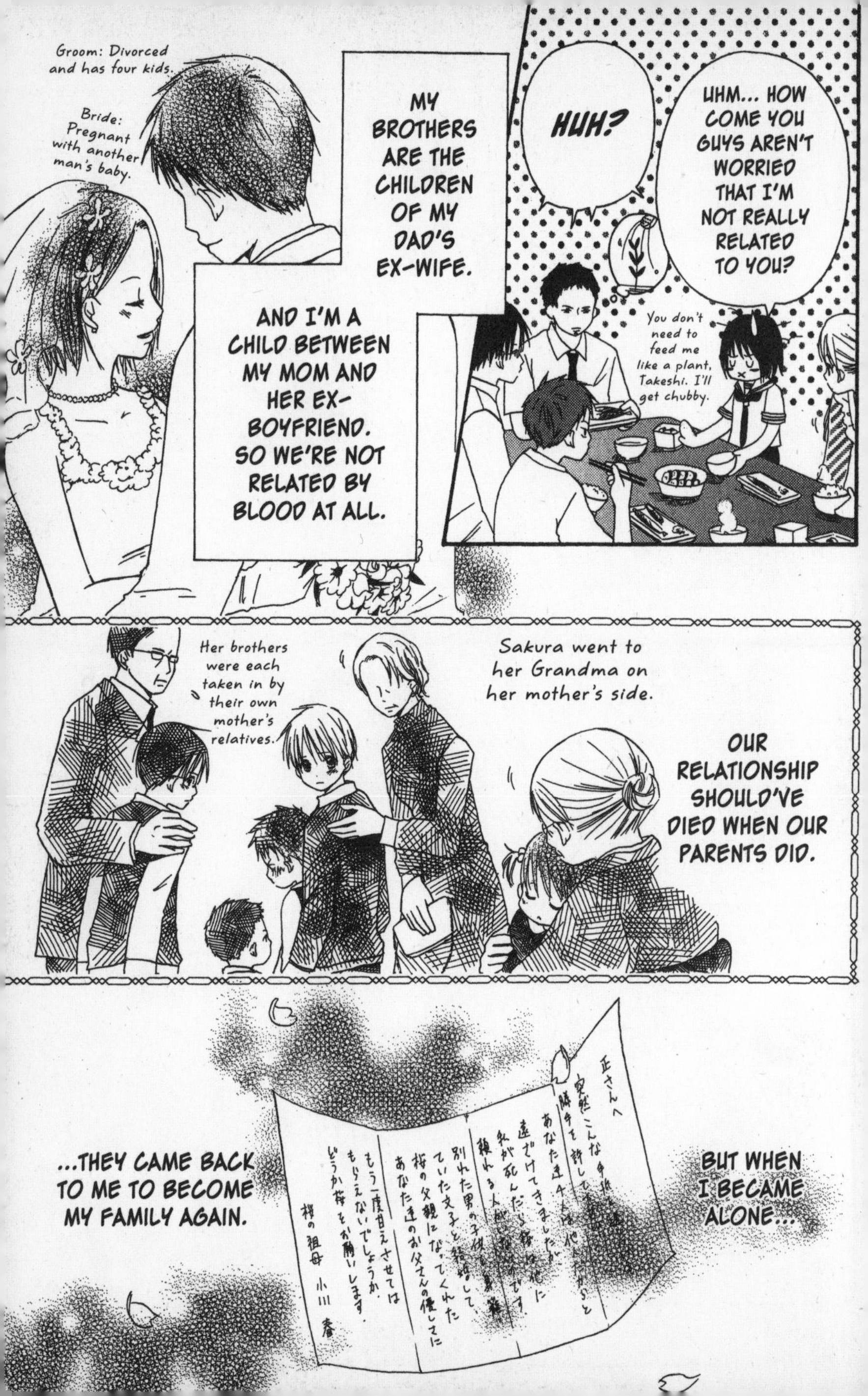
UHM... HOW COME YOU GUYS AREN'T WORRIED THAT I'M NOT REALLY RELATED TO YOU?
HUH?
You don't need to feed me like a plant, Takeshi. I'll get chubby.
MY BROTHERS ARE THE CHILDREN OF MY DAD'S EX-WIFE.
AND I'M A CHILD BETWEEN MY MOM AND HER EX-BOYFRIEND. SO WE'RE NOT RELATED BY BLOOD AT ALL.
Groom: Divorced and has four kids.
Bride: Pregnant with another man's baby.
Sakura went to her Grandma on her mother's side.
OUR RELATIONSHIP SHOULD'VE DIED WHEN OUR PARENTS DID.
Her brothers were each taken in by their own mother's relatives.
BUT WHEN I BECAME ALONE...
正さんへ
あなた達４人は他人だからと
遠ざけてきましたが
桜の父親になってくれた
あなた達のお父さんの優しさに
もう一度甘えさせては
もらえないでしょうか。
どうか桜をお願いします。
桜の祖母　小川　春
...THEY CAME BACK TO ME TO BECOME MY FAMILY AGAIN.

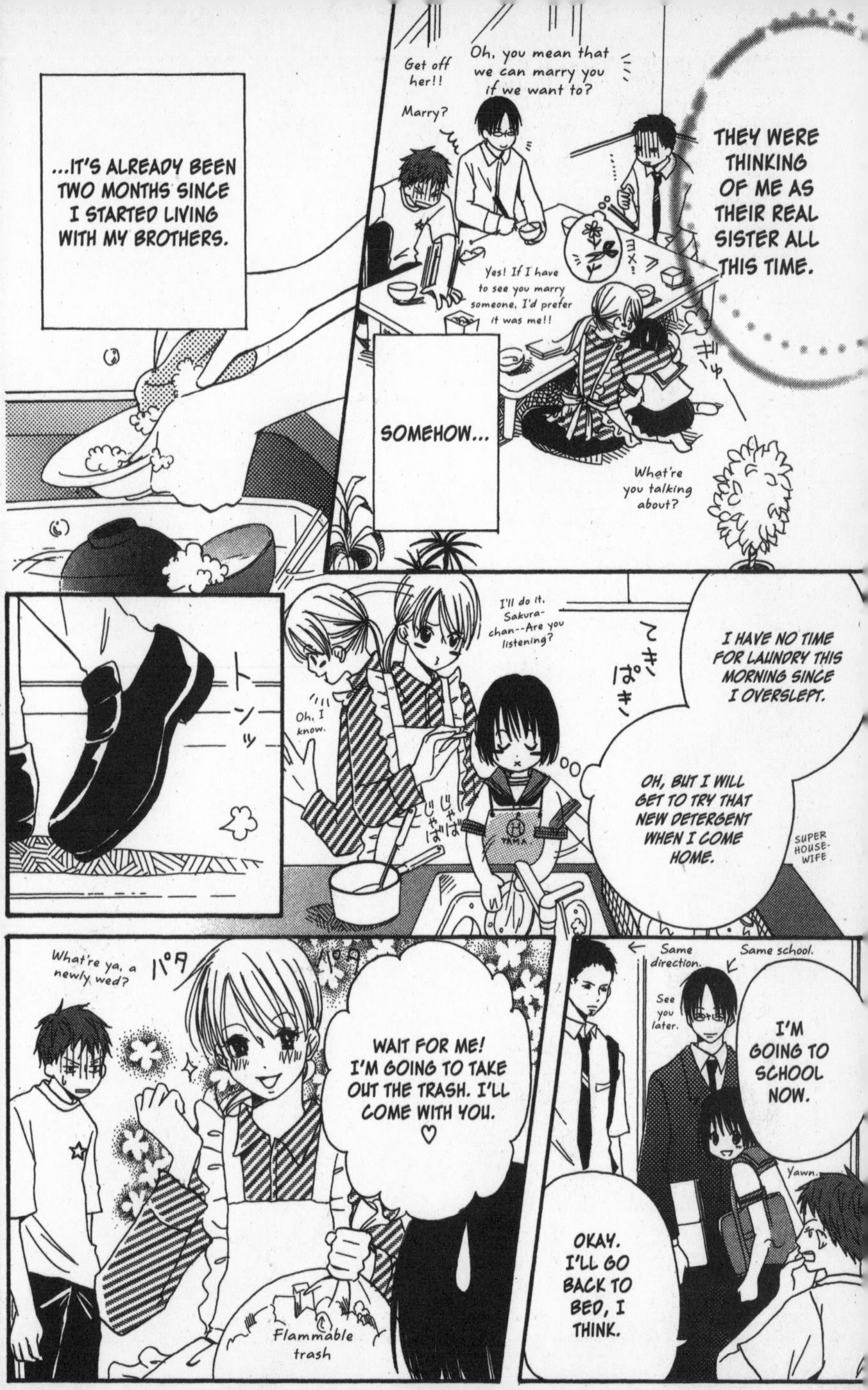
THEY WERE THINKING OF ME AS THEIR REAL SISTER ALL THIS TIME.
Oh, you mean that we can marry you if we want to?
Get off her!!
Marry?
Yes! If I have to see you marry someone, I'd prefer it was me!!
ギュー
SOMEHOW...
What're you talking about?
...IT'S ALREADY BEEN TWO MONTHS SINCE I STARTED LIVING WITH MY BROTHERS.
I HAVE NO TIME FOR LAUNDRY THIS MORNING SINCE I OVERSLEPT.
SUPER HOUSE-WIFE
OH, BUT I WILL GET TO TRY THAT NEW DETERGENT WHEN I COME HOME.
てきぱき
I'll do it, Sakura-chan--Are you listening?
Oh, I know.
じゃばじゃば
トンッ
Same school.
I'M GOING TO SCHOOL NOW.
Same direction.
See you later.
Yawn.
OKAY. I'LL GO BACK TO BED, I THINK.
WAIT FOR ME! I'M GOING TO TAKE OUT THE TRASH. I'LL COME WITH YOU. ♡
パタ
What're ya, a newly wed?
Flammable trash

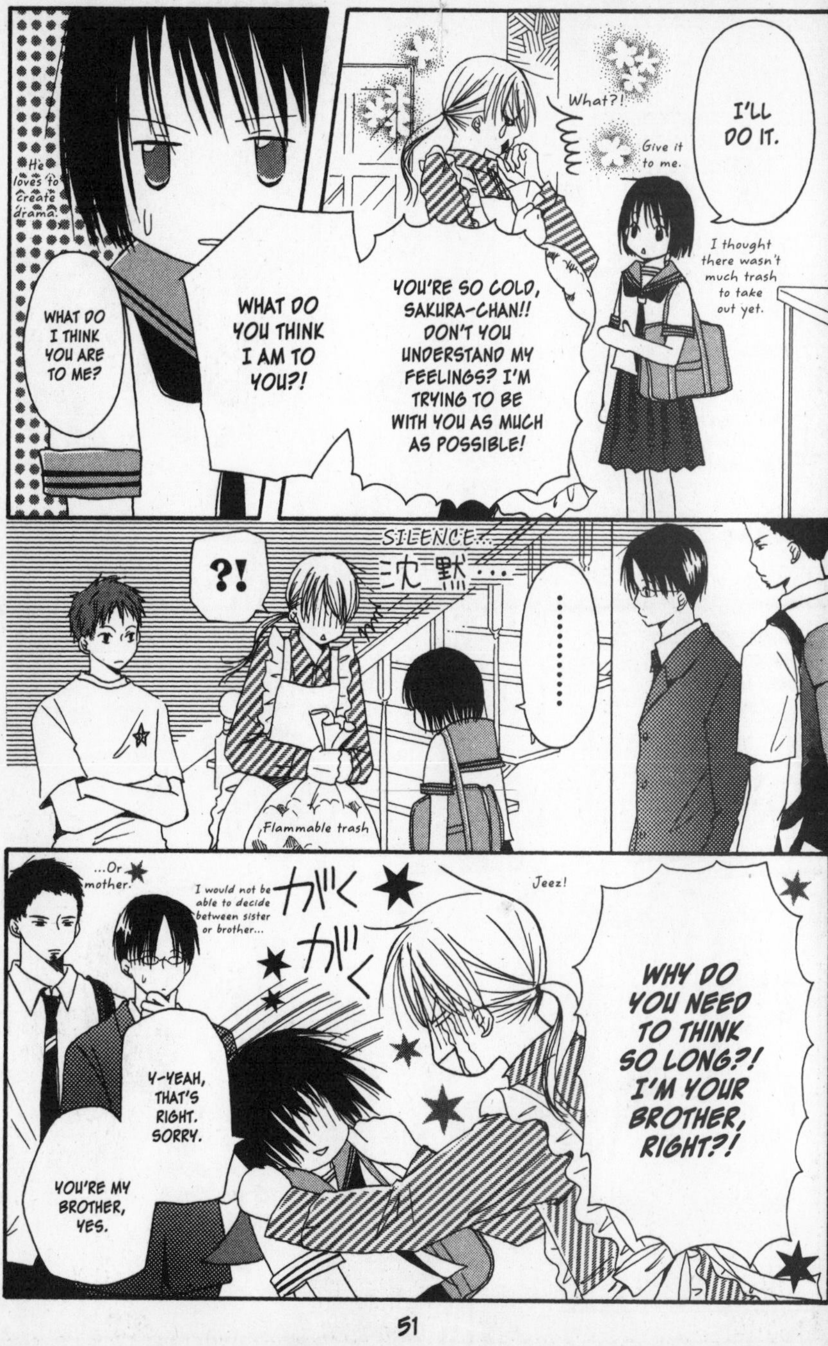
I'LL DO IT.
Give it to me.
What?!
I thought there wasn't much trash to take out yet.
YOU'RE SO COLD, SAKURA-CHAN!! DON'T YOU UNDERSTAND MY FEELINGS? I'M TRYING TO BE WITH YOU AS MUCH AS POSSIBLE!
WHAT DO YOU THINK I AM TO YOU?!
He loves to create drama.
WHAT DO I THINK YOU ARE TO ME?
......
SILENCE...
沈黙…
?!
Flammable trash
WHY DO YOU NEED TO THINK SO LONG?! I'M YOUR BROTHER, RIGHT?!
Jeez!
がくがく
I would not be able to decide between sister or brother...
...Or mother.
Y-YEAH, THAT'S RIGHT. SORRY.
YOU'RE MY BROTHER, YES.

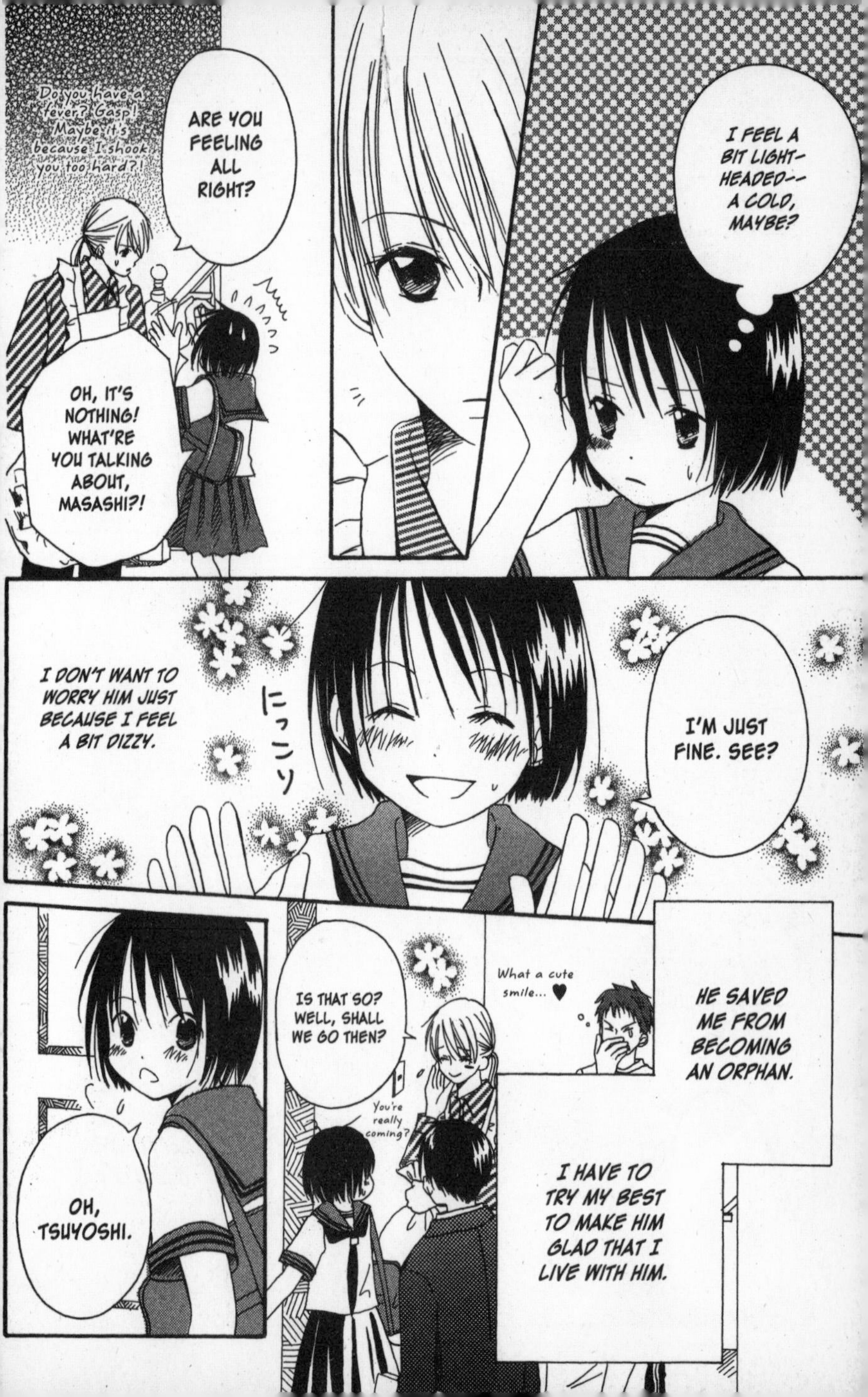
I FEEL A BIT LIGHT-HEADED-- A COLD, MAYBE?
ARE YOU FEELING ALL RIGHT?
Do you have a fever? Gasp! Maybe it's because I shook you too hard?!
OH, IT'S NOTHING! WHAT'RE YOU TALKING ABOUT, MASASHI?!
I'M JUST FINE. SEE?
にっこり
I DON'T WANT TO WORRY HIM JUST BECAUSE I FEEL A BIT DIZZY.
HE SAVED ME FROM BECOMING AN ORPHAN.
What a cute smile... ♥
I HAVE TO TRY MY BEST TO MAKE HIM GLAD THAT I LIVE WITH HIM.
IS THAT SO? WELL, SHALL WE GO THEN?
You're really coming?
OH, TSUYOSHI.

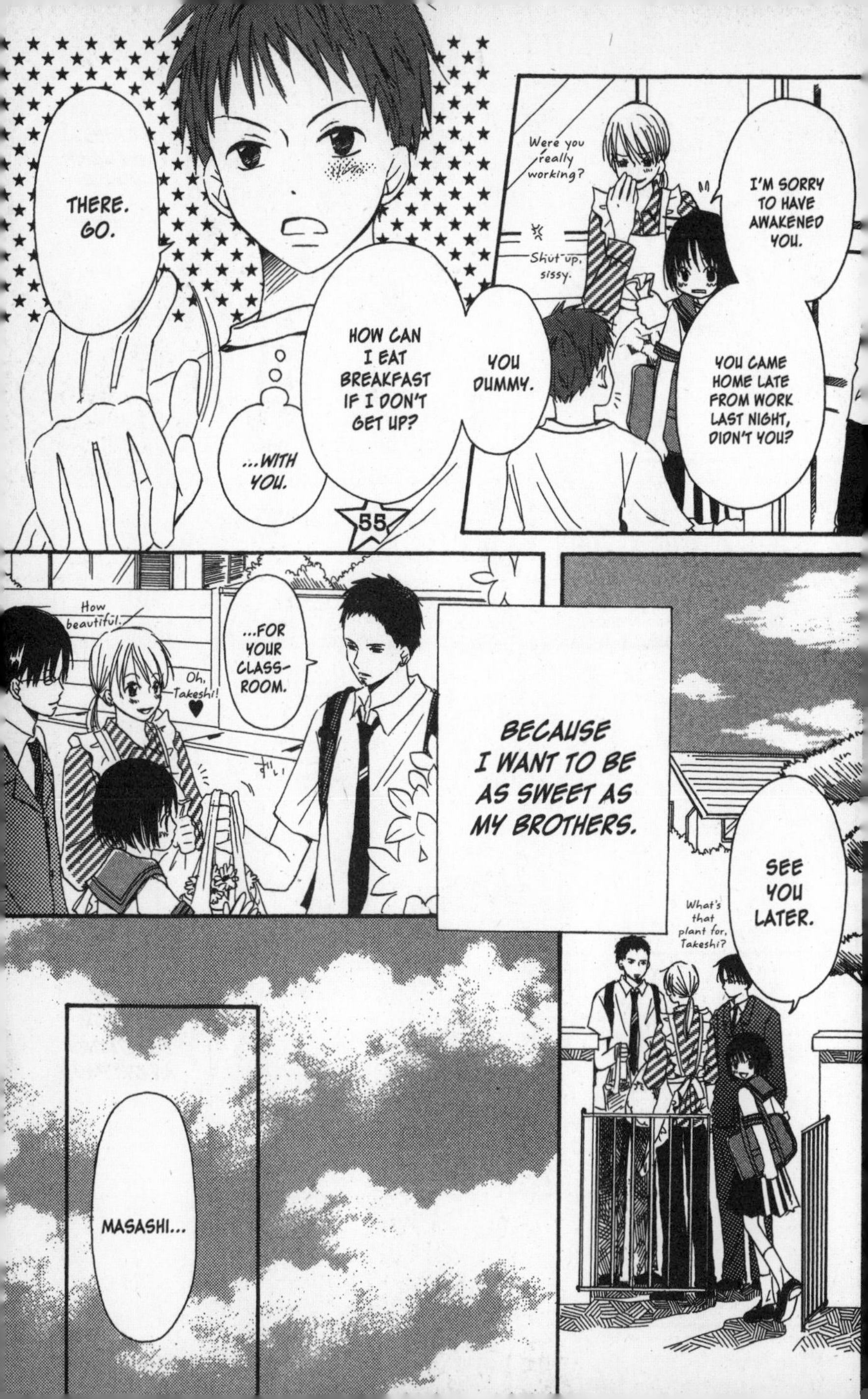
I'M SORRY TO HAVE AWAKENED YOU.
Were you really working?
Shut up, sissy.
YOU CAME HOME LATE FROM WORK LAST NIGHT, DIDN'T YOU?
YOU DUMMY.
HOW CAN I EAT BREAKFAST IF I DON'T GET UP?
...WITH YOU.
THERE. GO.
SEE YOU LATER.
What's that plant for, Takeshi?
...FOR YOUR CLASSROOM.
Oh, Takeshi! ♥
How beautiful.
BECAUSE I WANT TO BE AS SWEET AS MY BROTHERS.
MASASHI...

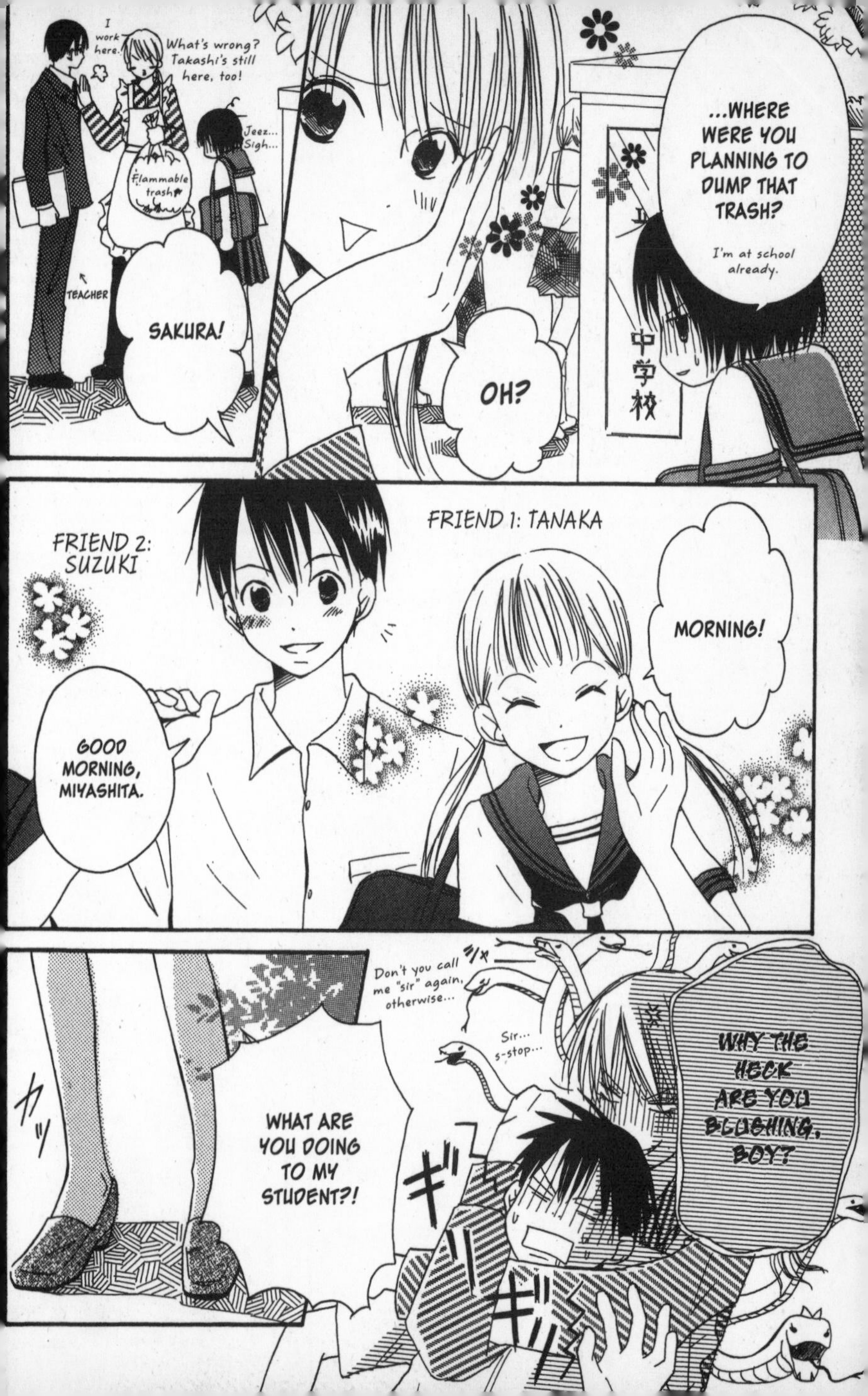
...WHERE WERE YOU PLANNING TO DUMP THAT TRASH?
I'm at school already.
中学校
OH?
I work here.
What's wrong? Takashi's still here, too!
Jeez... Sigh...
Flammable trash
TEACHER
SAKURA!
FRIEND 1: TANAKA
MORNING!
FRIEND 2: SUZUKI
GOOD MORNING, MIYASHITA.
Don't you call me "sir" again, otherwise...
WHY THE HECK ARE YOU BLUSHING, BOY?
Sir... s-stop...
WHAT ARE YOU DOING TO MY STUDENT?!

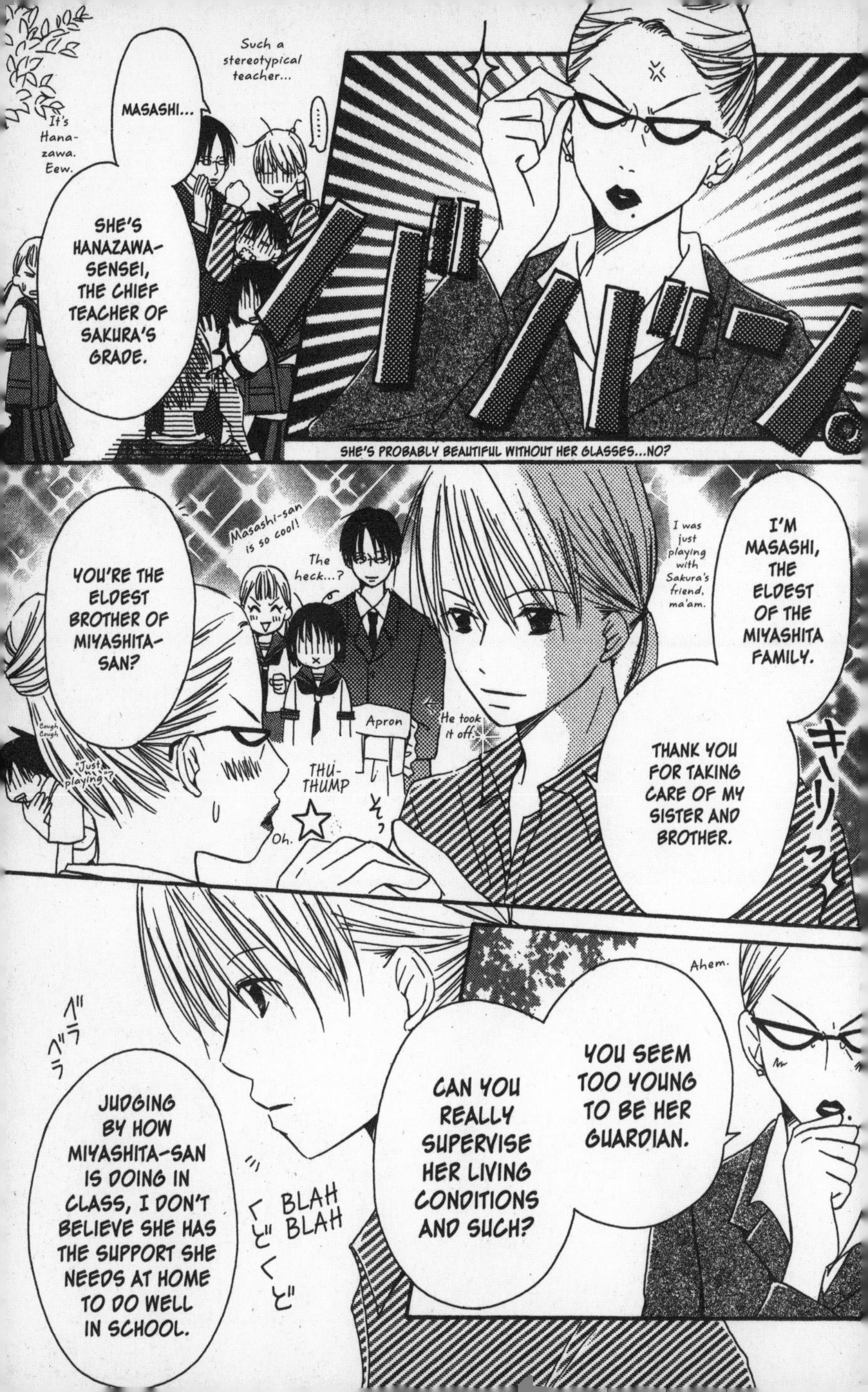

SHE'S PROBABLY BEAUTIFUL WITHOUT HER GLASSES...NO?
Such a stereotypical teacher...
......
MASASHI...
It's Hanazawa. Eew.
SHE'S HANAZAWA-SENSEI, THE CHIEF TEACHER OF SAKURA'S GRADE.
I'M MASASHI, THE ELDEST OF THE MIYASHITA FAMILY.
I was just playing with Sakura's friend, ma'am.
THANK YOU FOR TAKING CARE OF MY SISTER AND BROTHER.
He took it off.
Masashi-san is so cool!
The heck...?
Apron
YOU'RE THE ELDEST BROTHER OF MIYASHITA-SAN?
THU-THUMP
Oh.
Cough Cough
"Just playing"?
Ahem.
YOU SEEM TOO YOUNG TO BE HER GUARDIAN.
CAN YOU REALLY SUPERVISE HER LIVING CONDITIONS AND SUCH?
BLAH BLAH
JUDGING BY HOW MIYASHITA-SAN IS DOING IN CLASS, I DON'T BELIEVE SHE HAS THE SUPPORT SHE NEEDS AT HOME TO DO WELL IN SCHOOL.

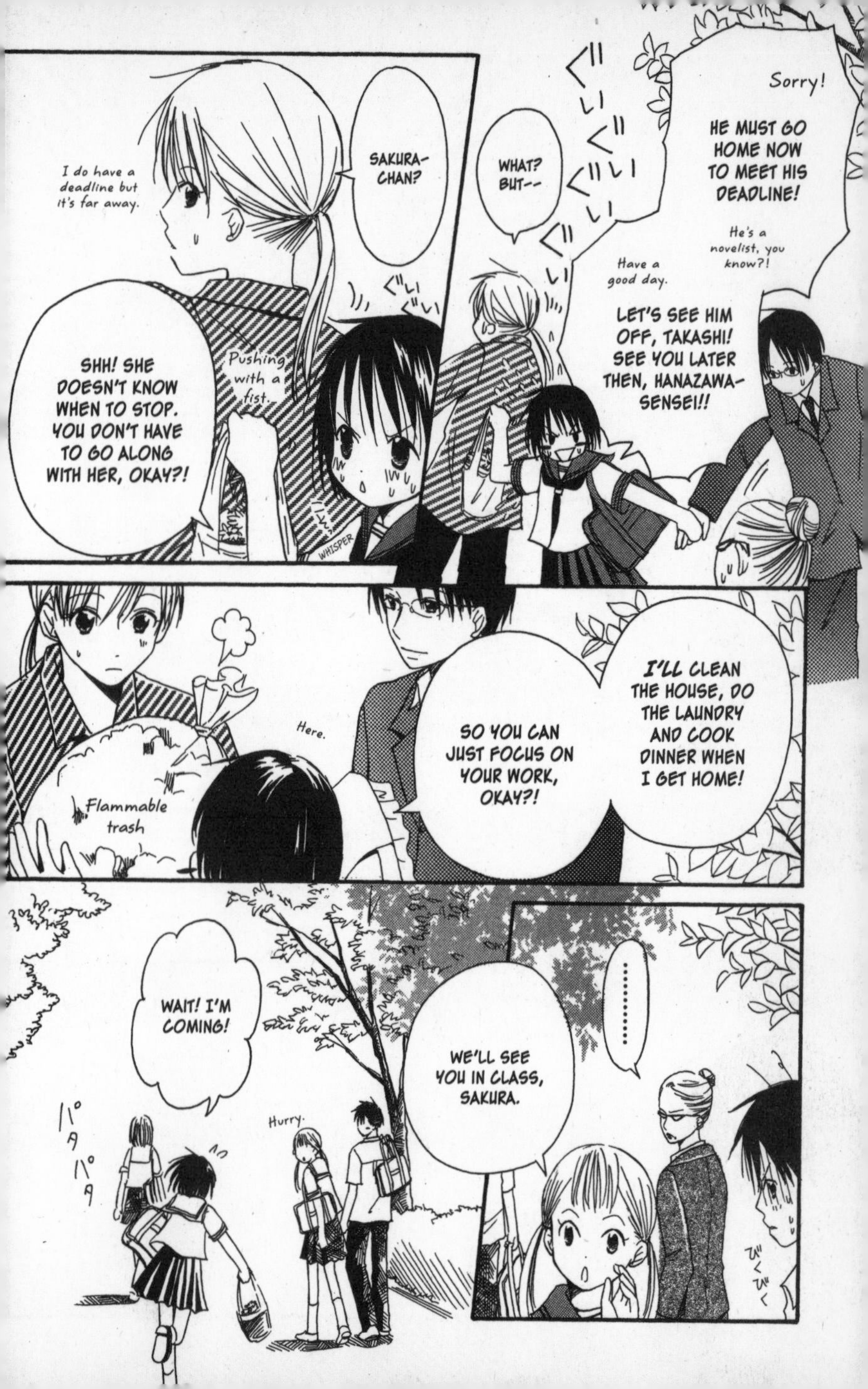
Sorry!
HE MUST GO HOME NOW TO MEET HIS DEADLINE!
He's a novelist, you know?!
Have a good day.
LET'S SEE HIM OFF, TAKASHI! SEE YOU LATER THEN, HANAZAWA-SENSEI!!
WHAT? BUT--
SAKURA-CHAN?
I do have a deadline but it's far away.
SHH! SHE DOESN'T KNOW WHEN TO STOP. YOU DON'T HAVE TO GO ALONG WITH HER, OKAY?!
Pushing with a fist.
WHISPER
I'LL CLEAN THE HOUSE, DO THE LAUNDRY AND COOK DINNER WHEN I GET HOME!
SO YOU CAN JUST FOCUS ON YOUR WORK, OKAY?!
Here.
Flammable trash
......
WE'LL SEE YOU IN CLASS, SAKURA.
WAIT! I'M COMING!
Hurry.

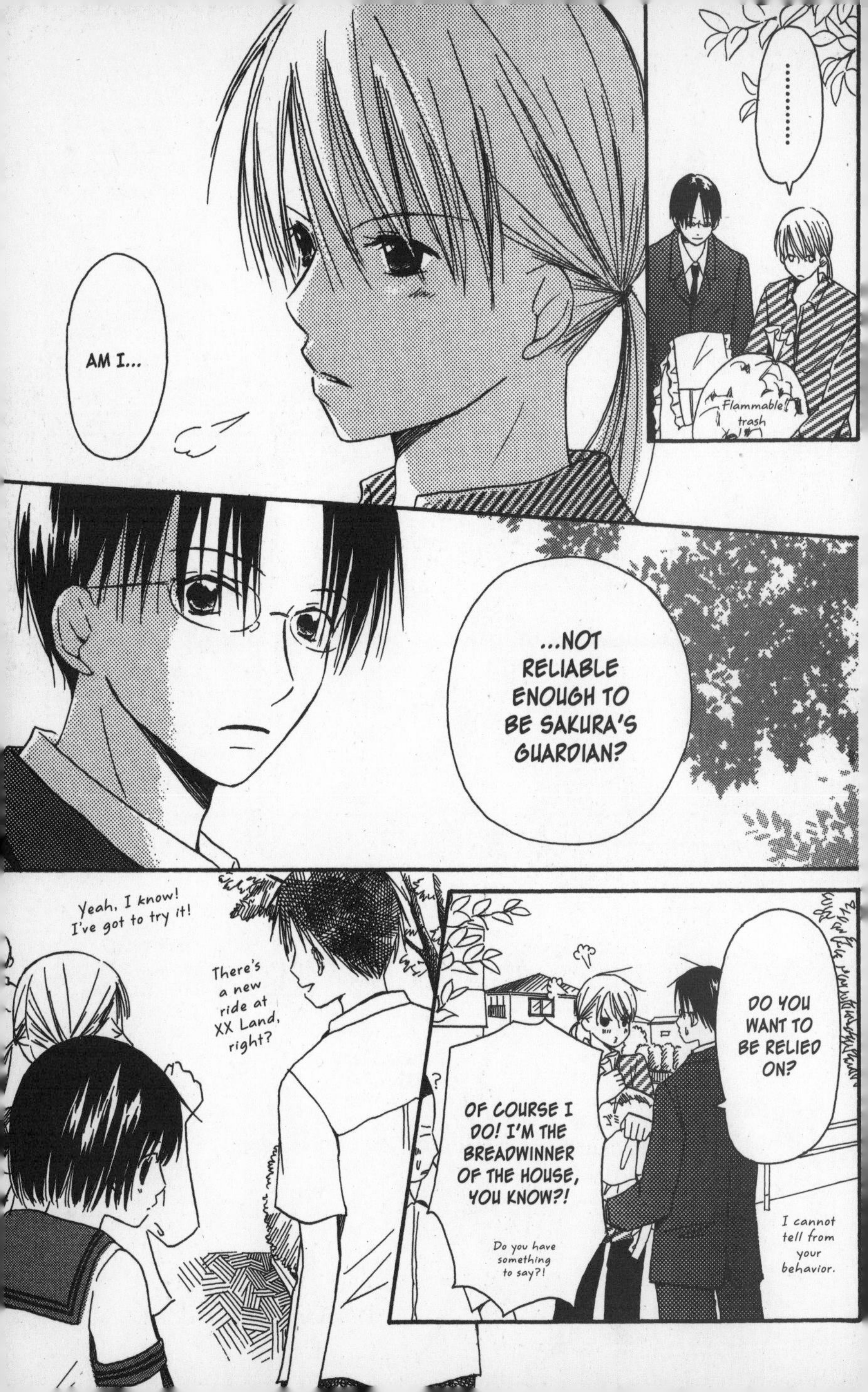
......
Flammable trash
AM I...
...NOT RELIABLE ENOUGH TO BE SAKURA'S GUARDIAN?
DO YOU WANT TO BE RELIED ON?
I cannot tell from your behavior.
OF COURSE I DO! I'M THE BREADWINNER OF THE HOUSE, YOU KNOW?!
Do you have something to say?!
There's a new ride at XX Land, right?
Yeah, I know! I've got to try it!

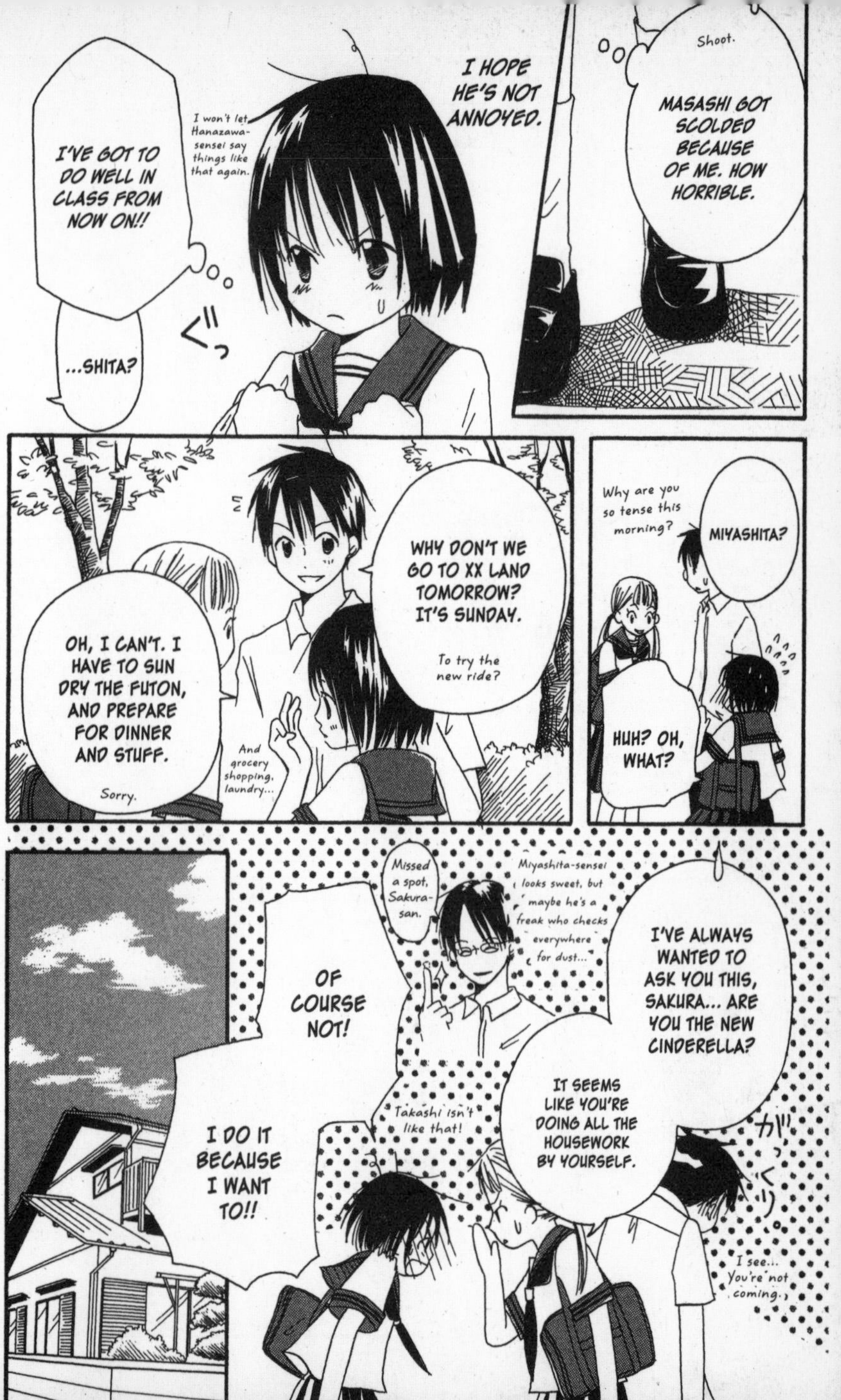

Shoot.
MASASHI GOT SCOLDED BECAUSE OF ME. HOW HORRIBLE.
I HOPE HE'S NOT ANNOYED.
I'VE GOT TO DO WELL IN CLASS FROM NOW ON!!
I won't let Hanazawa-sensei say things like that again.
...SHITA?
Why are you so tense this morning?
MIYASHITA?
HUH? OH, WHAT?
WHY DON'T WE GO TO XX LAND TOMORROW? IT'S SUNDAY.
To try the new ride?
OH, I CAN'T. I HAVE TO SUN DRY THE FUTON, AND PREPARE FOR DINNER AND STUFF.
And grocery shopping, laundry...
Sorry.
I'VE ALWAYS WANTED TO ASK YOU THIS, SAKURA... ARE YOU THE NEW CINDERELLA?
IT SEEMS LIKE YOU'RE DOING ALL THE HOUSEWORK BY YOURSELF.
I see... You're not coming.
OF COURSE NOT!
Miyashita-sensei looks sweet, but maybe he's a freak who checks everywhere for dust...
Missed a spot, Sakura-san.
Takashi isn't like that!
I DO IT BECAUSE I WANT TO!!

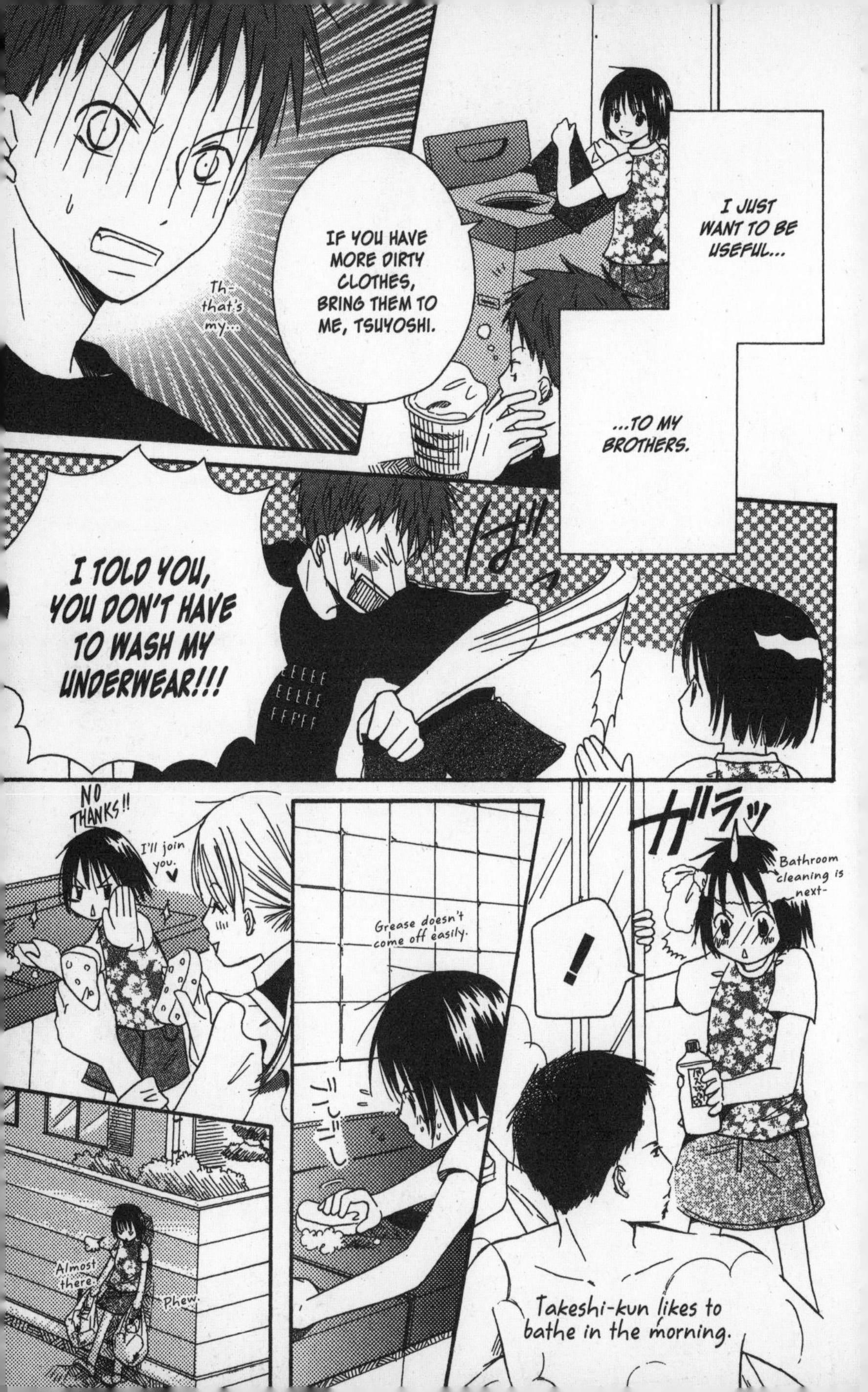

I JUST WANT TO BE USEFUL...
IF YOU HAVE MORE DIRTY CLOTHES, BRING THEM TO ME, TSUYOSHI.
...TO MY BROTHERS.
Th-that's my...
ばっ
I TOLD YOU, YOU DON'T HAVE TO WASH MY UNDERWEAR!!!
ガラッ
Bathroom cleaning is next-
!
Takeshi-kun likes to bathe in the morning.
Grease doesn't come off easily.
NO THANKS!!
I'll join you.
Almost there.
Phew.

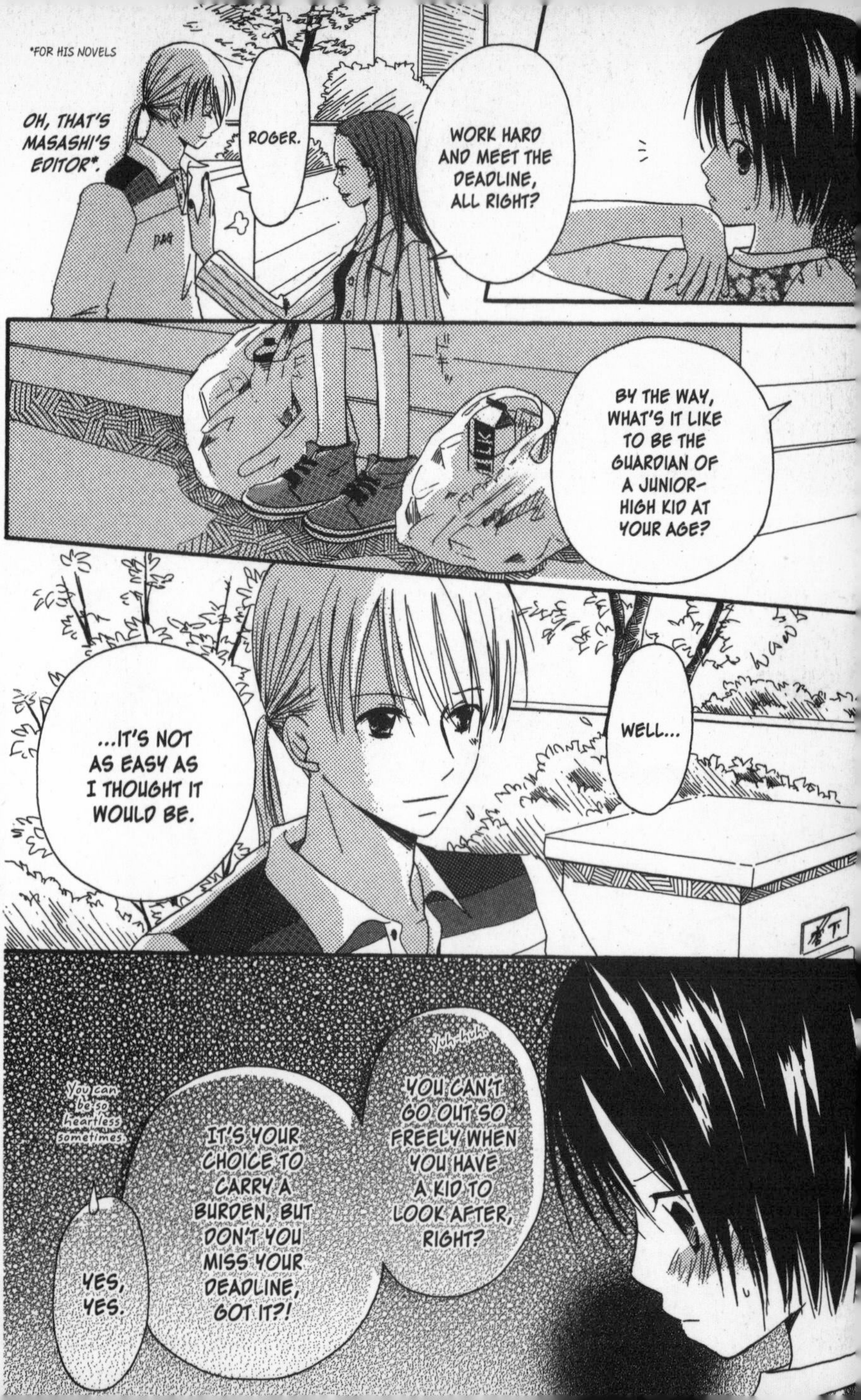
*FOR HIS NOVELS
WORK HARD AND MEET THE DEADLINE, ALL RIGHT?
ROGER.
OH, THAT'S MASASHI'S EDITOR*.
BY THE WAY, WHAT'S IT LIKE TO BE THE GUARDIAN OF A JUNIOR-HIGH KID AT YOUR AGE?
WELL...
...IT'S NOT AS EASY AS I THOUGHT IT WOULD BE.
Yuh-huh.
YOU CAN'T GO OUT SO FREELY WHEN YOU HAVE A KID TO LOOK AFTER, RIGHT?
IT'S YOUR CHOICE TO CARRY A BURDEN, BUT DON'T YOU MISS YOUR DEADLINE, GOT IT?!
You can be so heartless sometimes.
YES, YES.

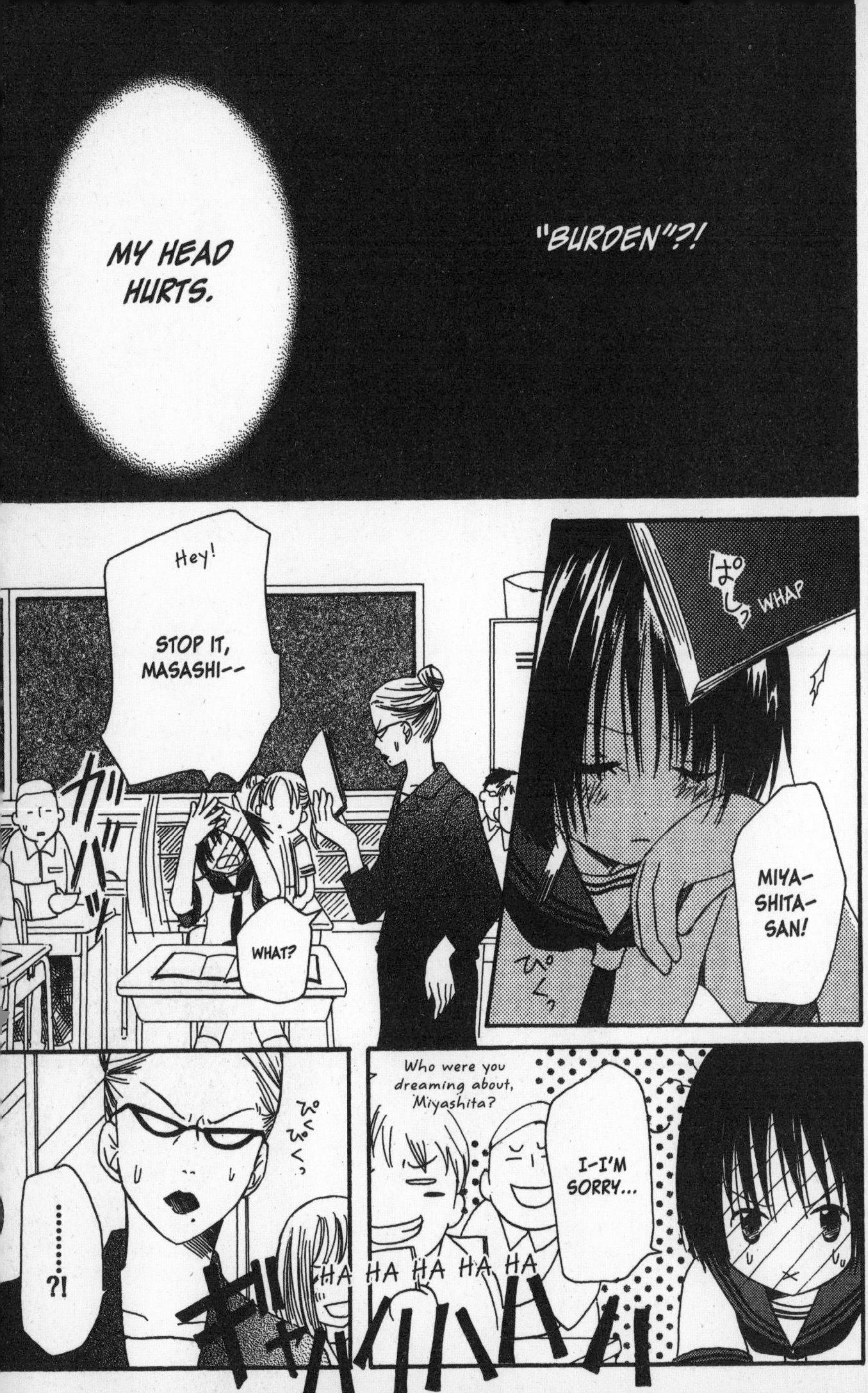
"BURDEN"?!
MY HEAD HURTS.
ぱしっ WHAP
MIYA-SHITA-SAN!
ぴくっ
Hey!
STOP IT, MASASHI--
WHAT?
Who were you dreaming about, Miyashita?
I-I'M SORRY...
HA HA HA HA HA
ぴくぴくっ
......?!

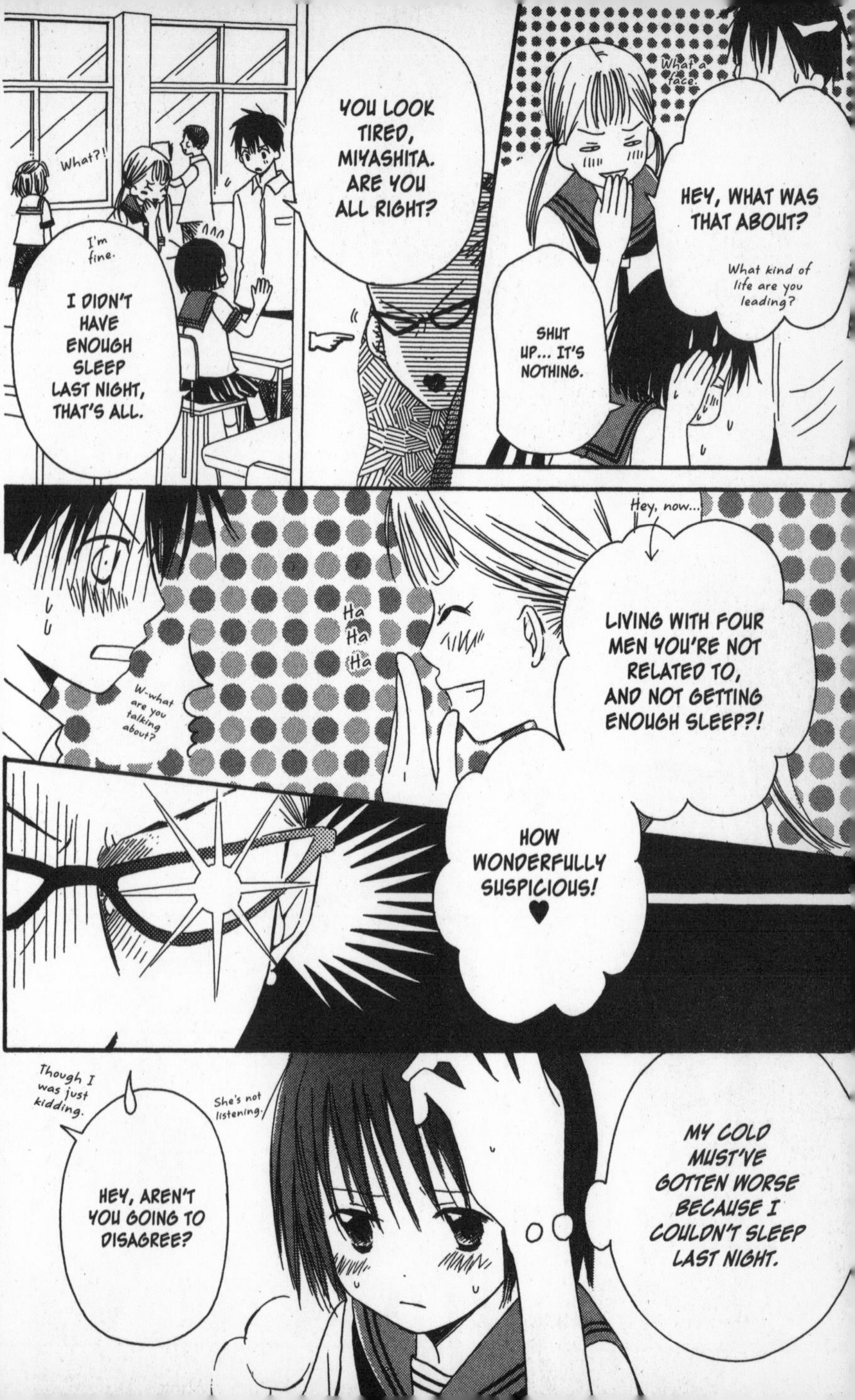
What a face.
HEY, WHAT WAS THAT ABOUT?
What kind of life are you leading?
SHUT UP... IT'S NOTHING.
YOU LOOK TIRED, MIYASHITA. ARE YOU ALL RIGHT?
What?!
I'm fine.
I DIDN'T HAVE ENOUGH SLEEP LAST NIGHT, THAT'S ALL.
Hey, now...
LIVING WITH FOUR MEN YOU'RE NOT RELATED TO, AND NOT GETTING ENOUGH SLEEP?!
Ha Ha Ha
W-what are you talking about?
HOW WONDERFULLY SUSPICIOUS! ♥
MY COLD MUST'VE GOTTEN WORSE BECAUSE I COULDN'T SLEEP LAST NIGHT.
She's not listening.
HEY, AREN'T YOU GOING TO DISAGREE?
Though I was just kidding.

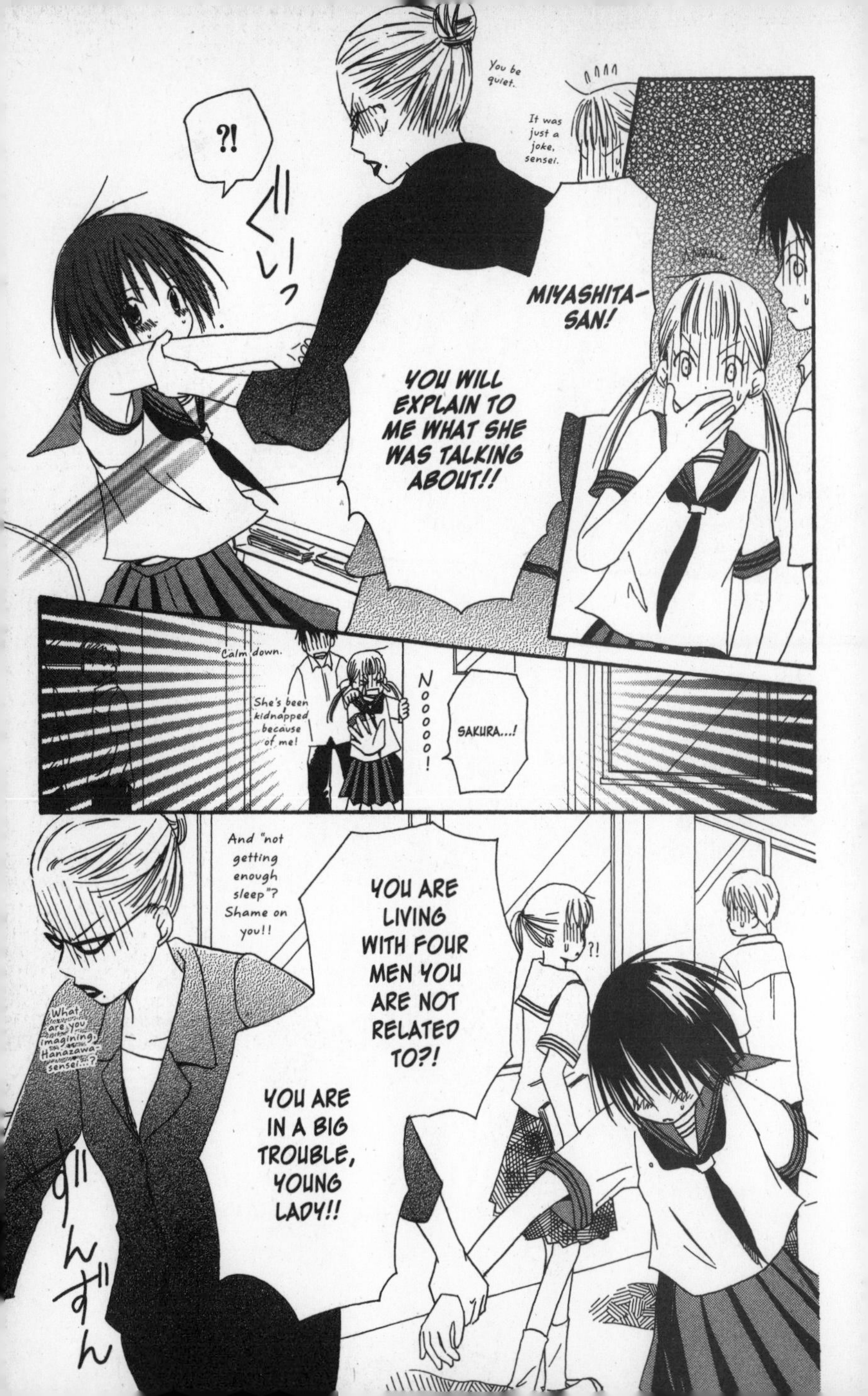
You be quiet.
It was just a joke, sensei.
MIYASHITA-SAN!
YOU WILL EXPLAIN TO ME WHAT SHE WAS TALKING ABOUT!!
?!
ぐいっ
SAKURA...!
Noooooo!
She's been kidnapped because of me!
Calm down.
YOU ARE LIVING WITH FOUR MEN YOU ARE NOT RELATED TO?!
And "not getting enough sleep"? Shame on you!!
?!
YOU ARE IN A BIG TROUBLE, YOUNG LADY!!
What are you imagining, Hanazawa-sensei...?
ずんずん

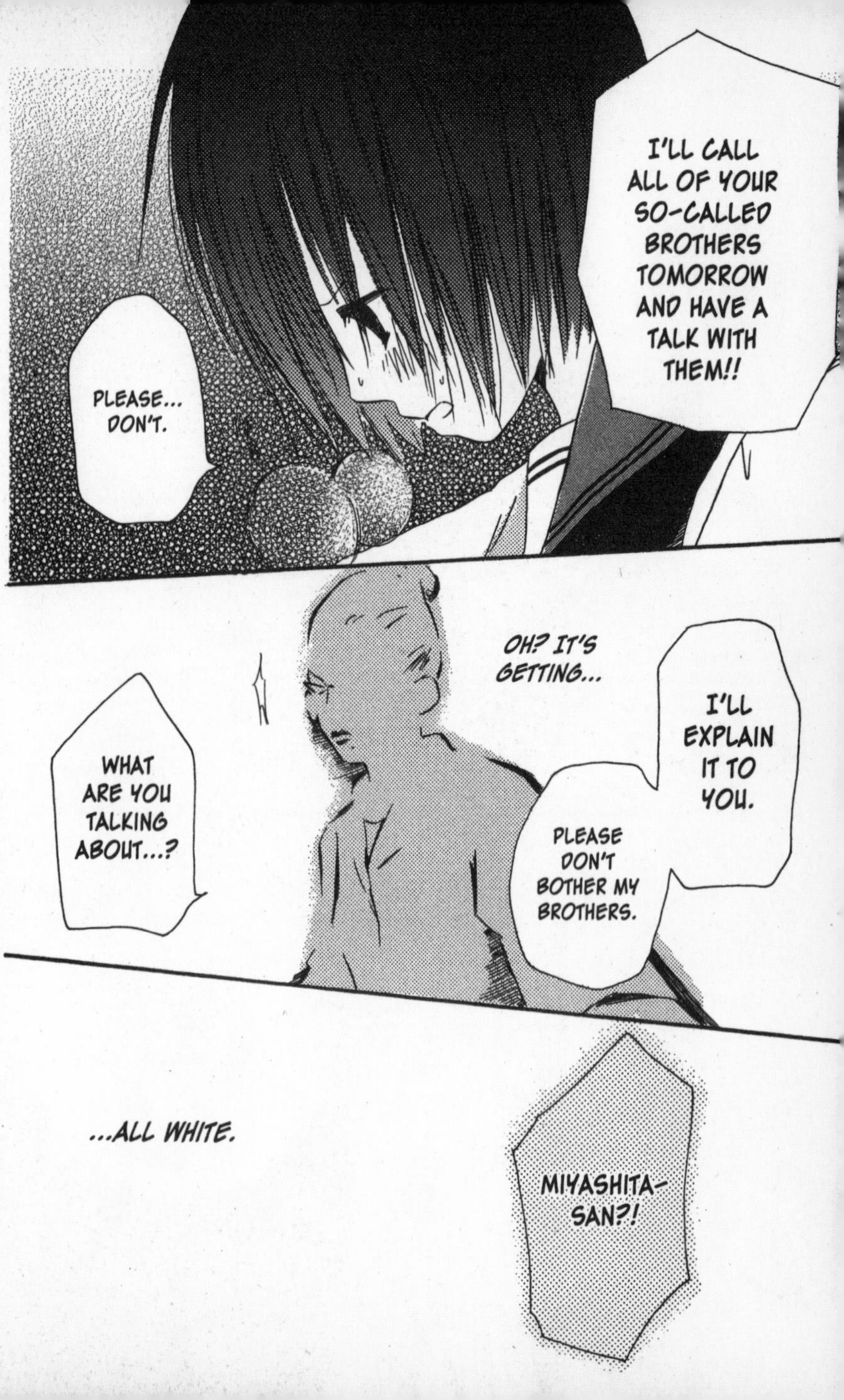
I'LL CALL ALL OF YOUR SO-CALLED BROTHERS TOMORROW AND HAVE A TALK WITH THEM!!
PLEASE... DON'T.
I'LL EXPLAIN IT TO YOU.
OH? IT'S GETTING...
PLEASE DON'T BOTHER MY BROTHERS.
WHAT ARE YOU TALKING ABOUT...?
MIYASHITA-SAN?!
...ALL WHITE.

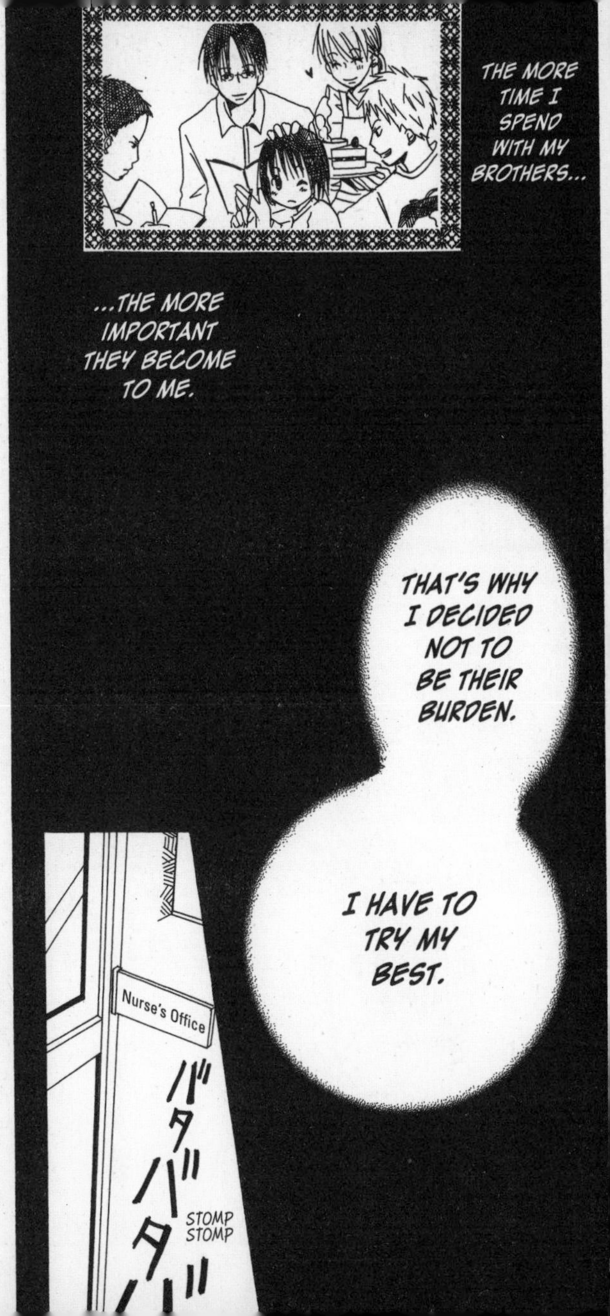
THE MORE TIME I SPEND WITH MY BROTHERS...
...THE MORE IMPORTANT THEY BECOME TO ME.
THAT'S WHY I DECIDED NOT TO BE THEIR BURDEN.
I HAVE TO TRY MY BEST.
Nurse's Office
バタバタ
STOMP STOMP

☆ 2 ☆

About the story.

Me & My Brothers is my first story with many characters, so I had a hard time. Phew! I first created those four brothers, thinking only about making them look different, but all my editors told me that none of them look good. Yes, there were many nights I wet my pillow with tears (exaggerating).

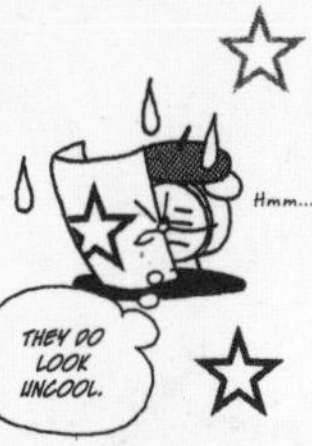
Hmm...
THEY DO LOOK UNCOOL.

Oh, but Takeshi has hardly changed, because he's my type. I can't compromise him. Ha ha ha. To be continued.

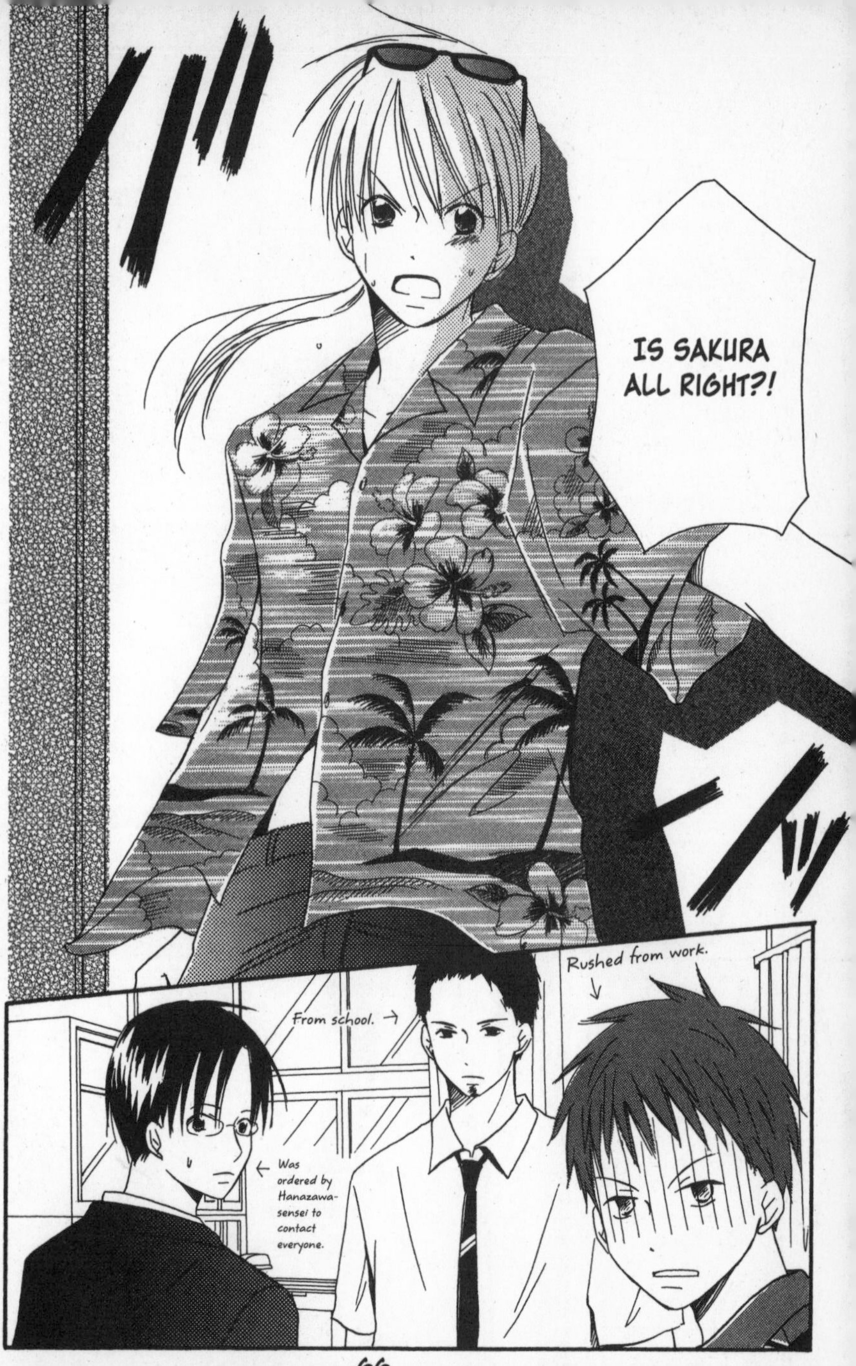
IS SAKURA ALL RIGHT?!
Rushed from work.
From school.
Was ordered by Hanazawa-sensei to contact everyone.

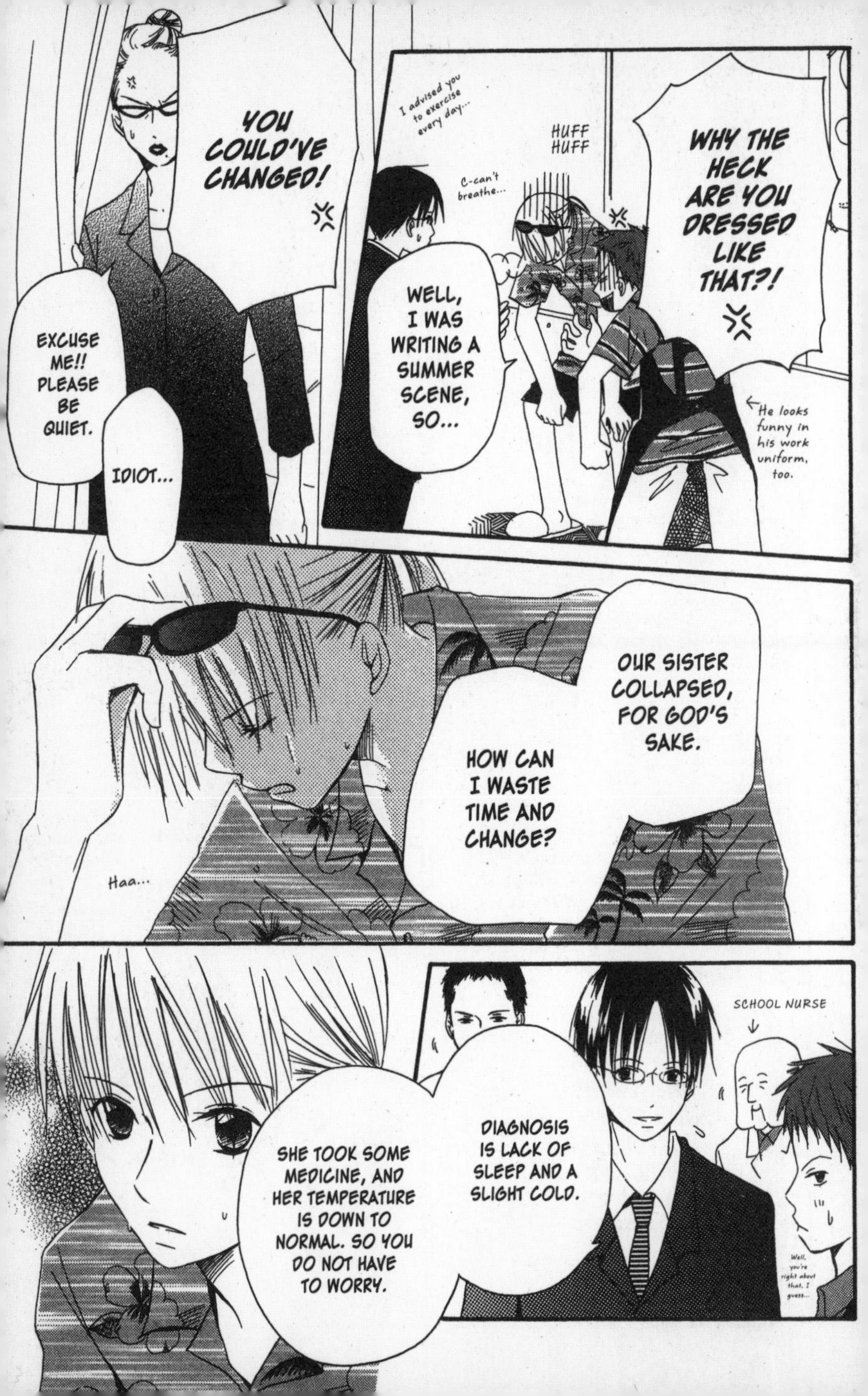
WHY THE HECK ARE YOU DRESSED LIKE THAT?!
He looks funny in his work uniform, too.
HUFF HUFF
I advised you to exercise every day...
C-can't breathe...
WELL, I WAS WRITING A SUMMER SCENE, SO...
YOU COULD'VE CHANGED!
IDIOT...
EXCUSE ME!! PLEASE BE QUIET.
OUR SISTER COLLAPSED, FOR GOD'S SAKE.
HOW CAN I WASTE TIME AND CHANGE?
Haa...
SCHOOL NURSE
Well, you're right about that, I guess...
DIAGNOSIS IS LACK OF SLEEP AND A SLIGHT COLD.
SHE TOOK SOME MEDICINE, AND HER TEMPERATURE IS DOWN TO NORMAL. SO YOU DO NOT HAVE TO WORRY.

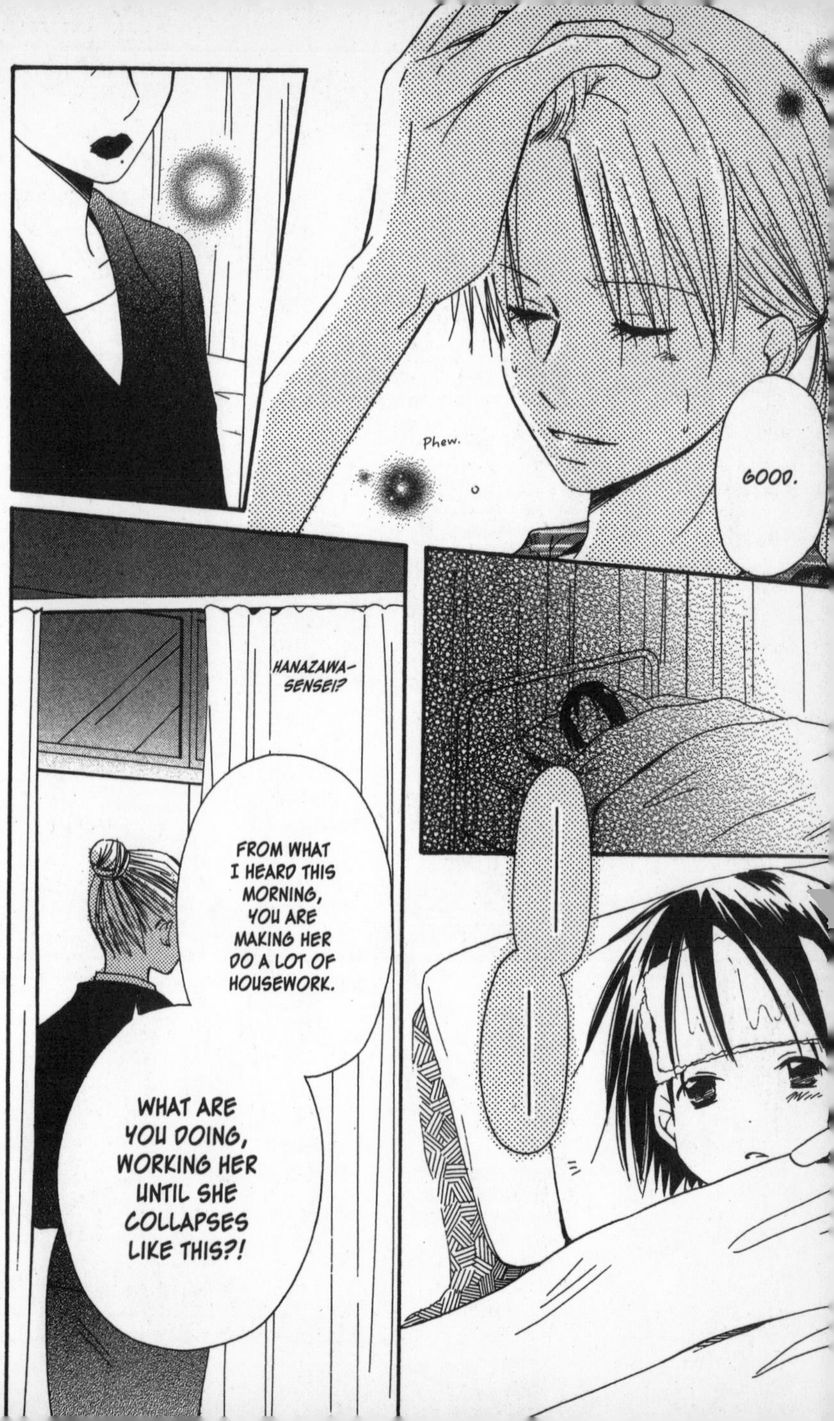
GOOD.
Phew.
HANAZAWA-SENSEI?
FROM WHAT I HEARD THIS MORNING, YOU ARE MAKING HER DO A LOT OF HOUSEWORK.
WHAT ARE YOU DOING, WORKING HER UNTIL SHE COLLAPSES LIKE THIS?!

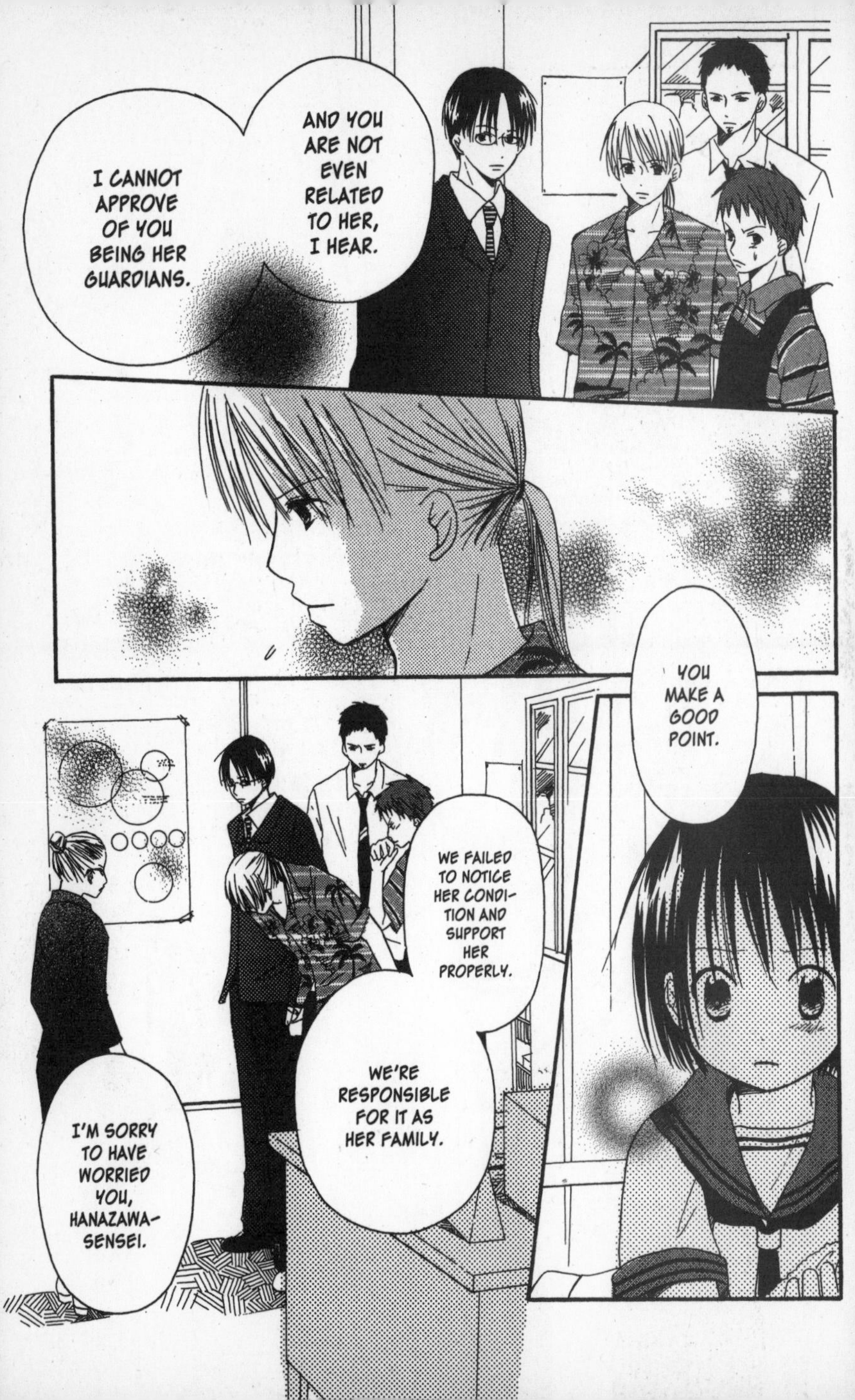
AND YOU ARE NOT EVEN RELATED TO HER, I HEAR.
I CANNOT APPROVE OF YOU BEING HER GUARDIANS.
YOU MAKE A GOOD POINT.
WE FAILED TO NOTICE HER CONDI-TION AND SUPPORT HER PROPERLY.
WE'RE RESPONSIBLE FOR IT AS HER FAMILY.
I'M SORRY TO HAVE WORRIED YOU, HANAZAWA-SENSEI.

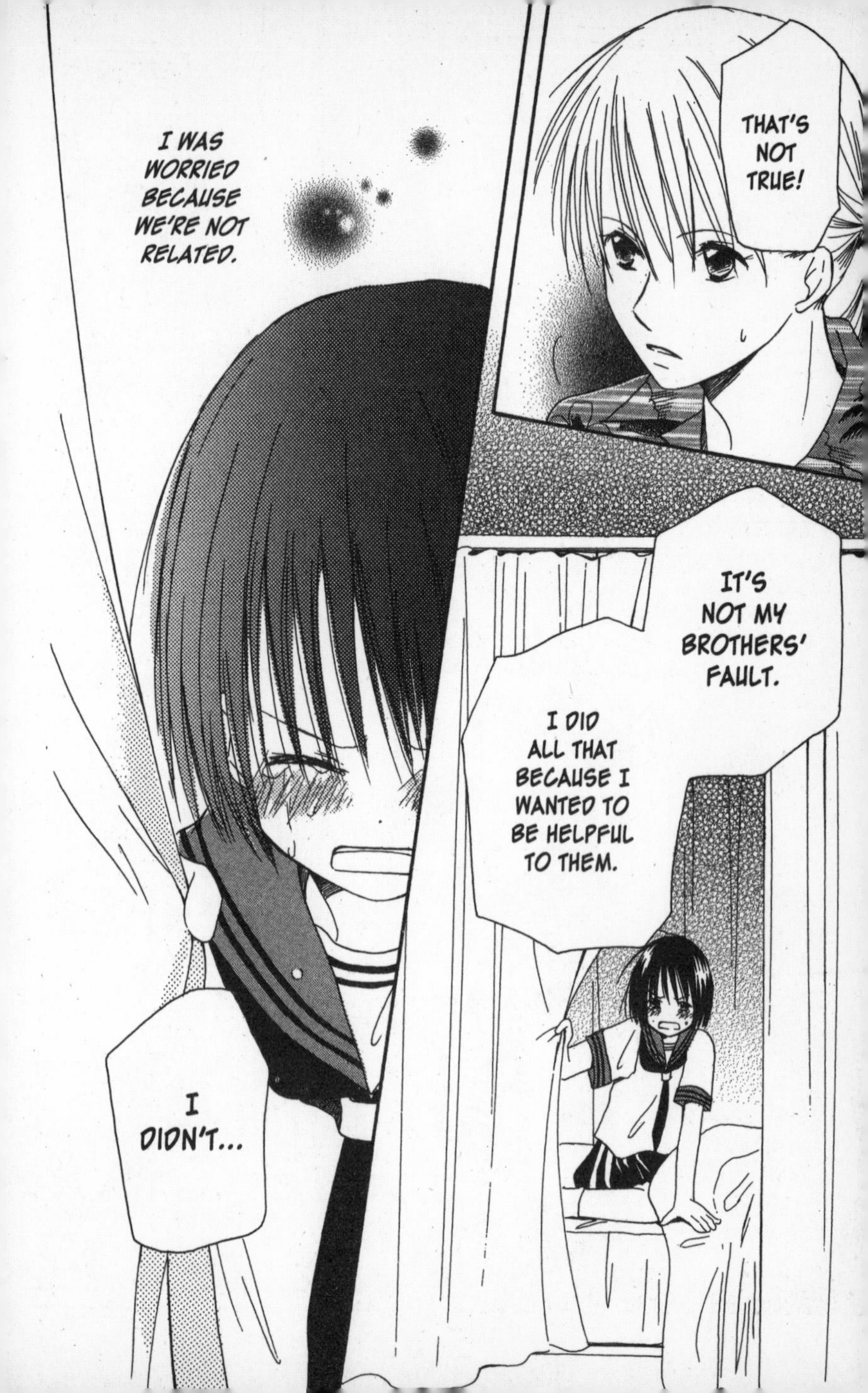
THAT'S NOT TRUE!
IT'S NOT MY BROTHERS' FAULT.
I DID ALL THAT BECAUSE I WANTED TO BE HELPFUL TO THEM.
I WAS WORRIED BECAUSE WE'RE NOT RELATED.
I DIDN'T...

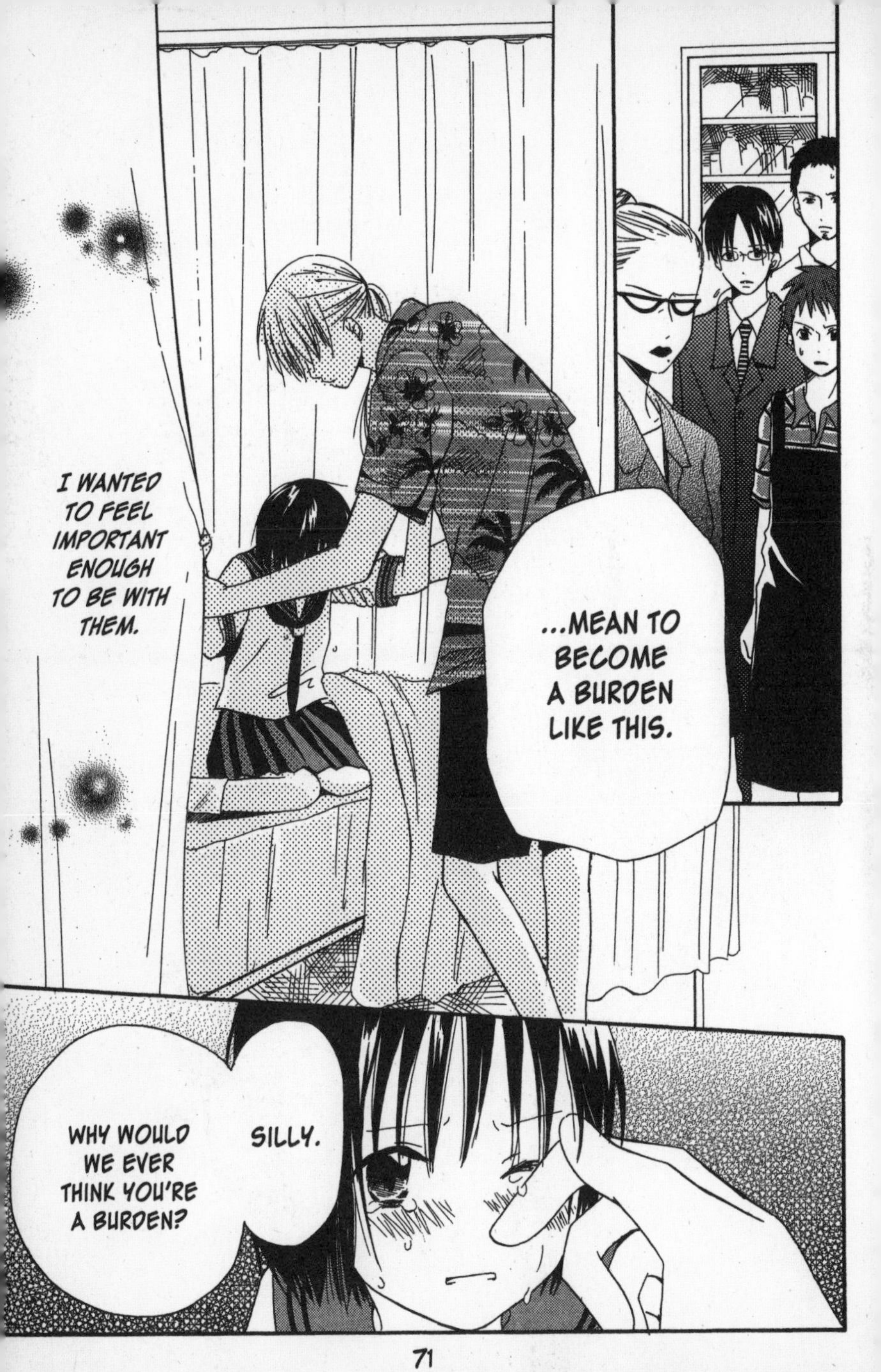
...MEAN TO BECOME A BURDEN LIKE THIS.
I WANTED TO FEEL IMPORTANT ENOUGH TO BE WITH THEM.
SILLY.
WHY WOULD WE EVER THINK YOU'RE A BURDEN?

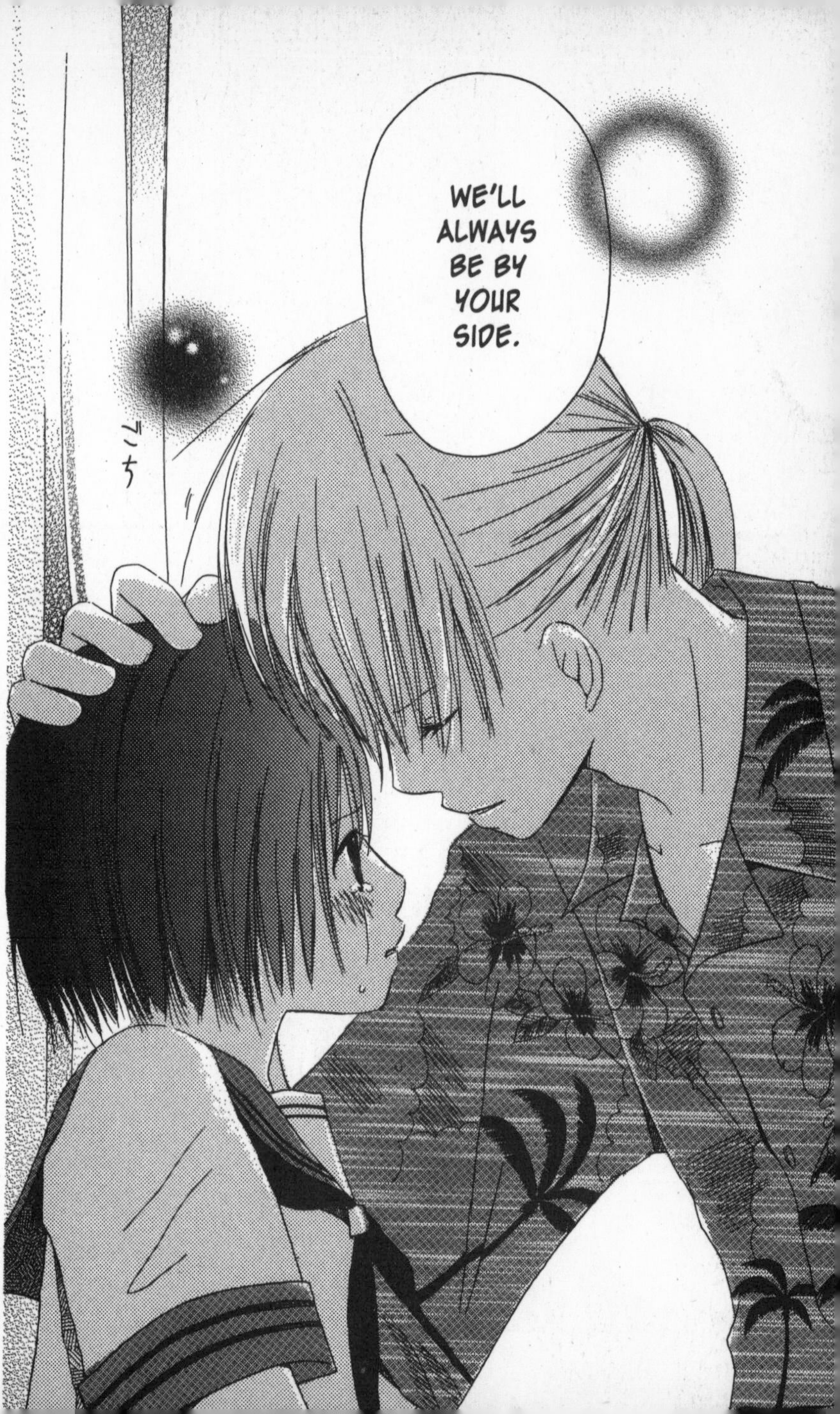
WE'LL ALWAYS BE BY YOUR SIDE.
ごち

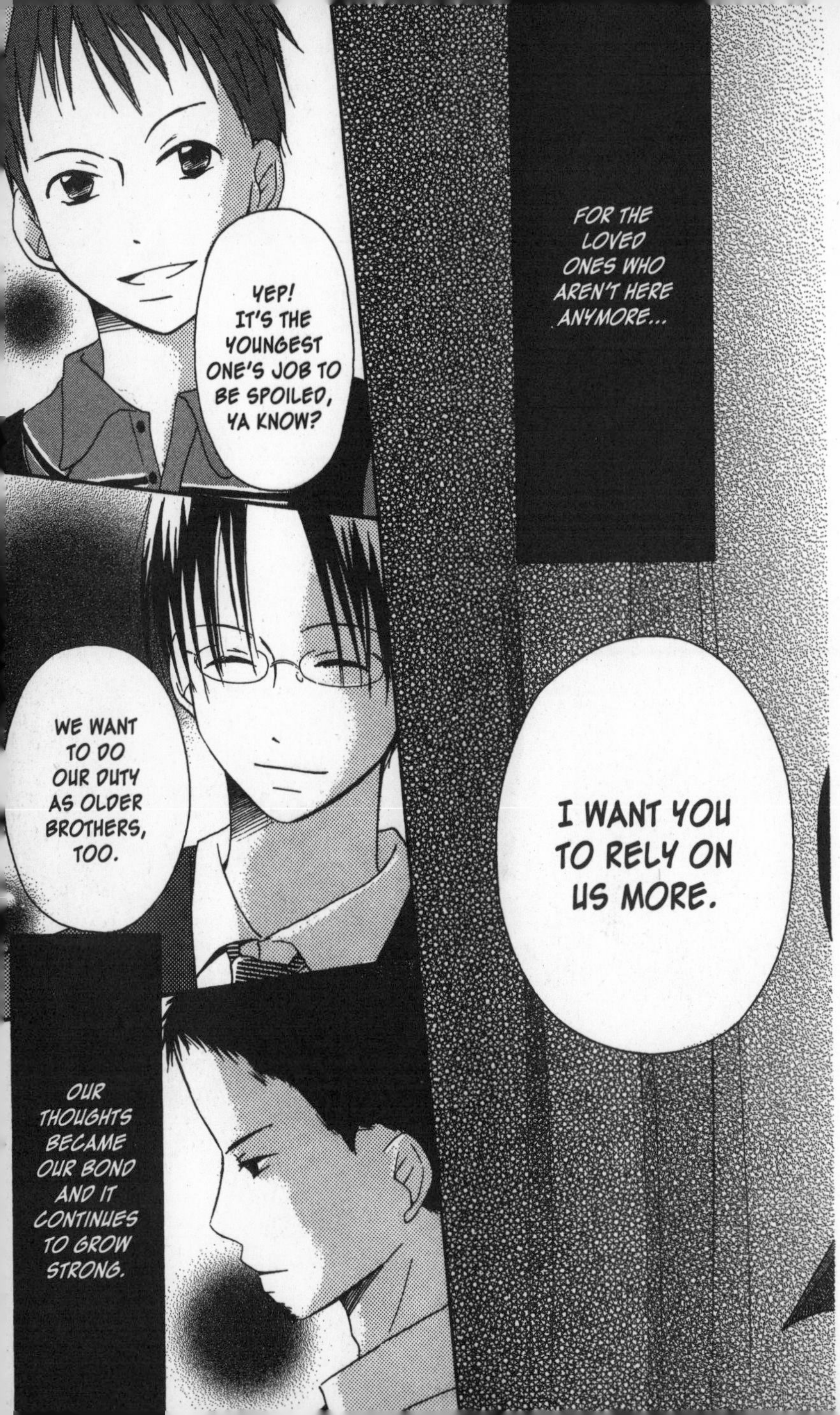
FOR THE LOVED ONES WHO AREN'T HERE ANYMORE...
I WANT YOU TO RELY ON US MORE.
YEP! IT'S THE YOUNGEST ONE'S JOB TO BE SPOILED, YA KNOW?
WE WANT TO DO OUR DUTY AS OLDER BROTHERS, TOO.
OUR THOUGHTS BECAME OUR BOND AND IT CONTINUES TO GROW STRONG.

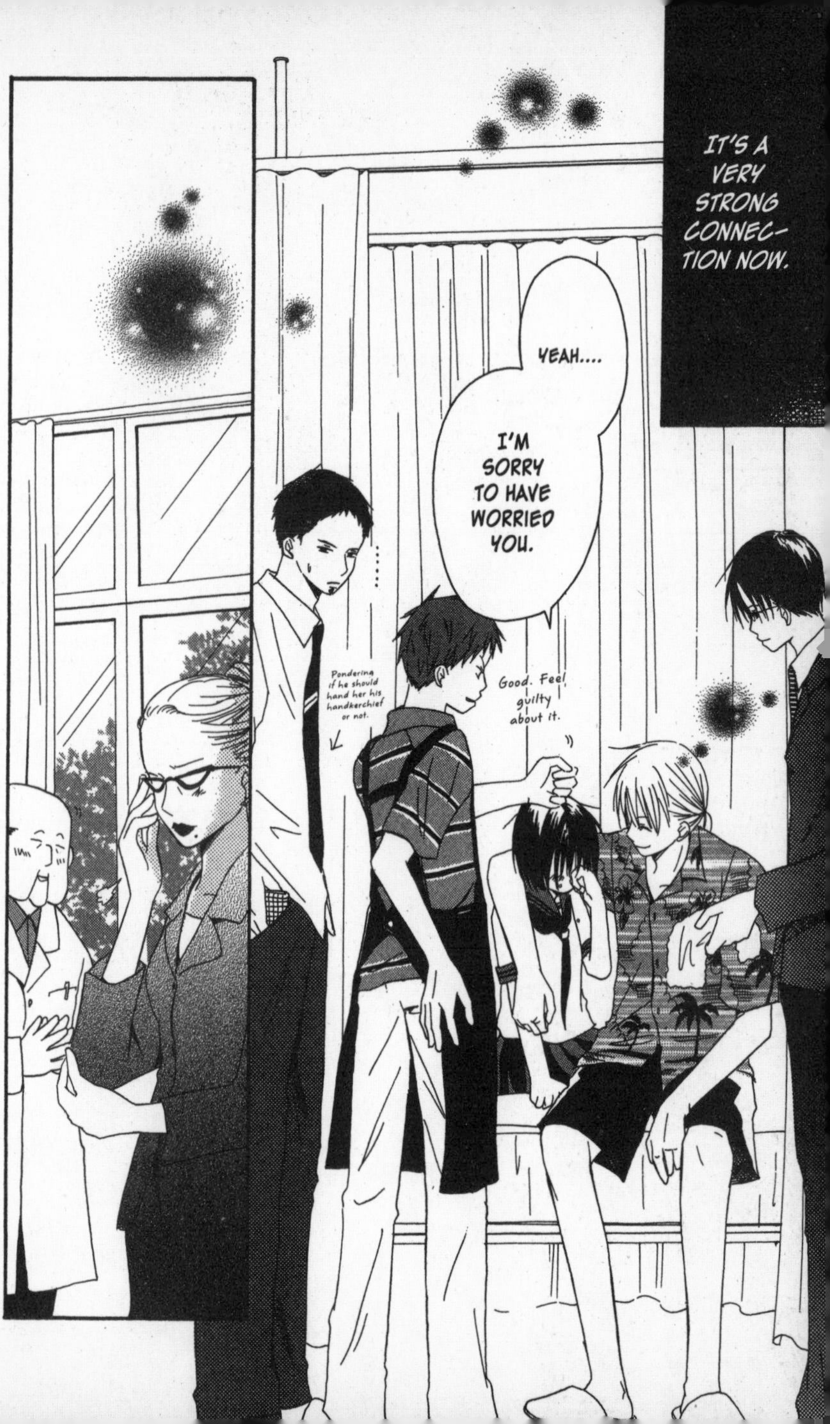
IT'S A VERY STRONG CONNECTION NOW.
YEAH.... I'M SORRY TO HAVE WORRIED YOU.
Good. Feel guilty about it.
Pondering if he should hand her his handkerchief or not.

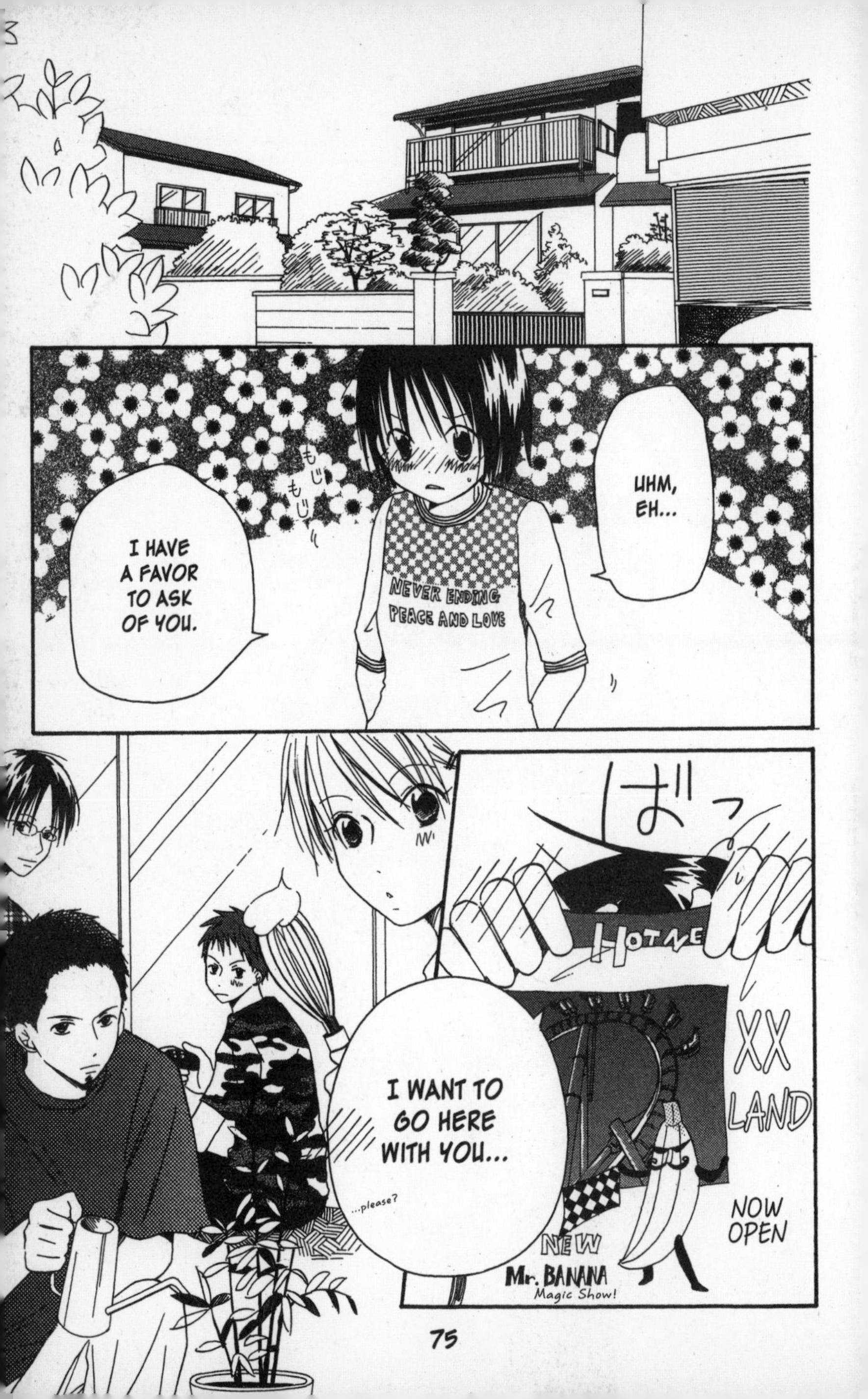
UHM, EH...
もじもじ
I HAVE A FAVOR TO ASK OF YOU.
ぱっ
HOTNE
XX LAND
NOW OPEN
NEW
Mr. BANANA
Magic Show!
I WANT TO GO HERE WITH YOU...
...please?

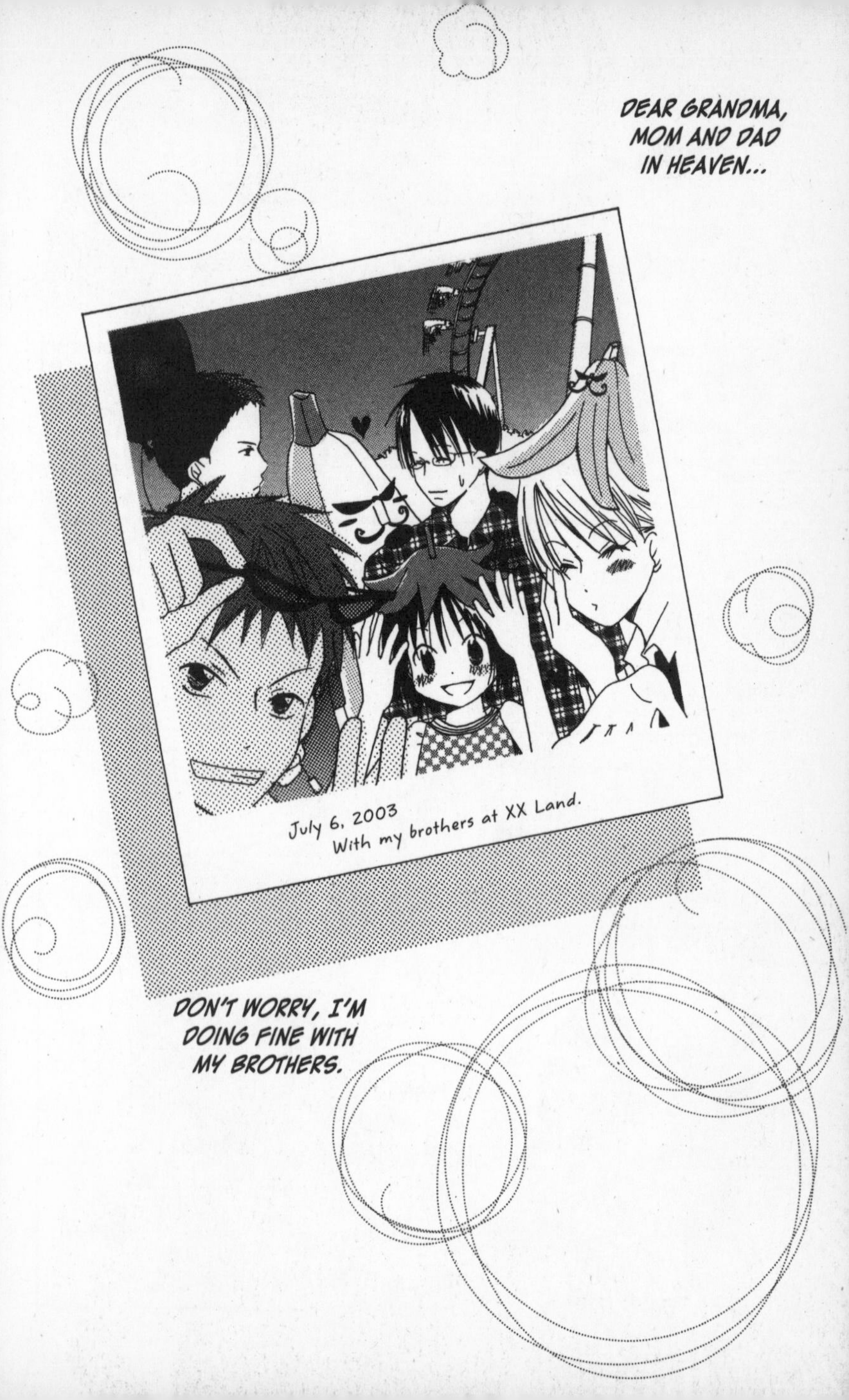
DEAR GRANDMA, MOM AND DAD IN HEAVEN...
July 6, 2003
With my brothers at XX Land.
DON'T WORRY, I'M DOING FINE WITH MY BROTHERS.

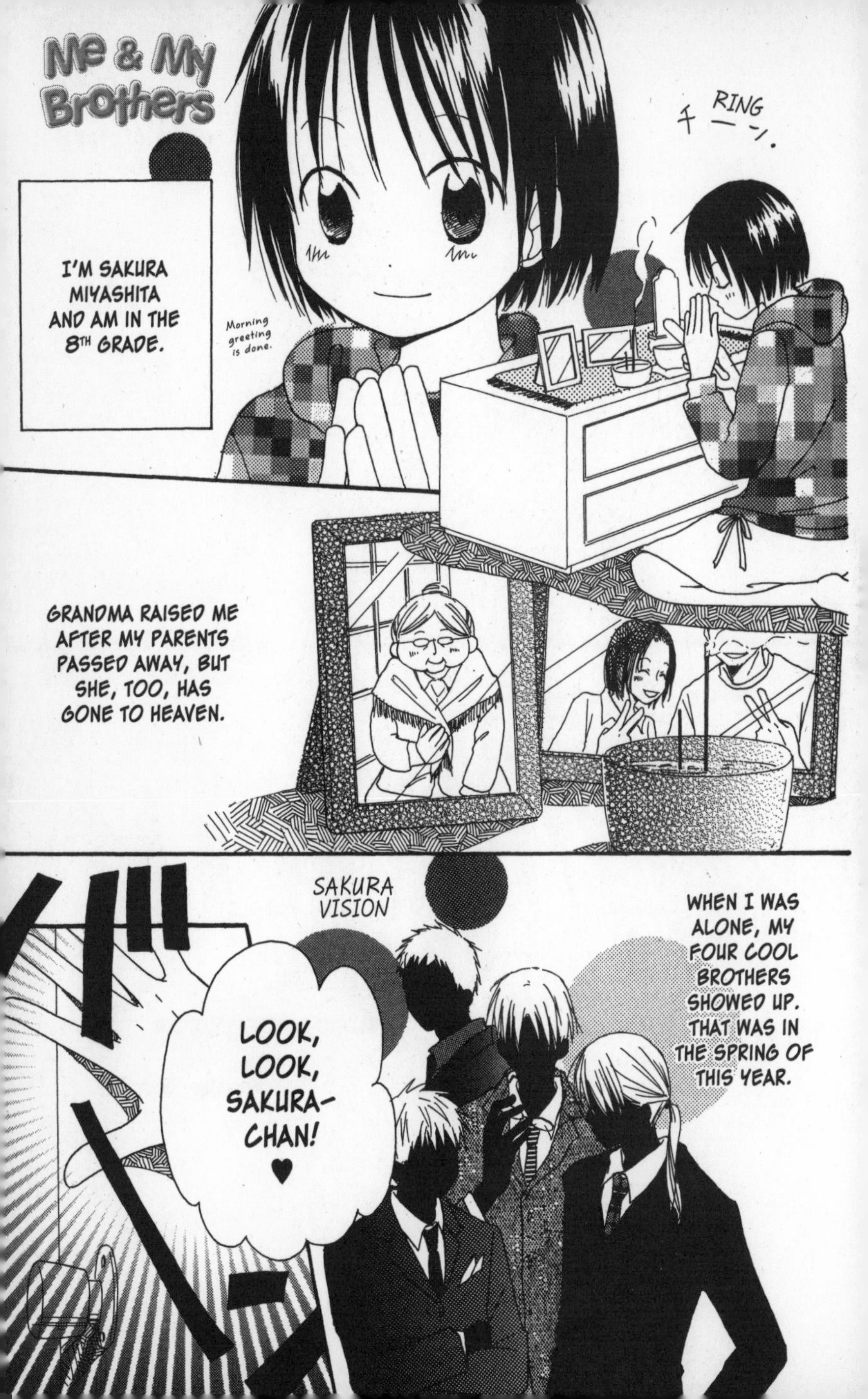
Me & My Brothers
RING
チーン.
Morning greeting is done.
I'M SAKURA MIYASHITA AND AM IN THE 8TH GRADE.
GRANDMA RAISED ME AFTER MY PARENTS PASSED AWAY, BUT SHE, TOO, HAS GONE TO HEAVEN.
WHEN I WAS ALONE, MY FOUR COOL BROTHERS SHOWED UP. THAT WAS IN THE SPRING OF THIS YEAR.
SAKURA VISION
LOOK, LOOK, SAKURA-CHAN! ♥

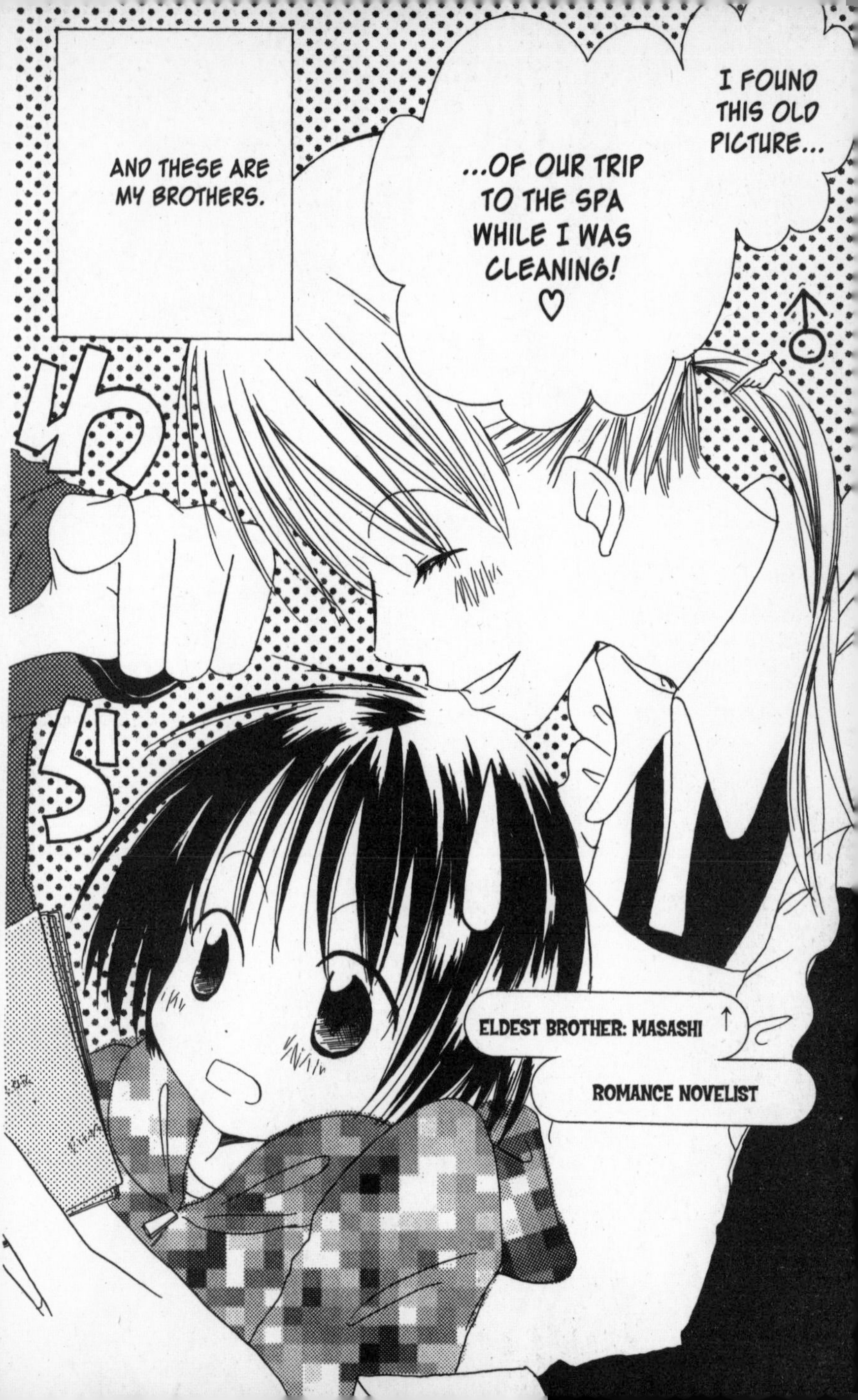
I FOUND THIS OLD PICTURE...
...OF OUR TRIP TO THE SPA WHILE I WAS CLEANING! ♡
AND THESE ARE MY BROTHERS.
ELDEST BROTHER: MASASHI ↑
ROMANCE NOVELIST

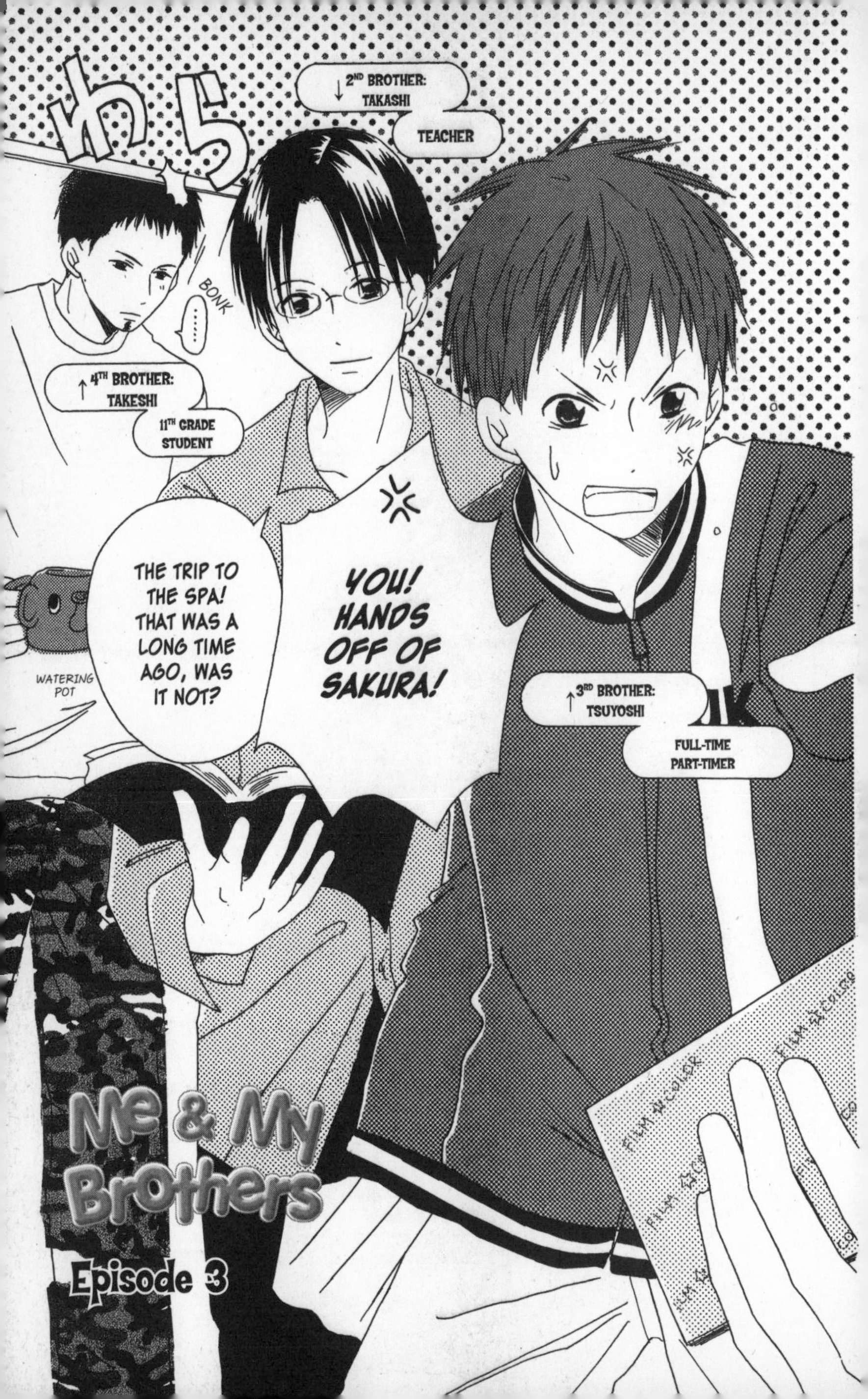
↓ 2ND BROTHER: TAKASHI
TEACHER
BONK
......
↑ 4TH BROTHER: TAKESHI
11TH GRADE STUDENT
YOU! HANDS OFF OF SAKURA!
THE TRIP TO THE SPA! THAT WAS A LONG TIME AGO, WAS IT NOT?
↑ 3RD BROTHER: TSUYOSHI
FULL-TIME PART-TIMER
WATERING POT
Me & My Brothers
Episode 3

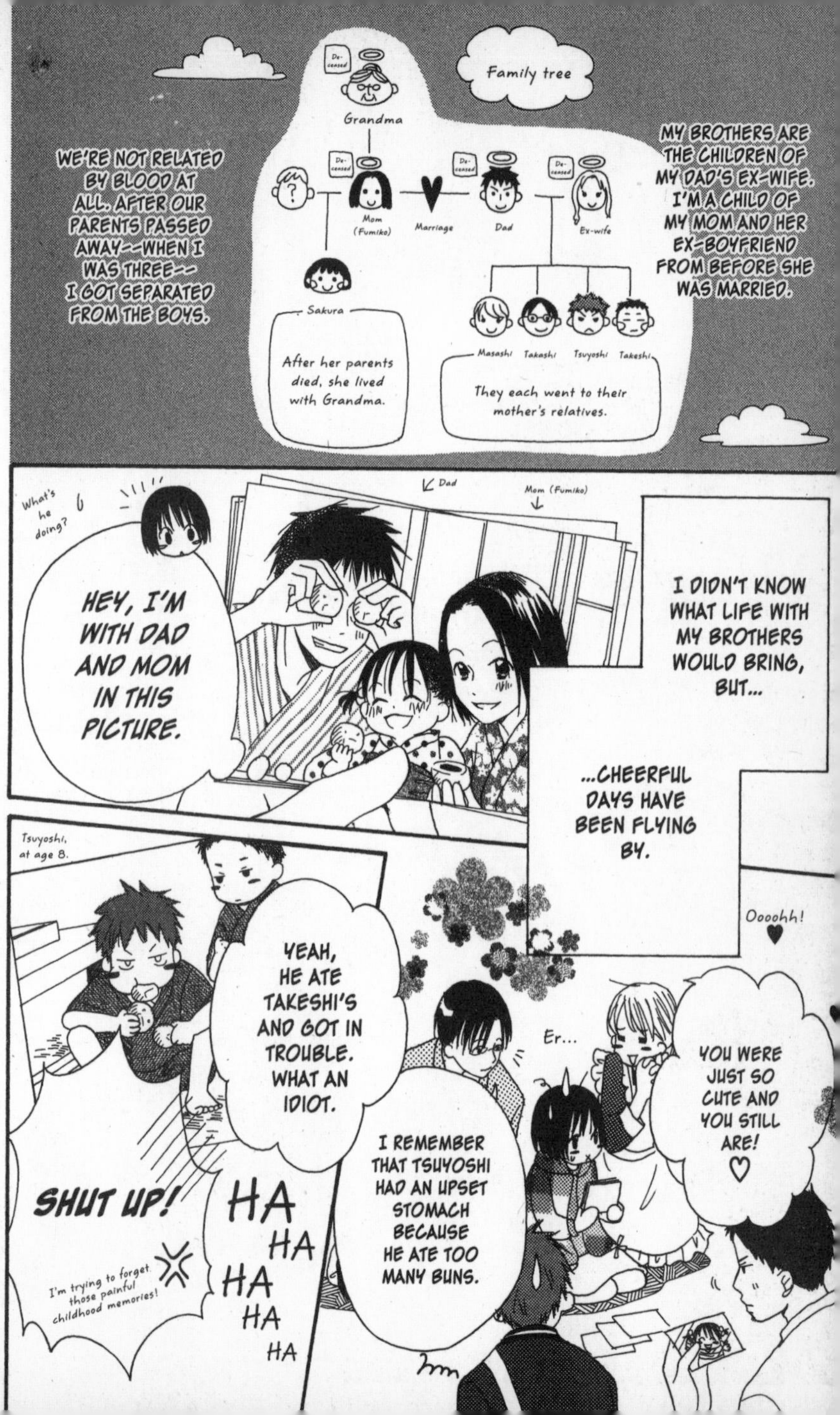

Family tree
MY BROTHERS ARE THE CHILDREN OF MY DAD'S EX-WIFE. I'M A CHILD OF MY MOM AND HER EX-BOYFRIEND FROM BEFORE SHE WAS MARRIED.
Deceased
Grandma
Deceased
Deceased
Deceased
?
Mom (Fumiko)
Marriage
Dad
Ex-wife
Sakura
After her parents died, she lived with Grandma.
Masashi
Takashi
Tsuyoshi
Takeshi
They each went to their mother's relatives.
WE'RE NOT RELATED BY BLOOD AT ALL. AFTER OUR PARENTS PASSED AWAY--WHEN I WAS THREE--I GOT SEPARATED FROM THE BOYS.
I DIDN'T KNOW WHAT LIFE WITH MY BROTHERS WOULD BRING, BUT...
...CHEERFUL DAYS HAVE BEEN FLYING BY.
Dad
Mom (Fumiko)
What's he doing?
HEY, I'M WITH DAD AND MOM IN THIS PICTURE.
Ooooh!
YOU WERE JUST SO CUTE AND YOU STILL ARE!
Er...
I REMEMBER THAT TSUYOSHI HAD AN UPSET STOMACH BECAUSE HE ATE TOO MANY BUNS.
YEAH, HE ATE TAKESHI'S AND GOT IN TROUBLE. WHAT AN IDIOT.
Tsuyoshi, at age 8.
HA HA HA HA HA
SHUT UP!
I'm trying to forget those painful childhood memories!

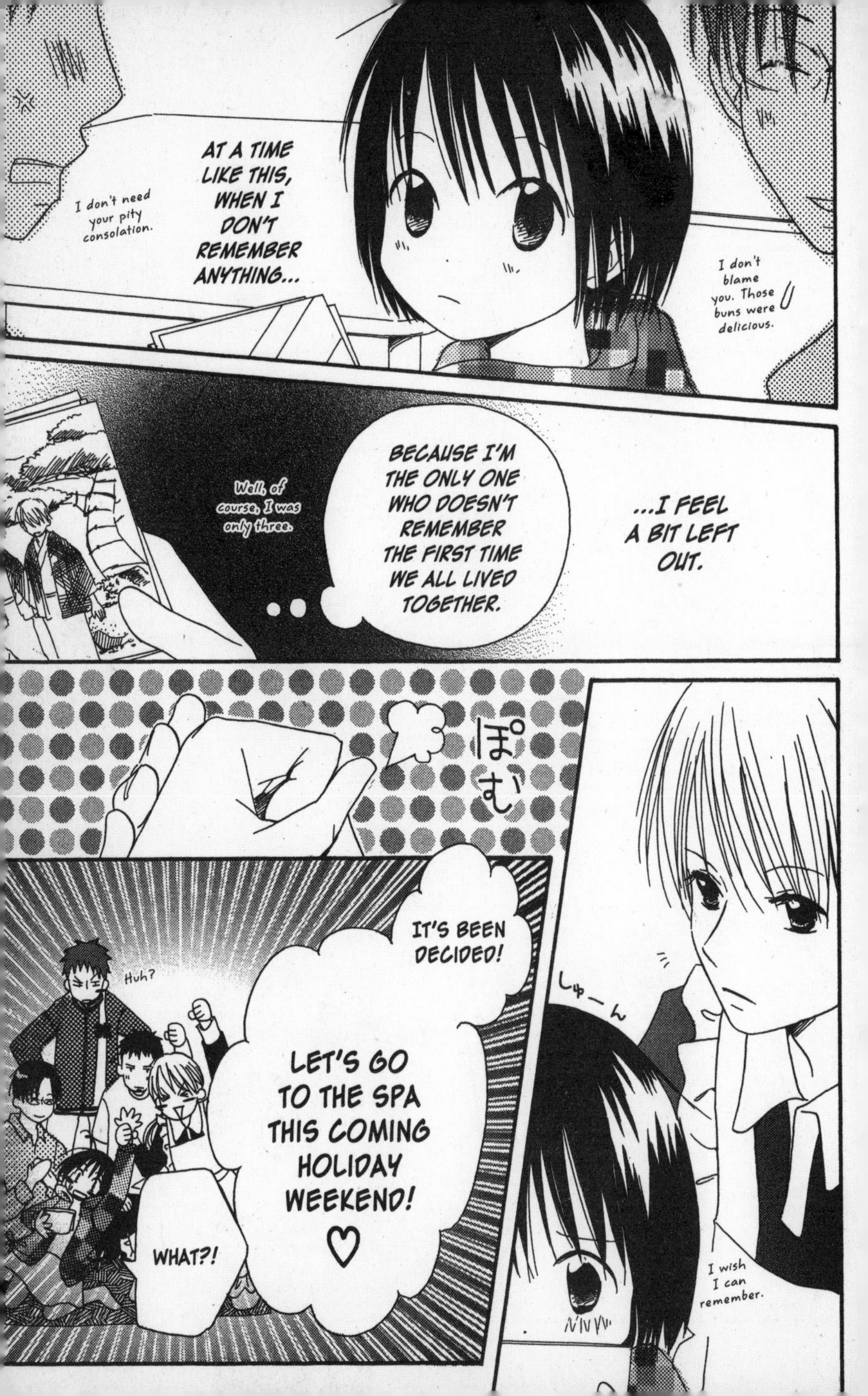
AT A TIME LIKE THIS, WHEN I DON'T REMEMBER ANYTHING...
I don't blame you. Those buns were delicious.
I don't need your pity consolation.
BECAUSE I'M THE ONLY ONE WHO DOESN'T REMEMBER THE FIRST TIME WE ALL LIVED TOGETHER.
...I FEEL A BIT LEFT OUT.
Well, of course, I was only three.
しゅーん
I wish I can remember.
ぽむ
IT'S BEEN DECIDED!
LET'S GO TO THE SPA THIS COMING HOLIDAY WEEKEND! ♡
Huh?
WHAT?!

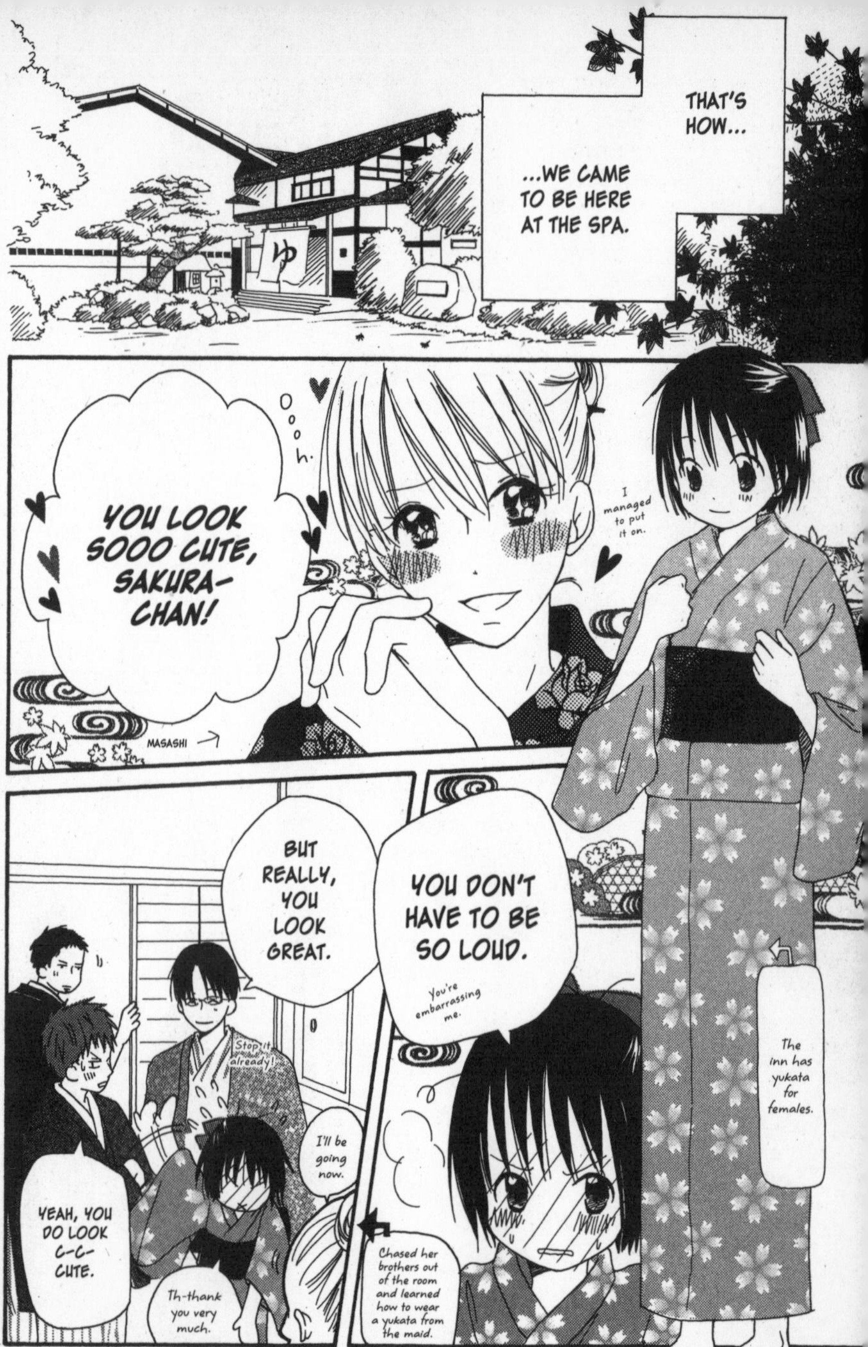

THAT'S HOW...
...WE CAME TO BE HERE AT THE SPA.
I managed to put it on.
The inn has yukata for females.
Oooh.
YOU LOOK SOOO CUTE, SAKURA-CHAN!
MASASHI
YOU DON'T HAVE TO BE SO LOUD.
You're embarrassing me.
Chased her brothers out of the room and learned how to wear a yukata from the maid.
BUT REALLY, YOU LOOK GREAT.
Stop it already!
I'll be going now.
YEAH, YOU DO LOOK C-C-CUTE.
Th-thank you very much.

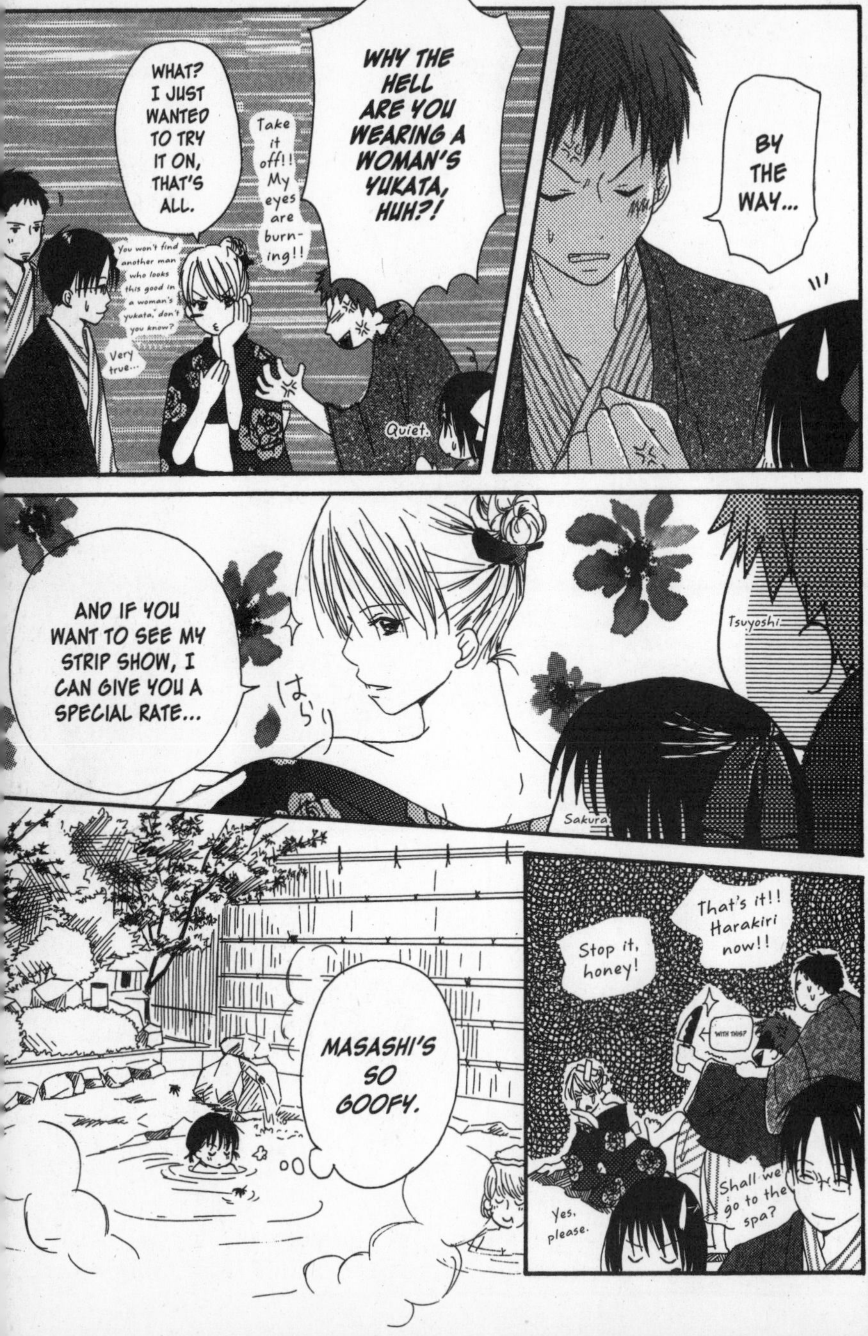
BY THE WAY...
WHY THE HELL ARE YOU WEARING A WOMAN'S YUKATA, HUH?!
Take it off!! My eyes are burning!!
WHAT? I JUST WANTED TO TRY IT ON, THAT'S ALL.
You won't find another man who looks this good in a woman's yukata, don't you know?
Very true...
Quiet.
Tsuyoshi
AND IF YOU WANT TO SEE MY STRIP SHOW, I CAN GIVE YOU A SPECIAL RATE...
はらり
Sakura
That's it!! Harakiri now!!
Stop it, honey!
WITH THIS?
Shall we go to the spa?
Yes, please.
MASASHI'S SO GOOFY.

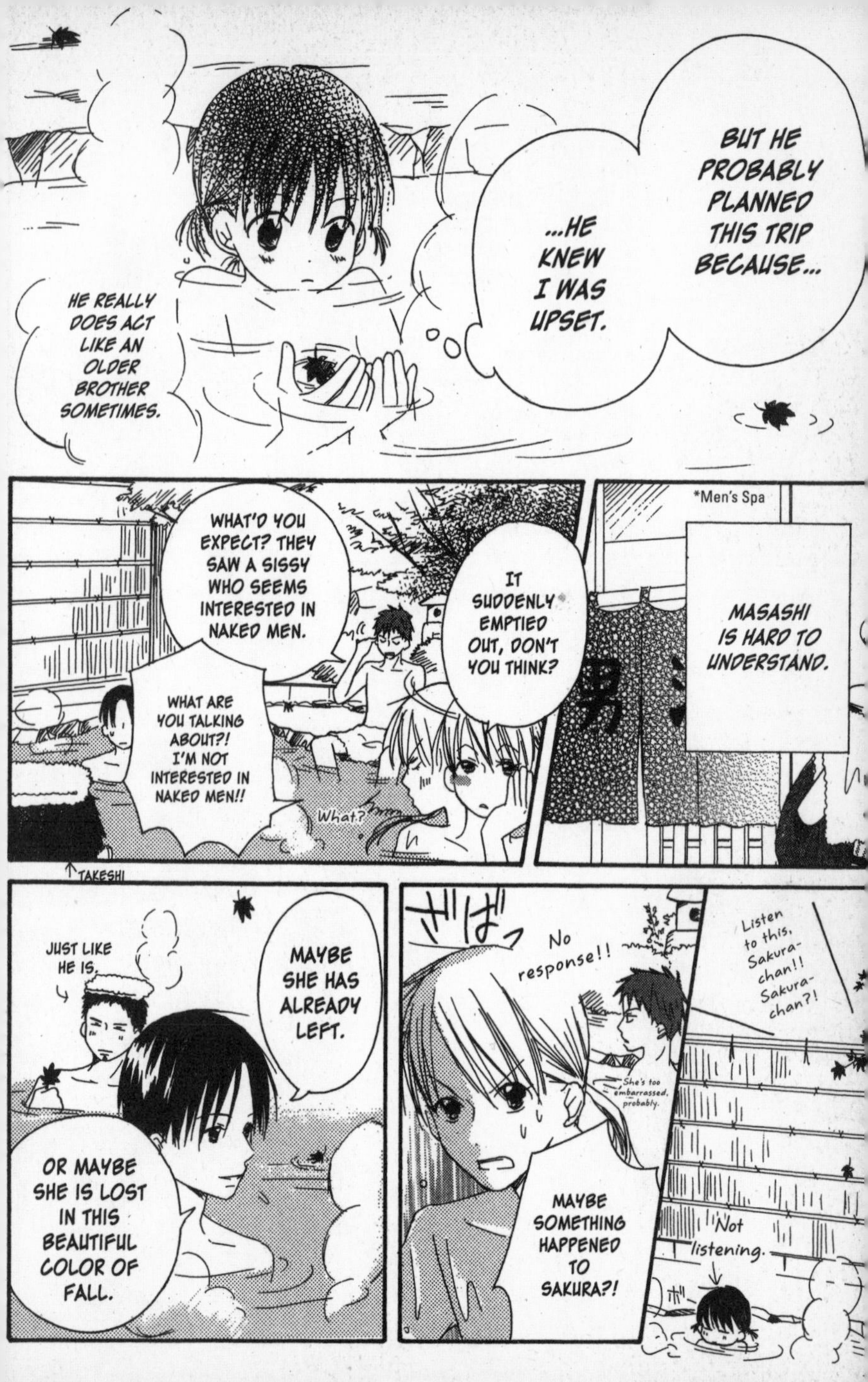
BUT HE PROBABLY PLANNED THIS TRIP BECAUSE...
...HE KNEW I WAS UPSET.
HE REALLY DOES ACT LIKE AN OLDER BROTHER SOMETIMES.
*Men's Spa
MASASHI IS HARD TO UNDERSTAND.
IT SUDDENLY EMPTIED OUT, DON'T YOU THINK?
WHAT'D YOU EXPECT? THEY SAW A SISSY WHO SEEMS INTERESTED IN NAKED MEN.
What?
WHAT ARE YOU TALKING ABOUT?! I'M NOT INTERESTED IN NAKED MEN!!
TAKESHI
Listen to this, Sakura-chan!! Sakura-chan?!
ざばっ
No response!!
She's too embarrassed, probably.
MAYBE SOMETHING HAPPENED TO SAKURA?!
Not listening.
ボー
MAYBE SHE HAS ALREADY LEFT.
JUST LIKE HE IS.
OR MAYBE SHE IS LOST IN THIS BEAUTIFUL COLOR OF FALL.

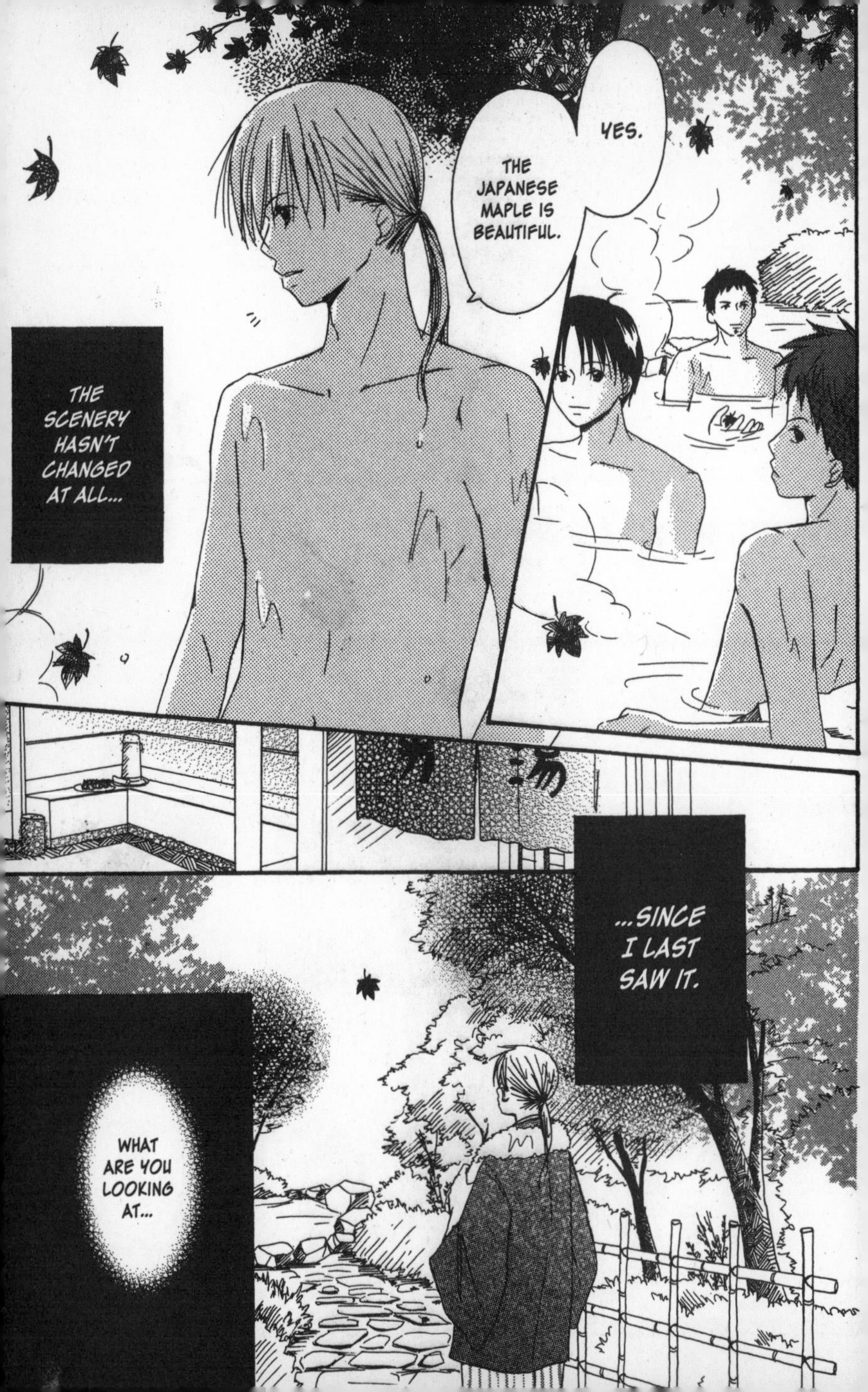
YES.
THE JAPANESE MAPLE IS BEAUTIFUL.
THE SCENERY HASN'T CHANGED AT ALL...
...SINCE I LAST SAW IT.
WHAT ARE YOU LOOKING AT...

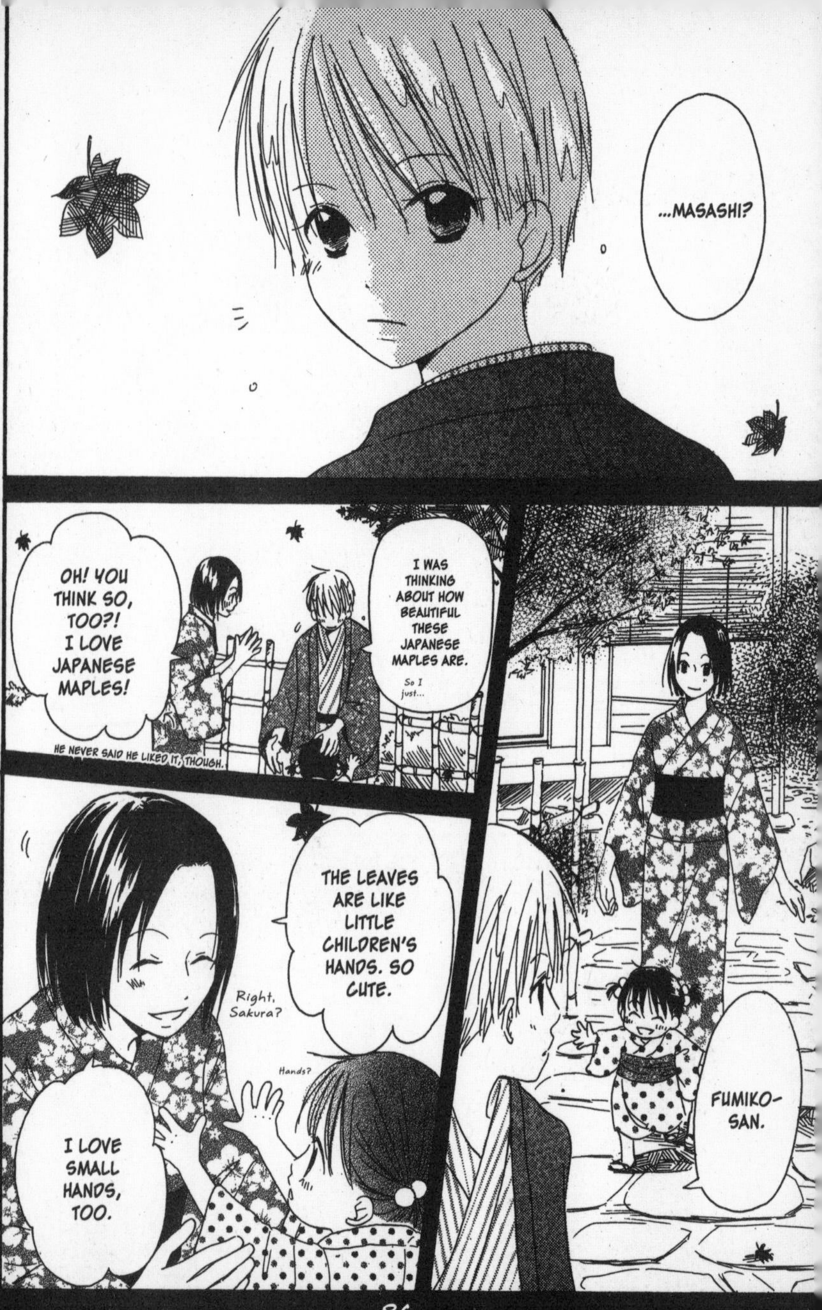
...MASASHI?
FUMIKO-SAN.
I WAS THINKING ABOUT HOW BEAUTIFUL THESE JAPANESE MAPLES ARE.
So I just...
OH! YOU THINK SO, TOO?! I LOVE JAPANESE MAPLES!
HE NEVER SAID HE LIKED IT, THOUGH.
THE LEAVES ARE LIKE LITTLE CHILDREN'S HANDS. SO CUTE.
Right, Sakura?
Hands?
I LOVE SMALL HANDS, TOO.

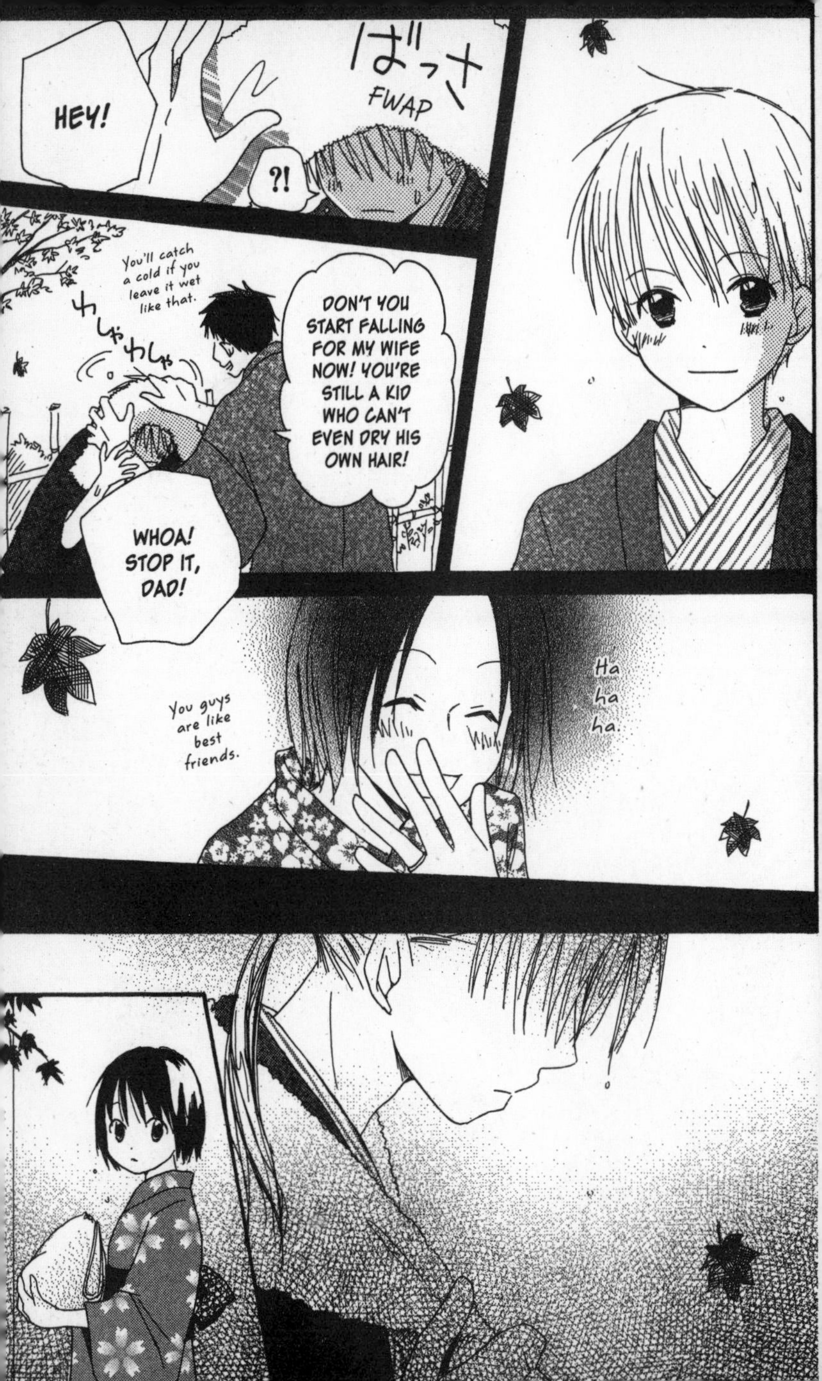
ばっさ
FWAP
HEY!
?!
DON'T YOU START FALLING FOR MY WIFE NOW! YOU'RE STILL A KID WHO CAN'T EVEN DRY HIS OWN HAIR!
You'll catch a cold if you leave it wet like that.
わしゃわしゃ
WHOA! STOP IT, DAD!
Ha ha ha.
You guys are like best friends.

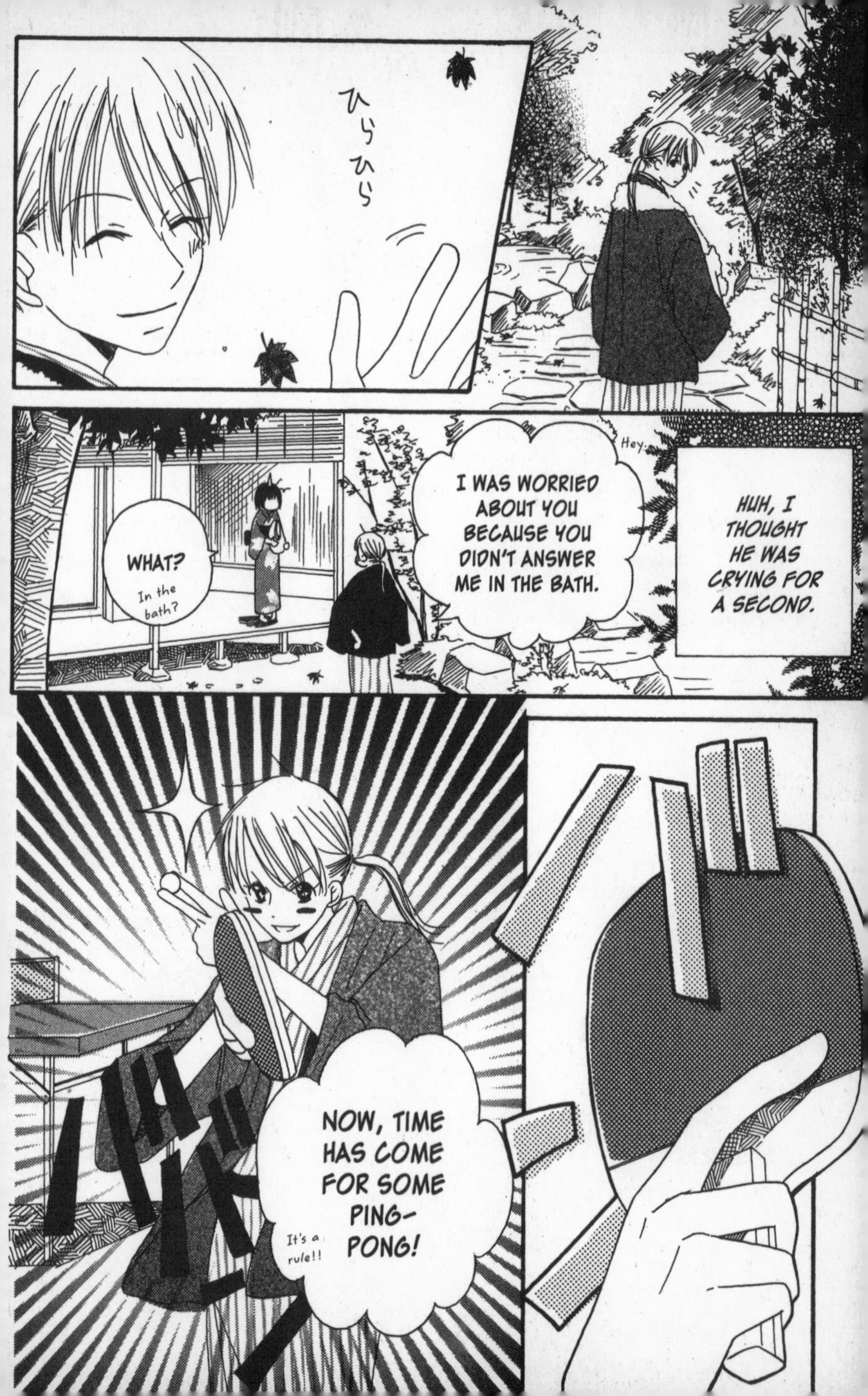

ひらひら
Hey.
HUH, I THOUGHT HE WAS CRYING FOR A SECOND.
I WAS WORRIED ABOUT YOU BECAUSE YOU DIDN'T ANSWER ME IN THE BATH.
WHAT?
In the bath?
NOW, TIME HAS COME FOR SOME PING-PONG!
It's a rule!!

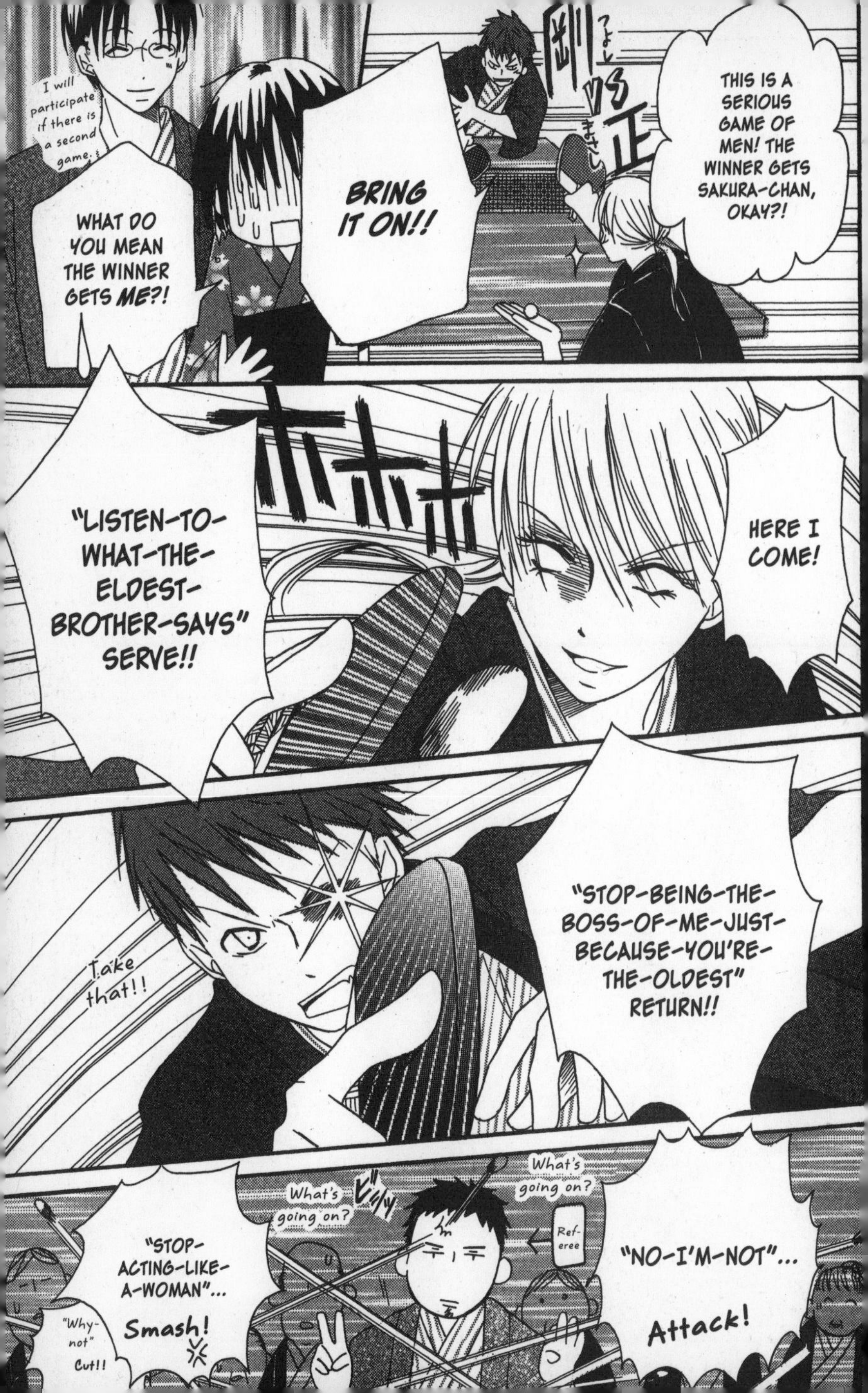
THIS IS A SERIOUS GAME OF MEN! THE WINNER GETS SAKURA-CHAN, OKAY?!
剛 つよし VS 正 まさし
BRING IT ON!!
WHAT DO YOU MEAN THE WINNER GETS ME?!
I will participate if there is a second game.
HERE I COME!
"LISTEN-TO-WHAT-THE-ELDEST-BROTHER-SAYS" SERVE!!
"STOP-BEING-THE-BOSS-OF-ME-JUST-BECAUSE-YOU'RE-THE-OLDEST" RETURN!!
Take that!!
"NO-I'M-NOT"...
Attack!
What's going on?
Referee
What's going on?
"STOP-ACTING-LIKE-A-WOMAN"...
Smash!
"Why-not"
Cut!!

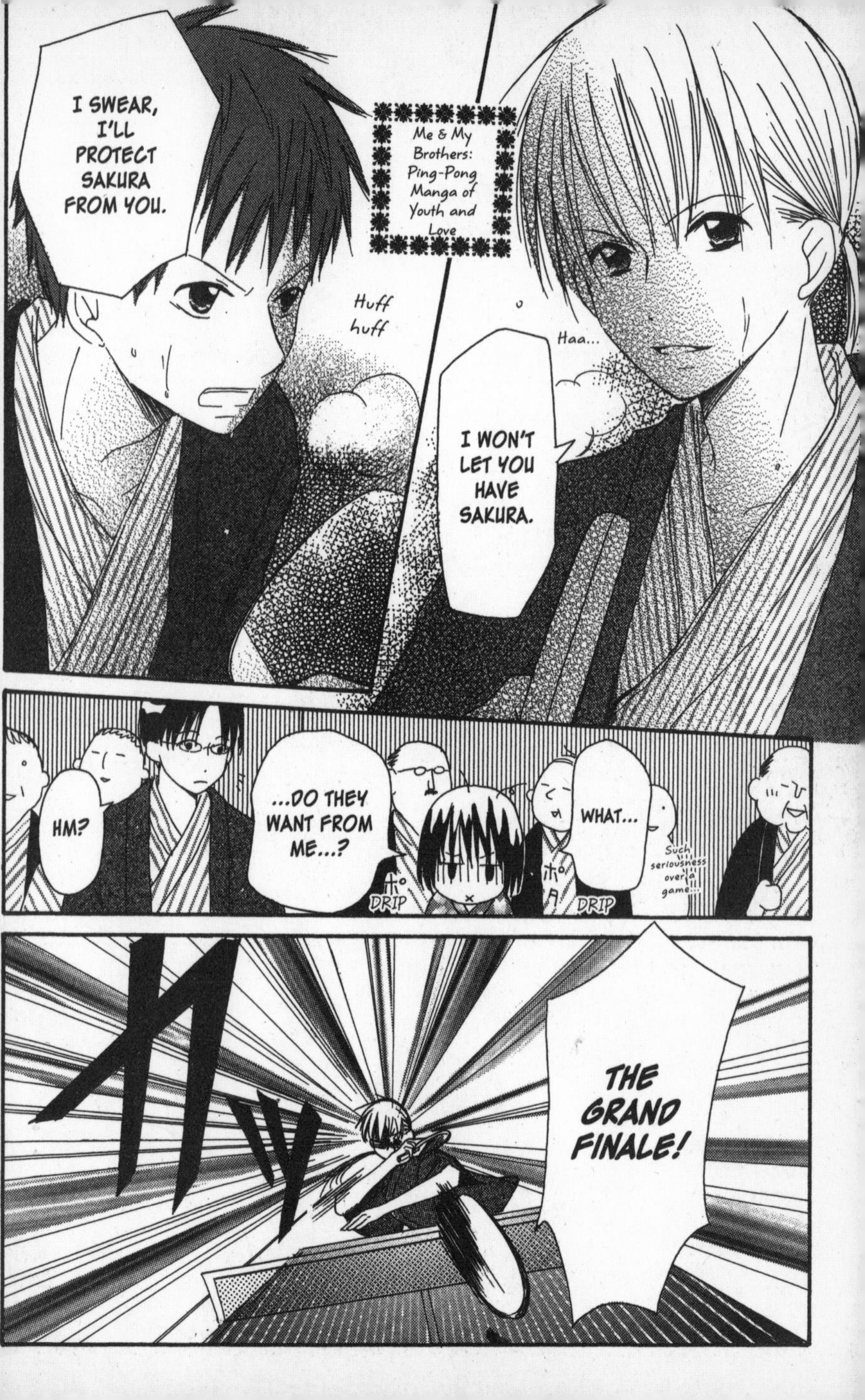
Me & My Brothers: Ping-Pong Manga of Youth and Love
Haa...
I WON'T LET YOU HAVE SAKURA.
Huff huff
I SWEAR, I'LL PROTECT SAKURA FROM YOU.
Such seriousness over a game...
WHAT...
DRIP
DRIP
...DO THEY WANT FROM ME...?
HM?
THE GRAND FINALE!
カッ

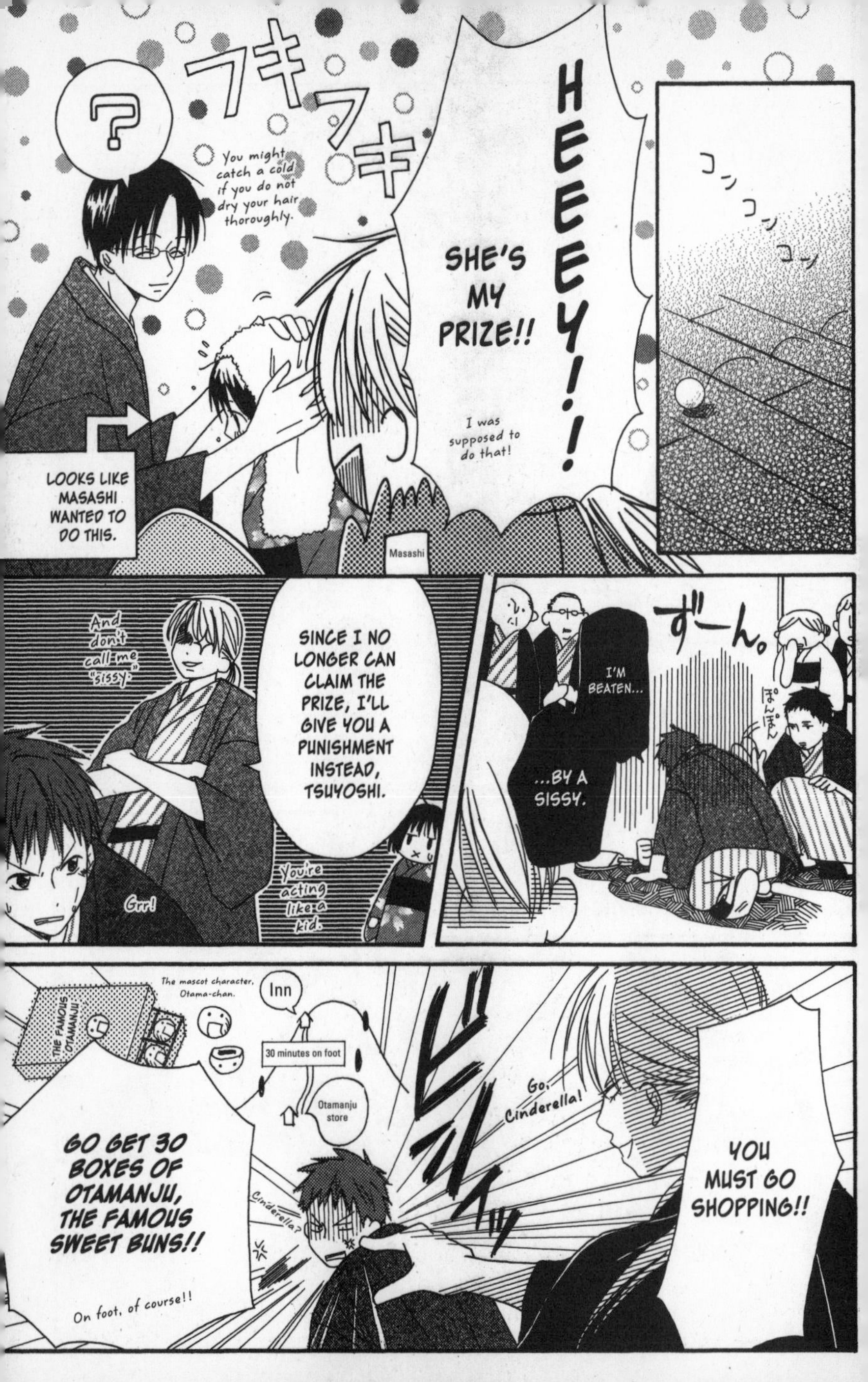
コン コン コン
HEEEEY!!
SHE'S MY PRIZE!!
I was supposed to do that!
フキフキ
?
You might catch a cold if you do not dry your hair thoroughly.
LOOKS LIKE MASASHI WANTED TO DO THIS.
Masashi
ずーん。
I'M BEATEN...
...BY A SISSY.
ぽんぽん
SINCE I NO LONGER CAN CLAIM THE PRIZE, I'LL GIVE YOU A PUNISHMENT INSTEAD, TSUYOSHI.
And don't call me "sissy."
You're acting like a kid.
Grr!
YOU MUST GO SHOPPING!!
Go, Cinderella!
Cinderella?
Inn
30 minutes on foot
Otamanju store
The mascot character, Otama-chan.
THE FAMOUS OTAMANJU
GO GET 30 BOXES OF OTAMANJU, THE FAMOUS SWEET BUNS!!
On foot, of course!!

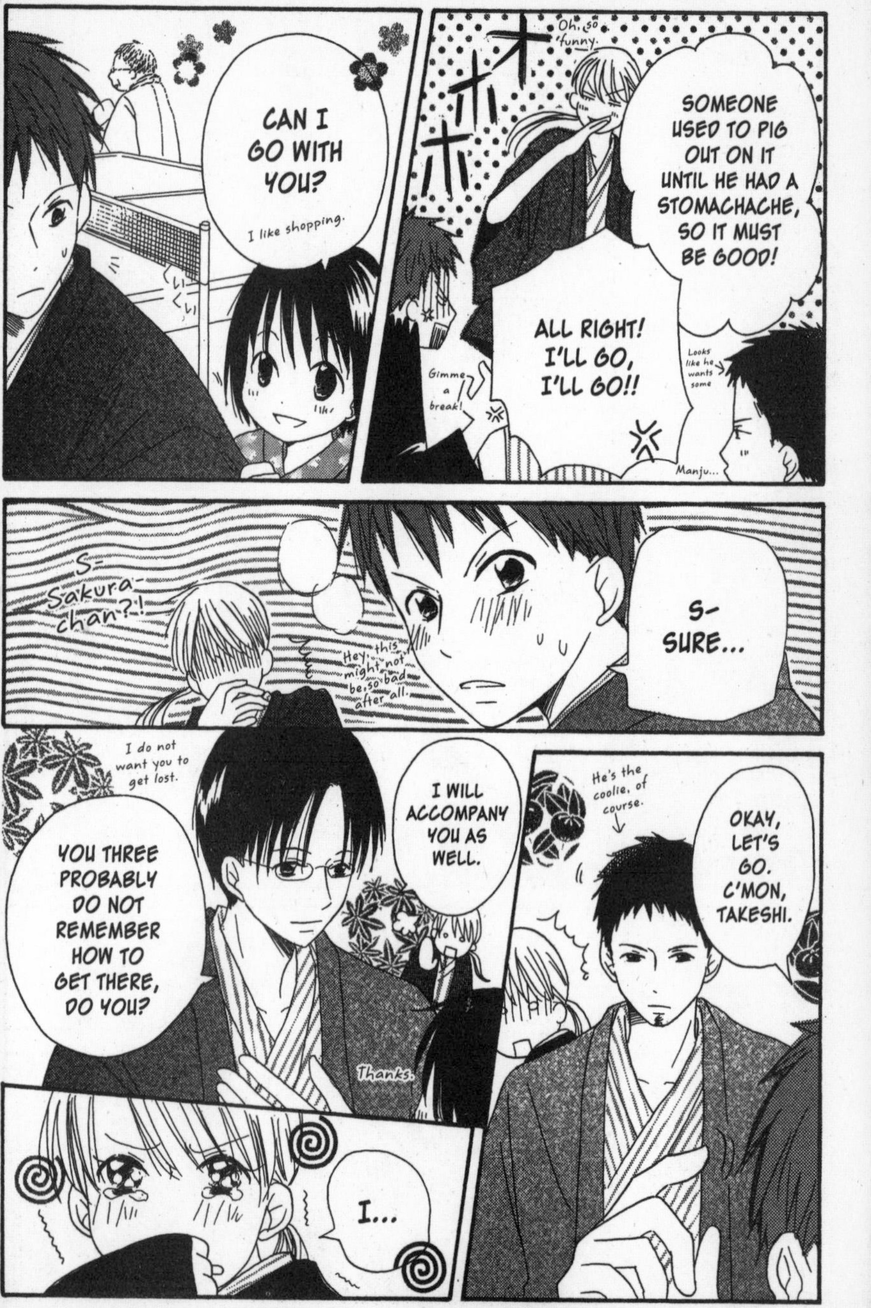
オホホ
Oh, so funny.
SOMEONE USED TO PIG OUT ON IT UNTIL HE HAD A STOMACHACHE, SO IT MUST BE GOOD!
ALL RIGHT! I'LL GO, I'LL GO!!
Gimme a break!
Looks like he wants some
Manju...
CAN I GO WITH YOU?
I like shopping.
S-SURE...
Hey, this might not be so bad after all.
S-Sakura-chan?!
He's the coolie, of course.
OKAY, LET'S GO. C'MON, TAKESHI.
I WILL ACCOMPANY YOU AS WELL.
I do not want you to get lost.
YOU THREE PROBABLY DO NOT REMEMBER HOW TO GET THERE, DO YOU?
Thanks.
I...

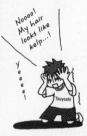

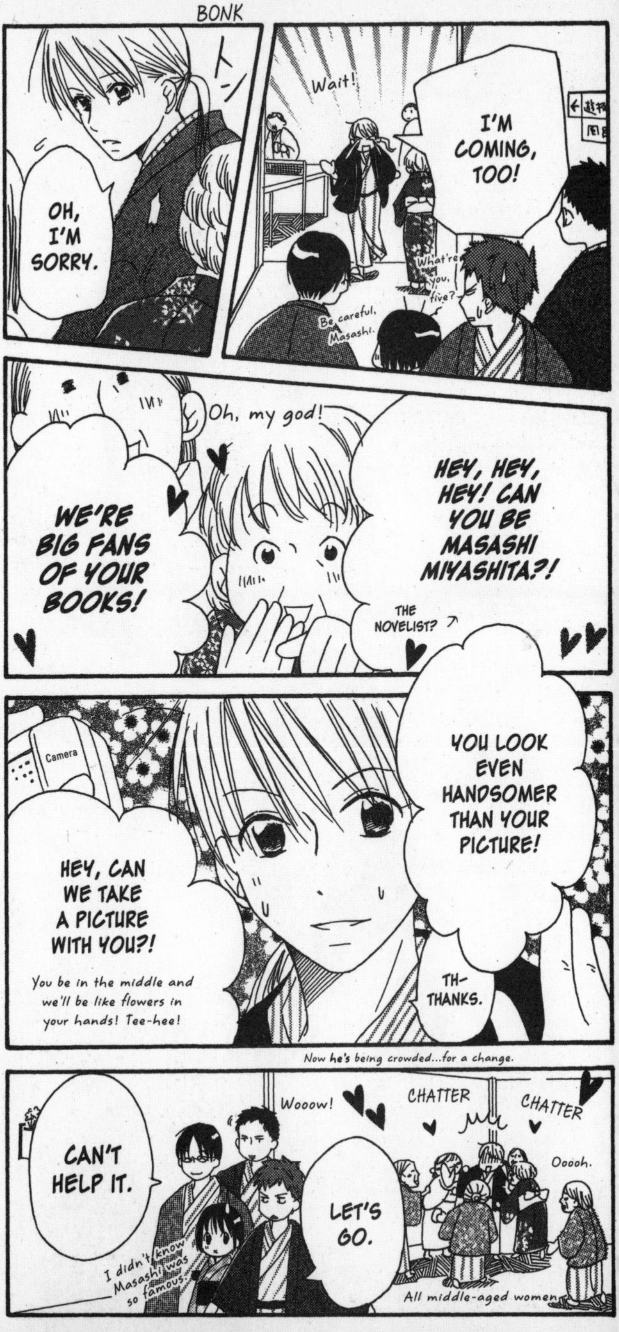
BONK
I'M COMING, TOO!
Wait!
What're you, five?
Be careful, Masashi.
OH, I'M SORRY.
HEY, HEY, HEY! CAN YOU BE MASASHI MIYASHITA?!
THE NOVELIST?
WE'RE BIG FANS OF YOUR BOOKS!
Oh, my god!
YOU LOOK EVEN HANDSOMER THAN YOUR PICTURE!
TH- THANKS.
HEY, CAN WE TAKE A PICTURE WITH YOU?!
You be in the middle and we'll be like flowers in your hands! Tee-hee!
Camera
Now he's being crowded...for a change.
CHATTER
CHATTER
Ooooh.
All middle-aged women
LET'S GO.
I didn't know Masashi was so famous.
Wooow!
CAN'T HELP IT.

☆ 3 ☆

Well, it's Tsuyoshi who changed the most. He used to look too... er... I guess I won't show you how he was, because I feel sorry for him.

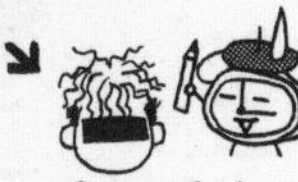

Oops, I drew it anyway.

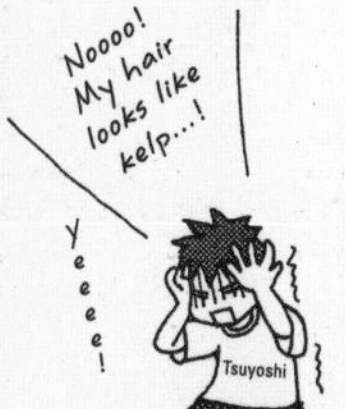
Noooo! My hair looks like kelp...!
Yeeeee!
Tsuyoshi

Yes, I'm glad I changed him—really.

☆ ☆ ☆

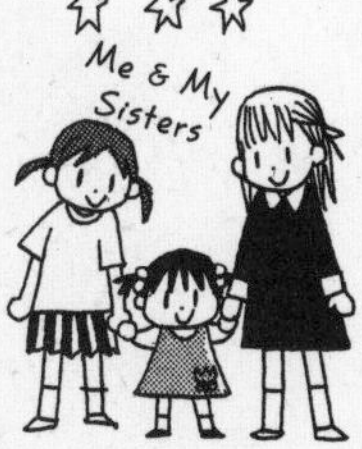
Me & My Sisters

☆ ☆ ☆

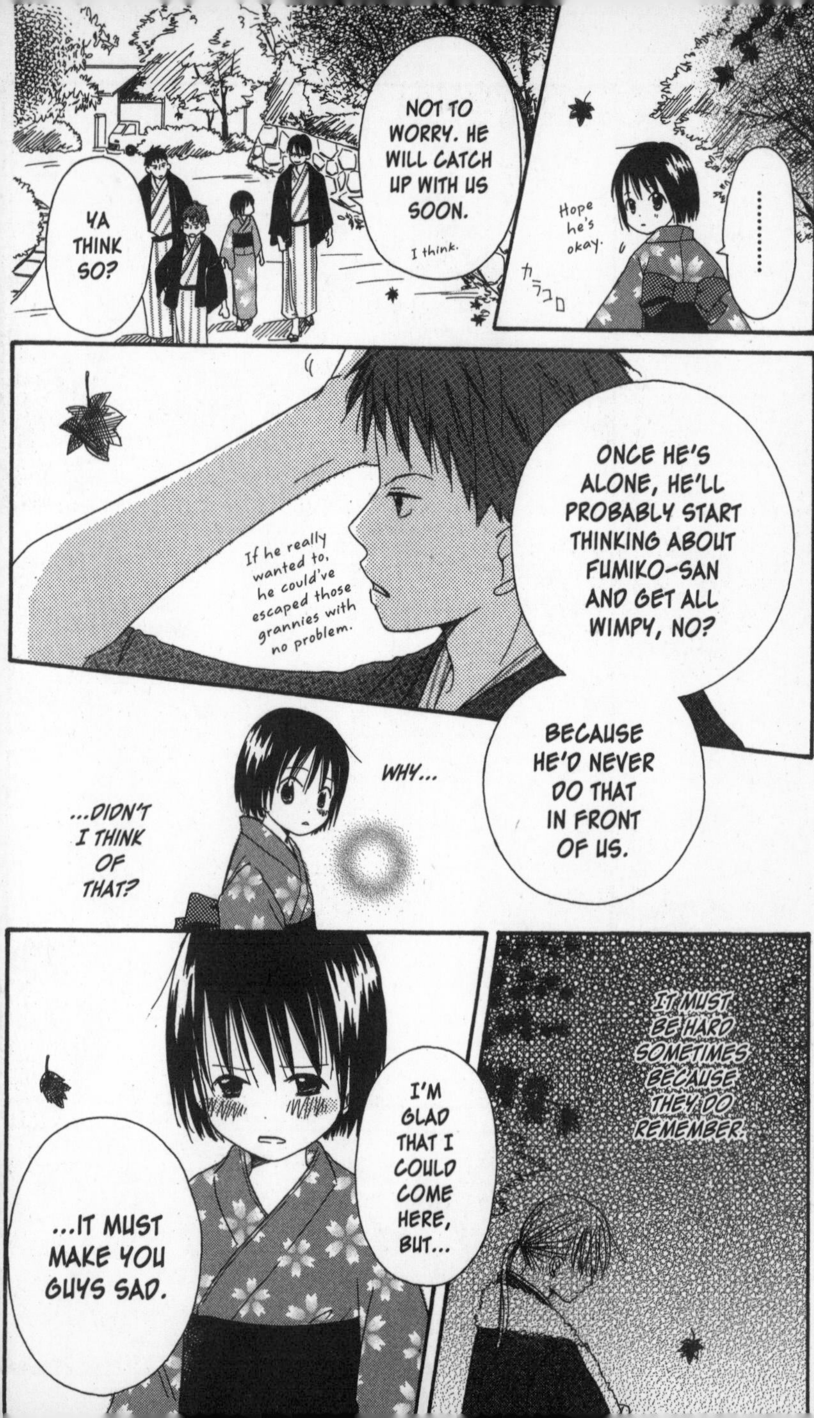
......
Hope he's okay.
カラコロ
NOT TO WORRY. HE WILL CATCH UP WITH US SOON.
I think.
YA THINK SO?
ONCE HE'S ALONE, HE'LL PROBABLY START THINKING ABOUT FUMIKO-SAN AND GET ALL WIMPY, NO?
If he really wanted to, he could've escaped those grannies with no problem.
BECAUSE HE'D NEVER DO THAT IN FRONT OF US.
WHY...
...DIDN'T I THINK OF THAT?
IT MUST BE HARD SOMETIMES BECAUSE THEY DO REMEMBER.
I'M GLAD THAT I COULD COME HERE, BUT...
...IT MUST MAKE YOU GUYS SAD.

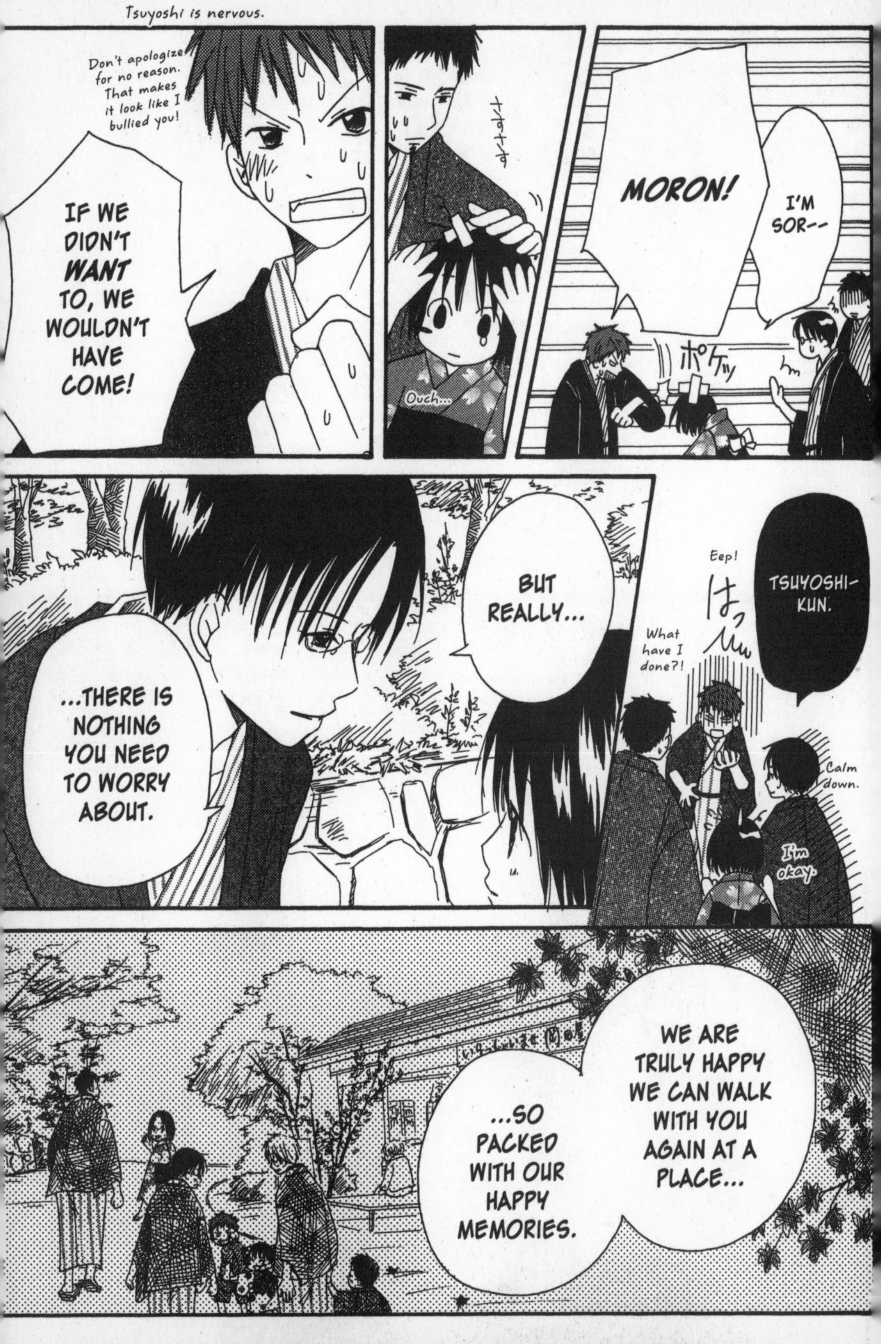
Tsuyoshi is nervous.
I'M SOR--
MORON!
ポケッ
さすさす
Ouch...
Don't apologize for no reason. That makes it look like I bullied you!
IF WE DIDN'T WANT TO, WE WOULDN'T HAVE COME!
TSUYOSHI-KUN.
Eep!
はっ
What have I done?!
Calm down.
I'm okay.
BUT REALLY...
...THERE IS NOTHING YOU NEED TO WORRY ABOUT.
WE ARE TRULY HAPPY WE CAN WALK WITH YOU AGAIN AT A PLACE...
...SO PACKED WITH OUR HAPPY MEMORIES.

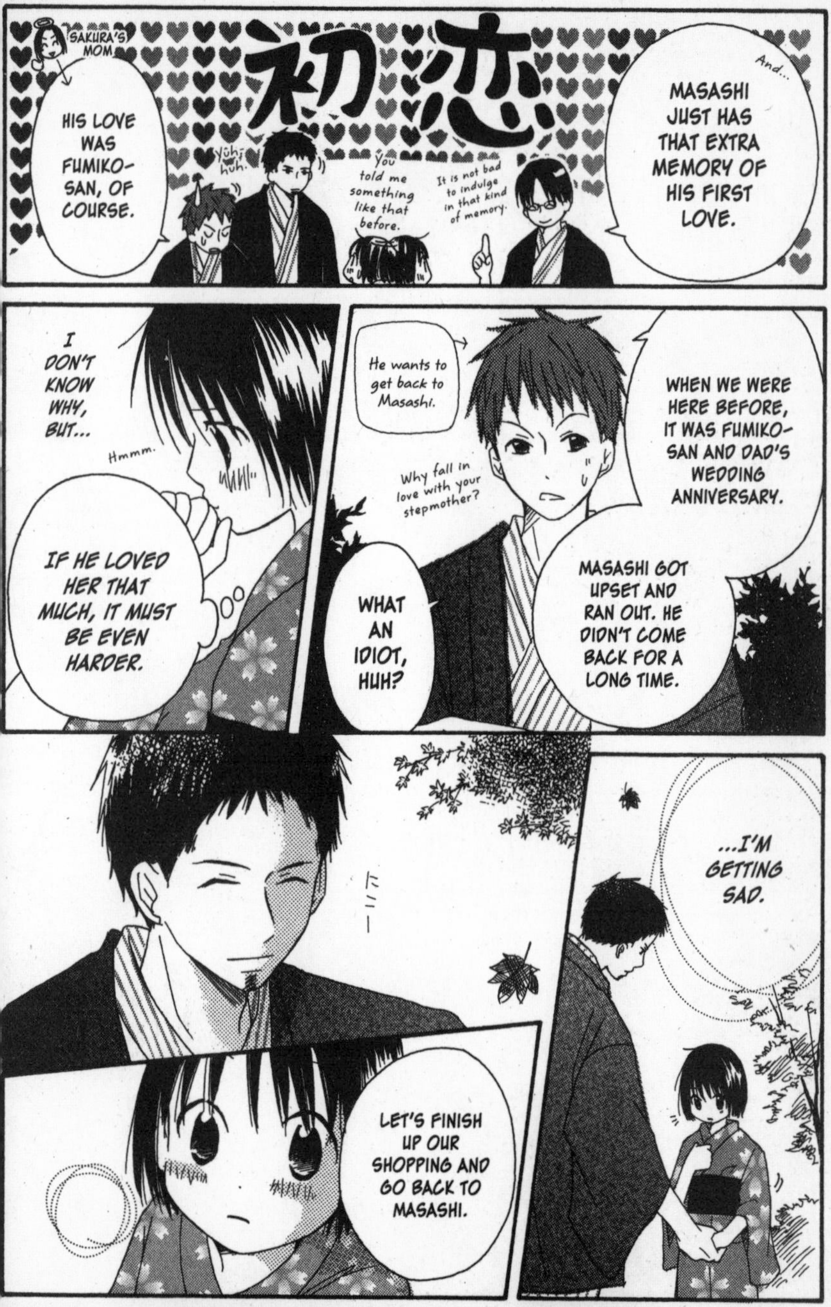
初恋
And...
MASASHI JUST HAS THAT EXTRA MEMORY OF HIS FIRST LOVE.
It is not bad to indulge in that kind of memory.
You told me something like that before.
Yuh-huh.
SAKURA'S MOM
HIS LOVE WAS FUMIKO-SAN, OF COURSE.
WHEN WE WERE HERE BEFORE, IT WAS FUMIKO-SAN AND DAD'S WEDDING ANNIVERSARY.
MASASHI GOT UPSET AND RAN OUT. HE DIDN'T COME BACK FOR A LONG TIME.
He wants to get back to Masashi.
Why fall in love with your stepmother?
WHAT AN IDIOT, HUH?
I DON'T KNOW WHY, BUT...
Hmmm.
IF HE LOVED HER THAT MUCH, IT MUST BE EVEN HARDER.
...I'M GETTING SAD.
にこー
LET'S FINISH UP OUR SHOPPING AND GO BACK TO MASASHI.

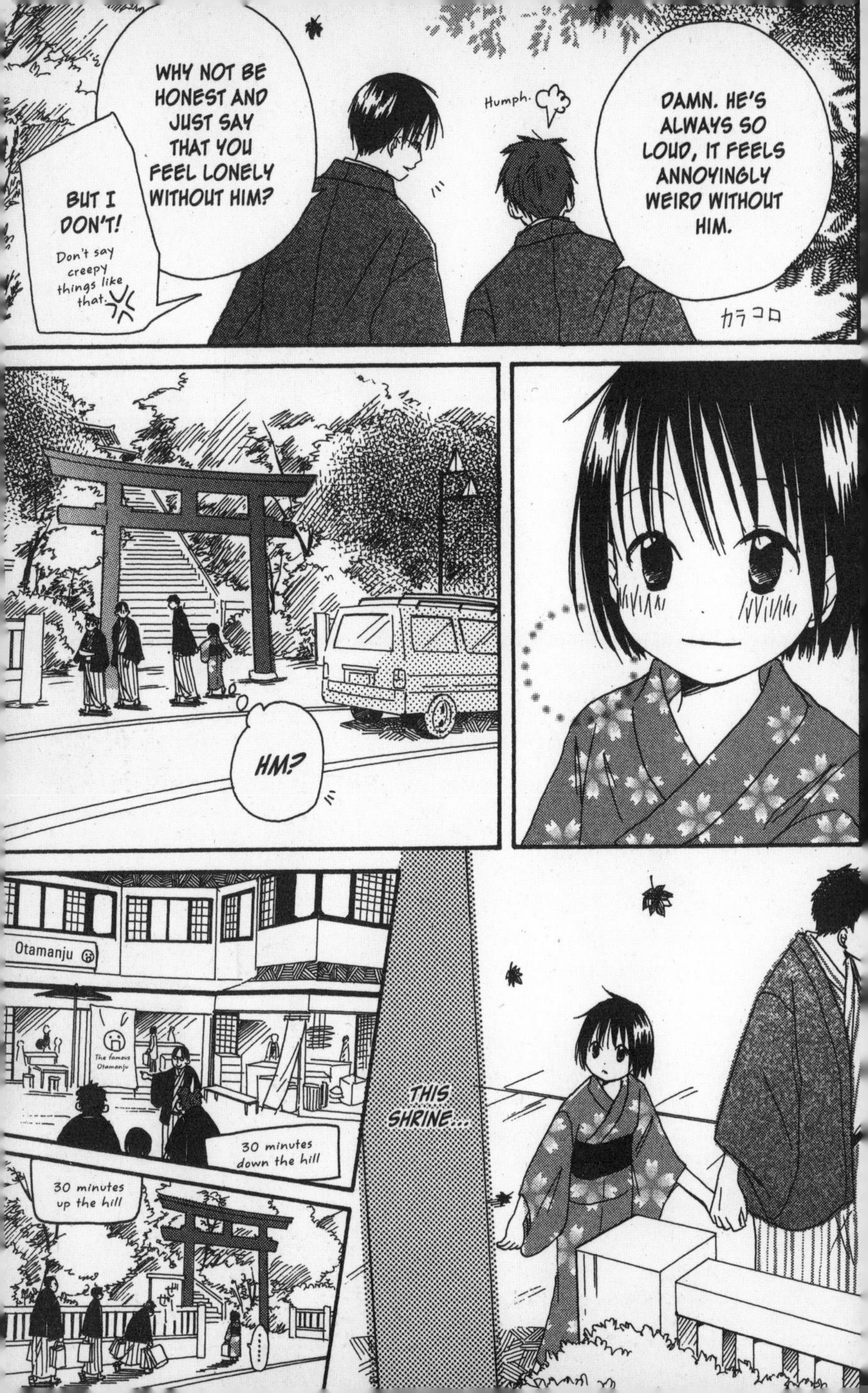
DAMN. HE'S ALWAYS SO LOUD, IT FEELS ANNOYINGLY WEIRD WITHOUT HIM.
カラコロ
Humph.
WHY NOT BE HONEST AND JUST SAY THAT YOU FEEL LONELY WITHOUT HIM?
BUT I DON'T!
Don't say creepy things like that.
HM?
THIS SHRINE...
Otamanju
The famous Otamanju
30 minutes down the hill
30 minutes up the hill
......

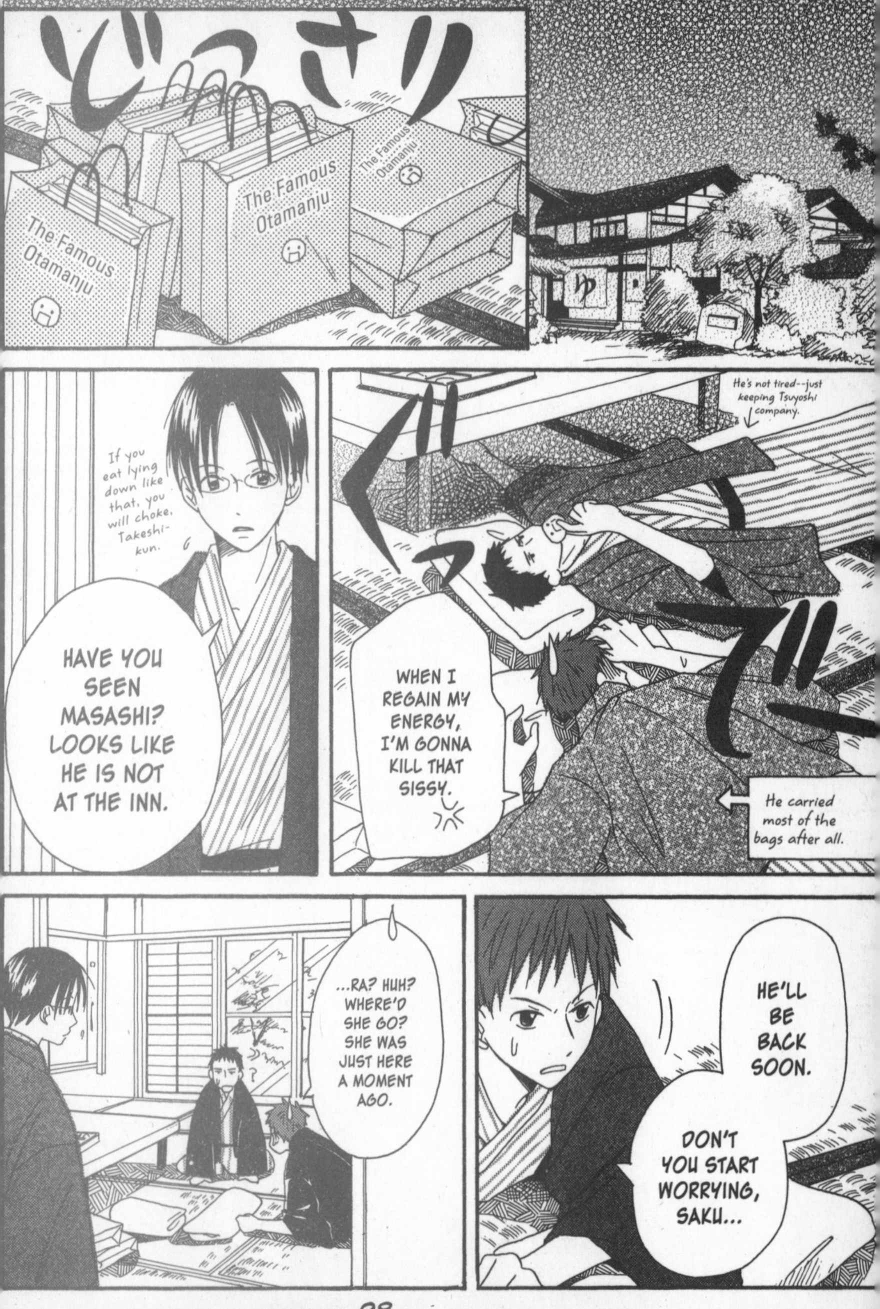

ゆ
どっさり
The Famous Otamanju
The Famous Otamanju
The Famous Otamanju
He's not tired--just keeping Tsuyoshi company.
WHEN I REGAIN MY ENERGY, I'M GONNA KILL THAT SISSY.
He carried most of the bags after all.
If you eat lying down like that, you will choke, Takeshi-kun.
HAVE YOU SEEN MASASHI? LOOKS LIKE HE IS NOT AT THE INN.
HE'LL BE BACK SOON.
DON'T YOU START WORRYING, SAKU...
...RA? HUH? WHERE'D SHE GO? SHE WAS JUST HERE A MOMENT AGO.

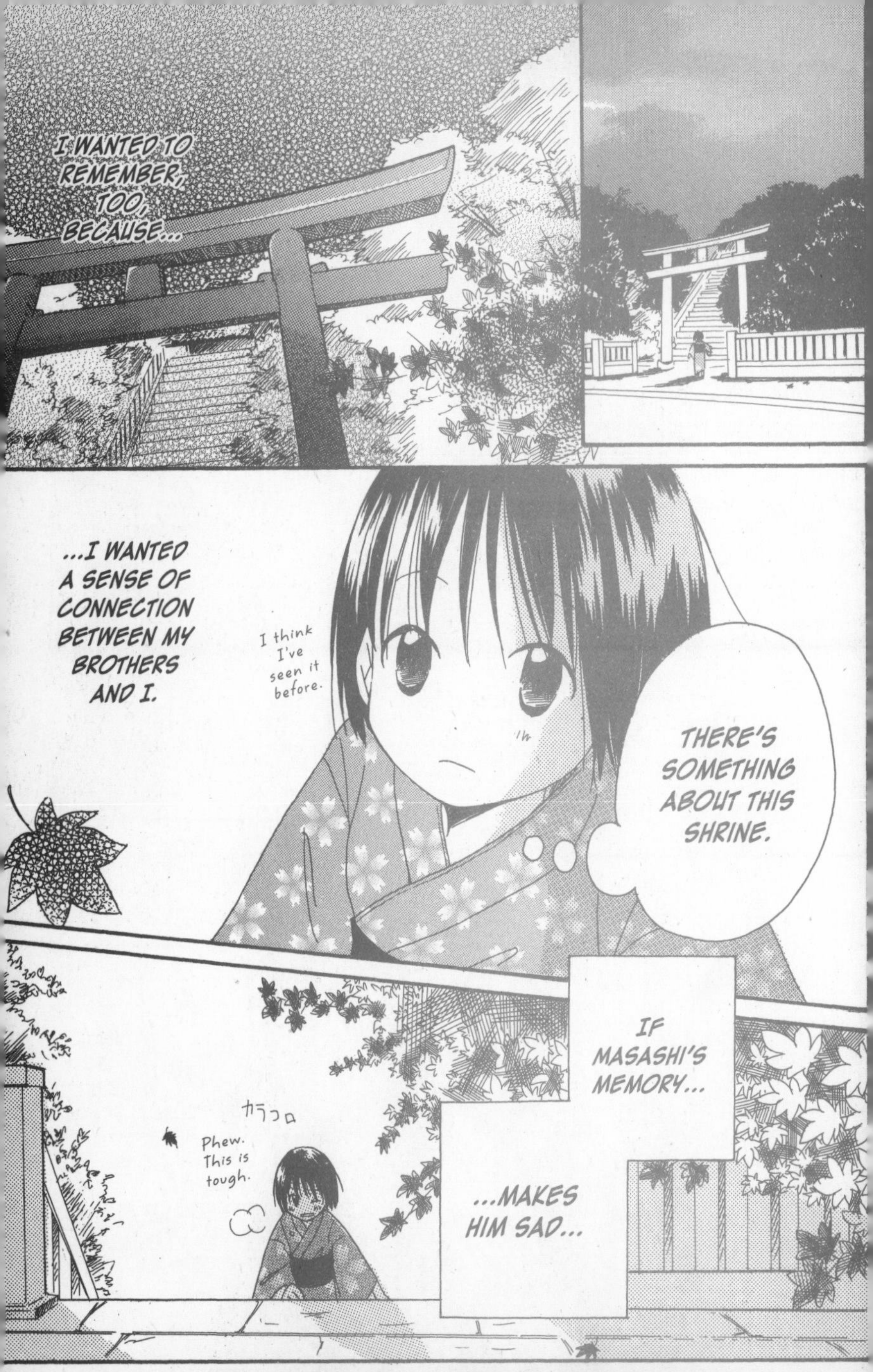
I WANTED TO REMEMBER, TOO, BECAUSE...
THERE'S SOMETHING ABOUT THIS SHRINE.
I think I've seen it before.
...I WANTED A SENSE OF CONNECTION BETWEEN MY BROTHERS AND I.
IF MASASHI'S MEMORY...
...MAKES HIM SAD...
カラコロ
Phew. This is tough.

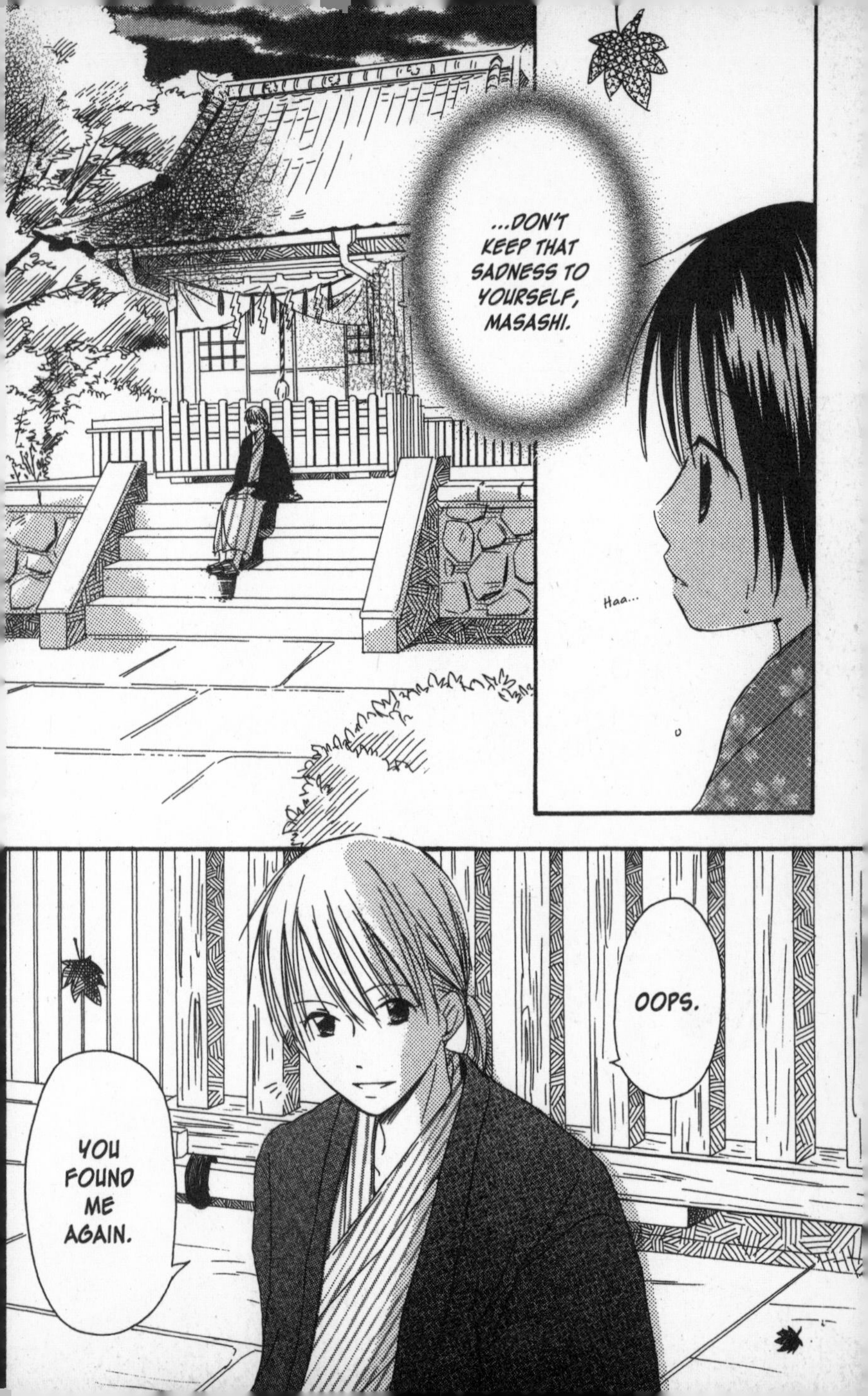
...DON'T KEEP THAT SADNESS TO YOURSELF, MASASHI.
Haa...
OOPS.
YOU FOUND ME AGAIN.

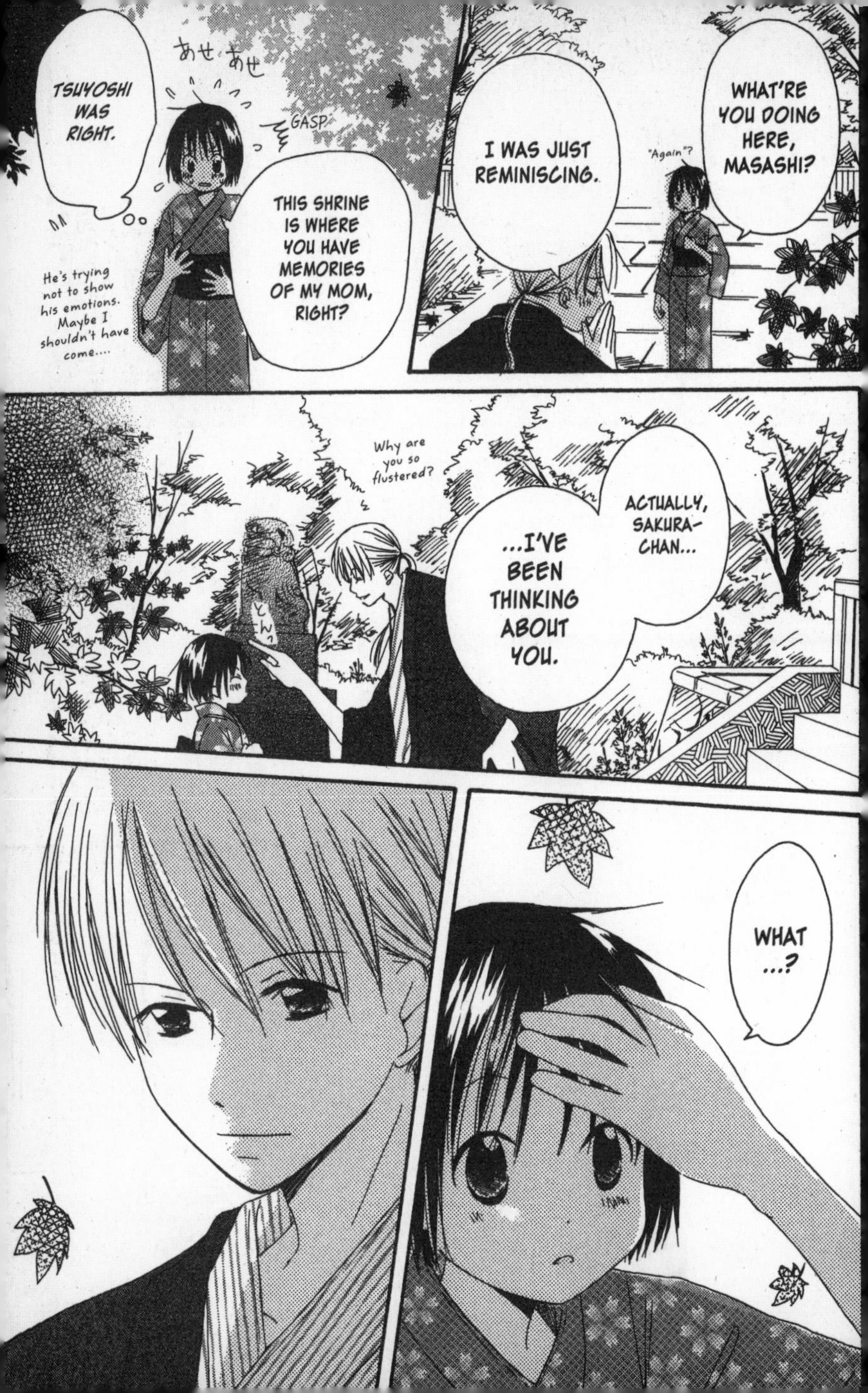
WHAT'RE YOU DOING HERE, MASASHI?
"Again"?
I WAS JUST REMINISCING.
あせ あせ
TSUYOSHI WAS RIGHT.
GASP
THIS SHRINE IS WHERE YOU HAVE MEMORIES OF MY MOM, RIGHT?
He's trying not to show his emotions. Maybe I shouldn't have come....
ACTUALLY, SAKURA-CHAN...
...I'VE BEEN THINKING ABOUT YOU.
Why are you so flustered?
とんっ
WHAT ...?

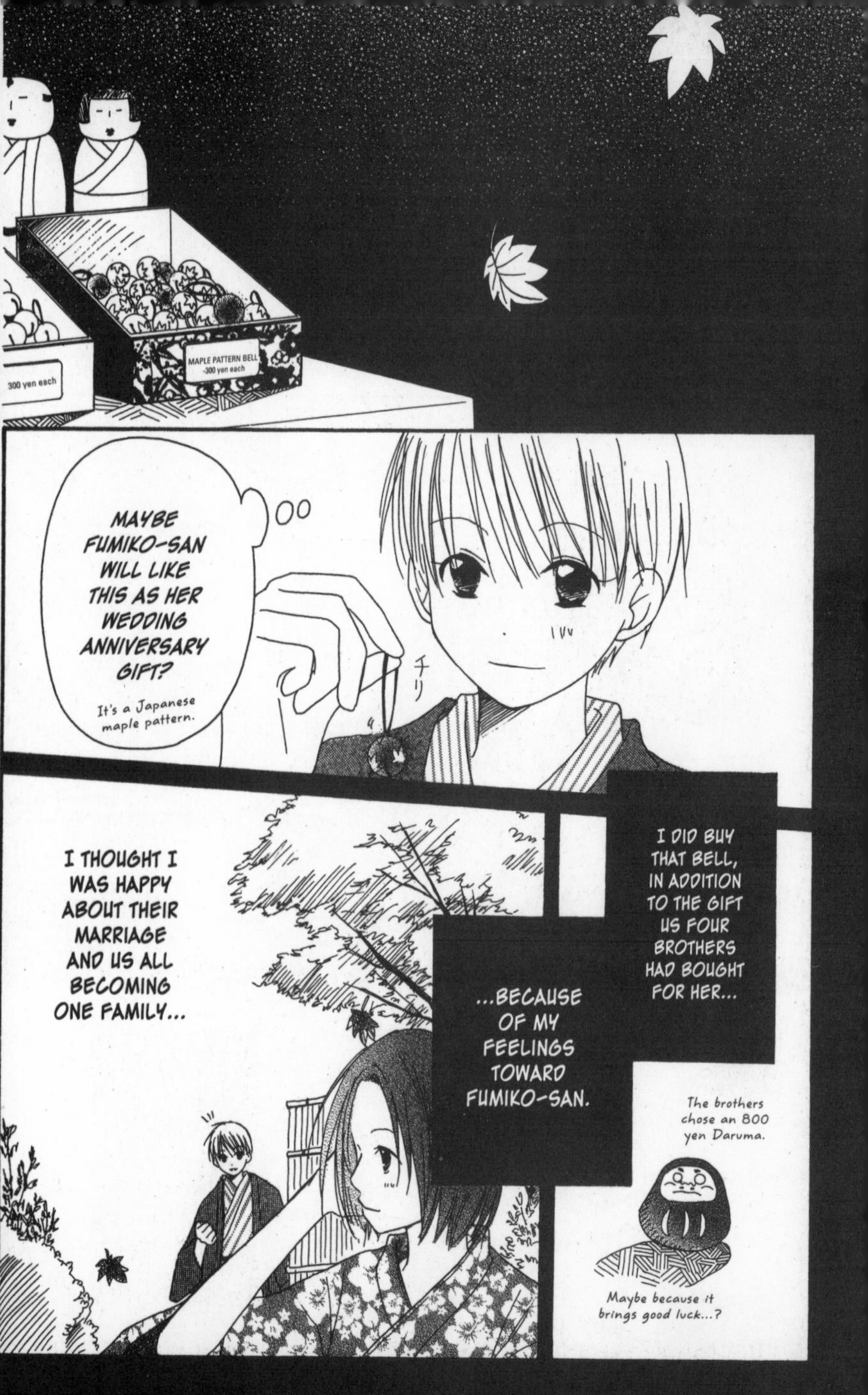

300 yen each
MAPLE PATTERN BELL -300 yen each
MAYBE FUMIKO-SAN WILL LIKE THIS AS HER WEDDING ANNIVERSARY GIFT?
It's a Japanese maple pattern.
チリ
I DID BUY THAT BELL, IN ADDITION TO THE GIFT US FOUR BROTHERS HAD BOUGHT FOR HER...
The brothers chose an 800 yen Daruma.
Maybe because it brings good luck...?
...BECAUSE OF MY FEELINGS TOWARD FUMIKO-SAN.
I THOUGHT I WAS HAPPY ABOUT THEIR MARRIAGE AND US ALL BECOMING ONE FAMILY...

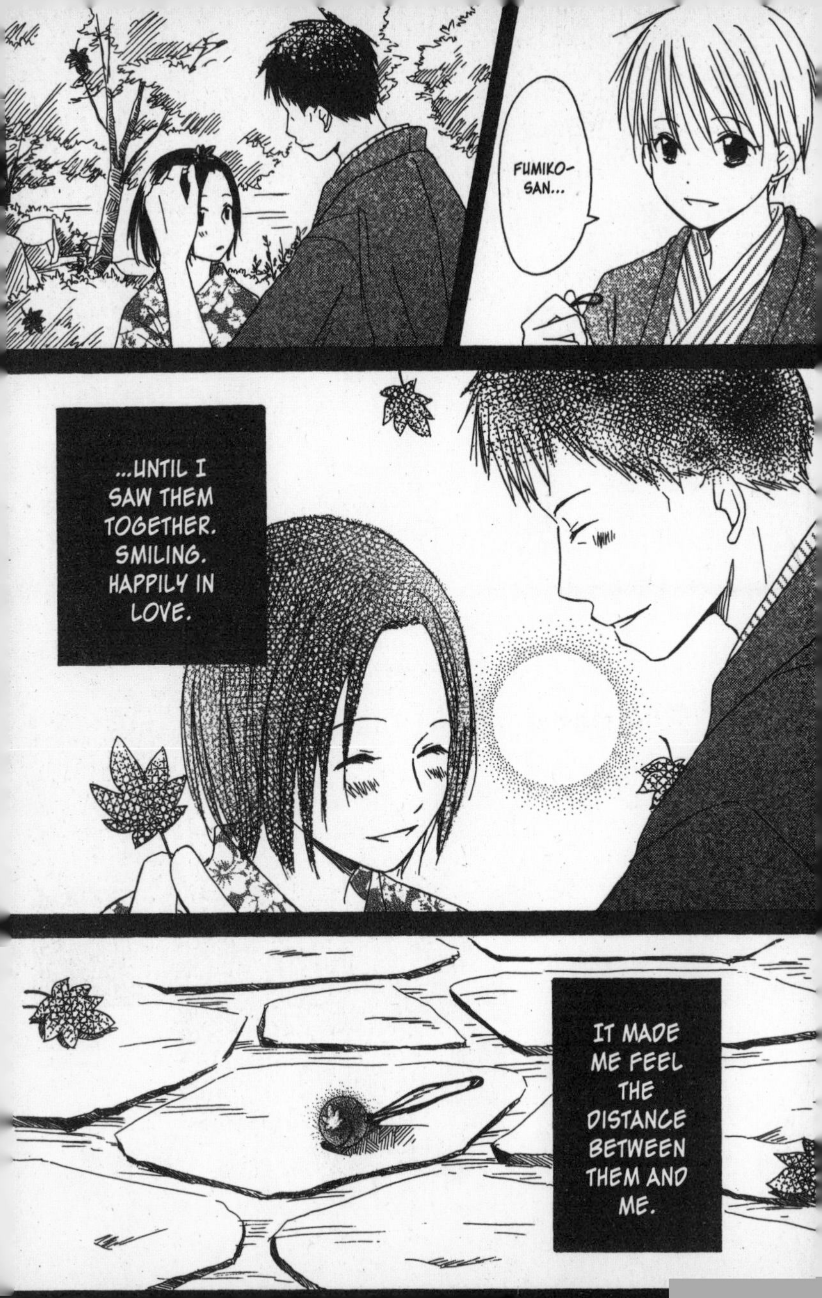
FUMIKO-SAN...
...UNTIL I SAW THEM TOGETHER. SMILING. HAPPILY IN LOVE.
IT MADE ME FEEL THE DISTANCE BETWEEN THEM AND ME.

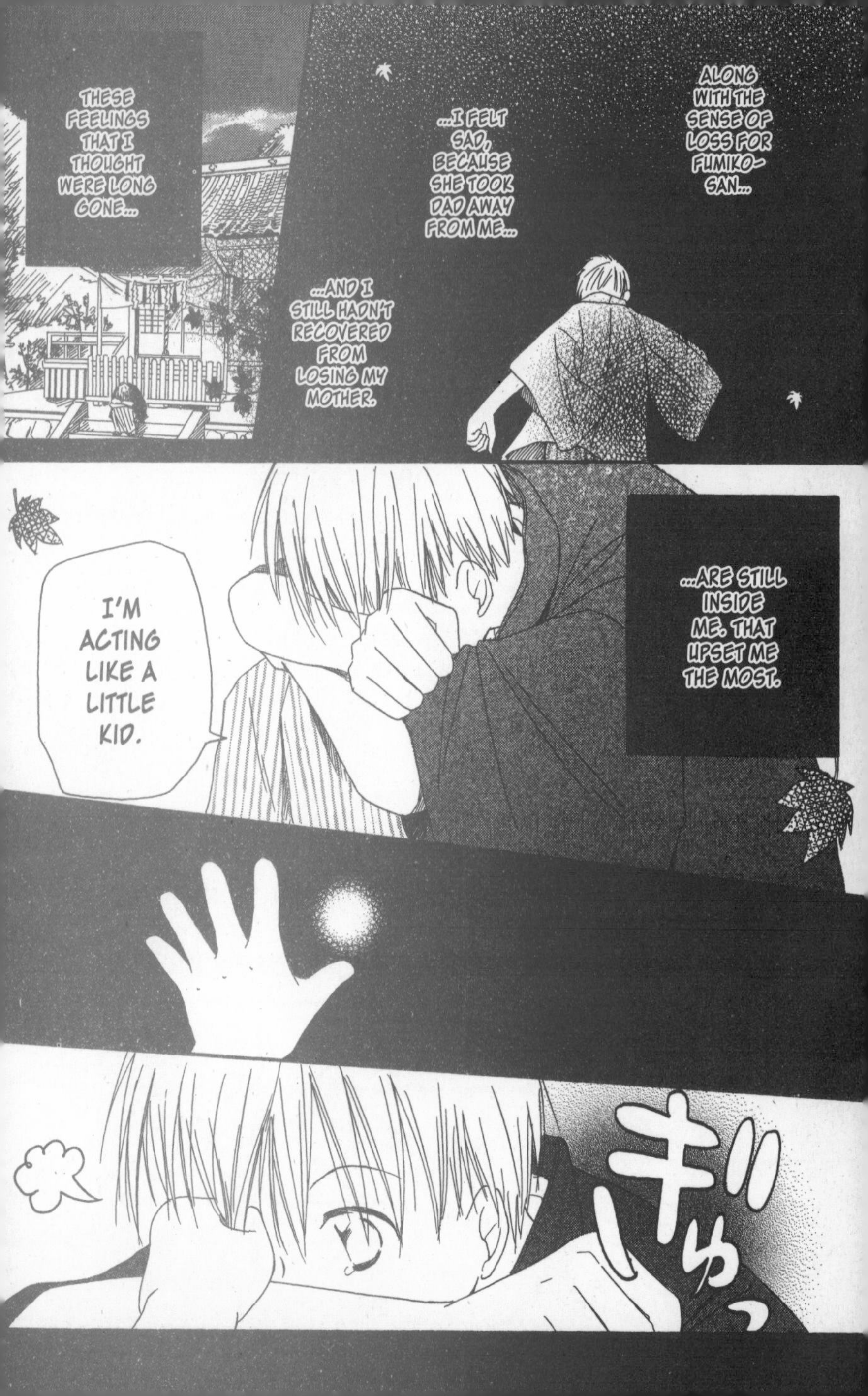
ALONG WITH THE SENSE OF LOSS FOR FUMIKO-SAN...
...I FELT SAD, BECAUSE SHE TOOK DAD AWAY FROM ME...
...AND I STILL HADN'T RECOVERED FROM LOSING MY MOTHER.
THESE FEELINGS THAT I THOUGHT WERE LONG GONE...
...ARE STILL INSIDE ME. THAT UPSET ME THE MOST.
I'M ACTING LIKE A LITTLE KID.
ぎゅっ

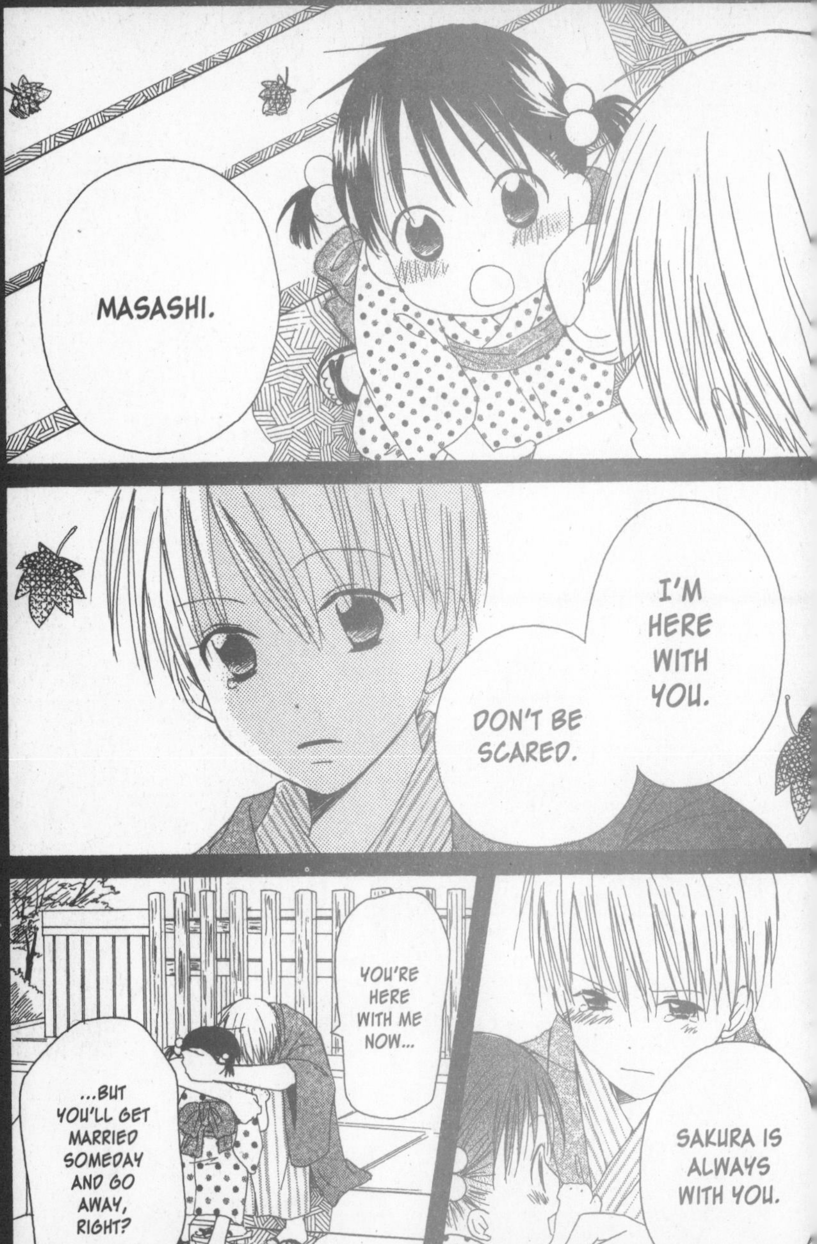
MASASHI.
I'M HERE WITH YOU.
DON'T BE SCARED.
SAKURA IS ALWAYS WITH YOU.
YOU'RE HERE WITH ME NOW...
...BUT YOU'LL GET MARRIED SOMEDAY AND GO AWAY, RIGHT?

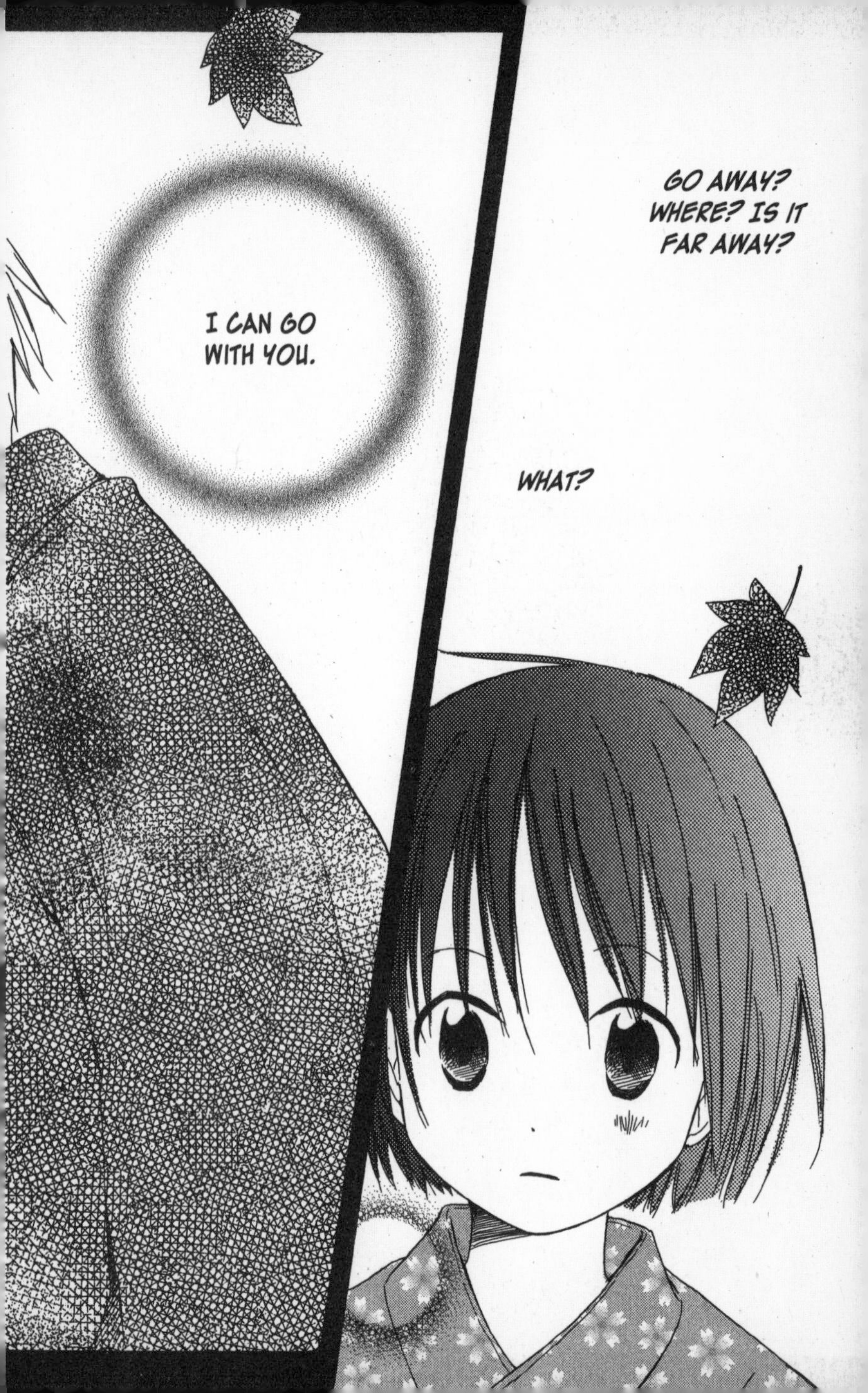
GO AWAY? WHERE? IS IT FAR AWAY?
WHAT?
I CAN GO WITH YOU.

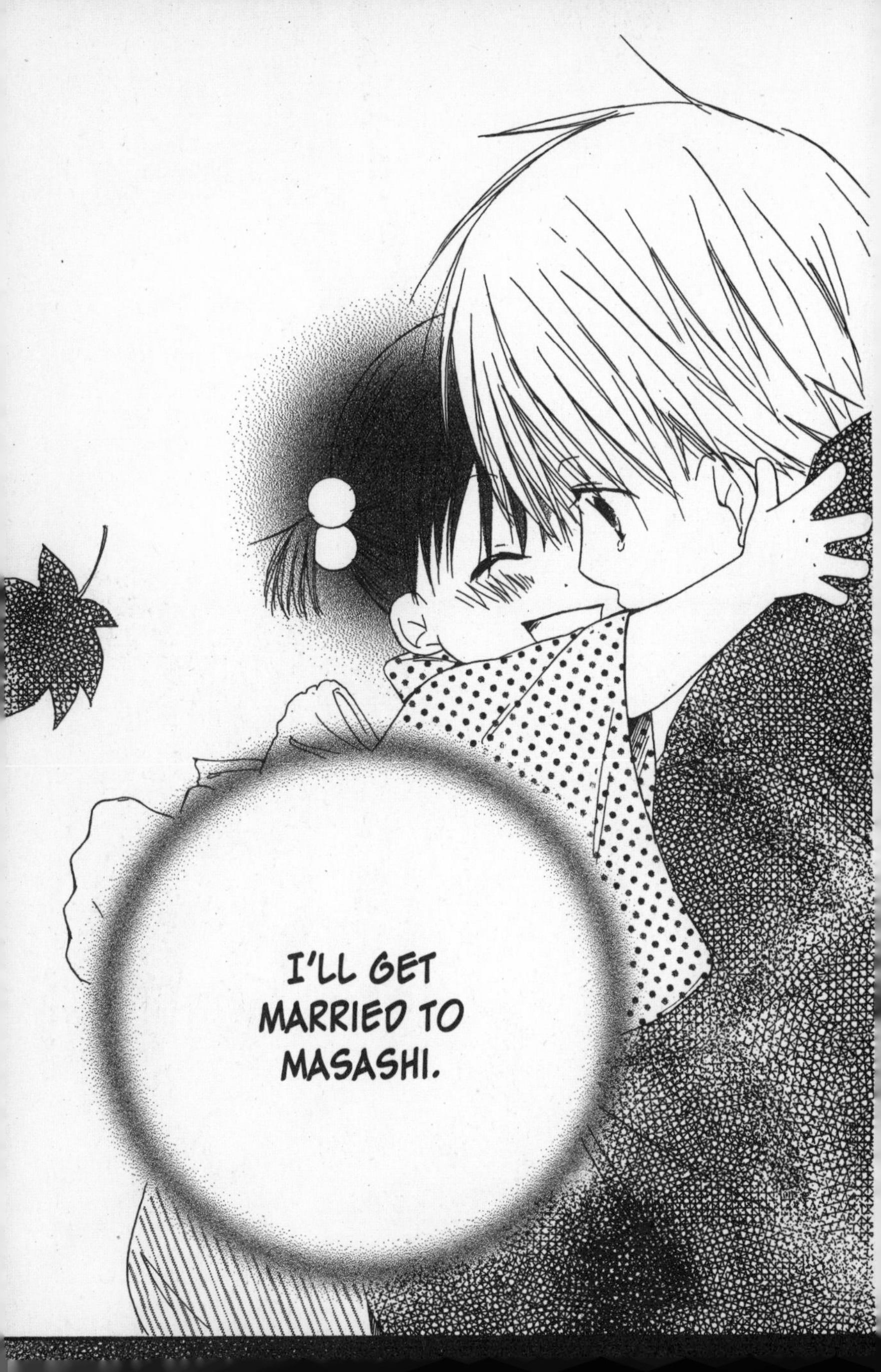
I'LL GET MARRIED TO MASASHI.

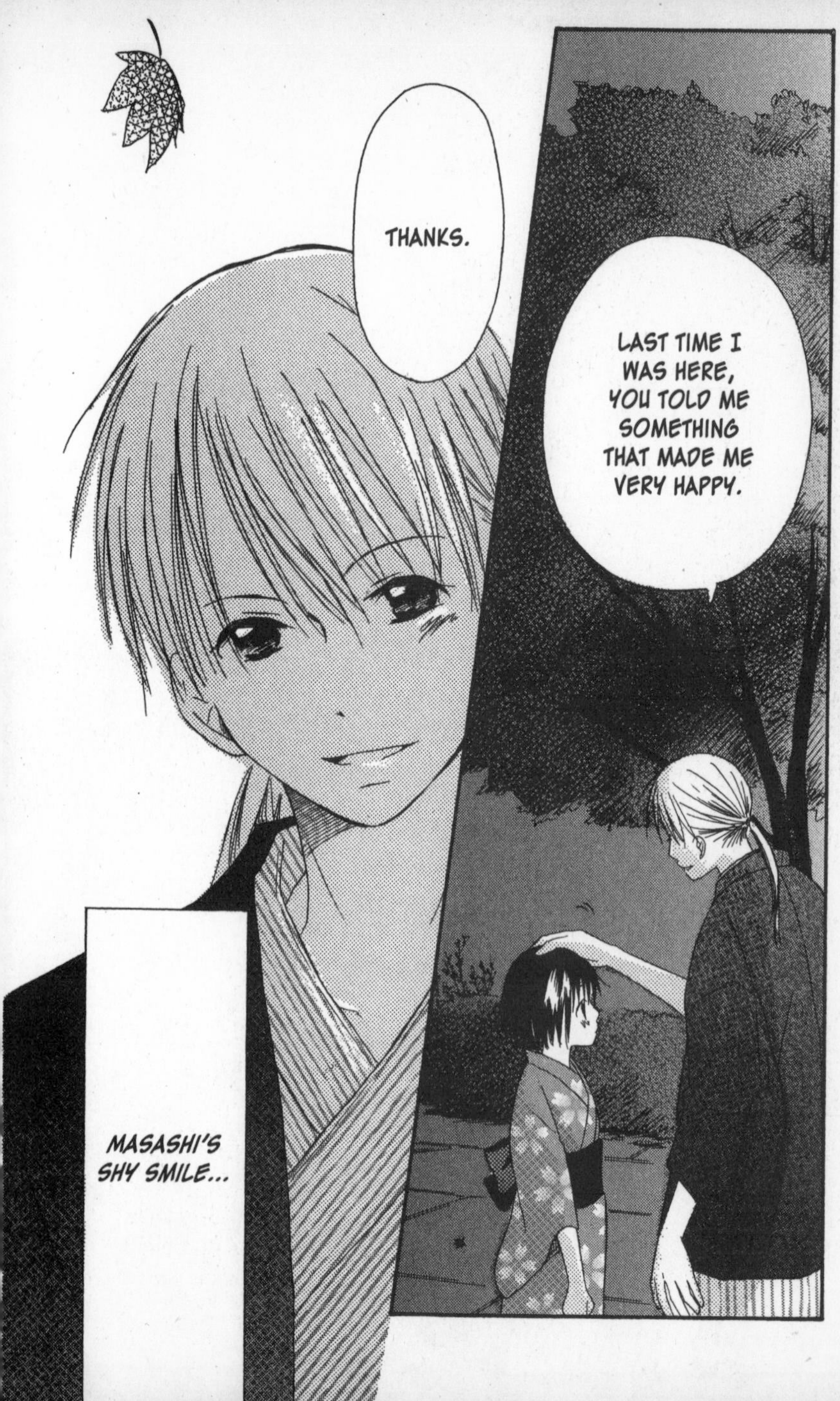
LAST TIME I WAS HERE, YOU TOLD ME SOMETHING THAT MADE ME VERY HAPPY.
THANKS.
MASASHI'S SHY SMILE...

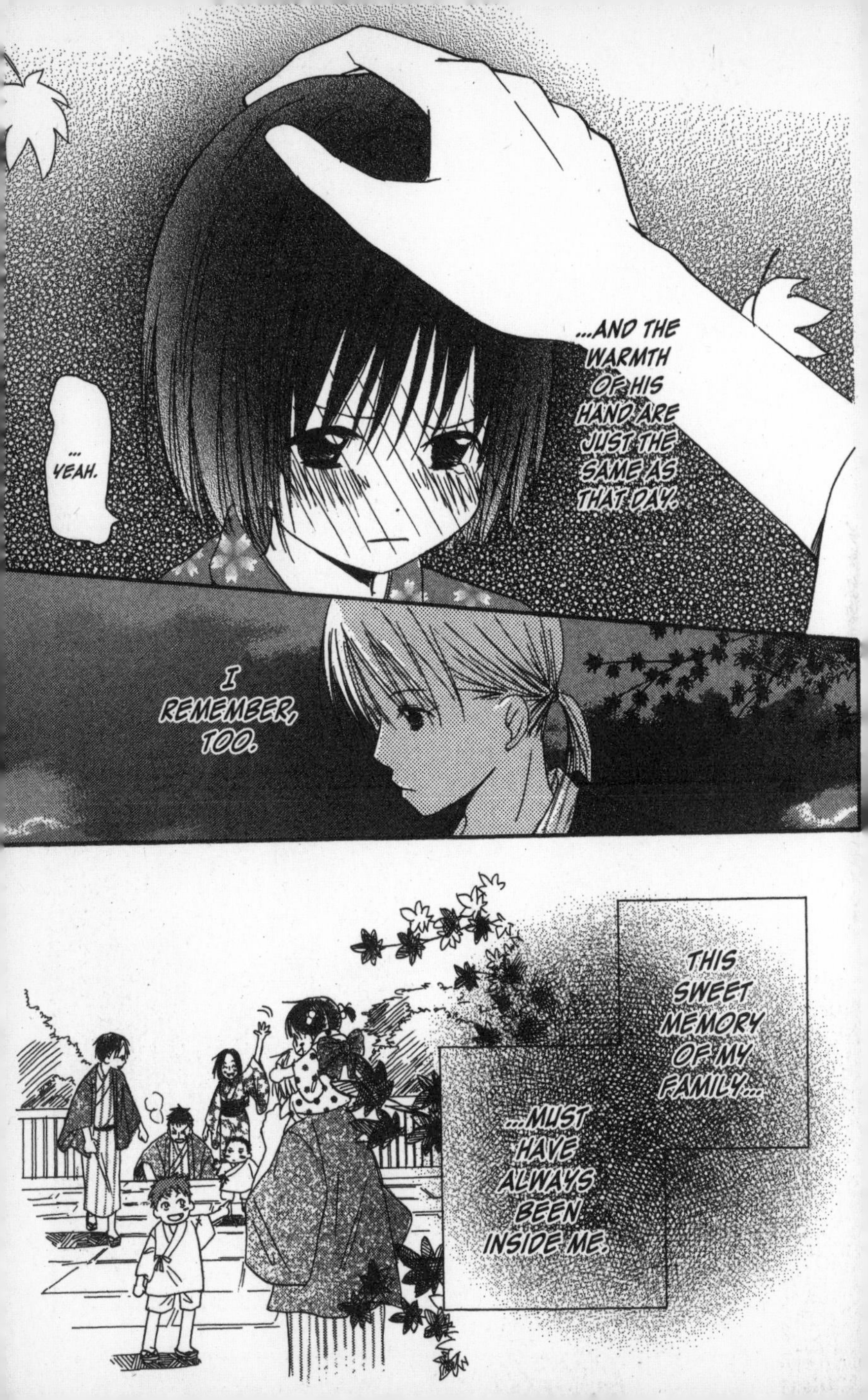
...AND THE WARMTH OF HIS HAND ARE JUST THE SAME AS THAT DAY.
... YEAH.
I REMEMBER, TOO.
THIS SWEET MEMORY OF MY FAMILY...
...MUST HAVE ALWAYS BEEN INSIDE ME.

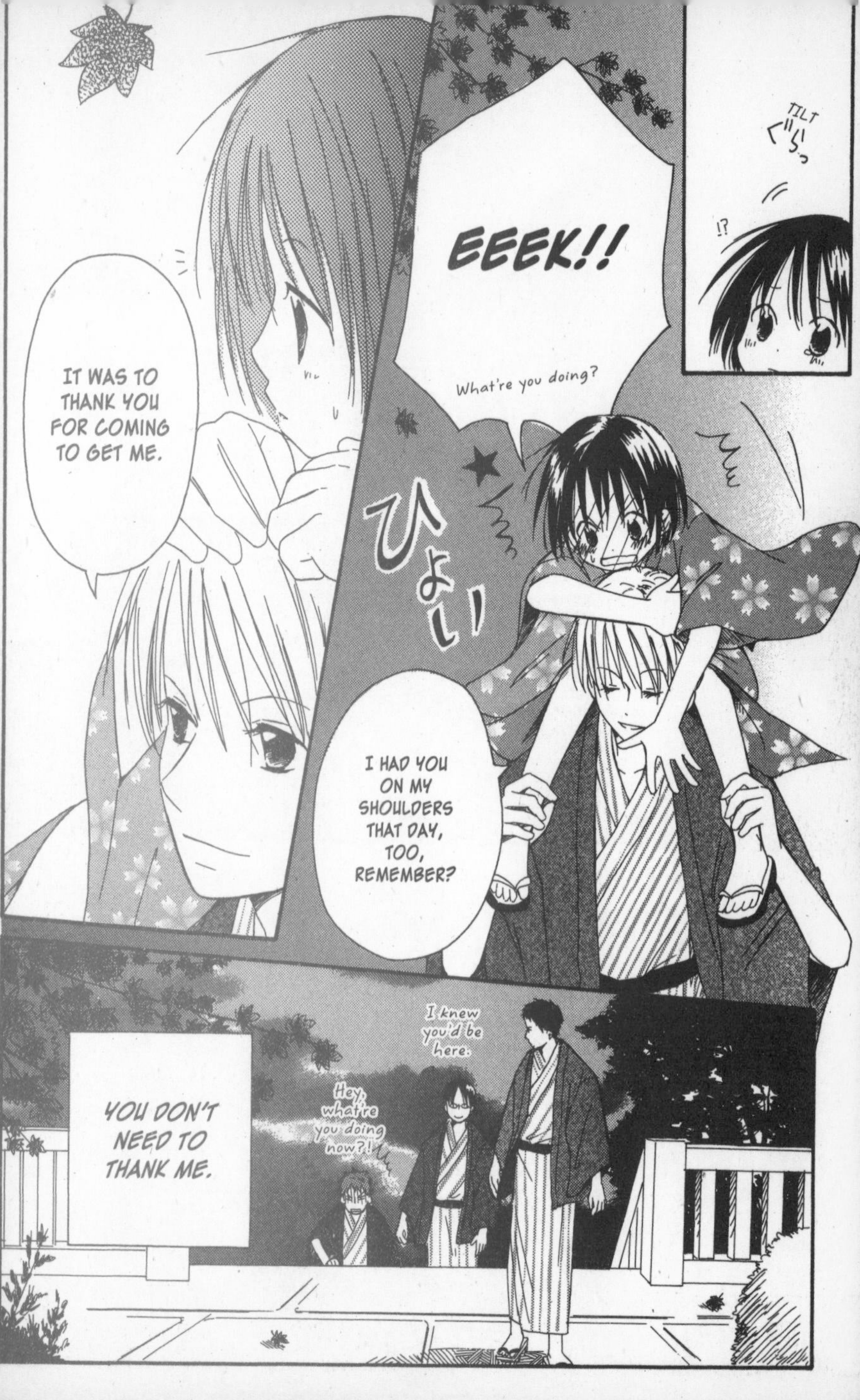
TILT
ぐらっ
!?
EEEK!!
What're you doing?
ひょい
I HAD YOU ON MY SHOULDERS THAT DAY, TOO, REMEMBER?
IT WAS TO THANK YOU FOR COMING TO GET ME.
I knew you'd be here.
Hey, what're you doing now?!
YOU DON'T NEED TO THANK ME.

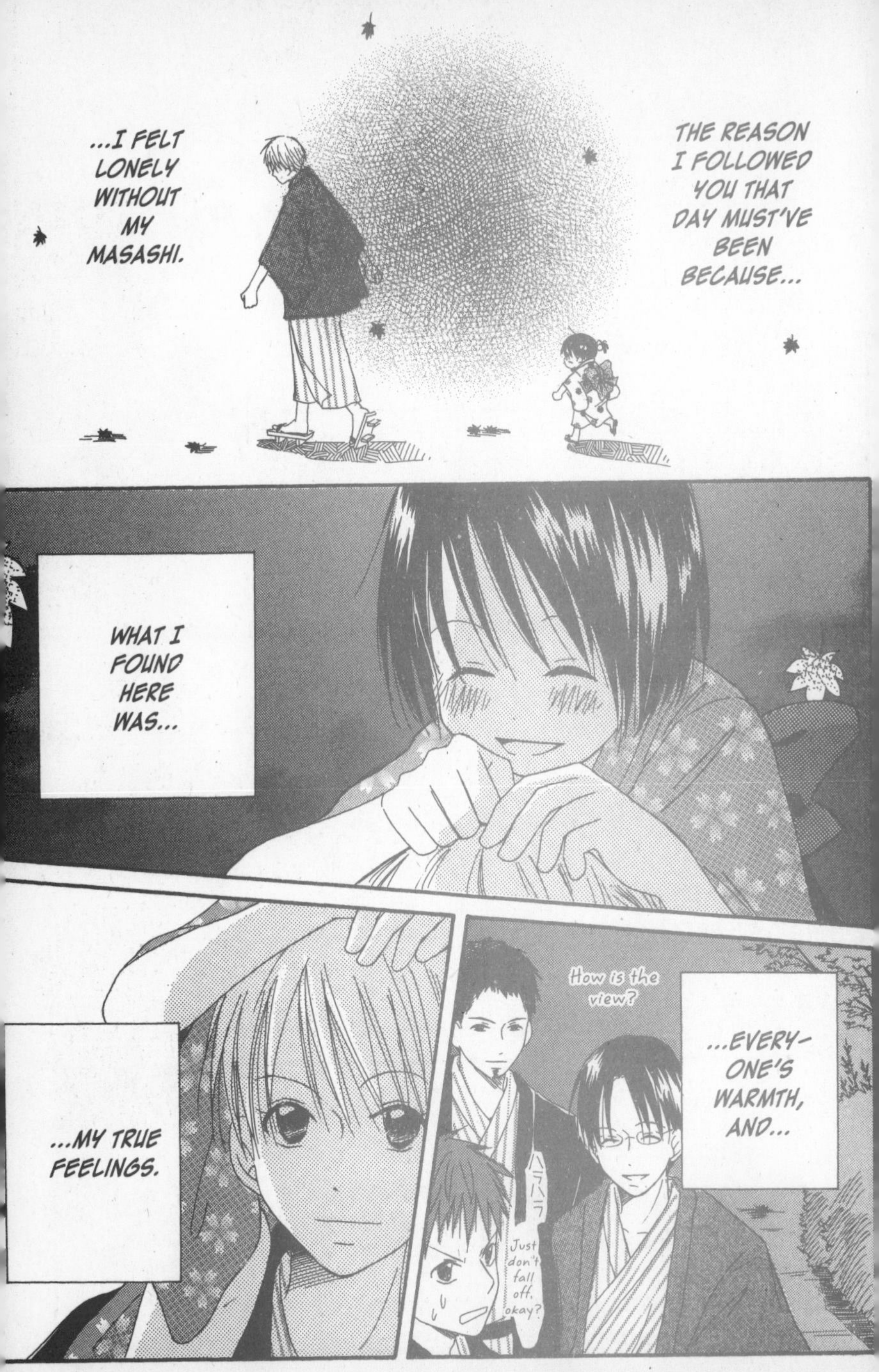
THE REASON I FOLLOWED YOU THAT DAY MUST'VE BEEN BECAUSE...
...I FELT LONELY WITHOUT MY MASASHI.
WHAT I FOUND HERE WAS...
How is the view?
...EVERY-ONE'S WARMTH, AND...
ハラハラ
Just don't fall off, okay?
...MY TRUE FEELINGS.

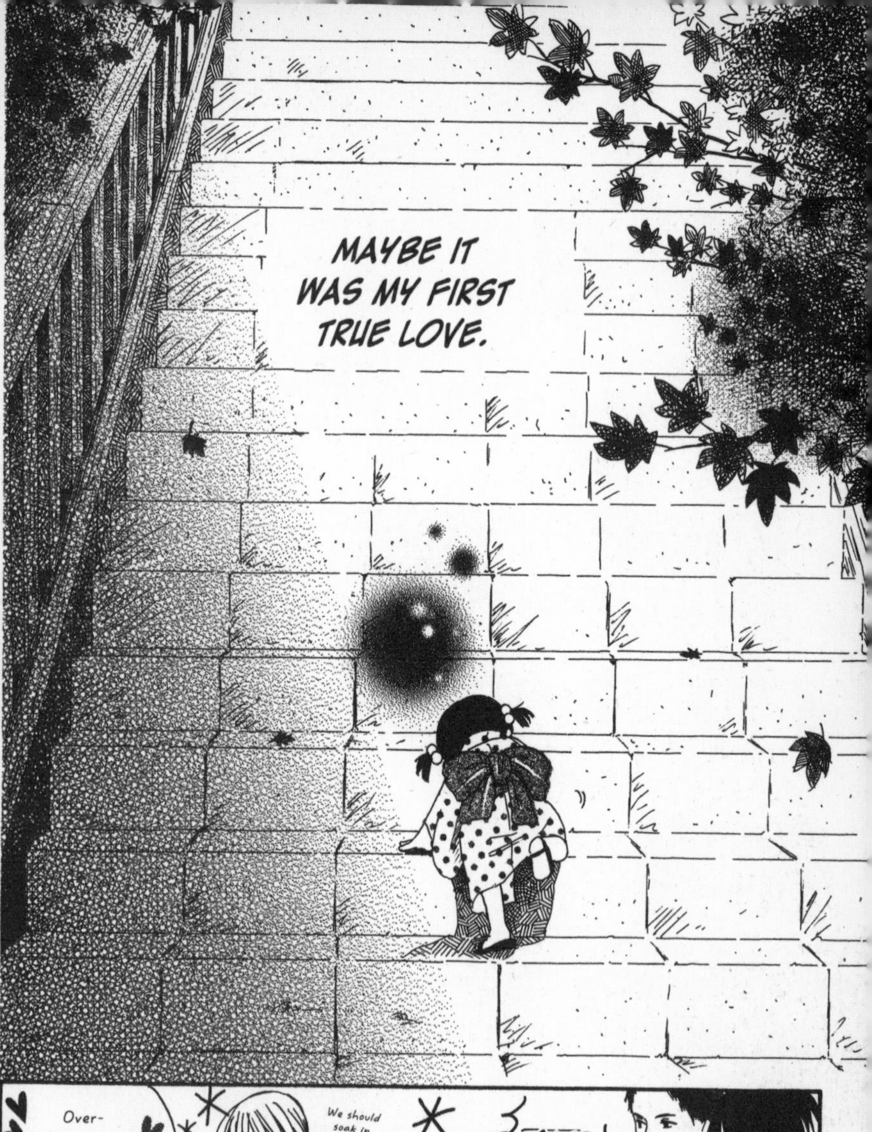
MAYBE IT WAS MY FIRST TRUE LOVE.

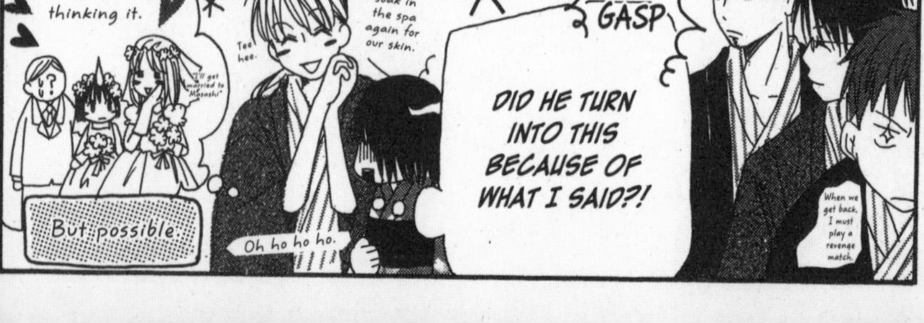
When we get back, I must play a revenge match.
GASP
DID HE TURN INTO THIS BECAUSE OF WHAT I SAID?!
We should soak in the spa again for our skin.
Tee hee.
Oh ho ho ho.
Over-thinking it.
"I'll get married to Mr Masashi"
But possible.

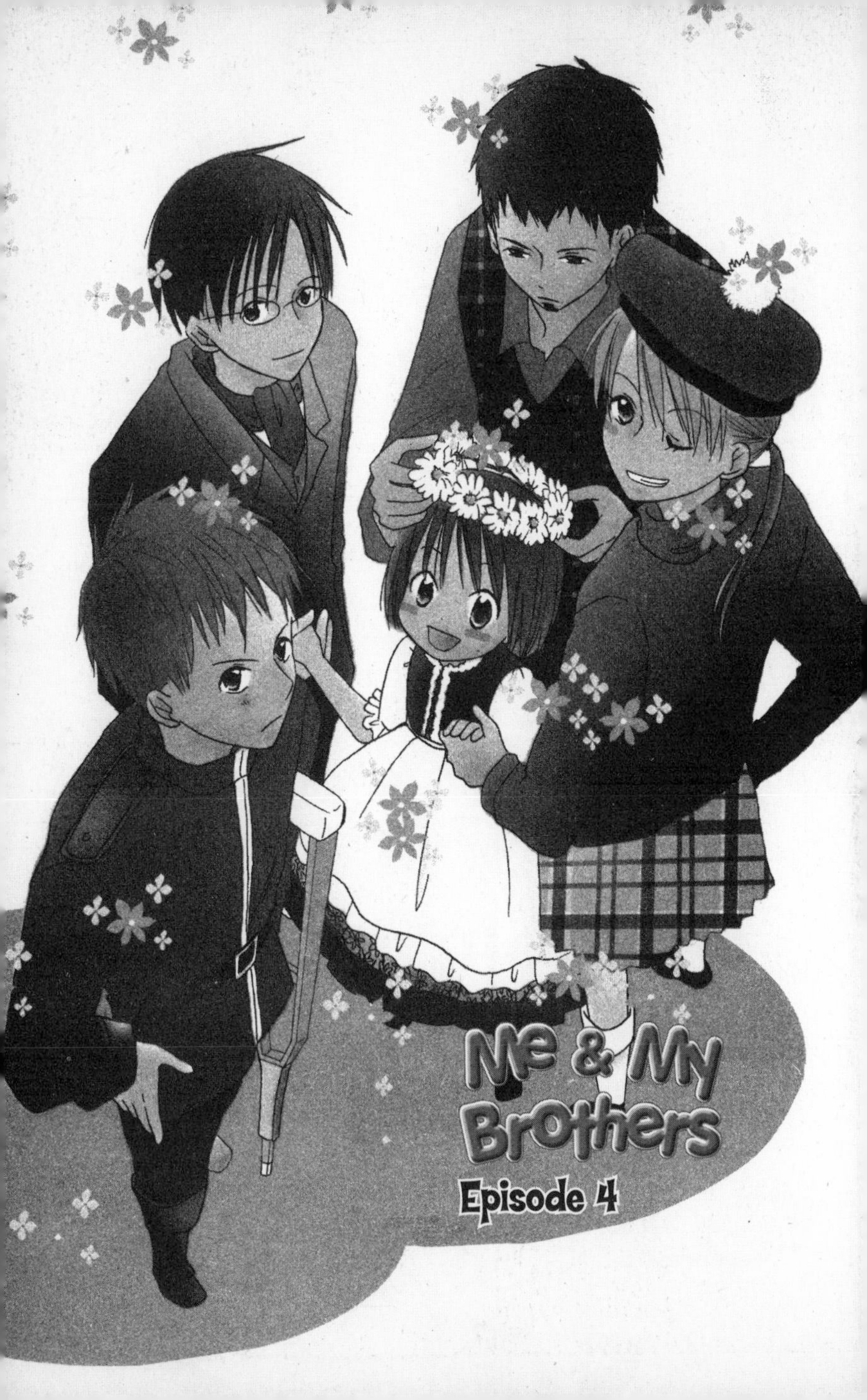
Me & My Brothers
Episode 4

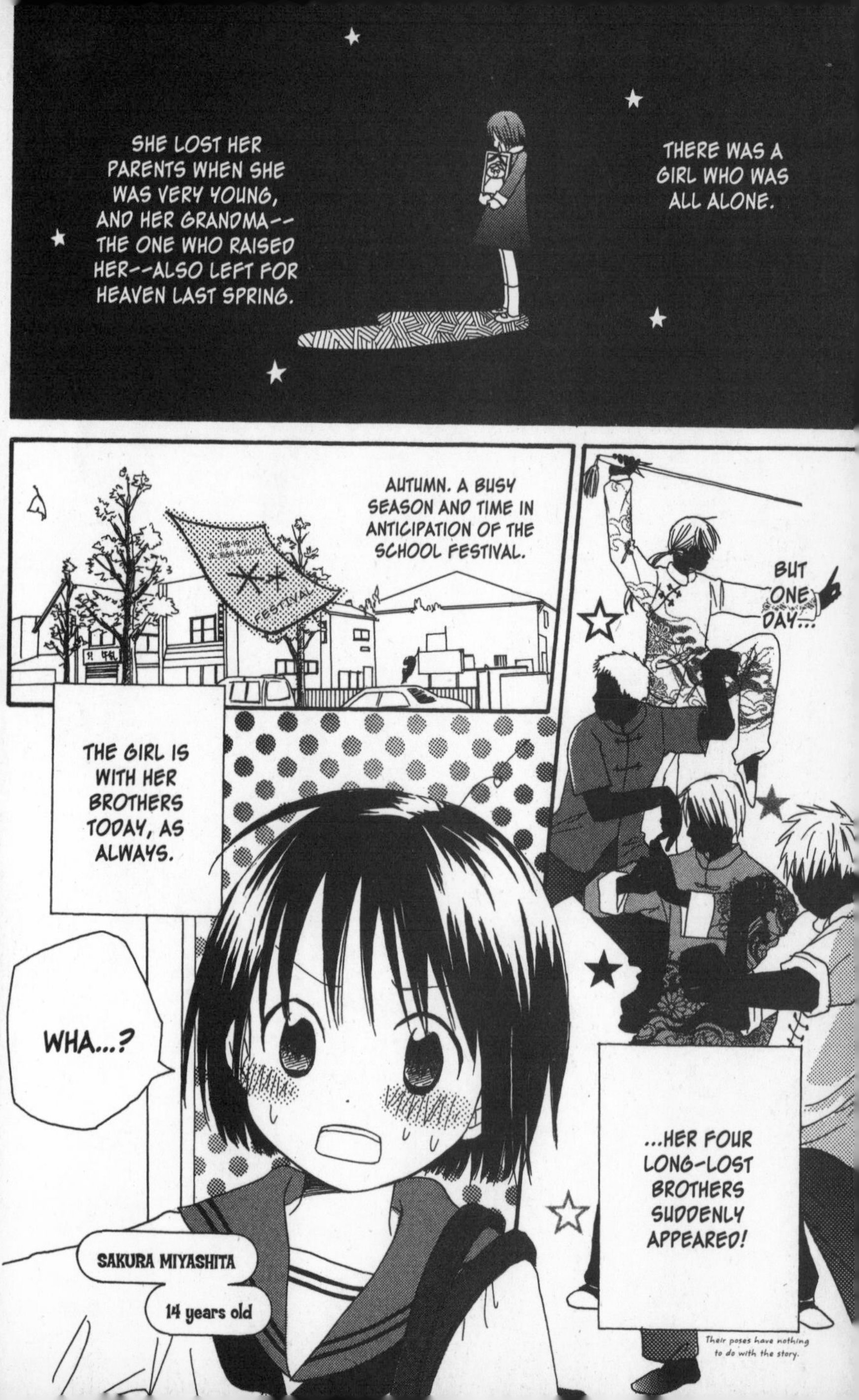
THERE WAS A GIRL WHO WAS ALL ALONE.
SHE LOST HER PARENTS WHEN SHE WAS VERY YOUNG, AND HER GRANDMA-- THE ONE WHO RAISED HER--ALSO LEFT FOR HEAVEN LAST SPRING.
BUT ONE DAY...
...HER FOUR LONG-LOST BROTHERS SUDDENLY APPEARED!
Their poses have nothing to do with the story.
AUTUMN. A BUSY SEASON AND TIME IN ANTICIPATION OF THE SCHOOL FESTIVAL.
THE 19TH JR. HIGH SCHOOL
FESTIVAL
THE GIRL IS WITH HER BROTHERS TODAY, AS ALWAYS.
WHA...?
SAKURA MIYASHITA
14 years old

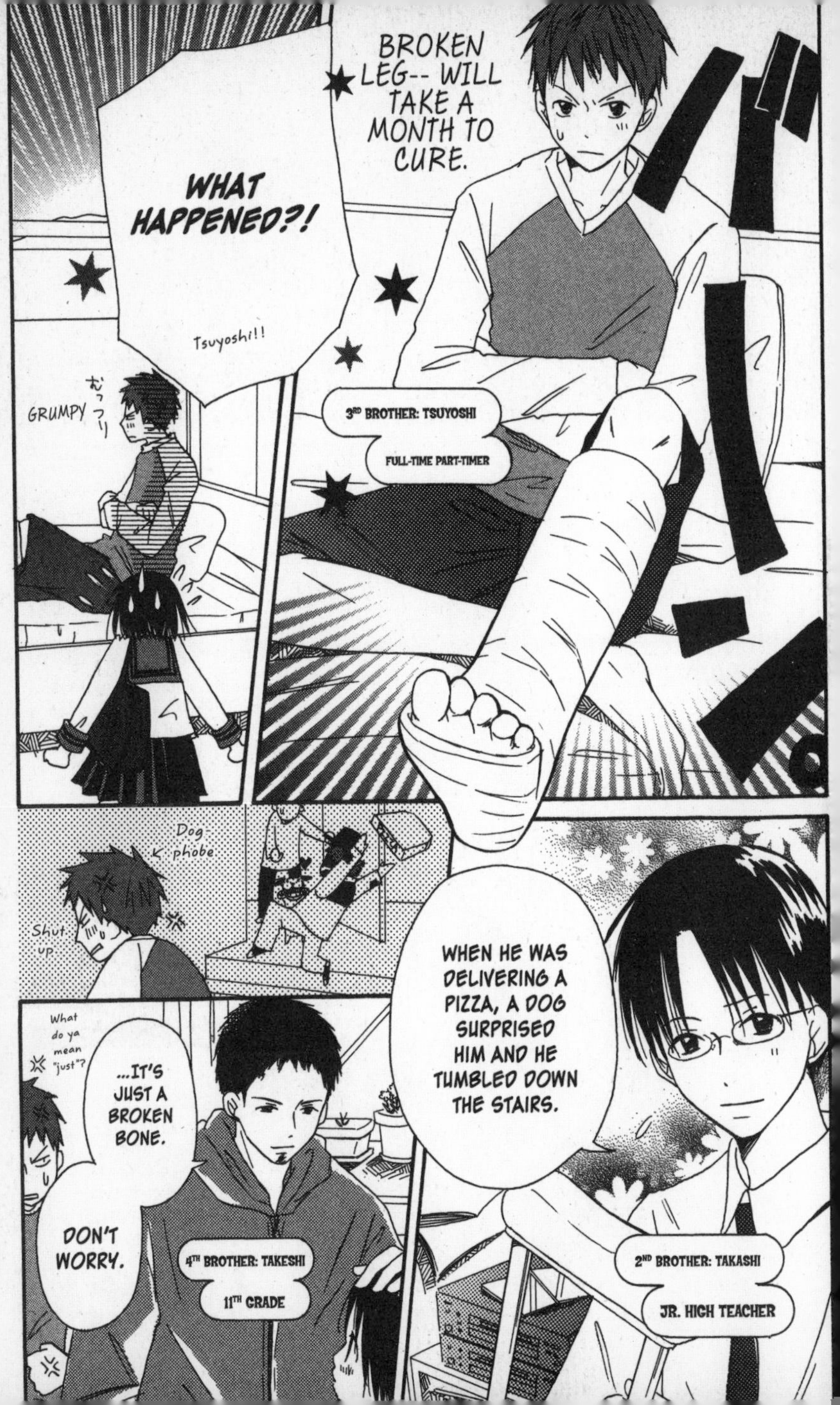
BROKEN LEG-- WILL TAKE A MONTH TO CURE.
3RD BROTHER: TSUYOSHI
FULL-TIME PART-TIMER
WHAT HAPPENED?!
Tsuyoshi!!
むっつり
GRUMPY
WHEN HE WAS DELIVERING A PIZZA, A DOG SURPRISED HIM AND HE TUMBLED DOWN THE STAIRS.
2ND BROTHER: TAKASHI
JR. HIGH TEACHER
Dog-phobe.
Shut up.
...IT'S JUST A BROKEN BONE.
DON'T WORRY.
4TH BROTHER: TAKESHI
11TH GRADE
What do ya mean "just"?

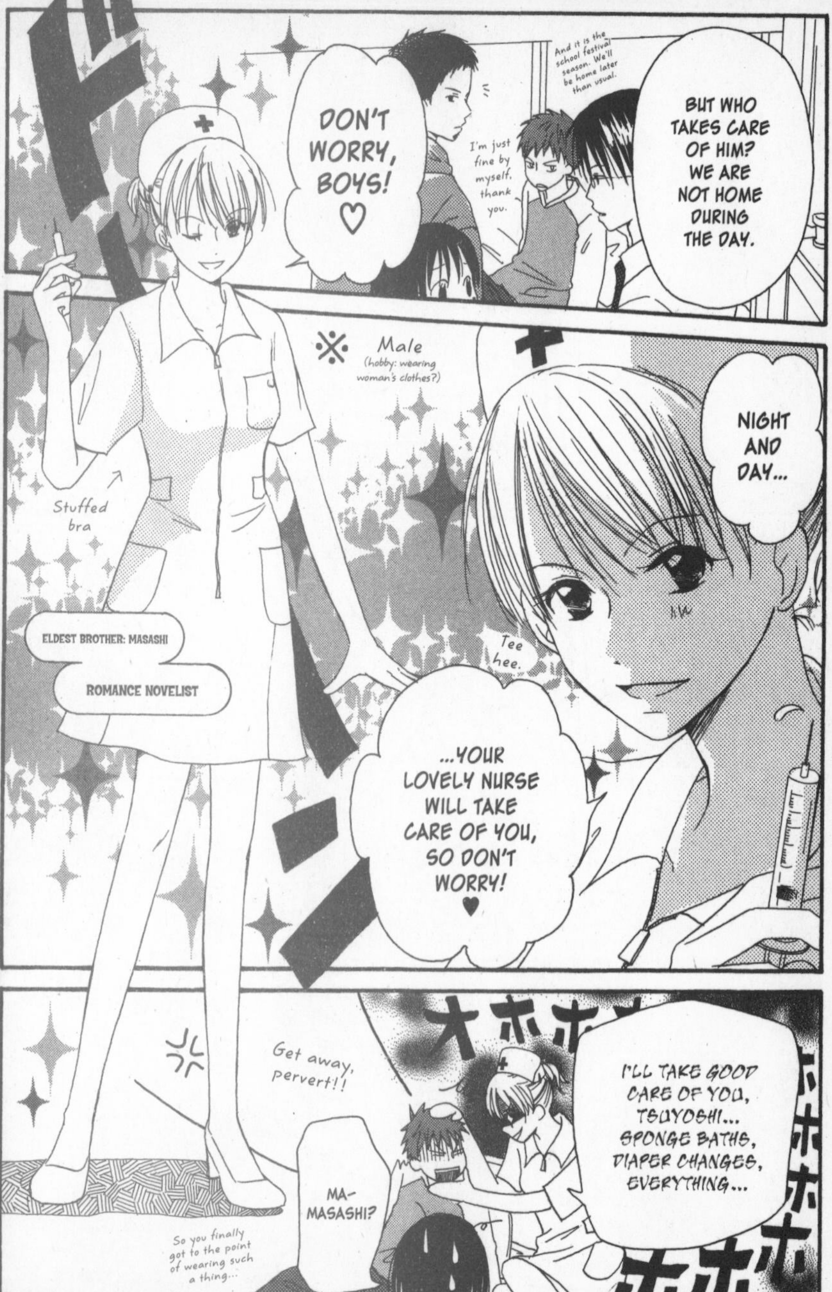
BUT WHO TAKES CARE OF HIM? WE ARE NOT HOME DURING THE DAY.
And it is the school festival season. We'll be home later than usual.
I'm just fine by myself, thank you.
DON'T WORRY, BOYS! ♡
NIGHT AND DAY...
Tee hee.
...YOUR LOVELY NURSE WILL TAKE CARE OF YOU, SO DON'T WORRY! ♥
※ Male (hobby: wearing woman's clothes?)
Stuffed bra
ELDEST BROTHER: MASASHI
ROMANCE NOVELIST
I'LL TAKE GOOD CARE OF YOU, TSUYOSHI... SPONGE BATHS, DIAPER CHANGES, EVERYTHING...
MA-MASASHI?
Get away, pervert!!
So you finally got to the point of wearing such a thing...

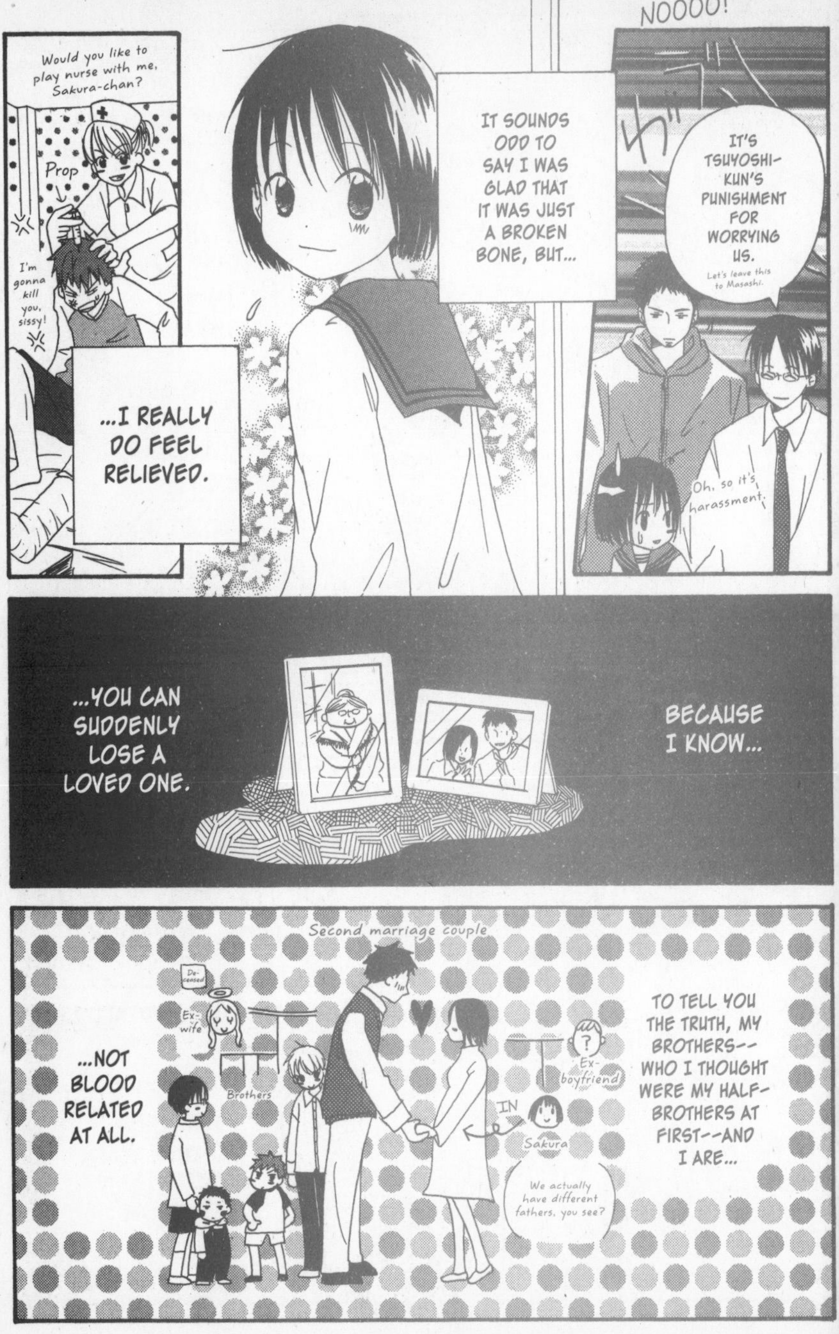
NOOOO!
IT'S TSUYOSHI-KUN'S PUNISHMENT FOR WORRYING US.
Let's leave this to Masashi.
Oh, so it's harassment.
IT SOUNDS ODD TO SAY I WAS GLAD THAT IT WAS JUST A BROKEN BONE, BUT...
Would you like to play nurse with me, Sakura-chan?
Prop
I'm gonna kill you, sissy!
...I REALLY DO FEEL RELIEVED.
BECAUSE I KNOW...
...YOU CAN SUDDENLY LOSE A LOVED ONE.
TO TELL YOU THE TRUTH, MY BROTHERS--WHO I THOUGHT WERE MY HALF-BROTHERS AT FIRST--AND I ARE...
Second marriage couple
?
Ex-boyfriend
IN
Sakura
We actually have different fathers, you see?
De-ceased
Ex-wife
Brothers
...NOT BLOOD RELATED AT ALL.

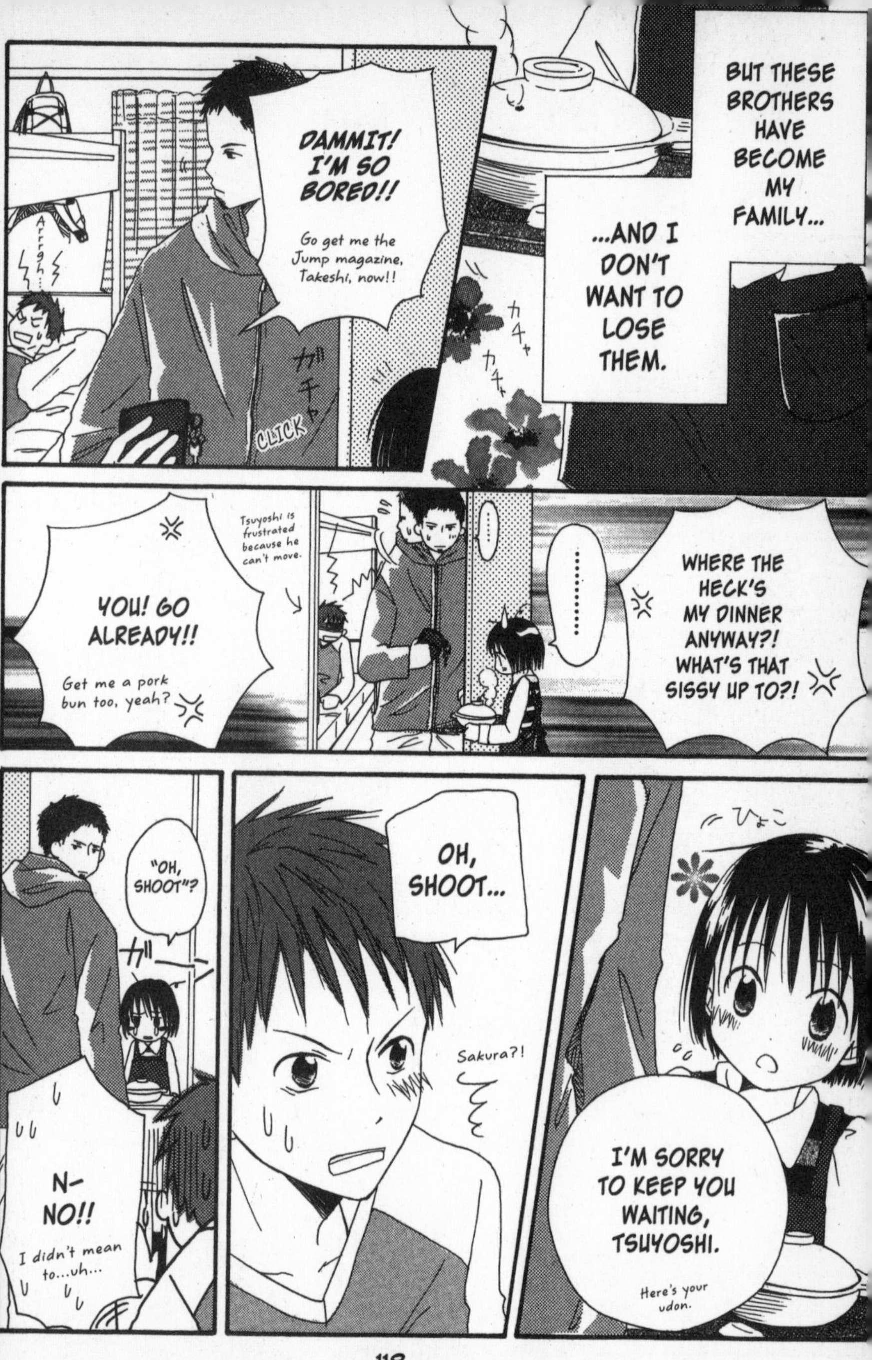
BUT THESE BROTHERS HAVE BECOME MY FAMILY...
...AND I DON'T WANT TO LOSE THEM.
カチャ
カチャ
DAMMIT! I'M SO BORED!!
Go get me the Jump magazine, Takeshi, now!!
Arrrgh...
ガチャ
CLICK
WHERE THE HECK'S MY DINNER ANYWAY?! WHAT'S THAT SISSY UP TO?!
......
Tsuyoshi is frustrated because he can't move.
YOU! GO ALREADY!!
Get me a pork bun too, yeah?
ひょこ
I'M SORRY TO KEEP YOU WAITING, TSUYOSHI.
Here's your udon.
OH, SHOOT...
Sakura?!
"OH, SHOOT"?
ガー
N-NO!!
I didn't mean to...uh...

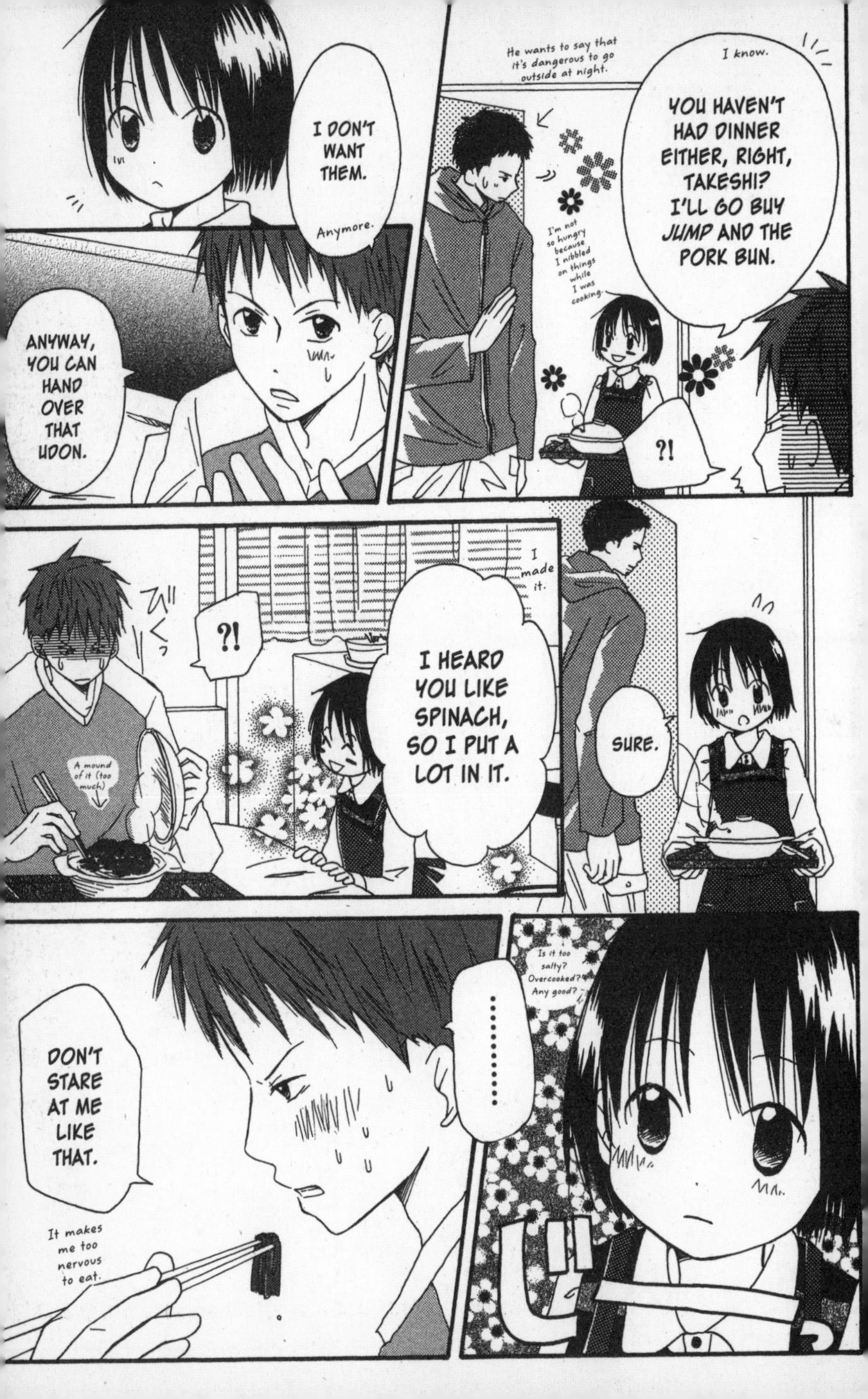
He wants to say that it's dangerous to go outside at night.
I know.
YOU HAVEN'T HAD DINNER EITHER, RIGHT, TAKESHI? I'LL GO BUY *JUMP* AND THE PORK BUN.
I'm not so hungry because I nibbled on things while I was cooking.
?!
I DON'T WANT THEM.
Anymore.
ANYWAY, YOU CAN HAND OVER THAT UDON.
I made it.
SURE.
I HEARD YOU LIKE SPINACH, SO I PUT A LOT IN IT.
?!
びくっ
A mound of it (too much)
Is it too salty? Overcooked? Any good?
......
DON'T STARE AT ME LIKE THAT.
It makes me too nervous to eat.

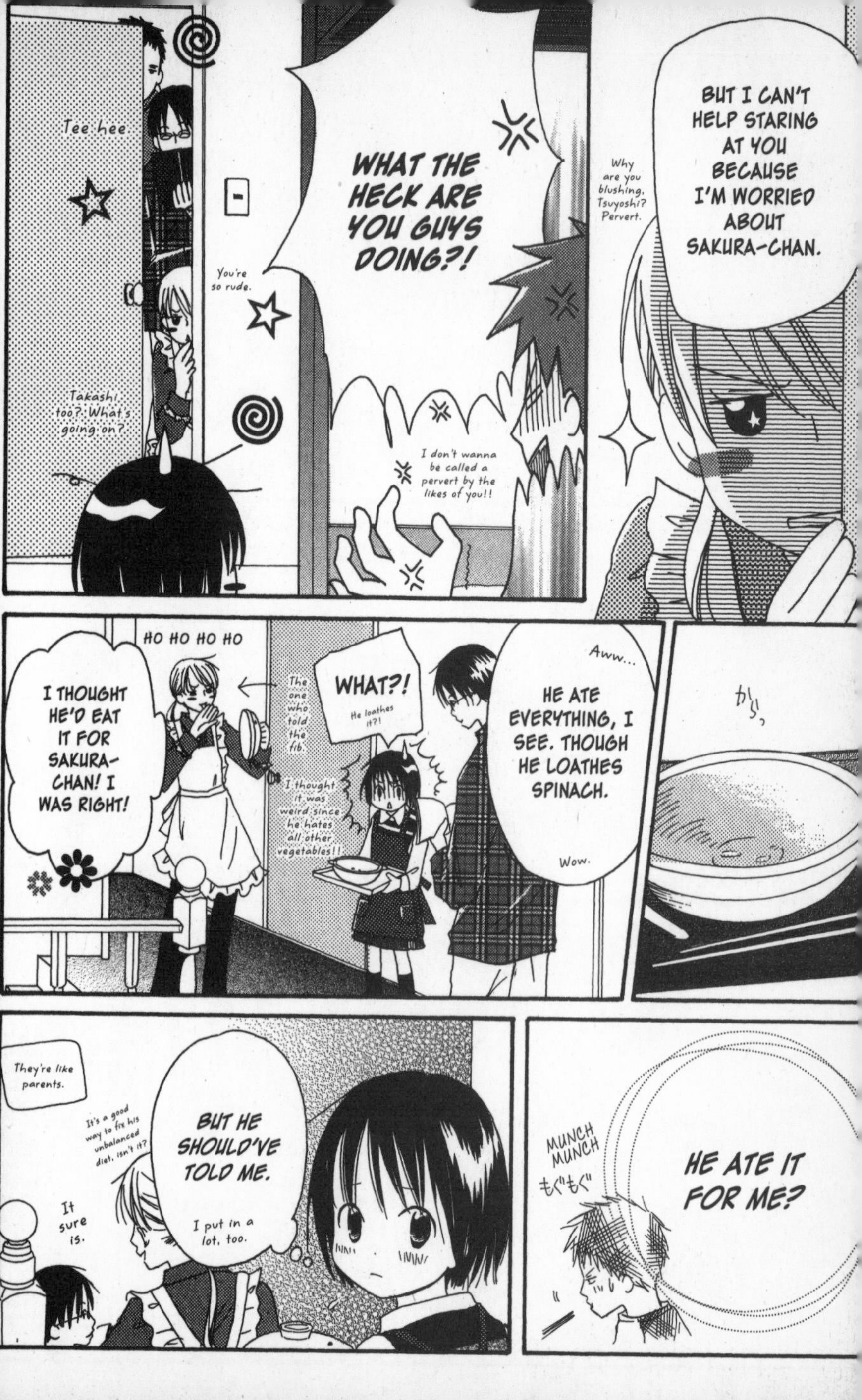
BUT I CAN'T HELP STARING AT YOU BECAUSE I'M WORRIED ABOUT SAKURA-CHAN.
Why are you blushing, Tsuyoshi? Pervert.
WHAT THE HECK ARE YOU GUYS DOING?!
I don't wanna be called a pervert by the likes of you!!
Tee hee
You're so rude.
Takashi too? What's going on?
からっ
Aww...
HE ATE EVERYTHING, I SEE. THOUGH HE LOATHES SPINACH.
Wow.
WHAT?!
He loathes it?!
I thought it was weird since he hates all other vegetables!!
The one who told the fib.
HO HO HO HO
I THOUGHT HE'D EAT IT FOR SAKURA-CHAN! I WAS RIGHT!
HE ATE IT FOR ME?
MUNCH MUNCH
もぐもぐ
BUT HE SHOULD'VE TOLD ME.
I put in a lot, too.
It's a good way to fix his unbalanced diet, isn't it?
It sure is.
They're like parents.

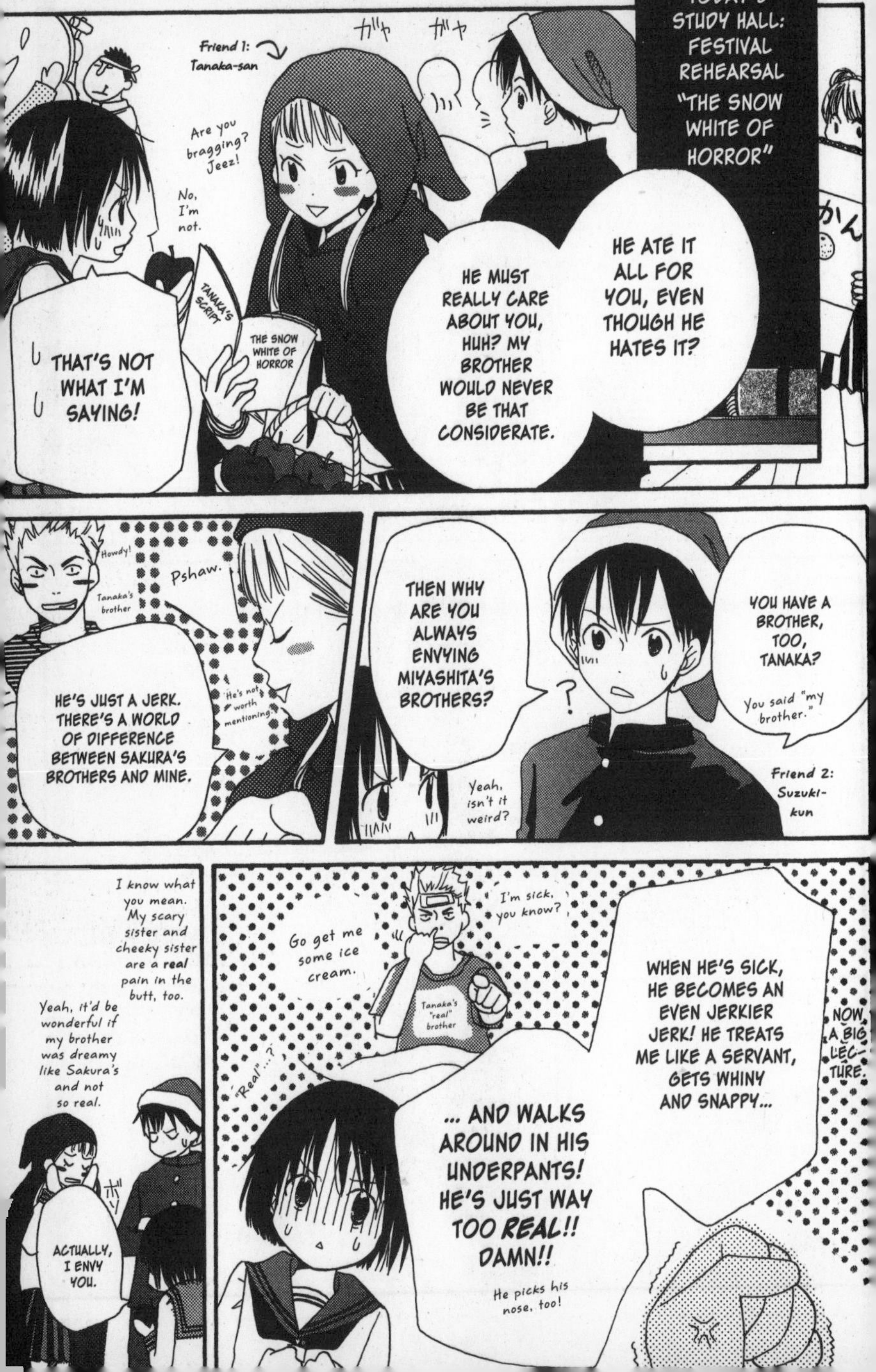
TODAY'S STUDY HALL: FESTIVAL REHEARSAL "THE SNOW WHITE OF HORROR"
ガヤ ガヤ
HE ATE IT ALL FOR YOU, EVEN THOUGH HE HATES IT?
HE MUST REALLY CARE ABOUT YOU, HUH? MY BROTHER WOULD NEVER BE THAT CONSIDERATE.
Friend 1: Tanaka-san
TANAKA'S SCRIPT
THE SNOW WHITE OF HORROR
Are you bragging? Jeez!
No, I'm not.
THAT'S NOT WHAT I'M SAYING!
YOU HAVE A BROTHER, TOO, TANAKA?
You said "my brother."
Friend 2: Suzuki-kun
THEN WHY ARE YOU ALWAYS ENVYING MIYASHITA'S BROTHERS?
?
Yeah, isn't it weird?
Pshaw.
Howdy!
Tanaka's brother
He's not worth mentioning.
HE'S JUST A JERK. THERE'S A WORLD OF DIFFERENCE BETWEEN SAKURA'S BROTHERS AND MINE.
NOW, A BIG LEC-TURE.
WHEN HE'S SICK, HE BECOMES AN EVEN JERKIER JERK! HE TREATS ME LIKE A SERVANT, GETS WHINY AND SNAPPY...
I'm sick, you know?
Go get me some ice cream.
Tanaka's "real" brother
"Real"...?
... AND WALKS AROUND IN HIS UNDERPANTS! HE'S JUST WAY TOO REAL!! DAMN!!
He picks his nose, too!
I know what you mean. My scary sister and cheeky sister are a real pain in the butt, too.
Yeah, it'd be wonderful if my brother was dreamy like Sakura's and not so real.
ACTUALLY, I ENVY YOU.

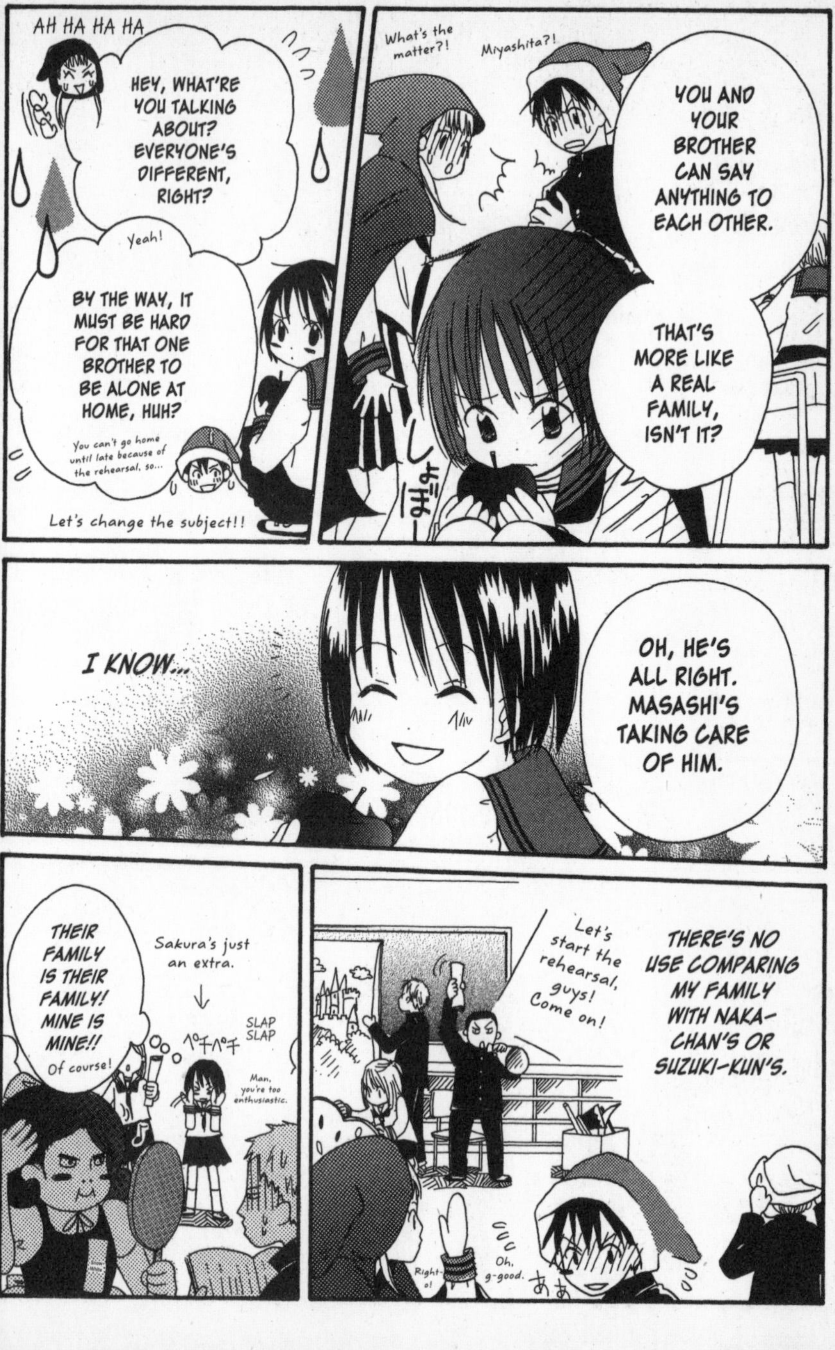

YOU AND YOUR BROTHER CAN SAY ANYTHING TO EACH OTHER.
Miyashita?!
What's the matter?!
THAT'S MORE LIKE A REAL FAMILY, ISN'T IT?
しょぼー
AH HA HA HA
HEY, WHAT'RE YOU TALKING ABOUT? EVERYONE'S DIFFERENT, RIGHT?
Yeah!
BY THE WAY, IT MUST BE HARD FOR THAT ONE BROTHER TO BE ALONE AT HOME, HUH?
You can't go home until late because of the rehearsal, so...
Let's change the subject!!
OH, HE'S ALL RIGHT. MASASHI'S TAKING CARE OF HIM.
I KNOW...
THERE'S NO USE COMPARING MY FAMILY WITH NAKA-CHAN'S OR SUZUKI-KUN'S.
Let's start the rehearsal, guys! Come on!
ああ
Oh, g-good.
Right-o!
Man, you're too enthusiastic.
SLAP SLAP
ペチペチ
Sakura's just an extra.
THEIR FAMILY IS THEIR FAMILY! MINE IS MINE!!
Of course!

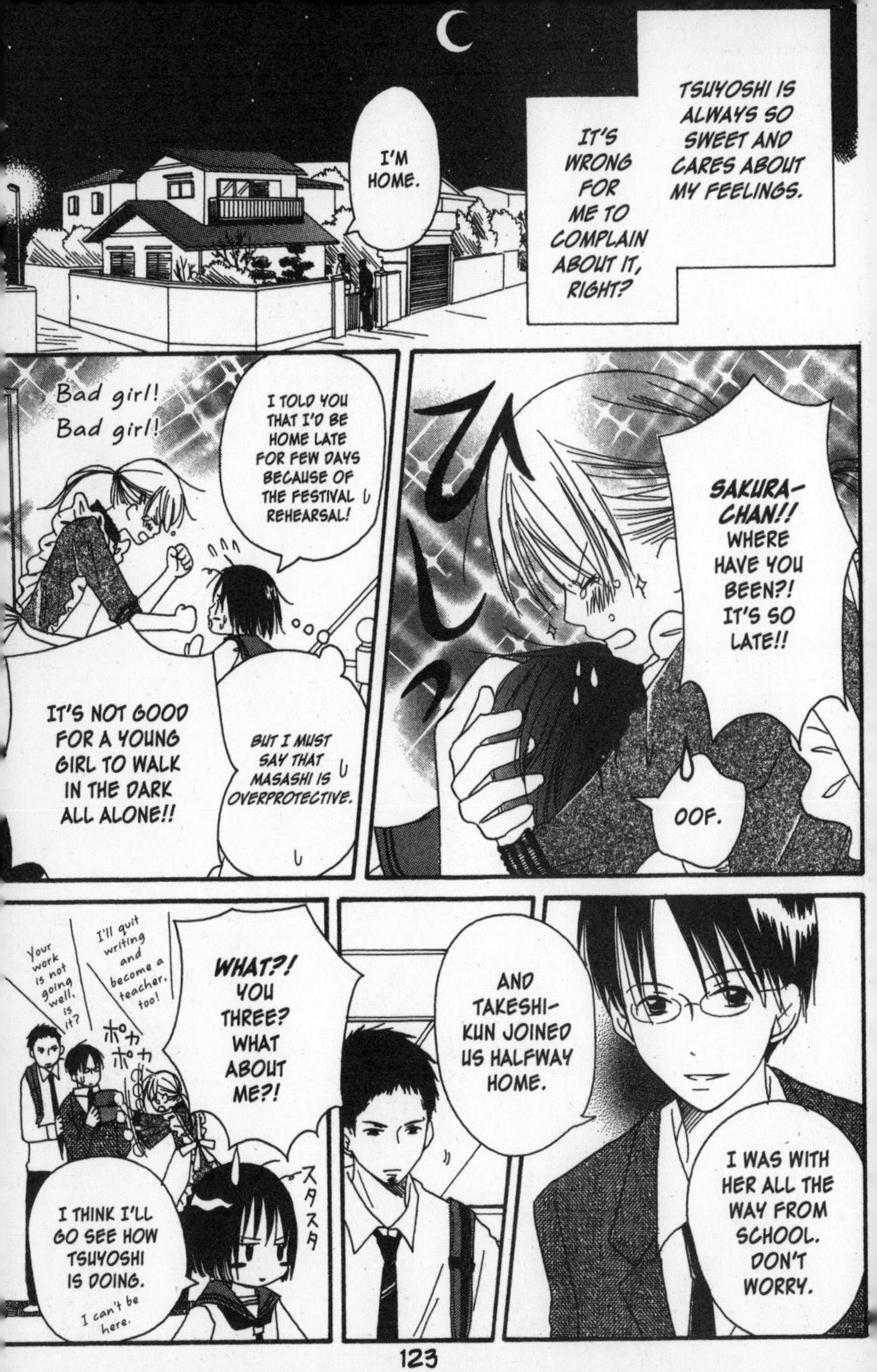
TSUYOSHI IS ALWAYS SO SWEET AND CARES ABOUT MY FEELINGS.
IT'S WRONG FOR ME TO COMPLAIN ABOUT IT, RIGHT?
I'M HOME.
SAKURA-CHAN!! WHERE HAVE YOU BEEN?! IT'S SO LATE!!
ひしっ
OOF.
I TOLD YOU THAT I'D BE HOME LATE FOR FEW DAYS BECAUSE OF THE FESTIVAL REHEARSAL!
Bad girl! Bad girl!
BUT I MUST SAY THAT MASASHI IS OVERPROTECTIVE.
IT'S NOT GOOD FOR A YOUNG GIRL TO WALK IN THE DARK ALL ALONE!!
I WAS WITH HER ALL THE WAY FROM SCHOOL. DON'T WORRY.
AND TAKESHI-KUN JOINED US HALFWAY HOME.
WHAT?! YOU THREE? WHAT ABOUT ME?!
I'll quit writing and become a teacher, too!
Your work is not going well, is it?
ポカポカ
スタスタ
I THINK I'LL GO SEE HOW TSUYOSHI IS DOING.
I can't be here.

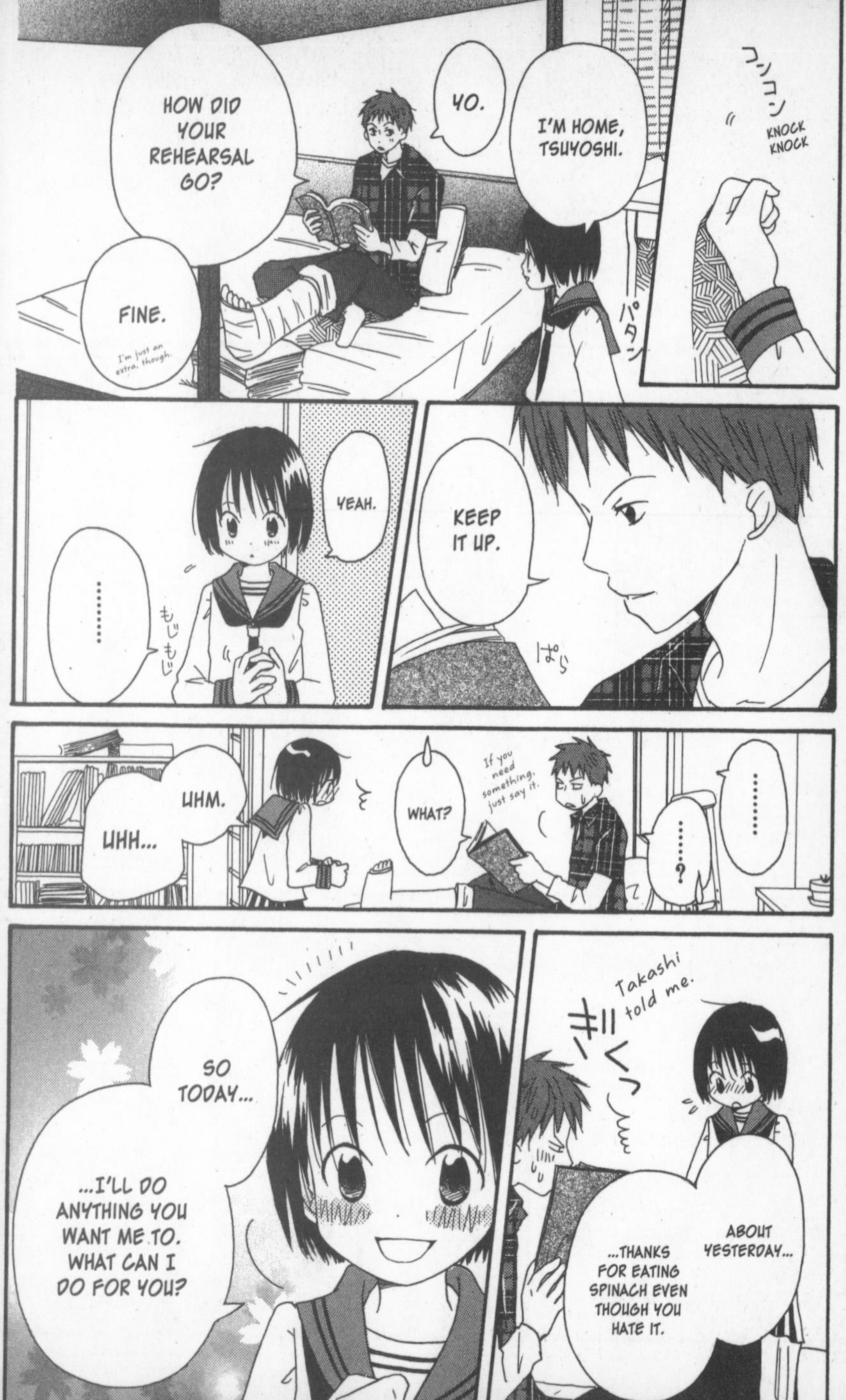
コンコン
KNOCK KNOCK
パタン
I'M HOME, TSUYOSHI.
YO.
HOW DID YOUR REHEARSAL GO?
FINE.
I'm just an extra, though.
KEEP IT UP.
ぱら
YEAH.
......
もじもじ
......
......?
WHAT?
If you need something, just say it.
UHM.
UHH...
Takashi told me.
ぎくっ
ABOUT YESTERDAY...
...THANKS FOR EATING SPINACH EVEN THOUGH YOU HATE IT.
SO TODAY...
...I'LL DO ANYTHING YOU WANT ME TO. WHAT CAN I DO FOR YOU?

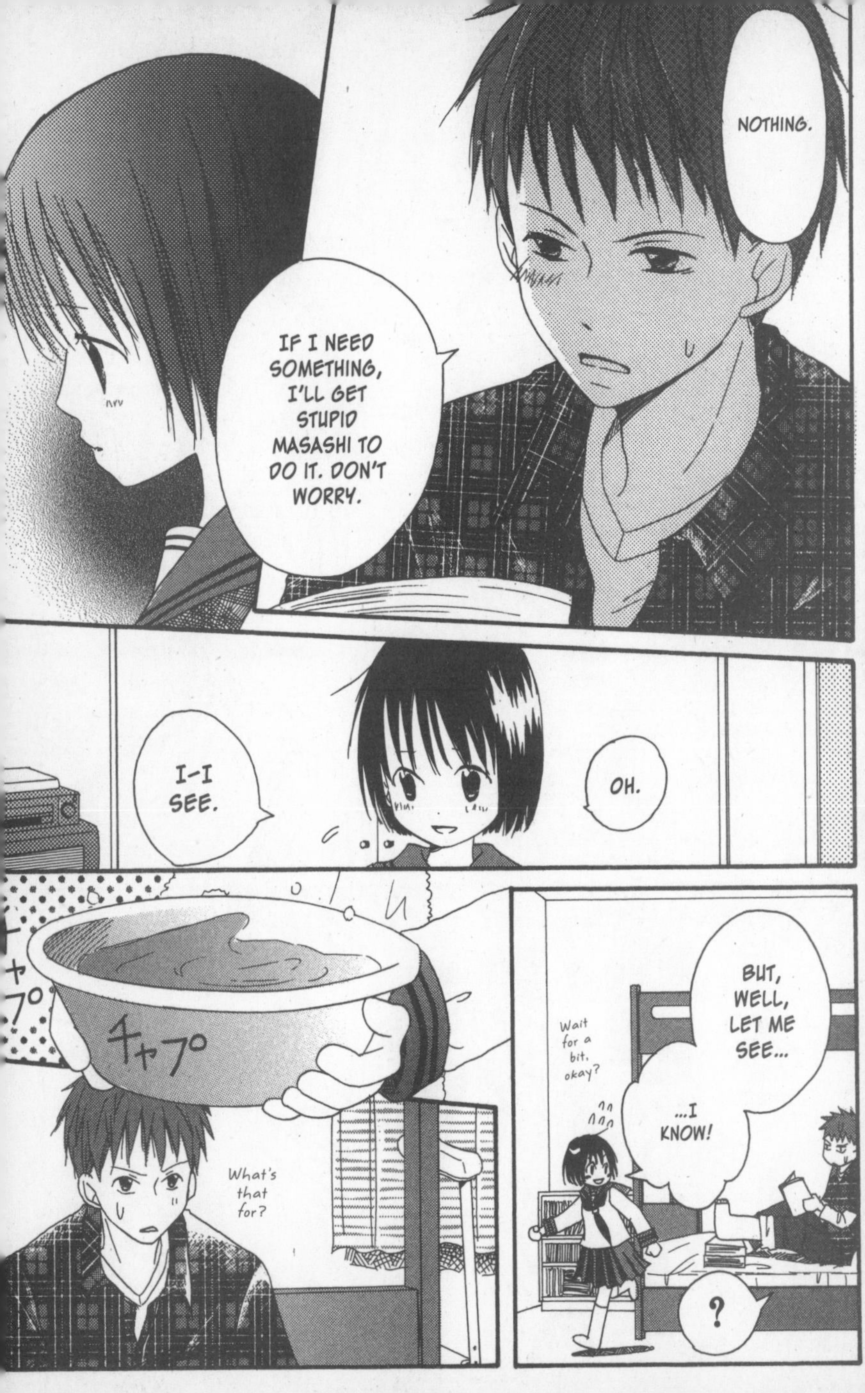
NOTHING.
IF I NEED SOMETHING, I'LL GET STUPID MASASHI TO DO IT. DON'T WORRY.
OH.
I-I SEE.
BUT, WELL, LET ME SEE...
...I KNOW!
Wait for a bit, okay?
?
チャプ
チャプ
What's that for?

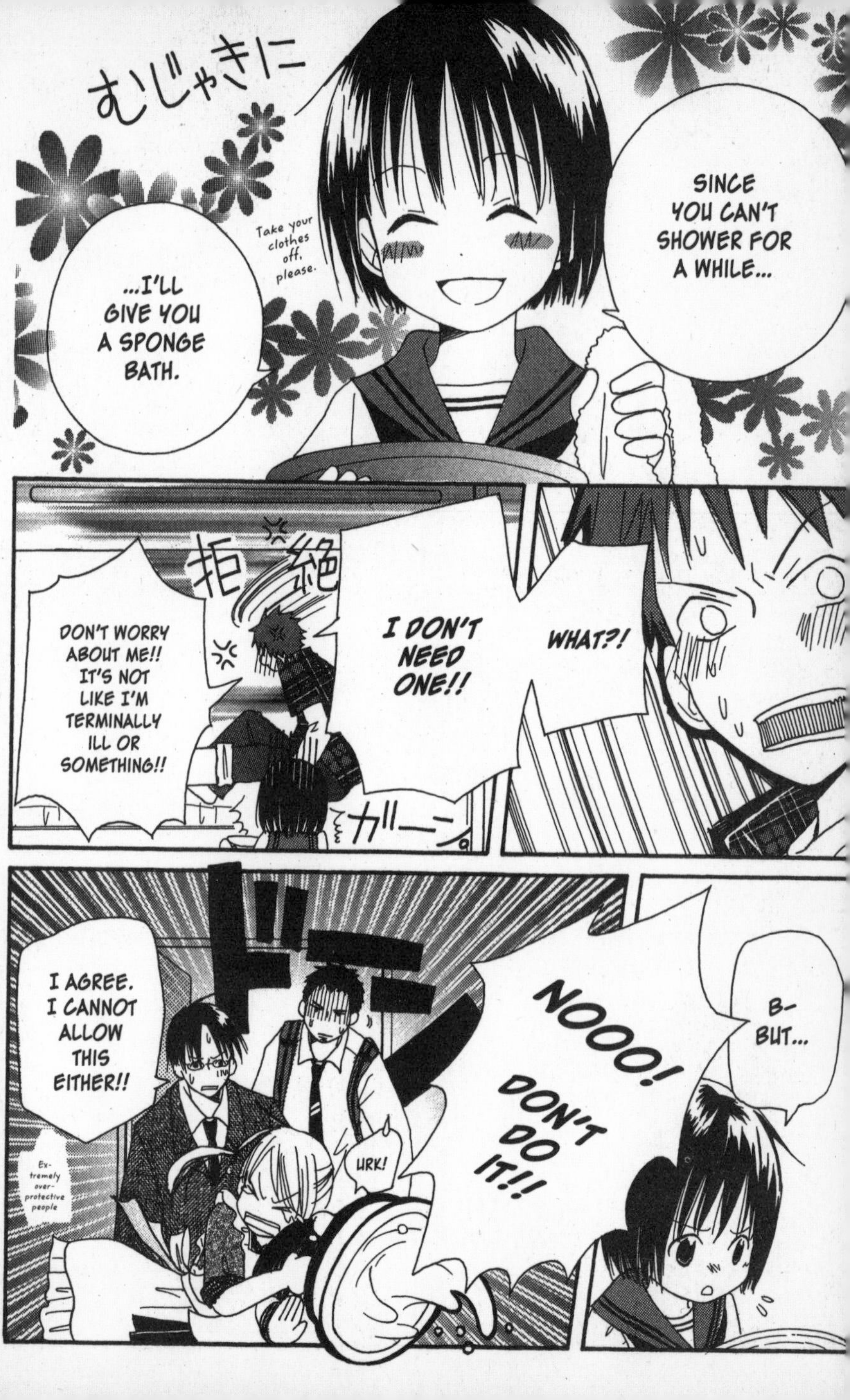
SINCE YOU CAN'T SHOWER FOR A WHILE...
むじゃきに
Take your clothes off, please.
...I'LL GIVE YOU A SPONGE BATH.
WHAT?!
I DON'T NEED ONE!!
拒絶
DON'T WORRY ABOUT ME!! IT'S NOT LIKE I'M TERMINALLY ILL OR SOMETHING!!
ガーン
B-BUT...
NOOOO! DON'T DO IT!!
I AGREE. I CANNOT ALLOW THIS EITHER!!
URK!
Extremely over-protective people

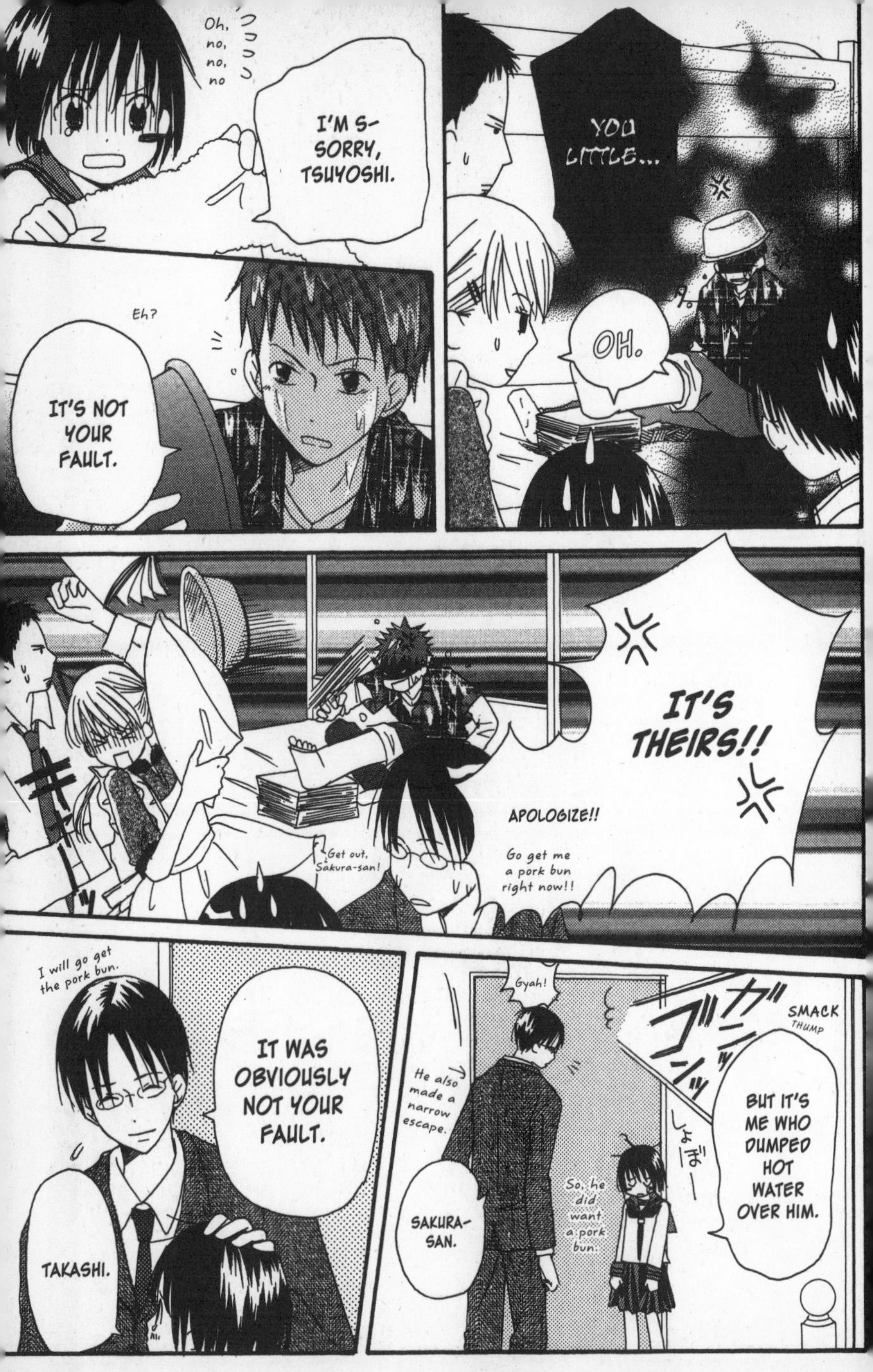
YOU LITTLE...
Oh, no, no, no
I'M S-SORRY, TSUYOSHI.
OH.
Eh?
IT'S NOT YOUR FAULT.
IT'S THEIRS!!
APOLOGIZE!!
Go get me a pork bun right now!!
Get out, Sakura-san!
SMACK
THUMP
Gyah!
BUT IT'S ME WHO DUMPED HOT WATER OVER HIM.
しょぼー
So, he did want a pork bun.
He also made a narrow escape.
SAKURA-SAN.
I will go get the pork bun.
IT WAS OBVIOUSLY NOT YOUR FAULT.
TAKASHI.

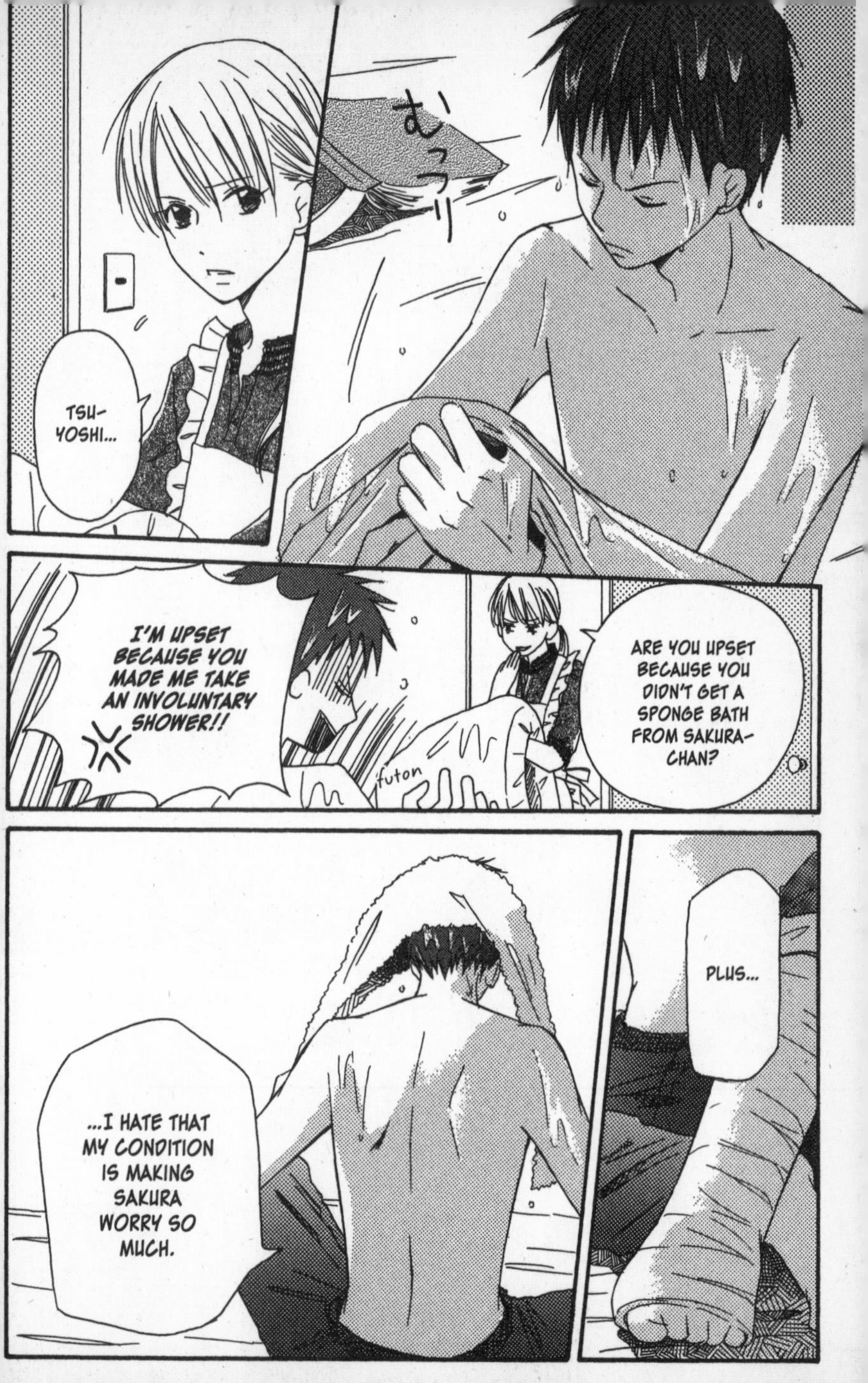

むっつり
TSU-YOSHI...
ARE YOU UPSET BECAUSE YOU DIDN'T GET A SPONGE BATH FROM SAKURA-CHAN?
I'M UPSET BECAUSE YOU MADE ME TAKE AN INVOLUNTARY SHOWER!!
futon
PLUS...
...I HATE THAT MY CONDITION IS MAKING SAKURA WORRY SO MUCH.

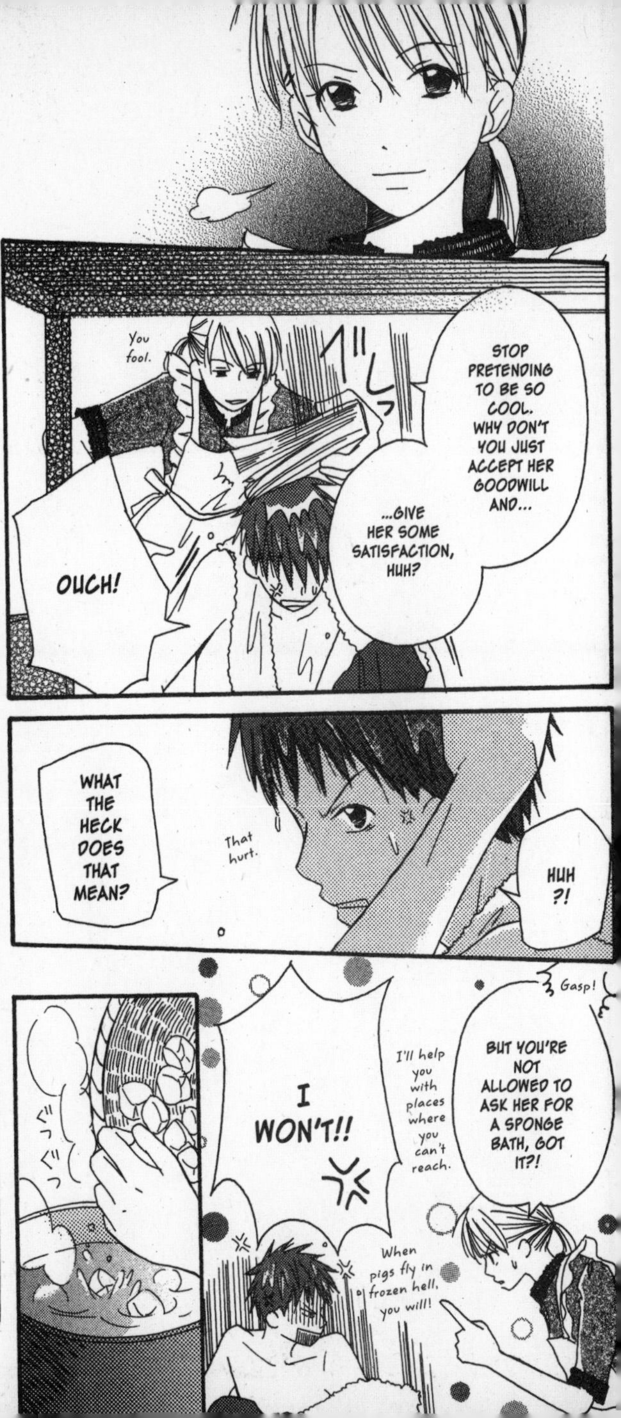
STOP PRETENDING TO BE SO COOL. WHY DON'T YOU JUST ACCEPT HER GOODWILL AND...
...GIVE HER SOME SATISFACTION, HUH?
You fool.
OUCH!
HUH ?!
That hurt.
WHAT THE HECK DOES THAT MEAN?
Gasp!
BUT YOU'RE NOT ALLOWED TO ASK HER FOR A SPONGE BATH, GOT IT?!
I'll help you with places where you can't reach.
I WON'T!!
When pigs fly in frozen hell, you will!

☆ 4 ☆

With one thing and another, it was difficult to create these brothers. I love them like my own children. (I'm such a doting parent! Although I've never given birth!) I hope you love them just as much. Oh, Sakura as well. I wasn't a child who helped with the housework like she does, so I'd like to follow her example.

☆

I appreciate the support from my editor, friends, family, my cousin Manami-chan (thanks, always!!) and of course, you readers!

☆ ☆ ☆

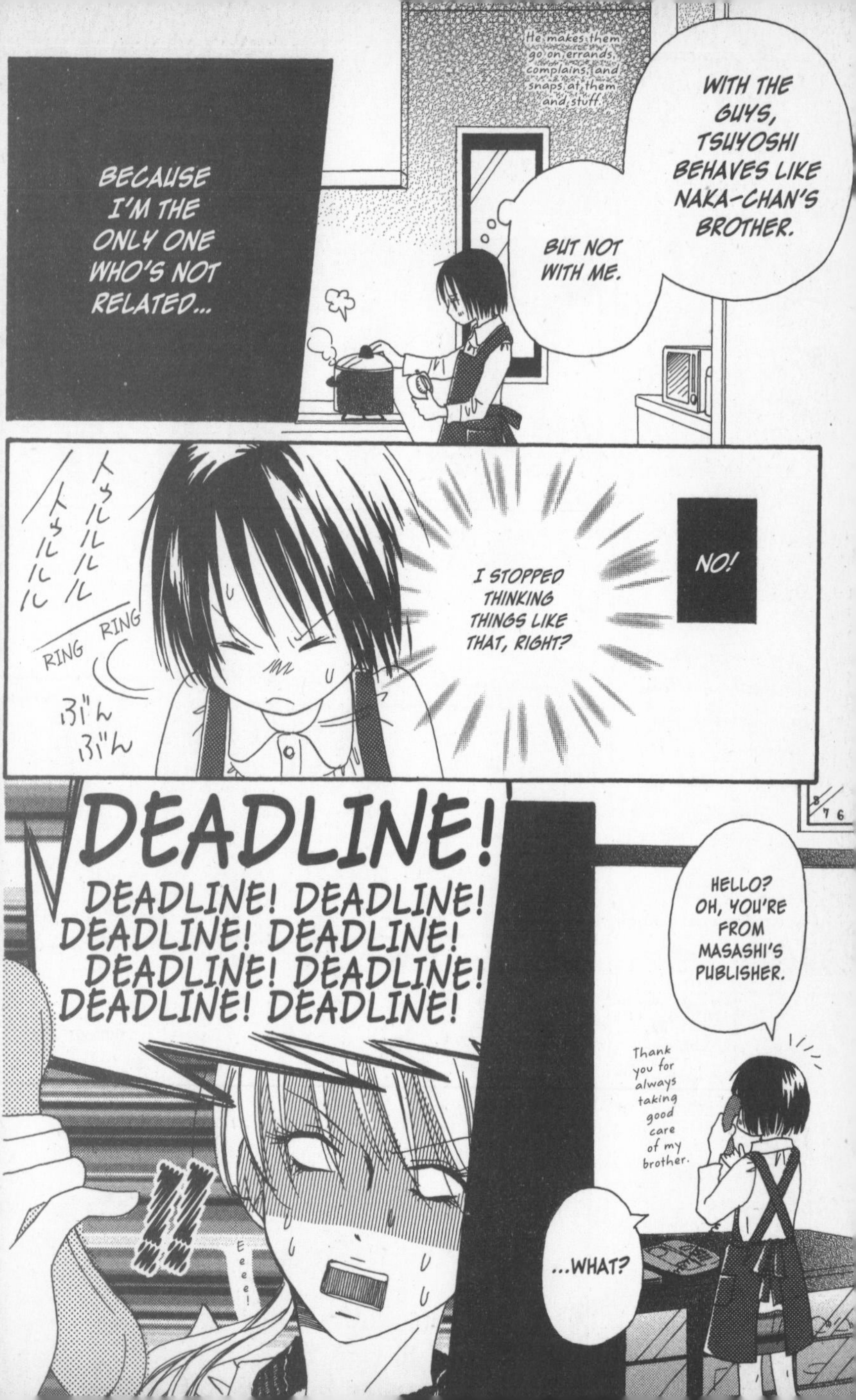
WITH THE GUYS, TSUYOSHI BEHAVES LIKE NAKA-CHAN'S BROTHER.
He makes them go on errands, complains, and snaps at them and stuff.
BUT NOT WITH ME.
BECAUSE I'M THE ONLY ONE WHO'S NOT RELATED...
NO!
I STOPPED THINKING THINGS LIKE THAT, RIGHT?
RING RING
ぶん ぶん
HELLO? OH, YOU'RE FROM MASASHI'S PUBLISHER.
Thank you for always taking good care of my brother.
...WHAT?
DEADLINE!
DEADLINE! DEADLINE! DEADLINE! DEADLINE! DEADLINE! DEADLINE! DEADLINE! DEADLINE!
Eeee!

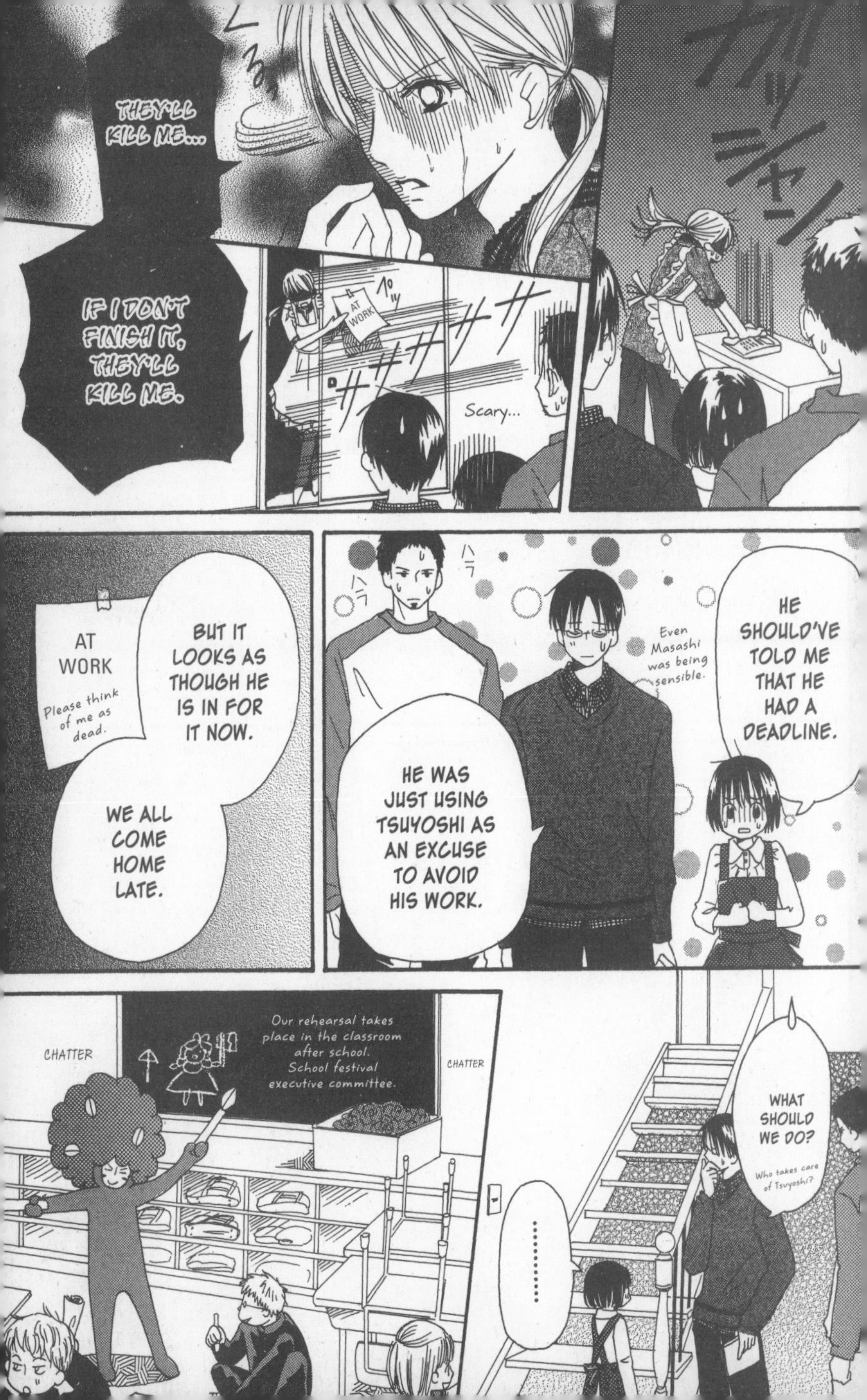
THEY'LL KILL ME...
AT WORK
Scary...
IF I DON'T FINISH IT, THEY'LL KILL ME.
HE SHOULD'VE TOLD ME THAT HE HAD A DEADLINE.
Even Masashi was being sensible.
HE WAS JUST USING TSUYOSHI AS AN EXCUSE TO AVOID HIS WORK.
AT WORK
Please think of me as dead.
BUT IT LOOKS AS THOUGH HE IS IN FOR IT NOW.
WE ALL COME HOME LATE.
WHAT SHOULD WE DO?
Who takes care of Tsuyoshi?
......
CHATTER
Our rehearsal takes place in the classroom after school. School festival executive committee.
CHATTER

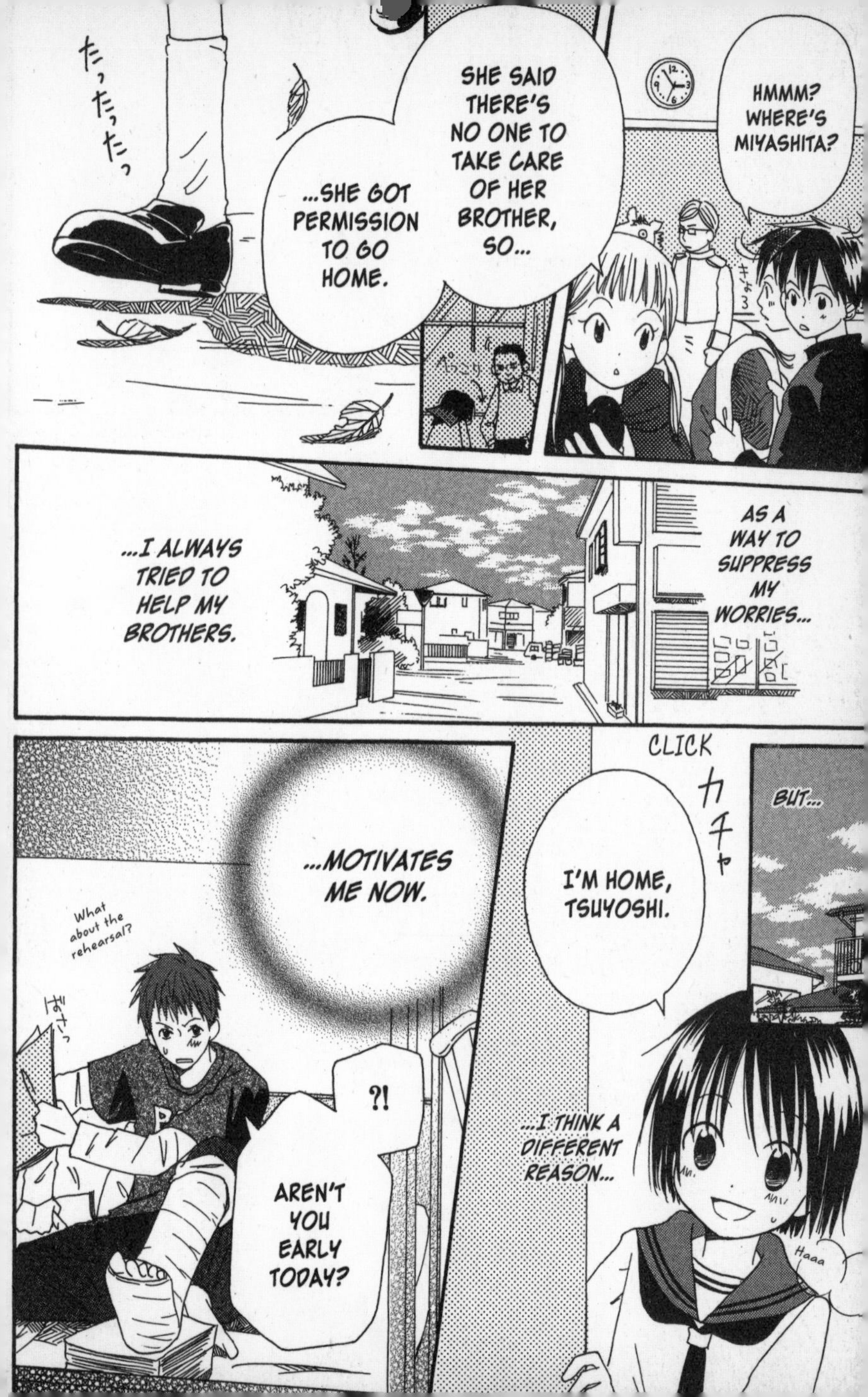
HMMM? WHERE'S MIYASHITA?
きょろ
SHE SAID THERE'S NO ONE TO TAKE CARE OF HER BROTHER, SO...
...SHE GOT PERMISSION TO GO HOME.
たったたっ
AS A WAY TO SUPPRESS MY WORRIES...
...I ALWAYS TRIED TO HELP MY BROTHERS.
BUT...
CLICK
カチャ
I'M HOME, TSUYOSHI.
...I THINK A DIFFERENT REASON...
Haaa
...MOTIVATES ME NOW.
?!
AREN'T YOU EARLY TODAY?
What about the rehearsal?
ばさっ

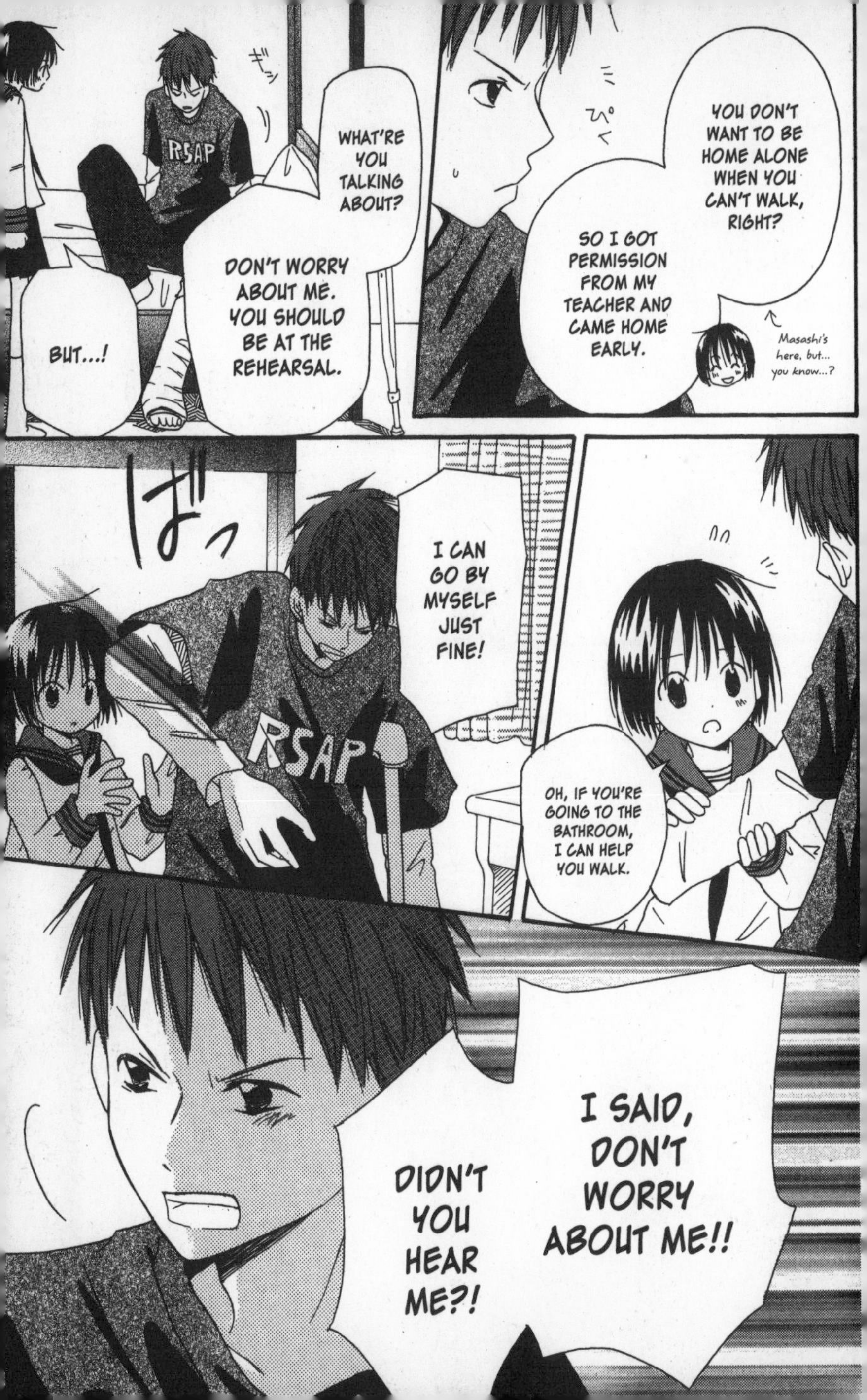
ぴく
YOU DON'T WANT TO BE HOME ALONE WHEN YOU CAN'T WALK, RIGHT?
SO I GOT PERMISSION FROM MY TEACHER AND CAME HOME EARLY.
Masashi's here, but... you know...?
ギッ
WHAT'RE YOU TALKING ABOUT?
DON'T WORRY ABOUT ME. YOU SHOULD BE AT THE REHEARSAL.
BUT...!
OH, IF YOU'RE GOING TO THE BATHROOM, I CAN HELP YOU WALK.
ばっ
I CAN GO BY MYSELF JUST FINE!
I SAID, DON'T WORRY ABOUT ME!!
DIDN'T YOU HEAR ME?!

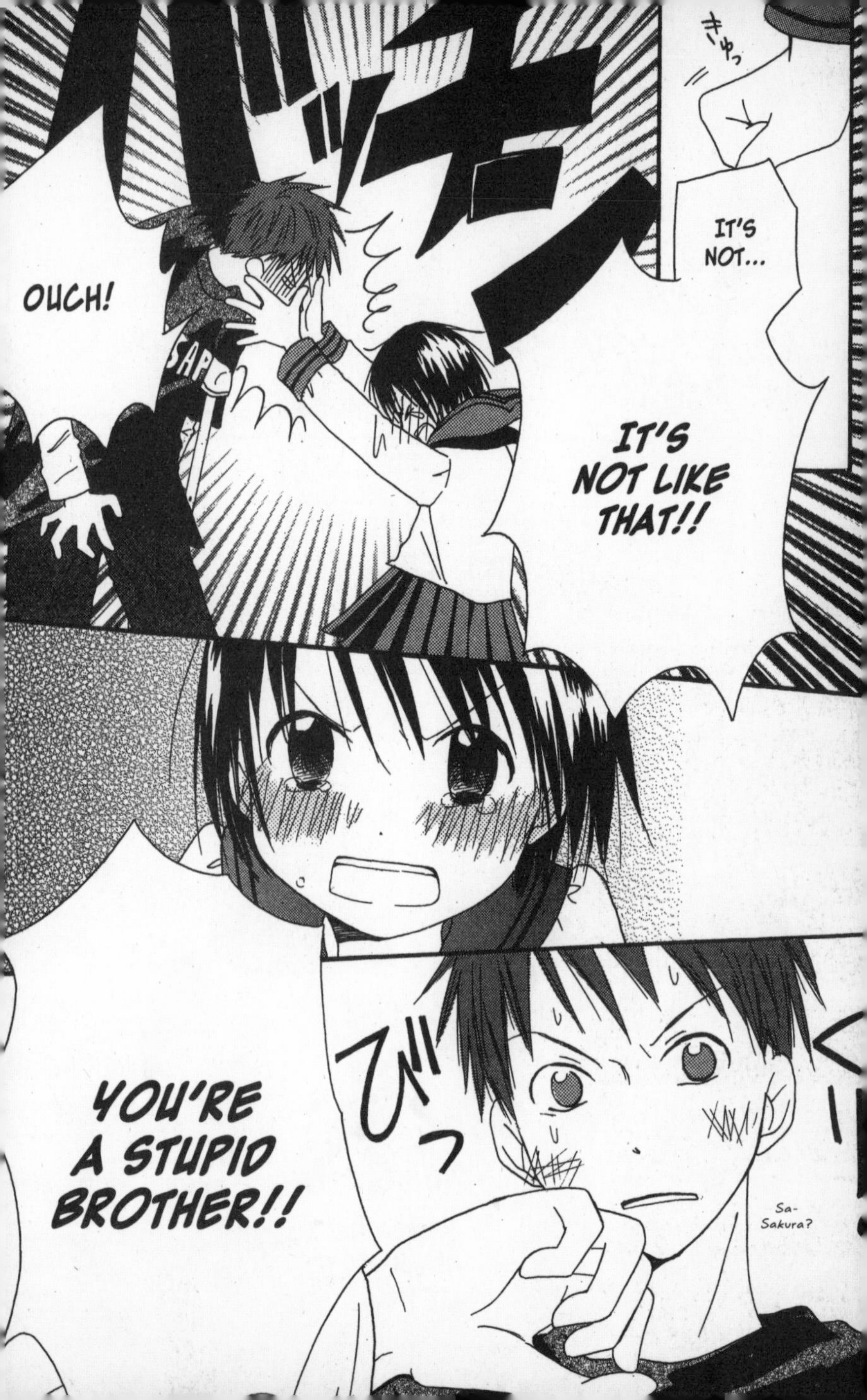
きゅっ
IT'S NOT...
IT'S NOT LIKE THAT!!
OUCH!
Sa- Sakura?
YOU'RE A STUPID BROTHER!!

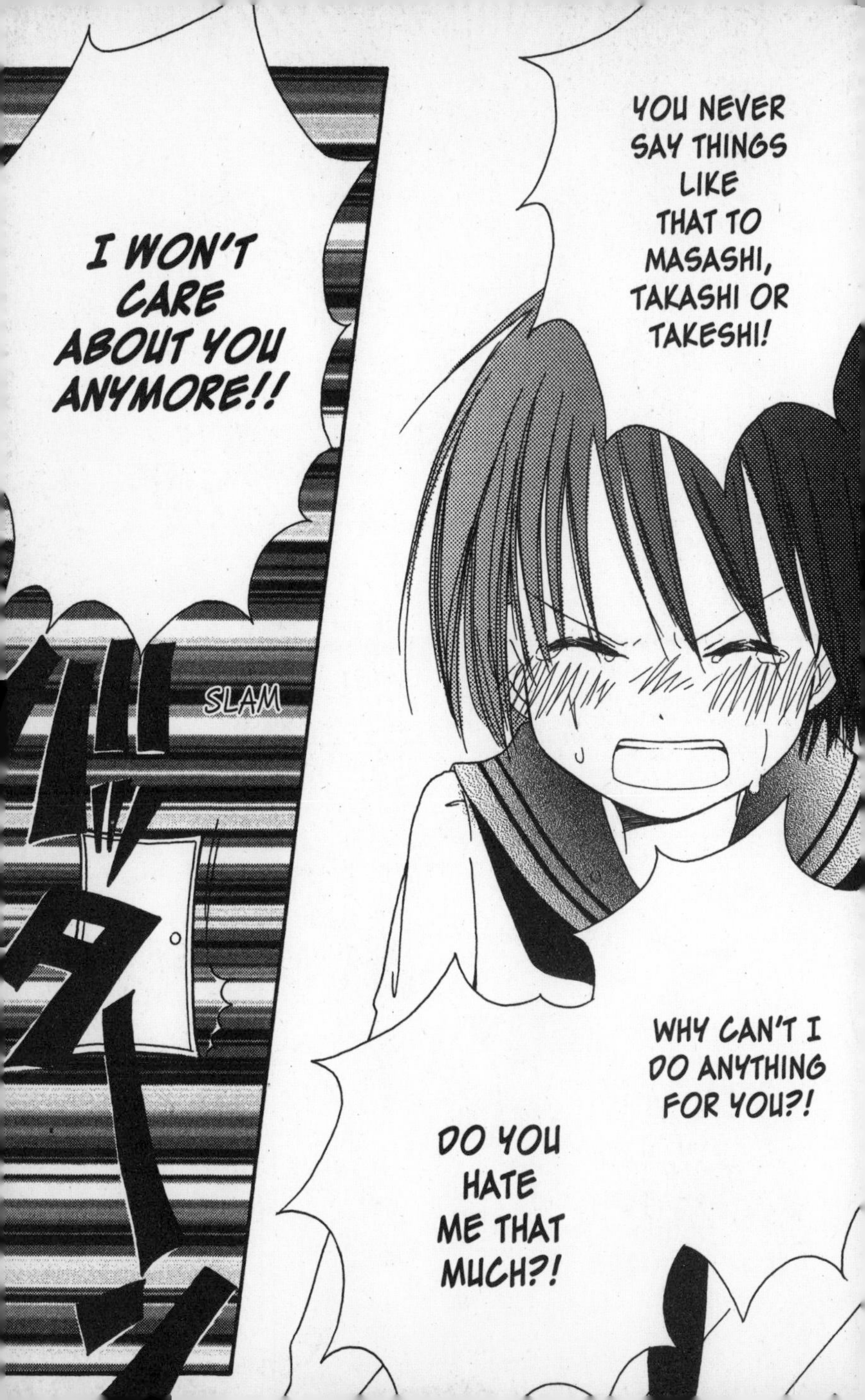
YOU NEVER SAY THINGS LIKE THAT TO MASASHI, TAKASHI OR TAKESHI!
WHY CAN'T I DO ANYTHING FOR YOU?!
DO YOU HATE ME THAT MUCH?!
I WON'T CARE ABOUT YOU ANYMORE!!
SLAM

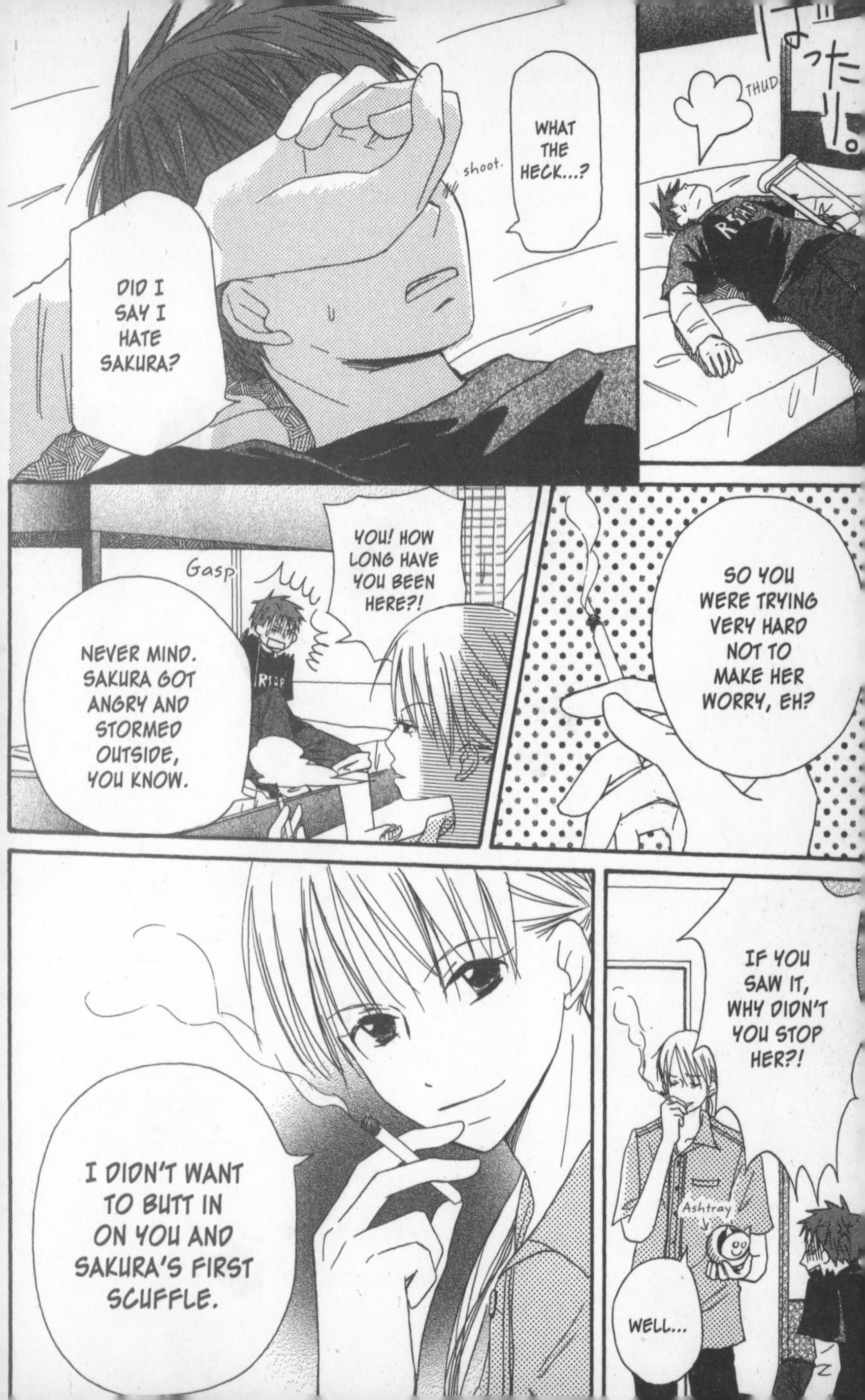
THUD
WHAT THE HECK...?
shoot.
DID I SAY I HATE SAKURA?
SO YOU WERE TRYING VERY HARD NOT TO MAKE HER WORRY, EH?
YOU! HOW LONG HAVE YOU BEEN HERE?!
Gasp
NEVER MIND. SAKURA GOT ANGRY AND STORMED OUTSIDE, YOU KNOW.
IF YOU SAW IT, WHY DIDN'T YOU STOP HER?!
Ashtray
WELL...
I DIDN'T WANT TO BUTT IN ON YOU AND SAKURA'S FIRST SCUFFLE.

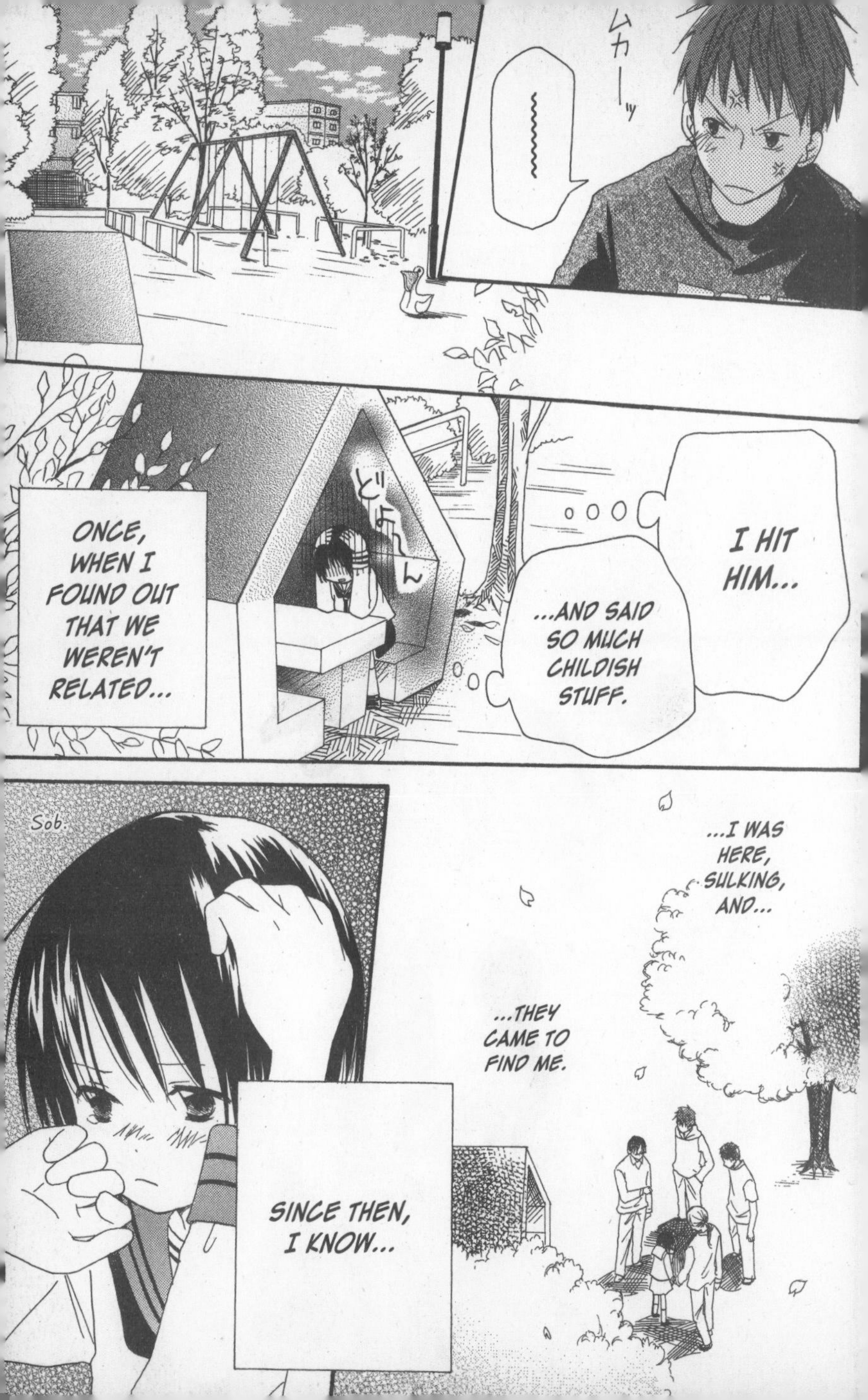
ムカーッ
I HIT HIM...
...AND SAID SO MUCH CHILDISH STUFF.
どよ〜ん
ONCE, WHEN I FOUND OUT THAT WE WEREN'T RELATED...
...I WAS HERE, SULKING, AND...
...THEY CAME TO FIND ME.
Sob.
SINCE THEN, I KNOW...

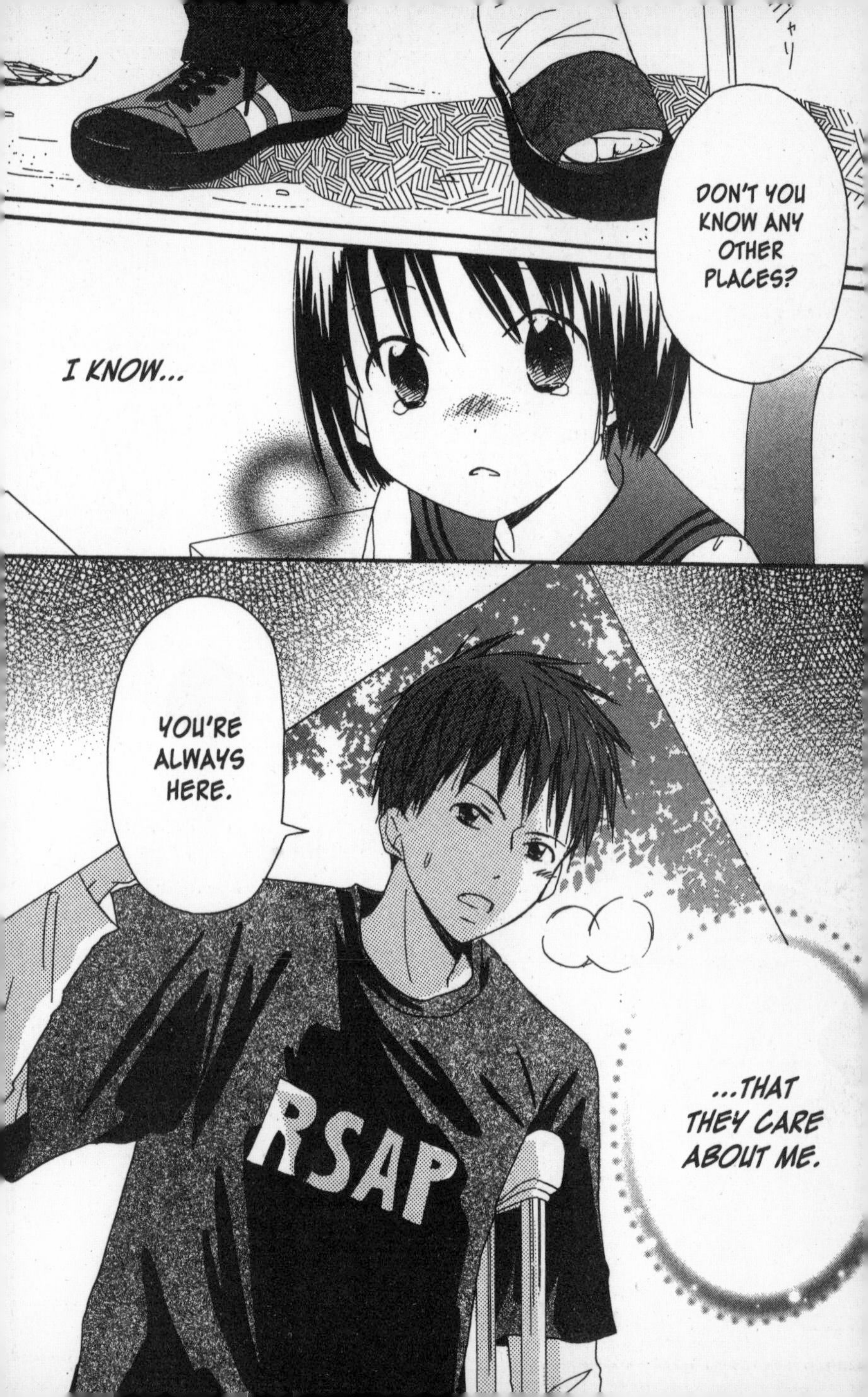
ジャリ
DON'T YOU KNOW ANY OTHER PLACES?
I KNOW...
YOU'RE ALWAYS HERE.
...THAT THEY CARE ABOUT ME.
RSAP

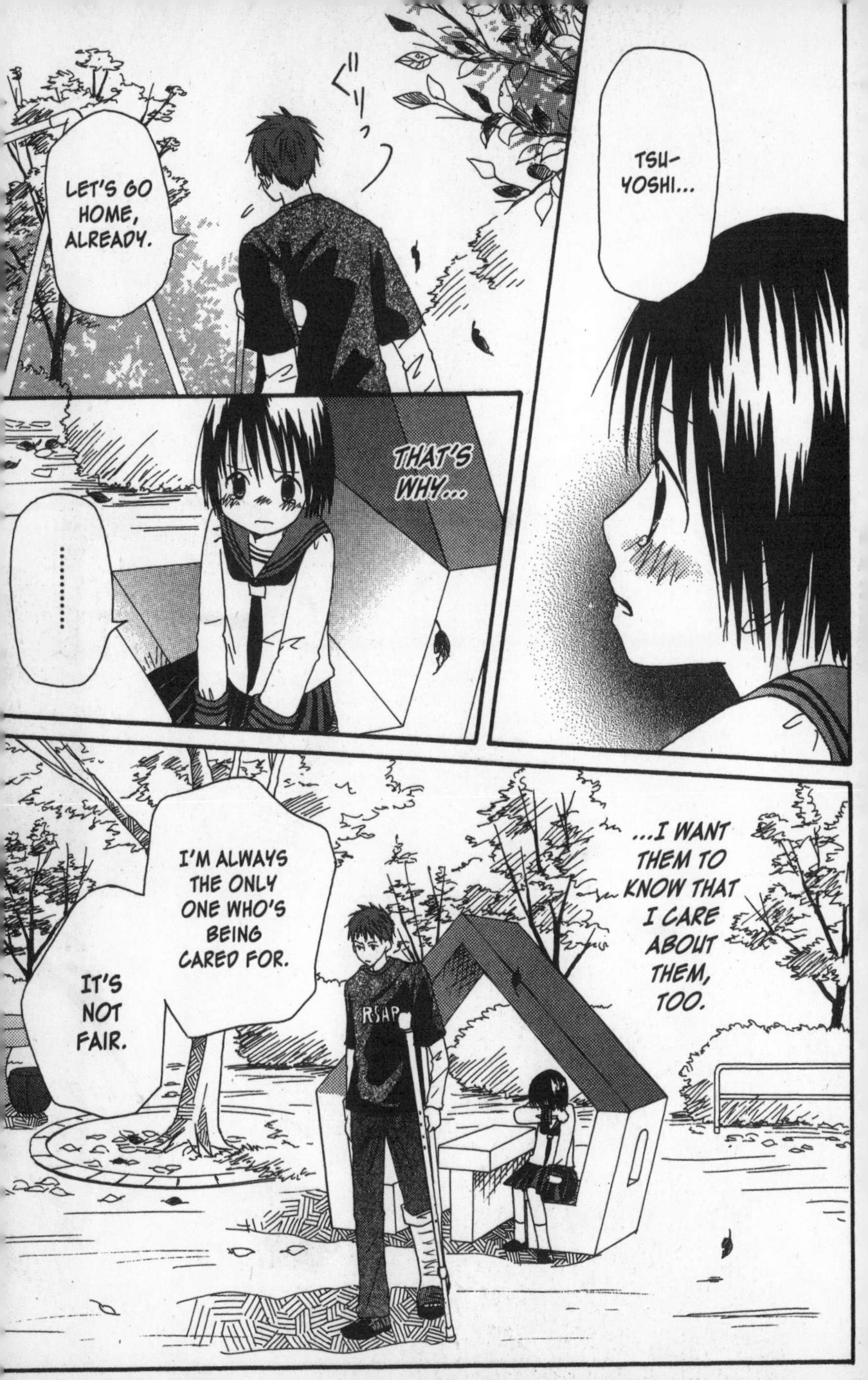
TSU-YOSHI...
LET'S GO HOME, ALREADY.
ぐッ
THAT'S WHY...
......
...I WANT THEM TO KNOW THAT I CARE ABOUT THEM, TOO.
I'M ALWAYS THE ONLY ONE WHO'S BEING CARED FOR.
IT'S NOT FAIR.

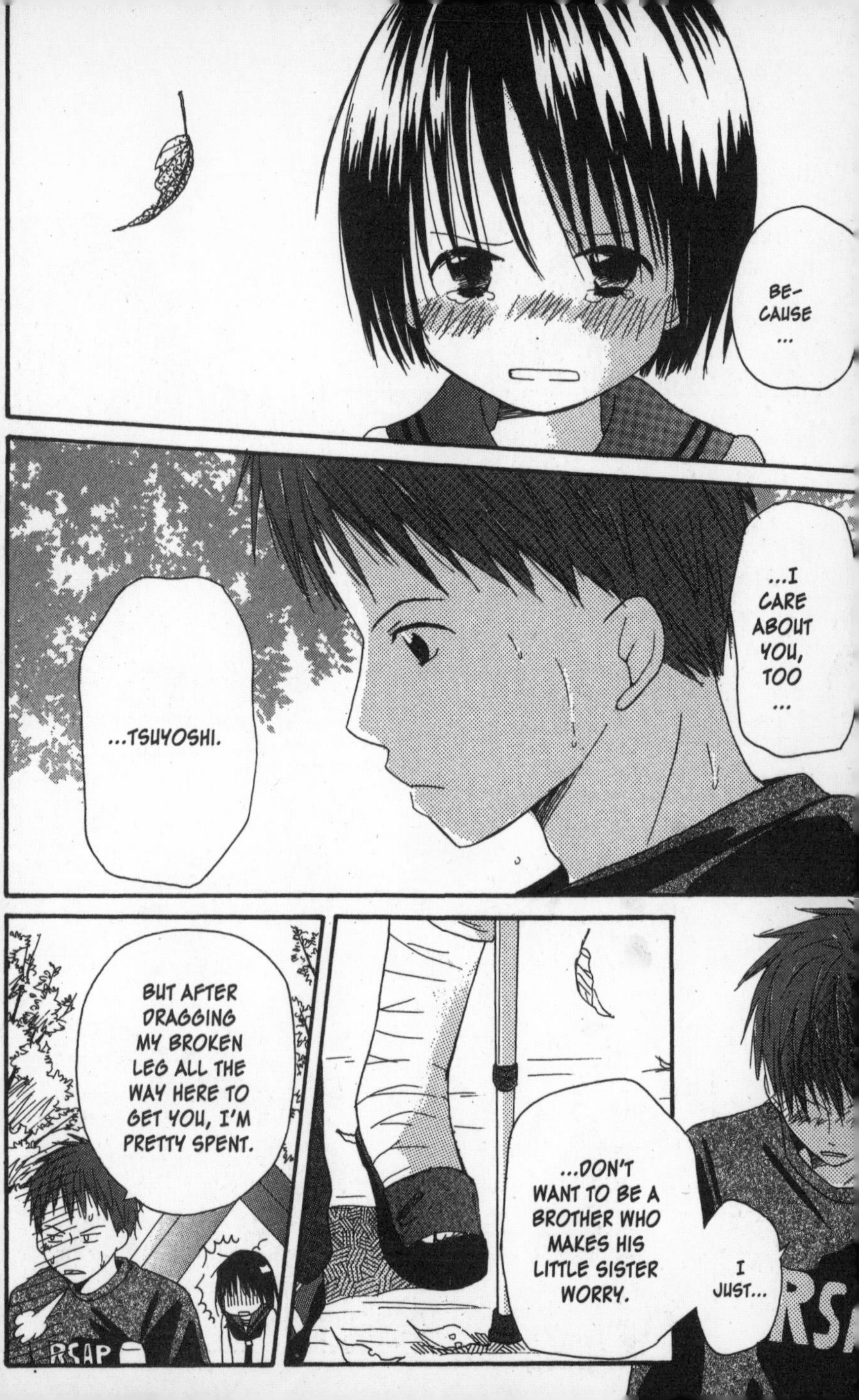
BE-CAUSE...
...I CARE ABOUT YOU, TOO...
...TSUYOSHI.
I JUST...
...DON'T WANT TO BE A BROTHER WHO MAKES HIS LITTLE SISTER WORRY.
BUT AFTER DRAGGING MY BROKEN LEG ALL THE WAY HERE TO GET YOU, I'M PRETTY SPENT.
RSAP

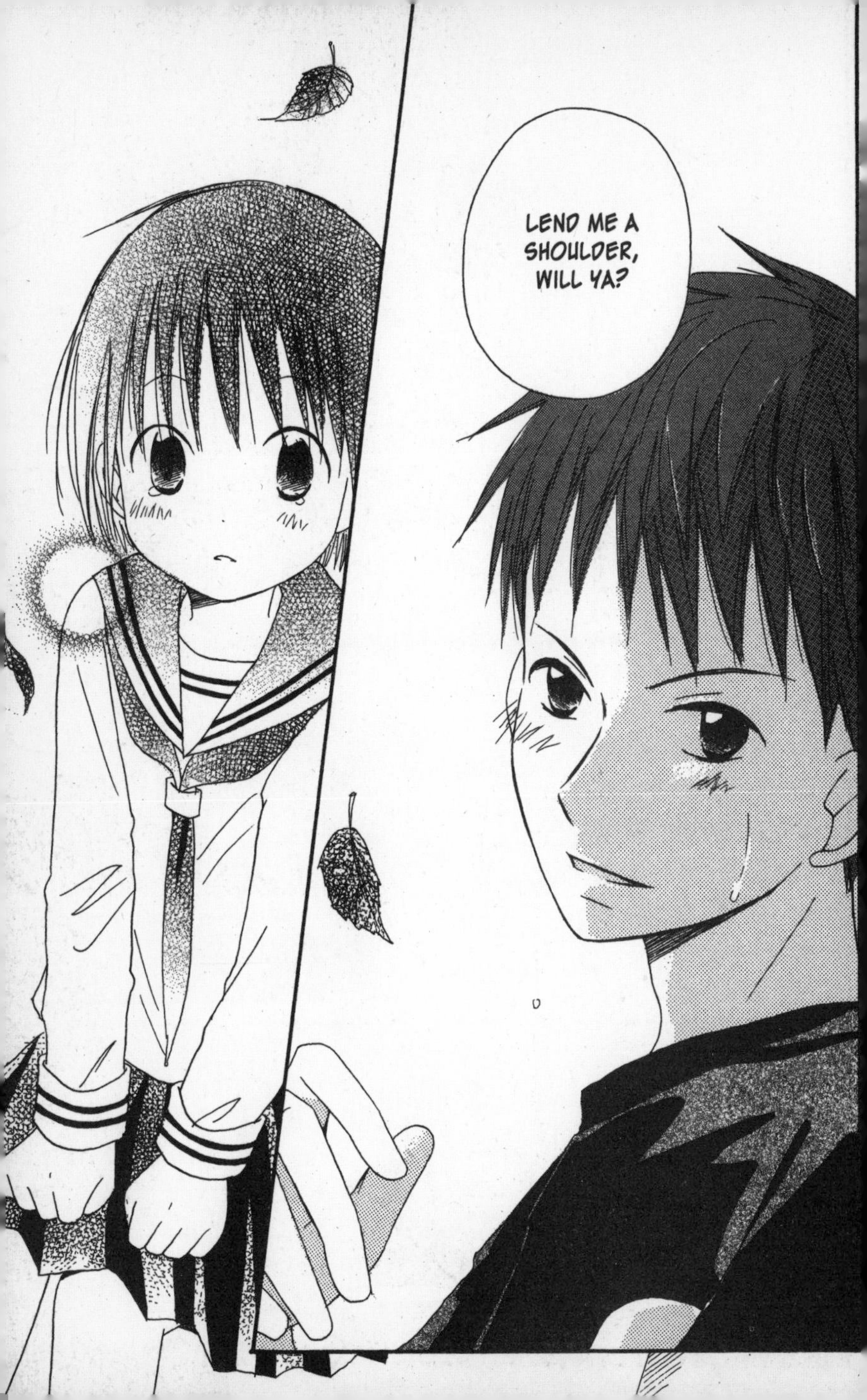
LEND ME A SHOULDER, WILL YA?

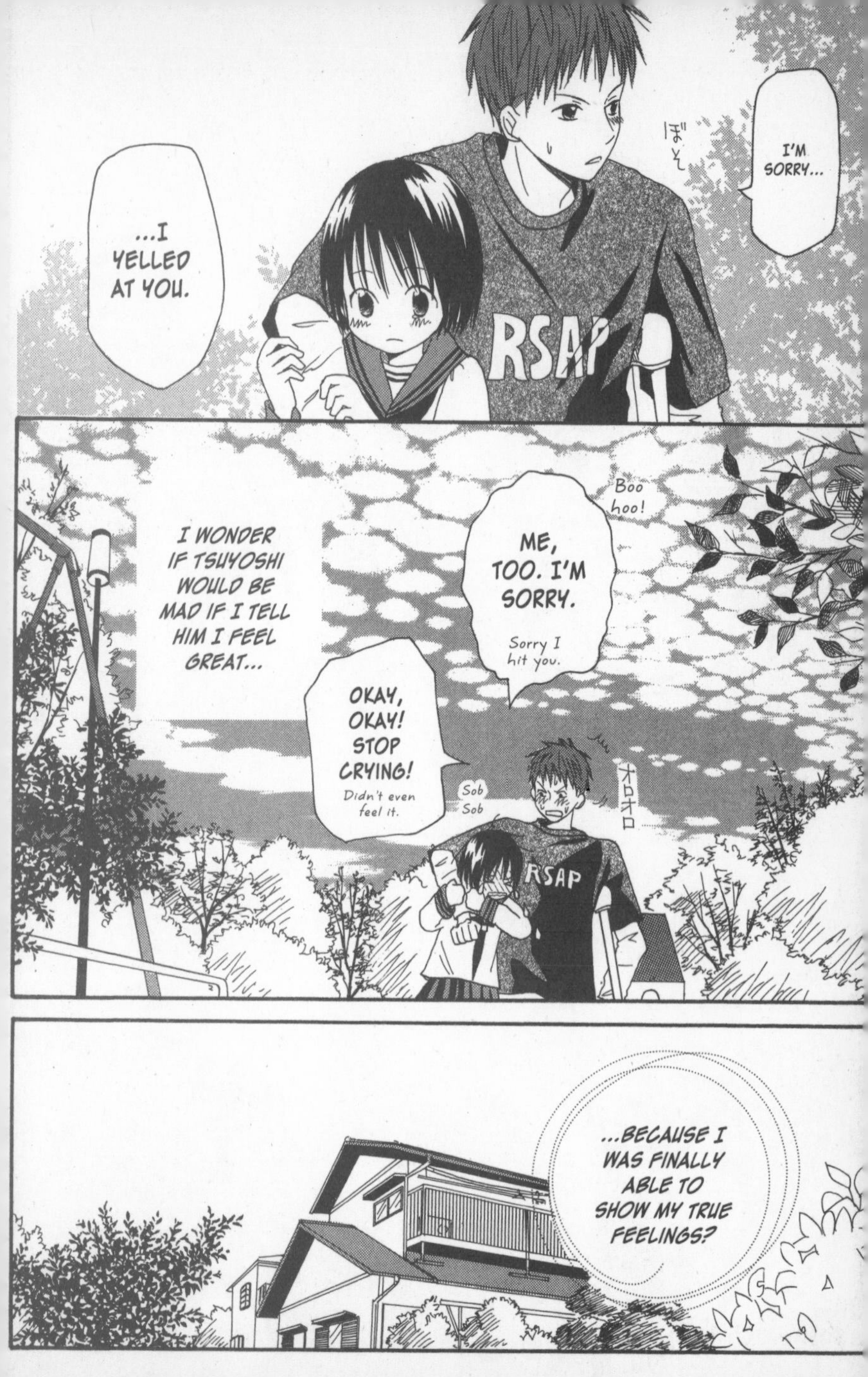
I'M SORRY...
ぼそ
...I YELLED AT YOU.
Boo hoo!
ME, TOO. I'M SORRY.
Sorry I hit you.
オロオロ
OKAY, OKAY! STOP CRYING!
Didn't even feel it.
Sob Sob
I WONDER IF TSUYOSHI WOULD BE MAD IF I TELL HIM I FEEL GREAT...
...BECAUSE I WAS FINALLY ABLE TO SHOW MY TRUE FEELINGS?

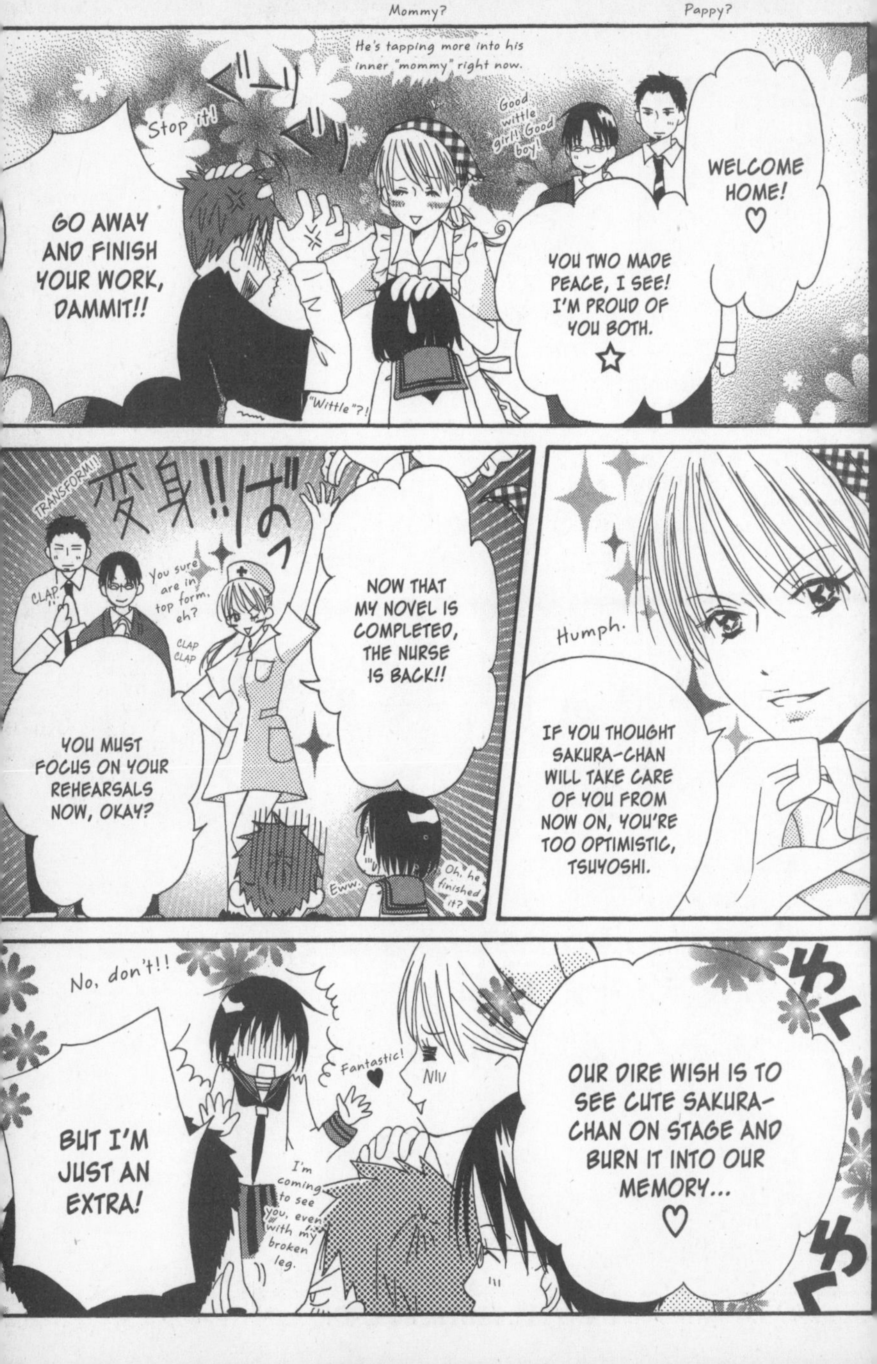
Pappy?
Mommy?
WELCOME HOME! ♡
YOU TWO MADE PEACE, I SEE! I'M PROUD OF YOU BOTH. ☆
Good wittle girl! Good boy!
He's tapping more into his inner "mommy" right now.
Stop it!
GO AWAY AND FINISH YOUR WORK, DAMMIT!!
"Wittle"?!
Humph.
IF YOU THOUGHT SAKURA-CHAN WILL TAKE CARE OF YOU FROM NOW ON, YOU'RE TOO OPTIMISTIC, TSUYOSHI.
NOW THAT MY NOVEL IS COMPLETED, THE NURSE IS BACK!!
変身!! ばっ
TRANSFORM!!
You sure are in top form, eh?
CLAP!!
CLAP CLAP
YOU MUST FOCUS ON YOUR REHEARSALS NOW, OKAY?
Oh, he finished it?
Eww.
OUR DIRE WISH IS TO SEE CUTE SAKURA-CHAN ON STAGE AND BURN IT INTO OUR MEMORY... ♡
Fantastic! ♥
No, don't!!
I'm coming to see you, even with my broken leg.
BUT I'M JUST AN EXTRA!

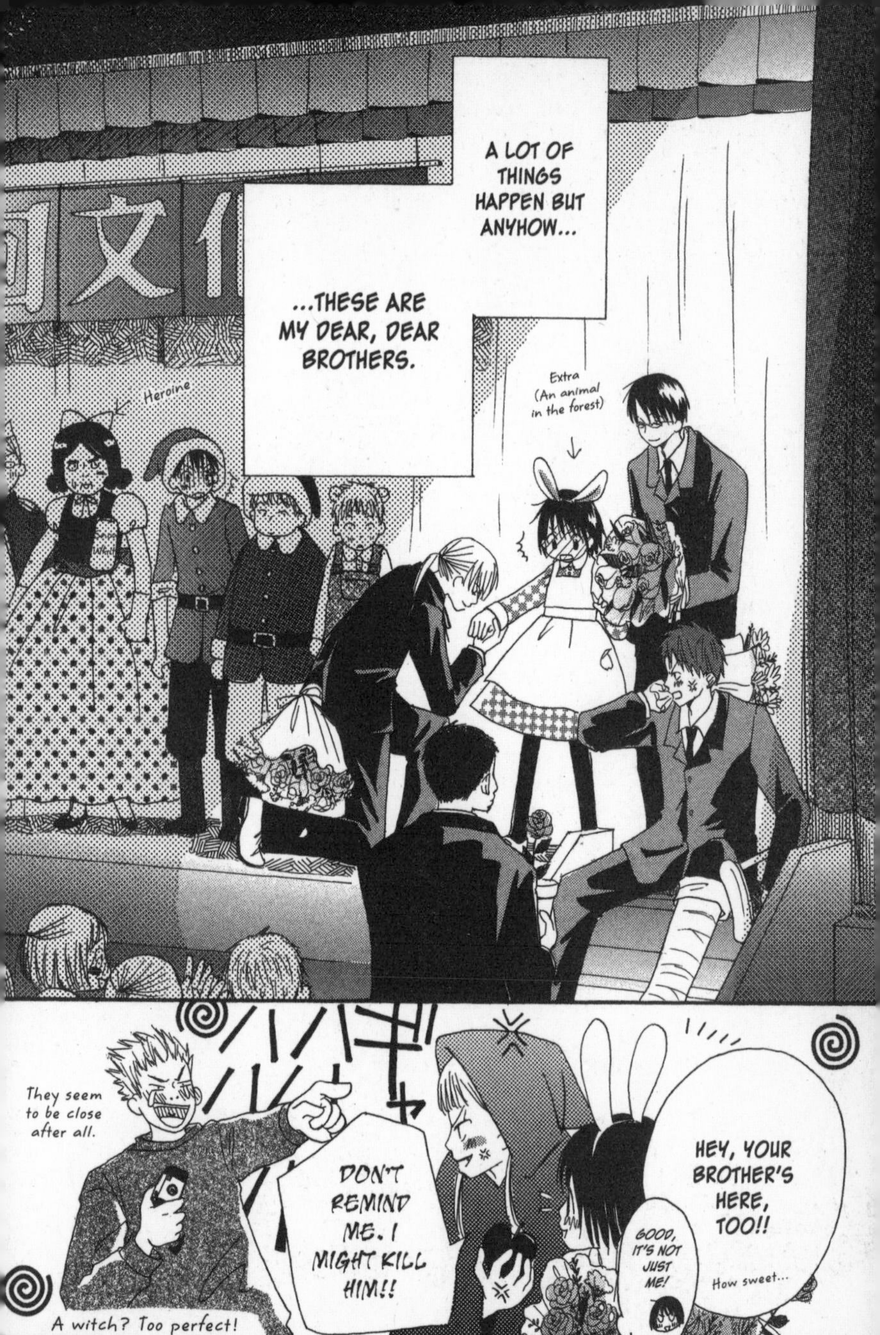
A LOT OF THINGS HAPPEN BUT ANYHOW...
...THESE ARE MY DEAR, DEAR BROTHERS.
Extra (An animal in the forest)
Heroine
HEY, YOUR BROTHER'S HERE, TOO!!
How sweet...
GOOD, IT'S NOT JUST ME!
DON'T REMIND ME. I MIGHT KILL HIM!!
They seem to be close after all.
A witch? Too perfect!

ME & MY BROTHERS 1/END

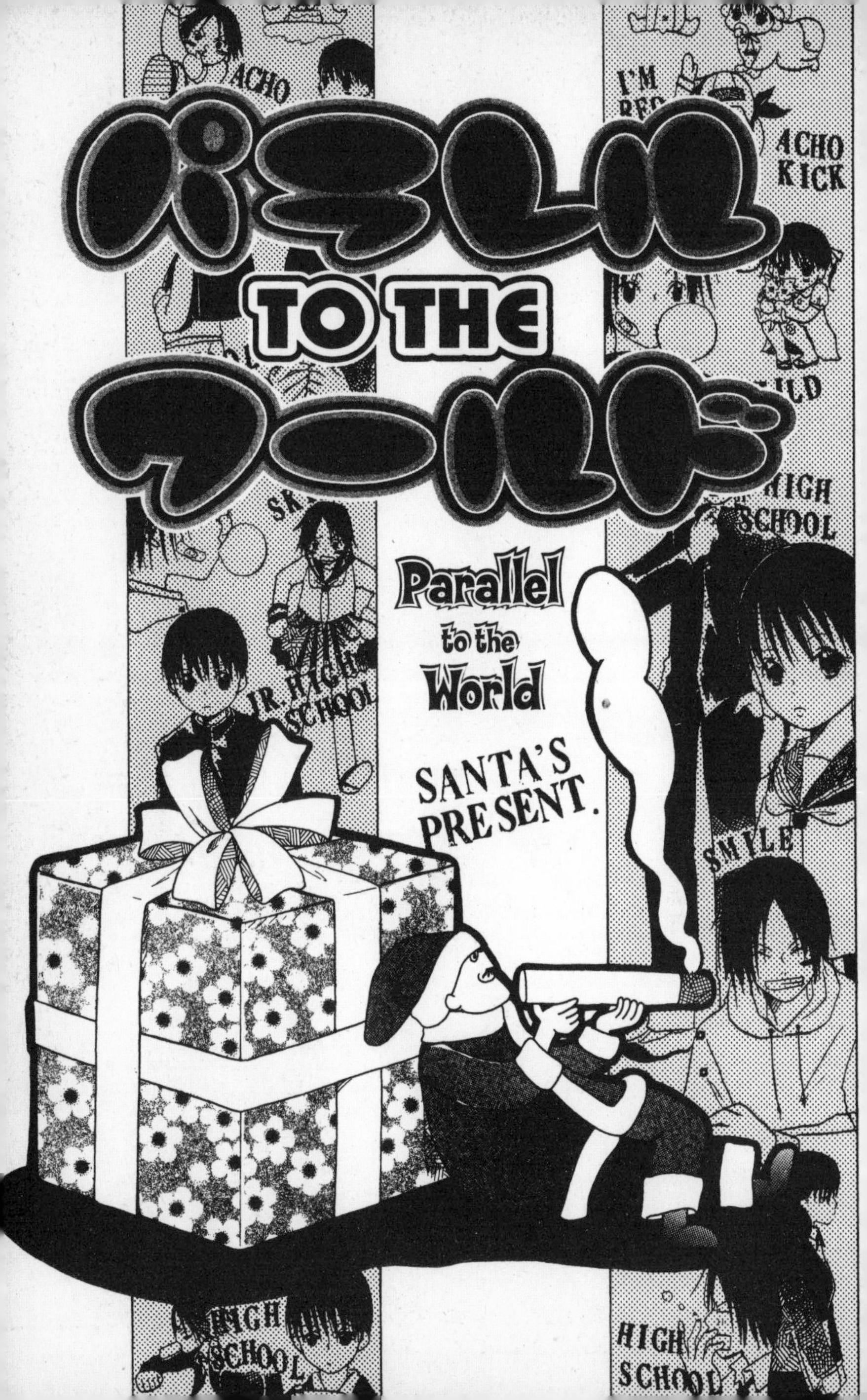
パラレル
TO THE
ワールド
Parallel to the World
SANTA'S PRESENT.
ACHO
ACHO KICK
HIGH SCHOOL
JR. HIGH SCHOOL
SMILE
HIGH SCHOOL
HIGH SCHOOL

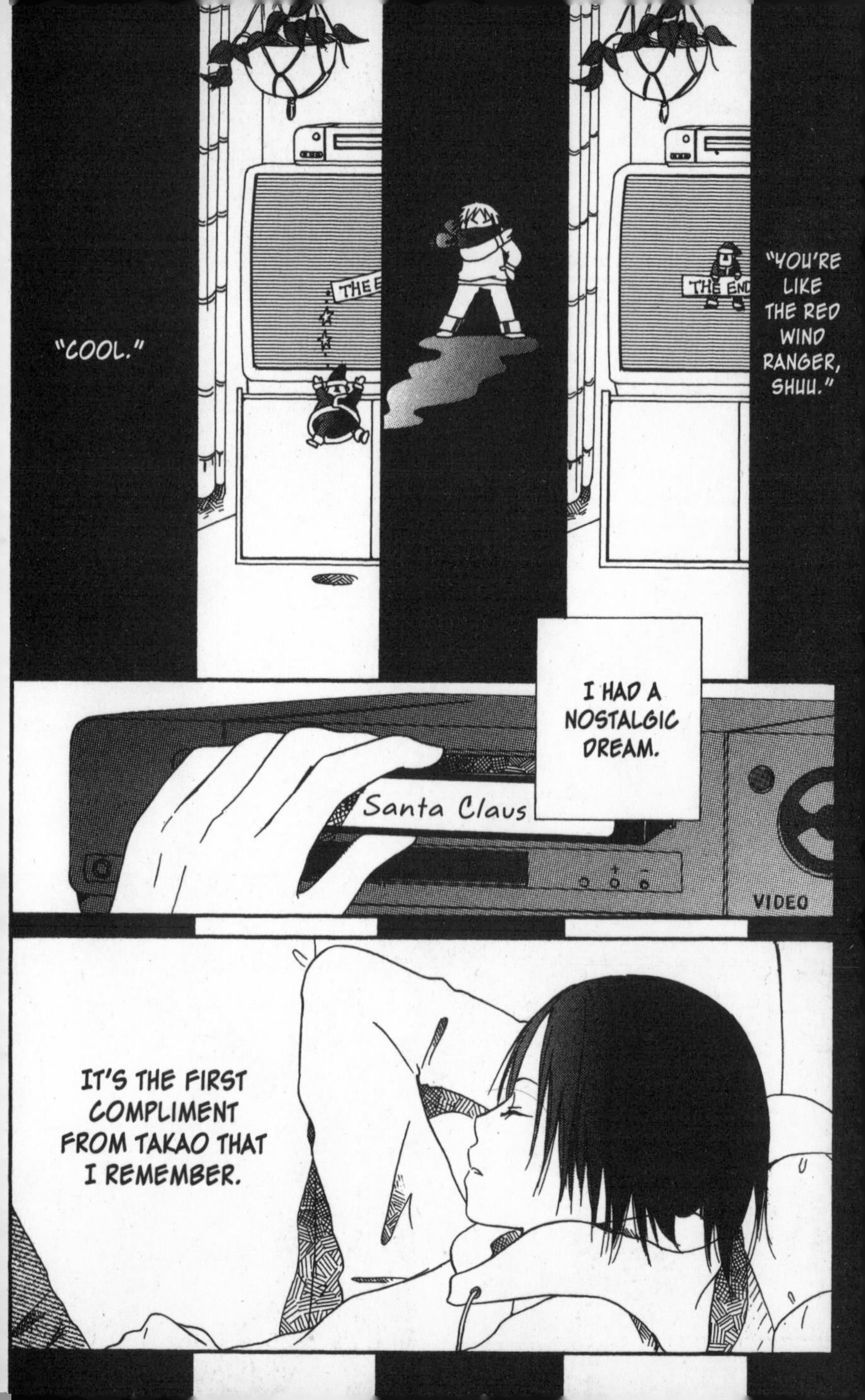
"YOU'RE LIKE THE RED WIND RANGER, SHUU."
THE END
"COOL."
I HAD A NOSTALGIC DREAM.
Santa Claus
VIDEO
IT'S THE FIRST COMPLIMENT FROM TAKAO THAT I REMEMBER.

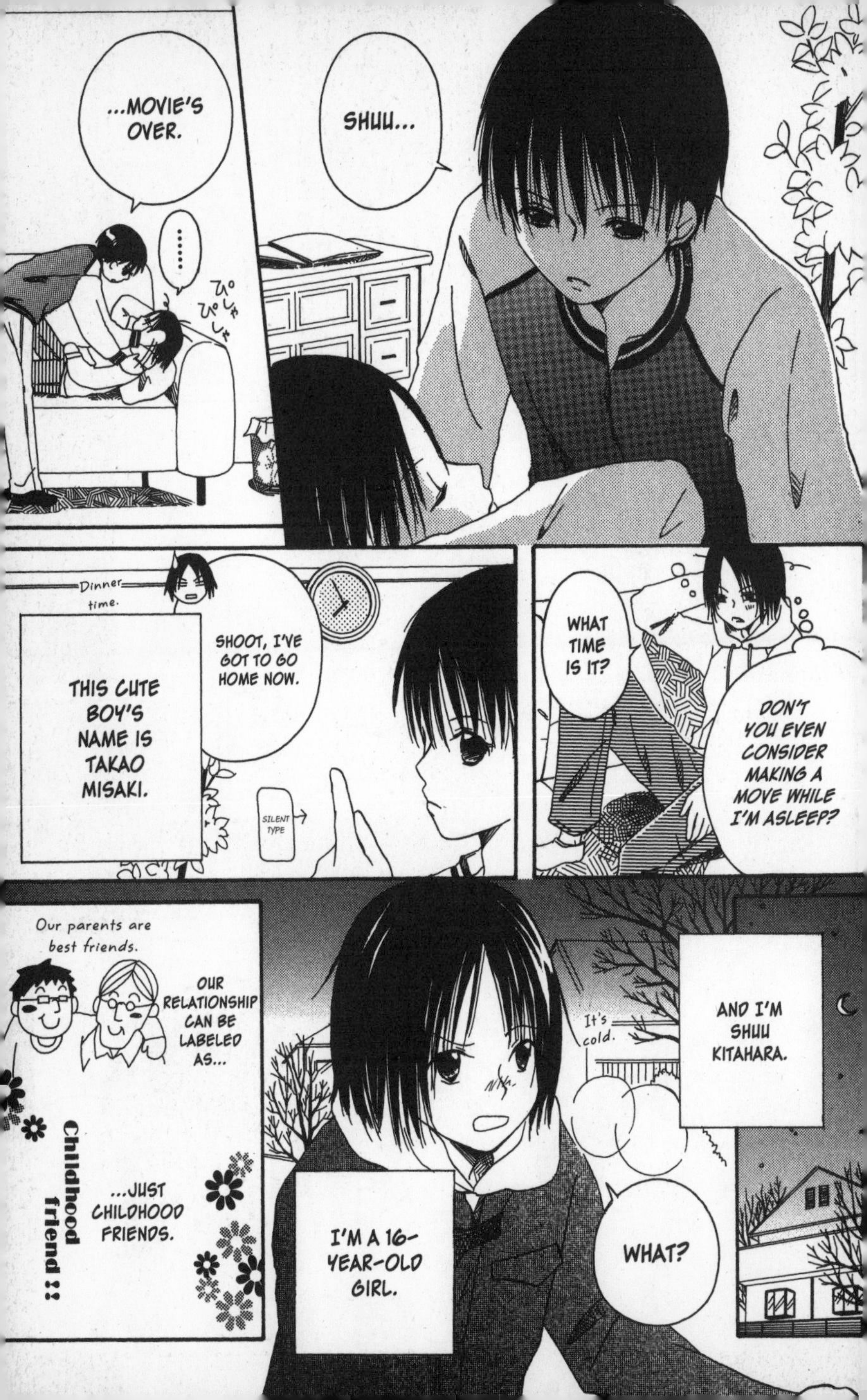
SHUU...
...MOVIE'S OVER.
......
ぴしゃ ぴしゃ
WHAT TIME IS IT?
DON'T YOU EVEN CONSIDER MAKING A MOVE WHILE I'M ASLEEP?
Dinner time.
SHOOT, I'VE GOT TO GO HOME NOW.
THIS CUTE BOY'S NAME IS TAKAO MISAKI.
SILENT TYPE
AND I'M SHUU KITAHARA.
It's cold.
WHAT?
I'M A 16-YEAR-OLD GIRL.
Our parents are best friends.
OUR RELATIONSHIP CAN BE LABELED AS...
...JUST CHILDHOOD FRIENDS.
Childhood friend!!

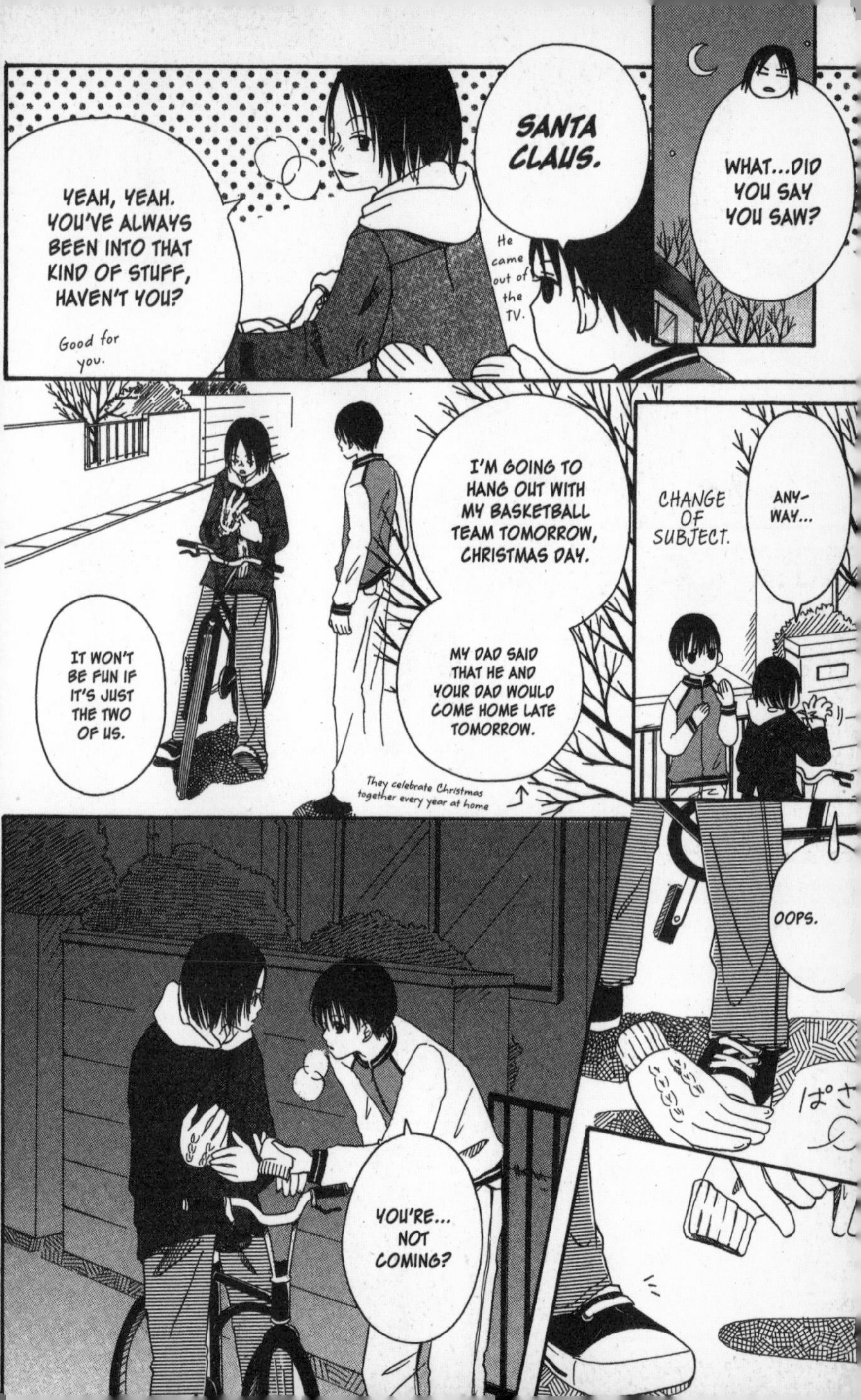
WHAT...DID YOU SAY YOU SAW?
SANTA CLAUS.
He came out of the TV.
YEAH, YEAH. YOU'VE ALWAYS BEEN INTO THAT KIND OF STUFF, HAVEN'T YOU?
Good for you.
ANY-WAY...
CHANGE OF SUBJECT.
I'M GOING TO HANG OUT WITH MY BASKETBALL TEAM TOMORROW, CHRISTMAS DAY.
MY DAD SAID THAT HE AND YOUR DAD WOULD COME HOME LATE TOMORROW.
They celebrate Christmas together every year at home
IT WON'T BE FUN IF IT'S JUST THE TWO OF US.
OOPS.
ぱさ
YOU'RE... NOT COMING?

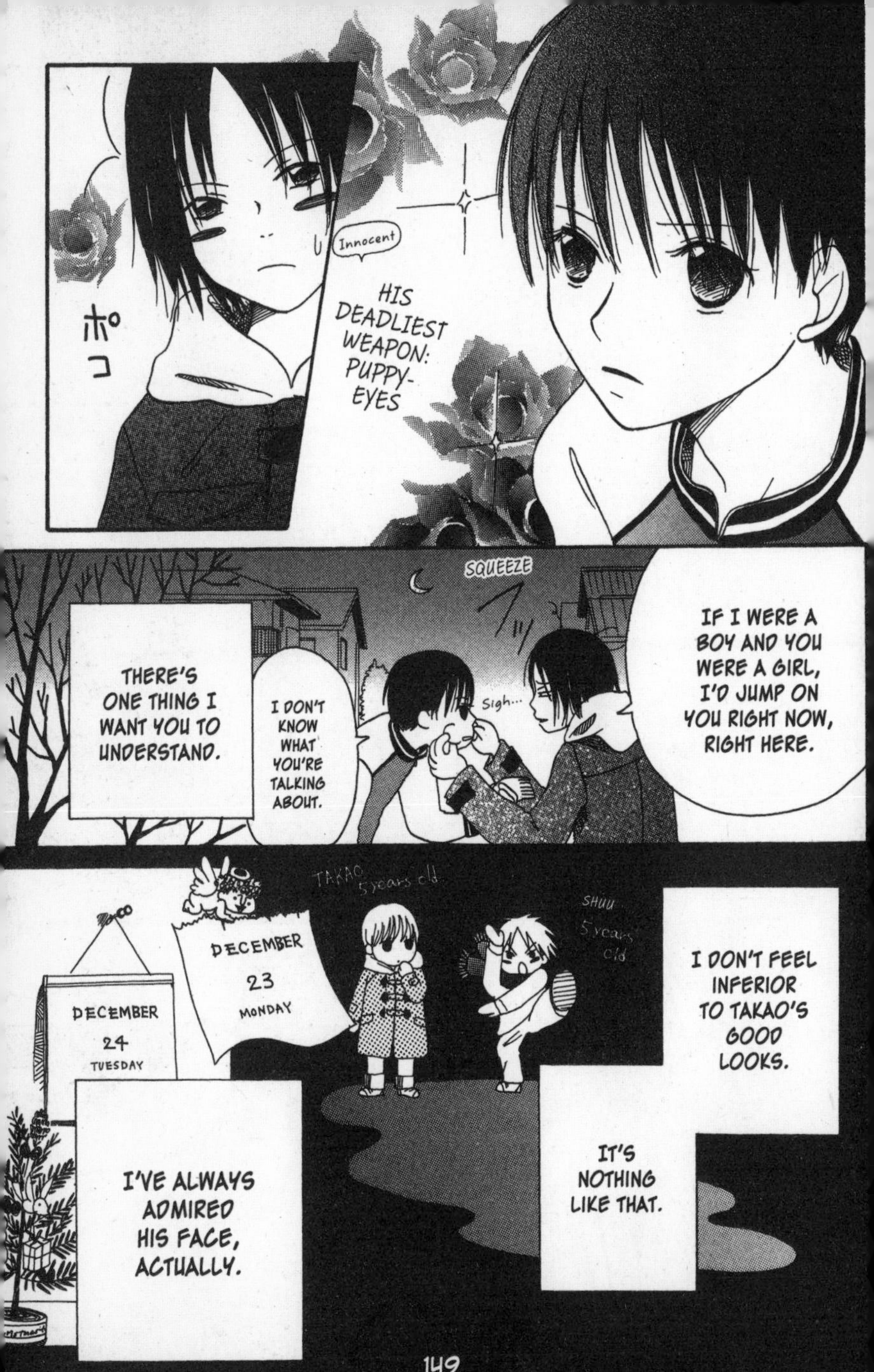
Innocent
HIS DEADLIEST WEAPON: PUPPY-EYES
ポコ
SQUEEZE
IF I WERE A BOY AND YOU WERE A GIRL, I'D JUMP ON YOU RIGHT NOW, RIGHT HERE.
Sigh...
I DON'T KNOW WHAT YOU'RE TALKING ABOUT.
THERE'S ONE THING I WANT YOU TO UNDERSTAND.
I DON'T FEEL INFERIOR TO TAKAO'S GOOD LOOKS.
SHUU 5 years old
TAKAO 5 years old
DECEMBER 23 MONDAY
DECEMBER 24 TUESDAY
IT'S NOTHING LIKE THAT.
I'VE ALWAYS ADMIRED HIS FACE, ACTUALLY.

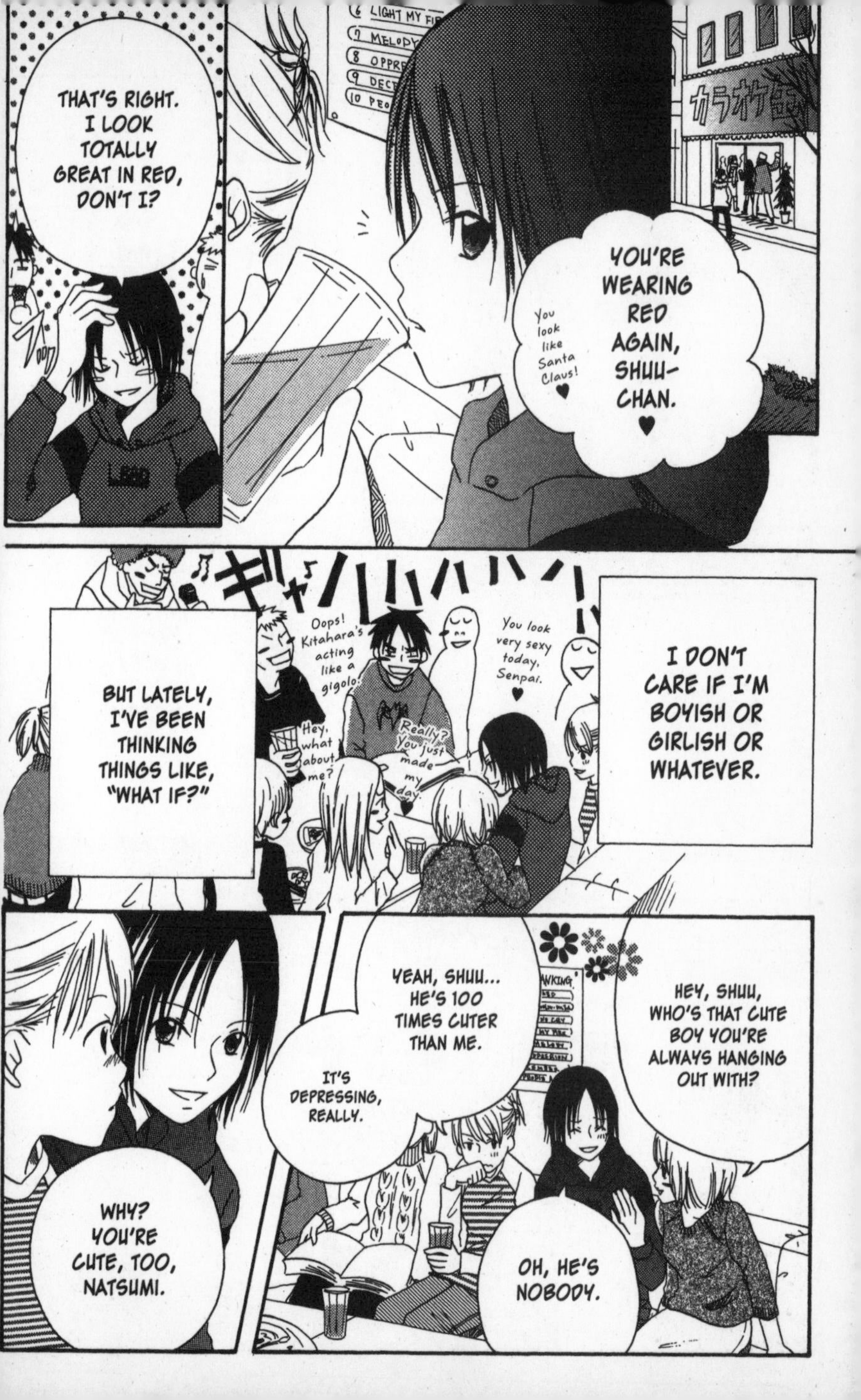
YOU'RE WEARING RED AGAIN, SHUU-CHAN. ♥
You look like Santa Claus! ♥
THAT'S RIGHT. I LOOK TOTALLY GREAT IN RED, DON'T I?
I DON'T CARE IF I'M BOYISH OR GIRLISH OR WHATEVER.
You look very sexy today, Senpai. ♥
ギャハハハハハ
Oops! Kitahara's acting like a gigolo!
Really? You just made my day. ♥
Hey, what about me?
BUT LATELY, I'VE BEEN THINKING THINGS LIKE, "WHAT IF?"
HEY, SHUU, WHO'S THAT CUTE BOY YOU'RE ALWAYS HANGING OUT WITH?
OH, HE'S NOBODY.
YEAH, SHUU... HE'S 100 TIMES CUTER THAN ME.
IT'S DEPRESSING, REALLY.
WHY? YOU'RE CUTE, TOO, NATSUMI.

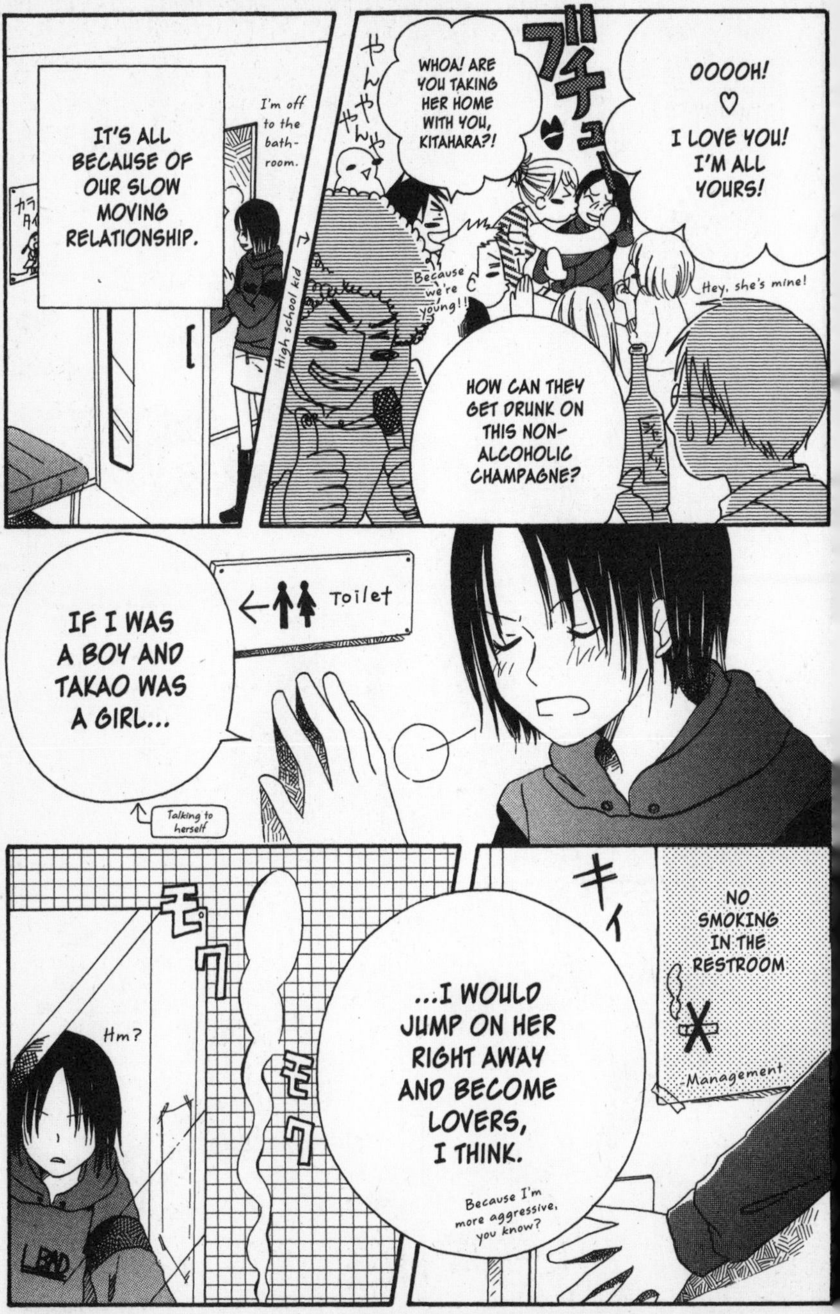
OOOOH! ♡ I LOVE YOU! I'M ALL YOURS!
ブチュ
WHOA! ARE YOU TAKING HER HOME WITH YOU, KITAHARA?!
Hey, she's mine!
Because we're young!!
High school kid
HOW CAN THEY GET DRUNK ON THIS NON-ALCOHOLIC CHAMPAGNE?
I'm off to the bathroom.
IT'S ALL BECAUSE OF OUR SLOW MOVING RELATIONSHIP.
Toilet
IF I WAS A BOY AND TAKAO WAS A GIRL...
Talking to herself
キィ
NO SMOKING IN THE RESTROOM
-Management
...I WOULD JUMP ON HER RIGHT AWAY AND BECOME LOVERS, I THINK.
Because I'm more aggressive, you know?
モクモク
Hm?

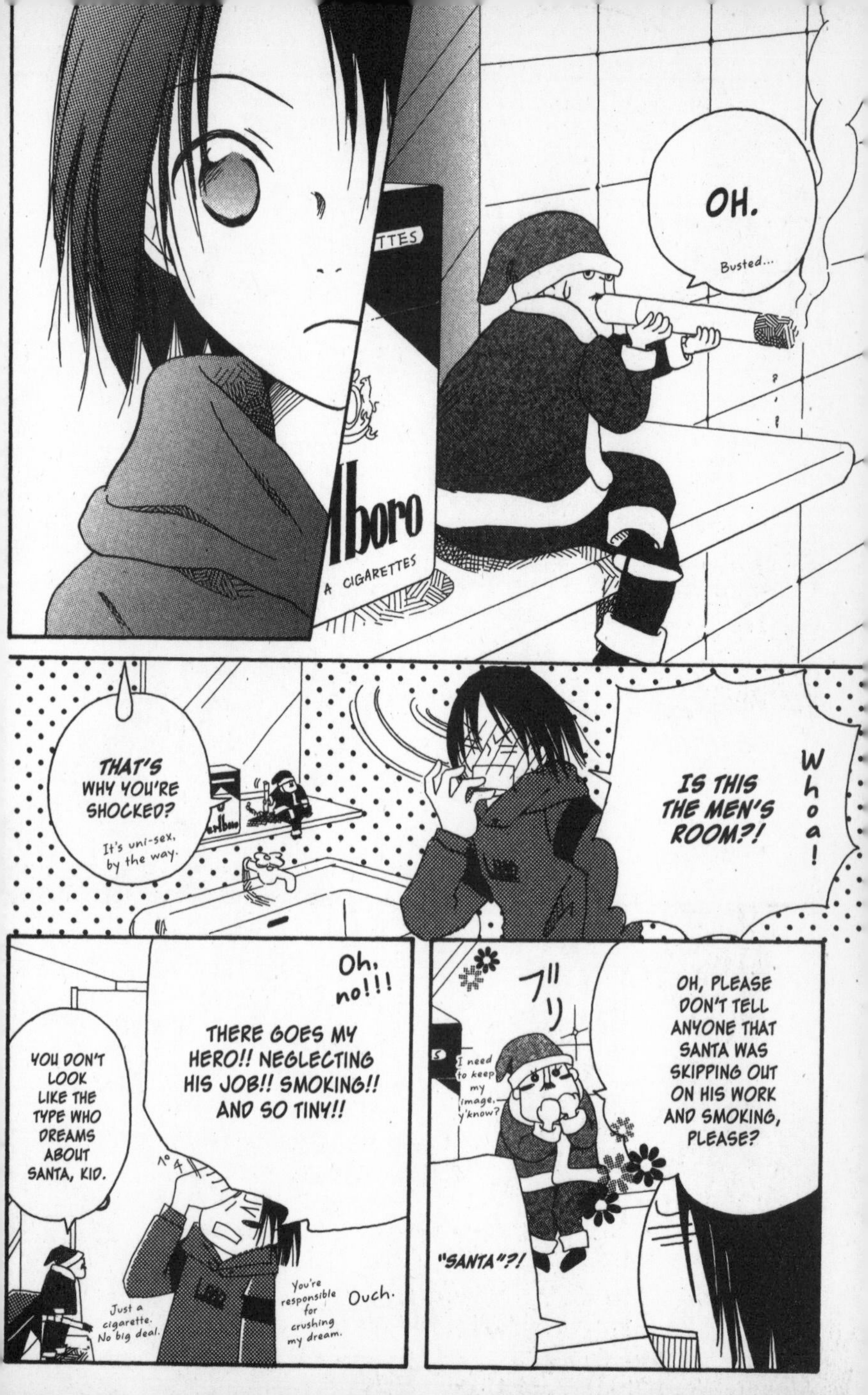
OH.
Busted...
TTES
lboro
A CIGARETTES
Whoa!
IS THIS THE MEN'S ROOM?!
THAT'S WHY YOU'RE SHOCKED?
It's uni-sex, by the way.
OH, PLEASE DON'T TELL ANYONE THAT SANTA WAS SKIPPING OUT ON HIS WORK AND SMOKING, PLEASE?
ブリ
I need to keep my image, y'know?
"SANTA"?!
Oh, no!!!
THERE GOES MY HERO!! NEGLECTING HIS JOB!! SMOKING!! AND SO TINY!!
YOU DON'T LOOK LIKE THE TYPE WHO DREAMS ABOUT SANTA, KID.
Ouch.
You're responsible for crushing my dream.
Just a cigarette. No big deal.

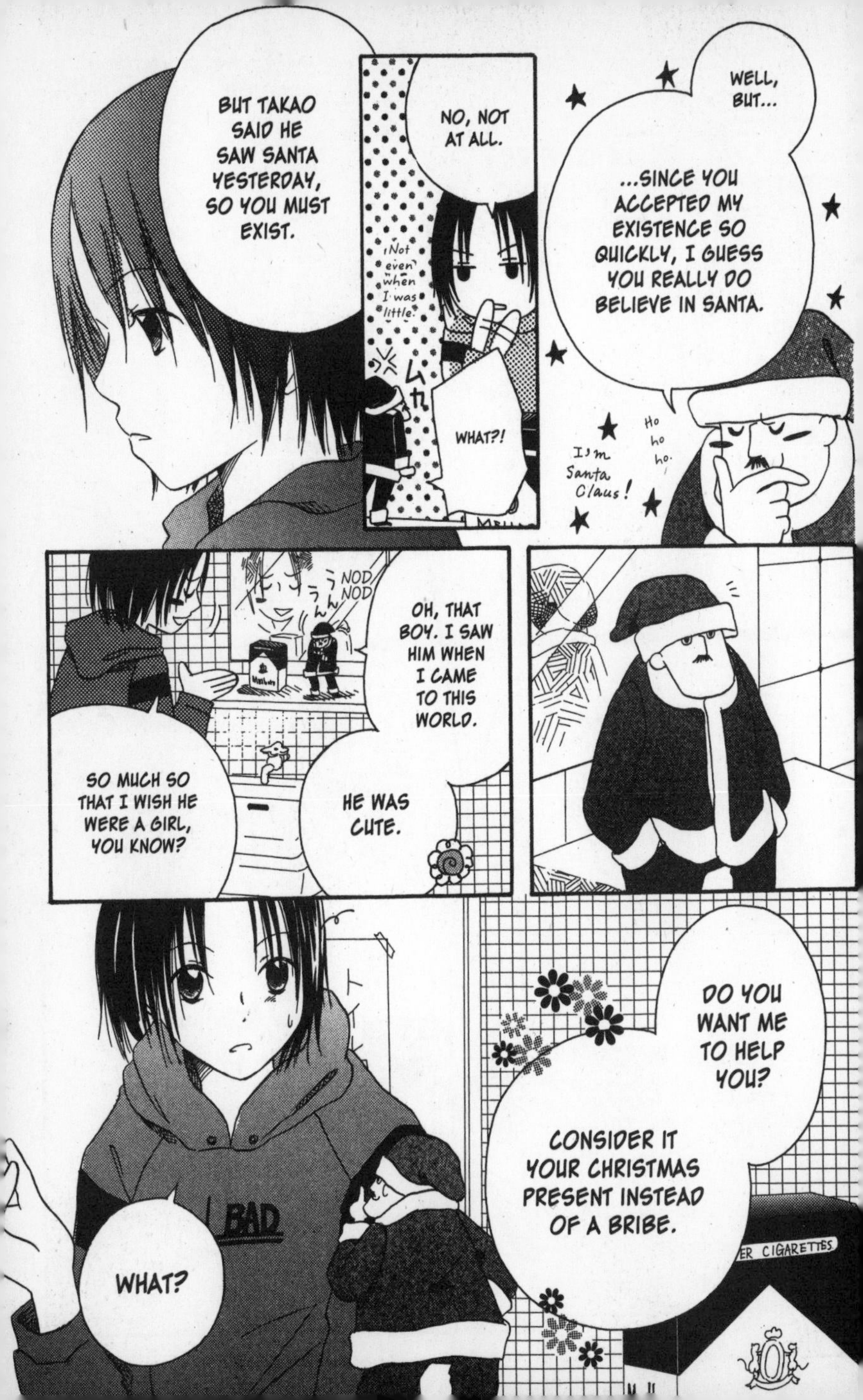
WELL, BUT...
...SINCE YOU ACCEPTED MY EXISTENCE SO QUICKLY, I GUESS YOU REALLY DO BELIEVE IN SANTA.
Ho ho ho.
I'm Santa Claus!
NO, NOT AT ALL.
Not even when I was little.
WHAT?!
BUT TAKAO SAID HE SAW SANTA YESTERDAY, SO YOU MUST EXIST.
NOD NOD
OH, THAT BOY. I SAW HIM WHEN I CAME TO THIS WORLD.
HE WAS CUTE.
SO MUCH SO THAT I WISH HE WERE A GIRL, YOU KNOW?
DO YOU WANT ME TO HELP YOU?
CONSIDER IT YOUR CHRISTMAS PRESENT INSTEAD OF A BRIBE.
BAD
WHAT?

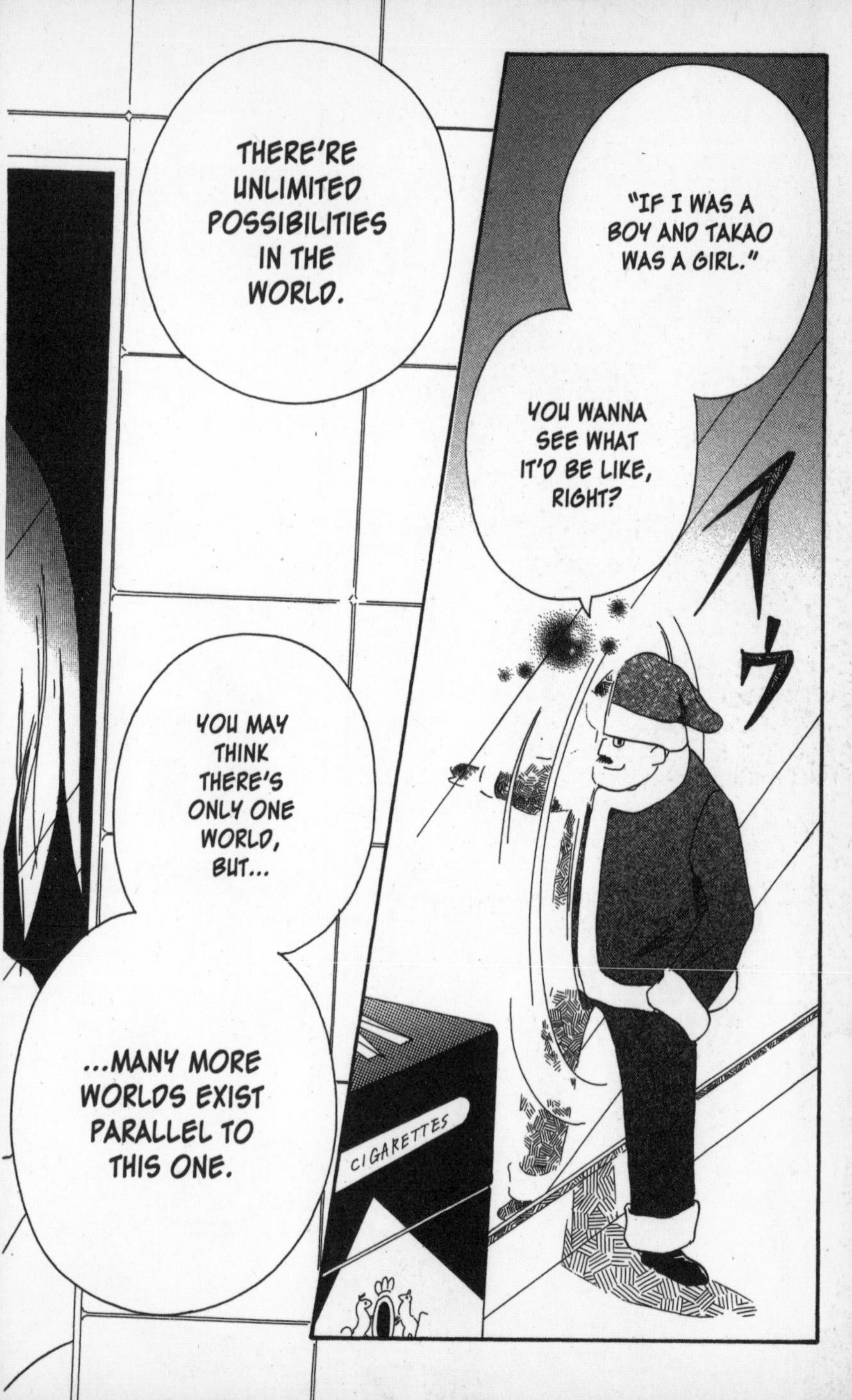
"IF I WAS A BOY AND TAKAO WAS A GIRL."
YOU WANNA SEE WHAT IT'D BE LIKE, RIGHT?
ウ
CIGARETTES
THERE'RE UNLIMITED POSSIBILITIES IN THE WORLD.
YOU MAY THINK THERE'S ONLY ONE WORLD, BUT...
...MANY MORE WORLDS EXIST PARALLEL TO THIS ONE.

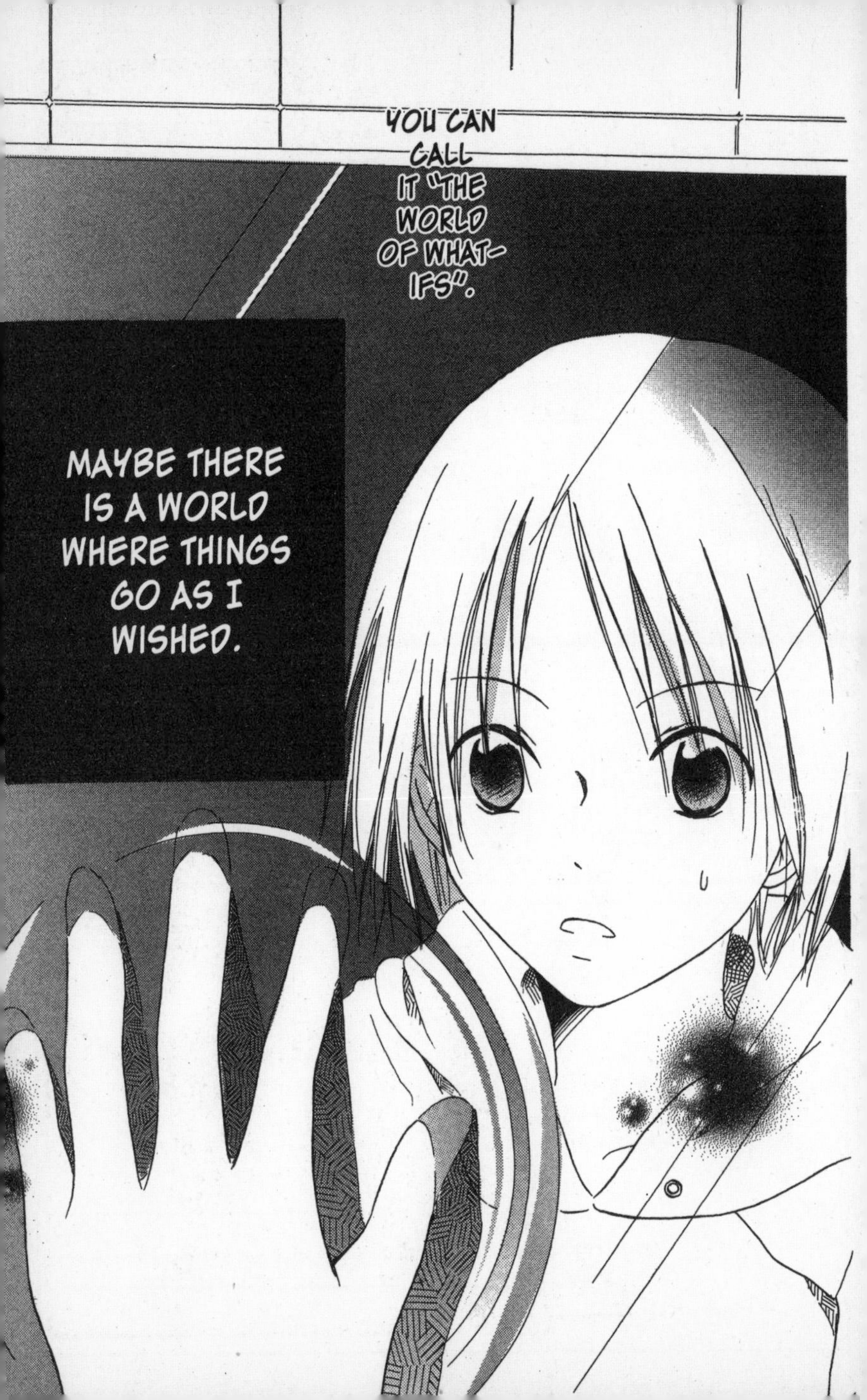
YOU CAN CALL IT "THE WORLD OF WHAT-IFS".
MAYBE THERE IS A WORLD WHERE THINGS GO AS I WISHED.

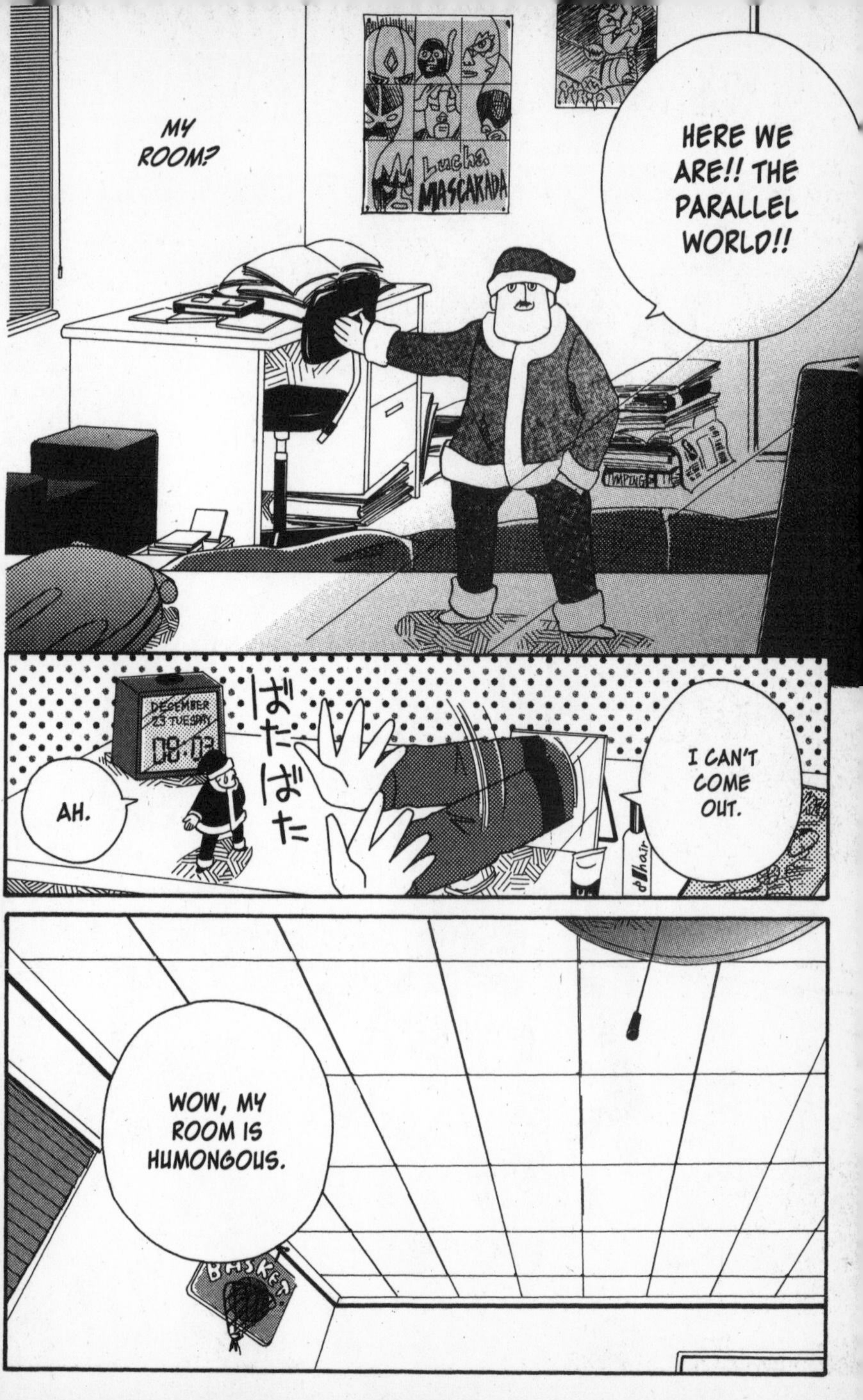
HERE WE ARE!! THE PARALLEL WORLD!!
MY ROOM?
Lucha MASCARADA
I CAN'T COME OUT.
ばたばた
DECEMBER 23 TUESDAY
08:03
AH.
WOW, MY ROOM IS HUMONGOUS.
BASKET

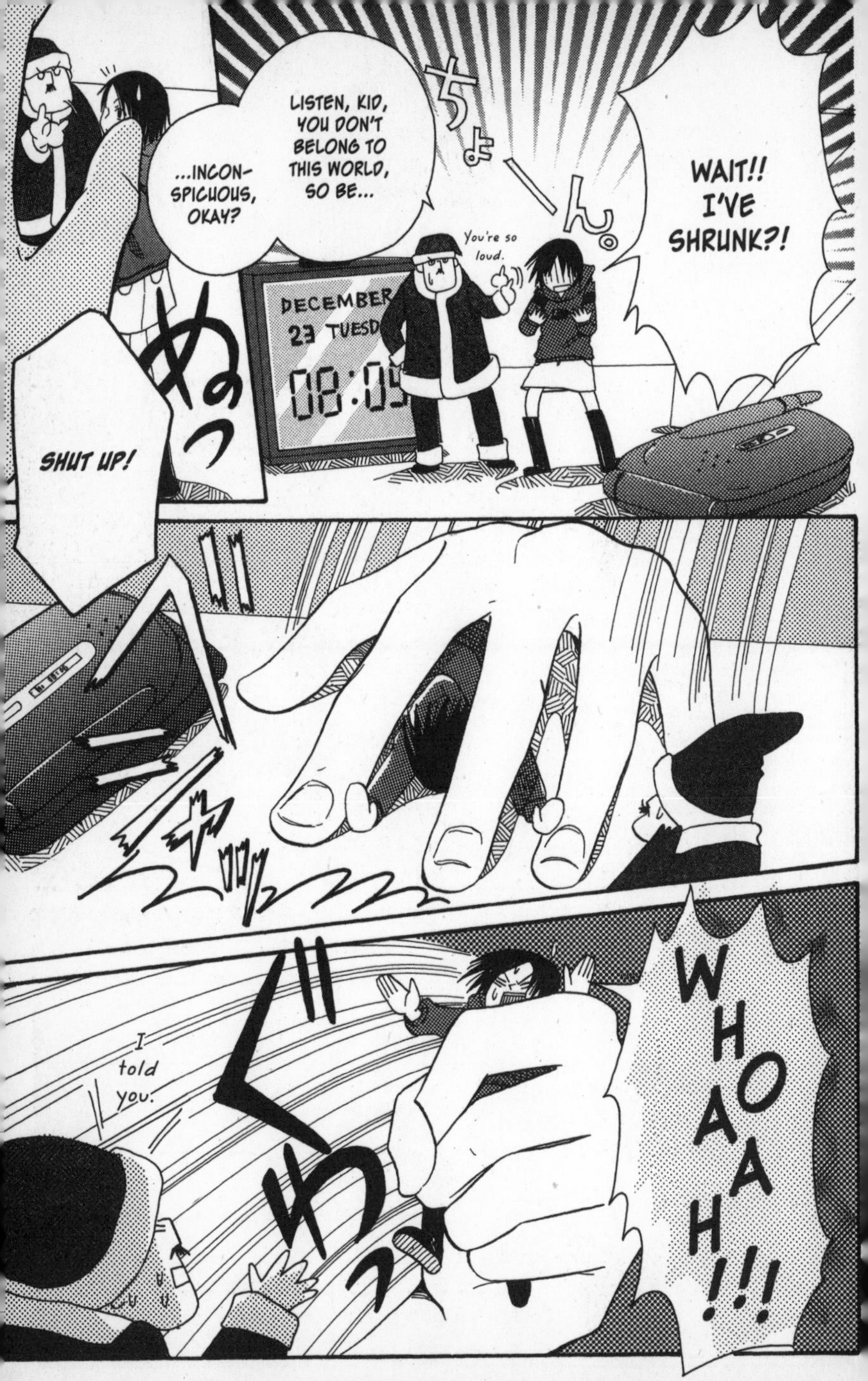
WAIT!! I'VE SHRUNK?!
ちょーん。
You're so loud.
LISTEN, KID, YOU DON'T BELONG TO THIS WORLD, SO BE...
...INCON-SPICUOUS, OKAY?
SHUT UP!
WHOAAAH!!!
I told you.

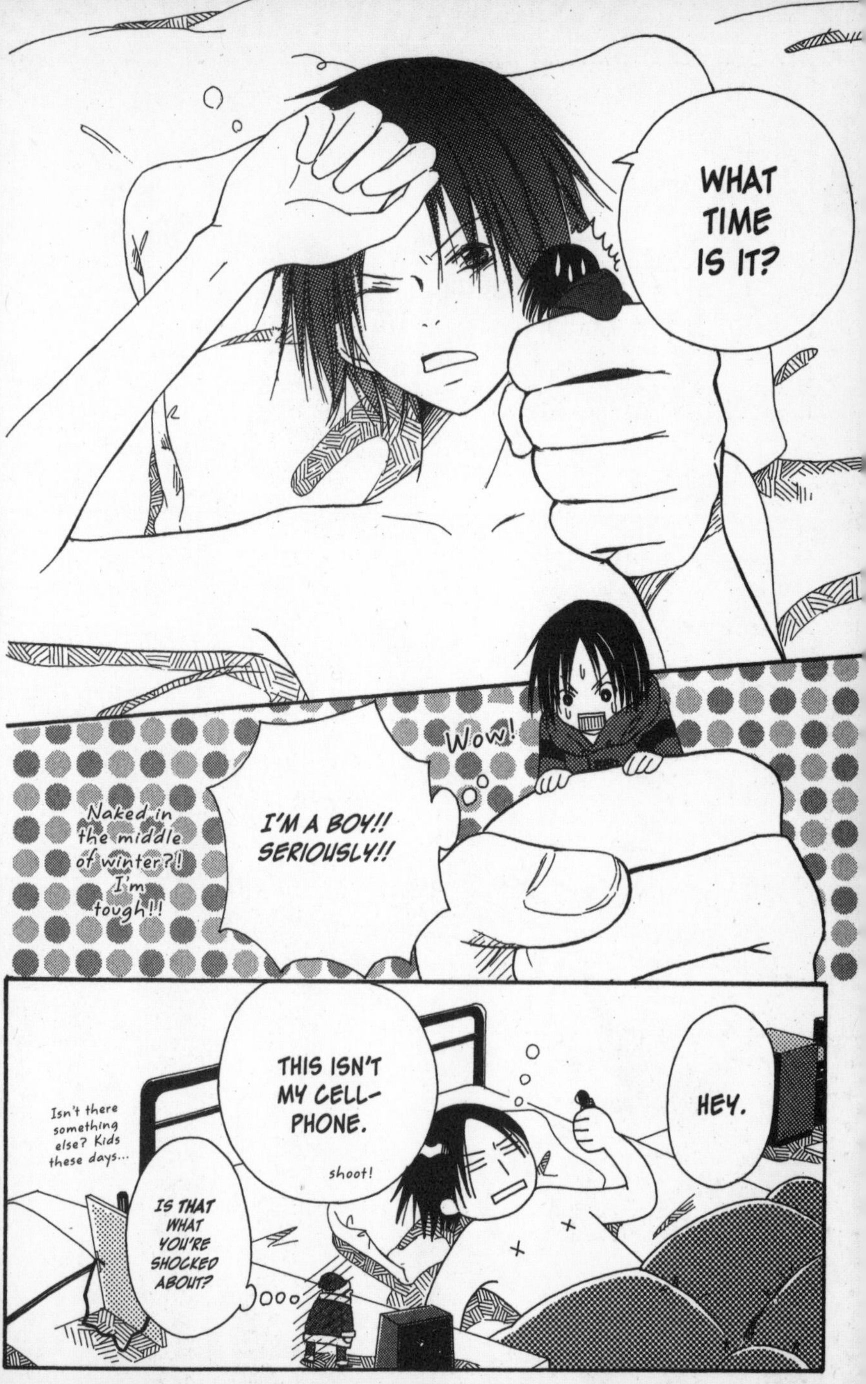
WHAT TIME IS IT?
Wow!
I'M A BOY!! SERIOUSLY!!
Naked in the middle of winter?! I'm tough!!
HEY.
THIS ISN'T MY CELL-PHONE.
shoot!
IS THAT WHAT YOU'RE SHOCKED ABOUT?
Isn't there something else? Kids these days...

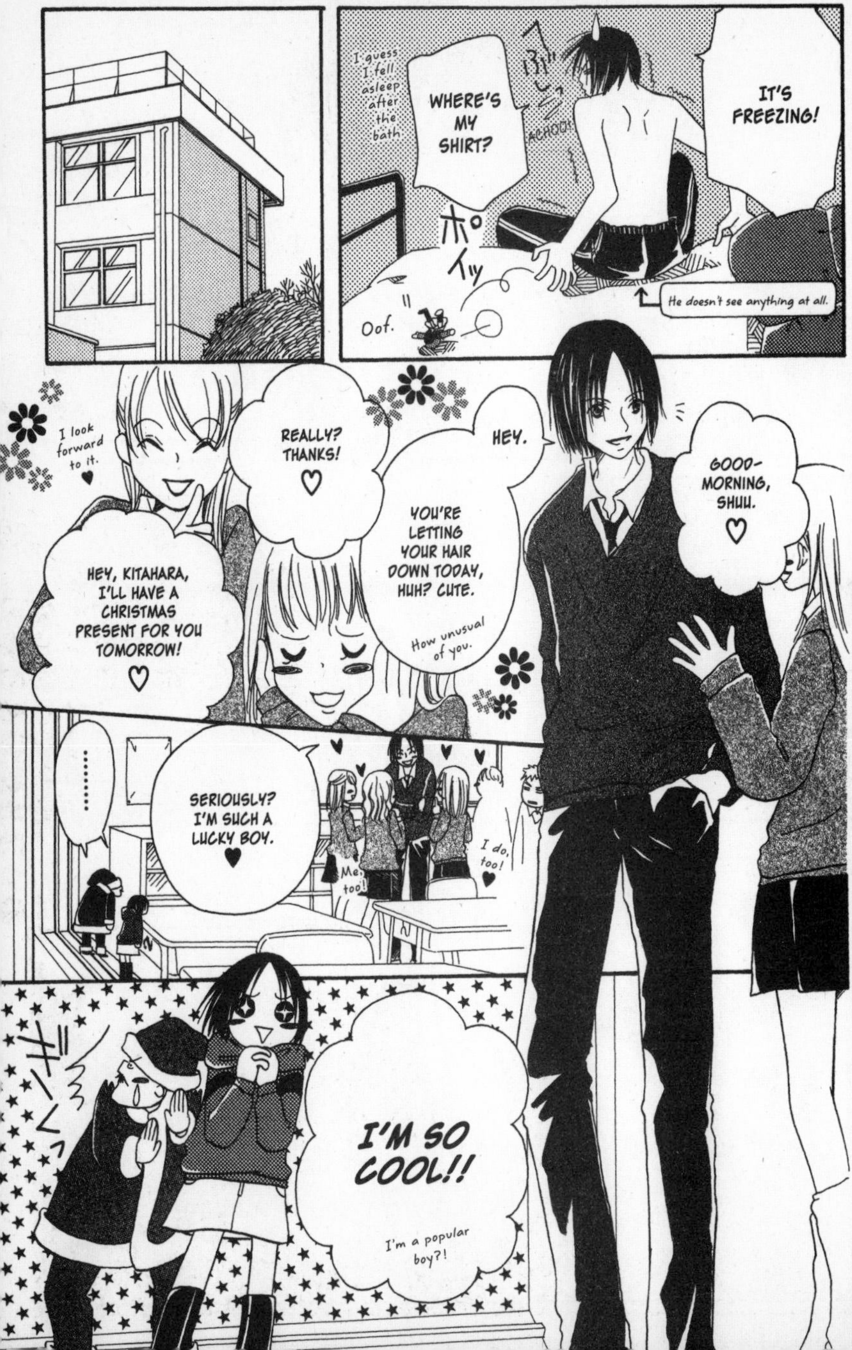
IT'S FREEZING!
ACHOO!
WHERE'S MY SHIRT?
I guess I fell asleep after the bath.
ポイッ
He doesn't see anything at all.
Oof.
GOOD-MORNING, SHUU. ♡
HEY.
YOU'RE LETTING YOUR HAIR DOWN TODAY, HUH? CUTE.
How unusual of you.
REALLY? THANKS! ♡
I look forward to it. ♥
HEY, KITAHARA, I'LL HAVE A CHRISTMAS PRESENT FOR YOU TOMORROW! ♡
SERIOUSLY? I'M SUCH A LUCKY BOY. ♥
I do, too! ♥
Me, too!
......
I'M SO COOL!!
I'm a popular boy?!

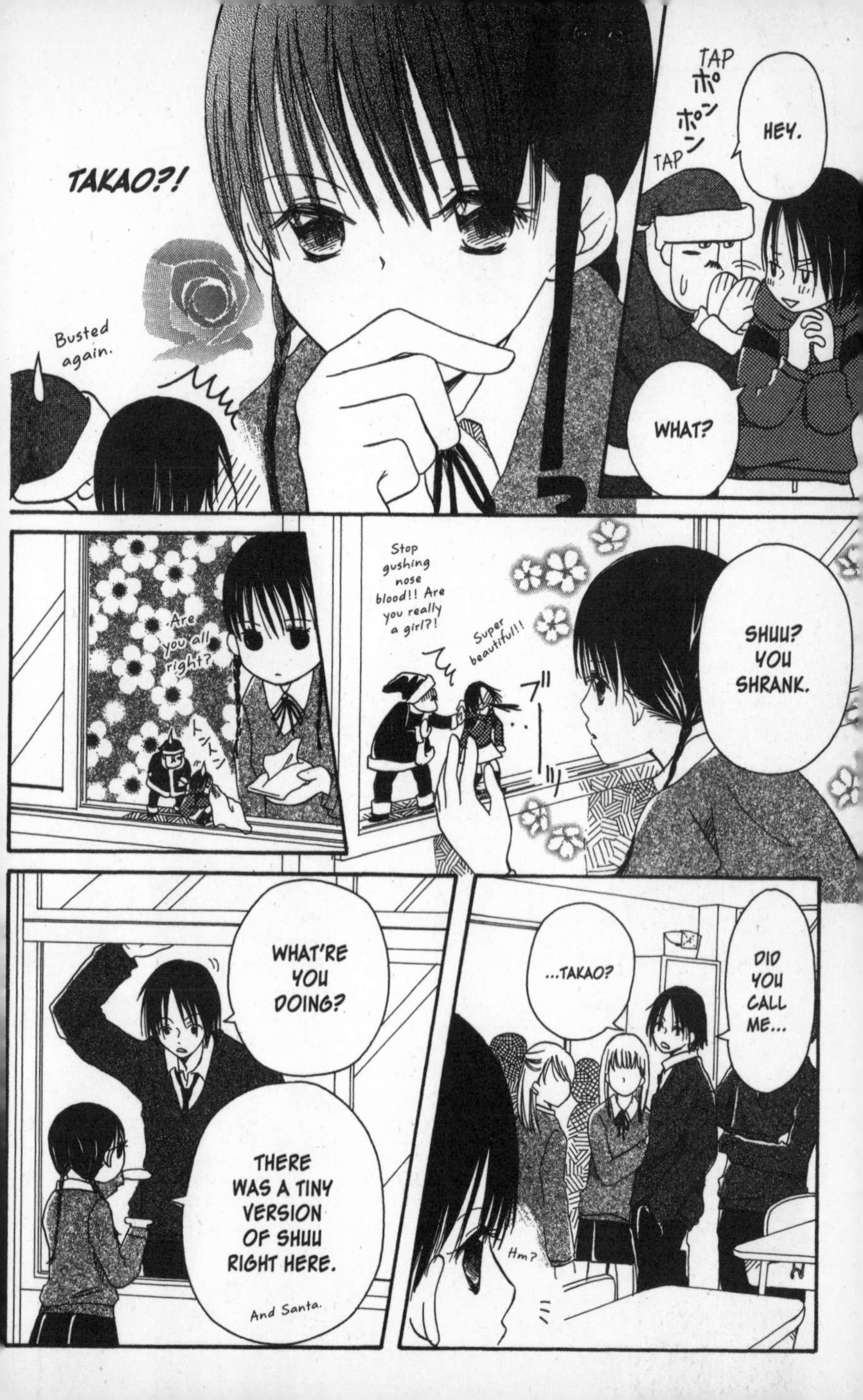
TAP
ポン
ポン
TAP
HEY.
WHAT?
TAKAO?!
Busted again.
SHUU? YOU SHRANK.
Stop gushing nose blood!! Are you really a girl?!
Super beautiful!!
Are you all right?
トントン
DID YOU CALL ME...
...TAKAO?
Hm?
WHAT'RE YOU DOING?
THERE WAS A TINY VERSION OF SHUU RIGHT HERE.
And Santa.

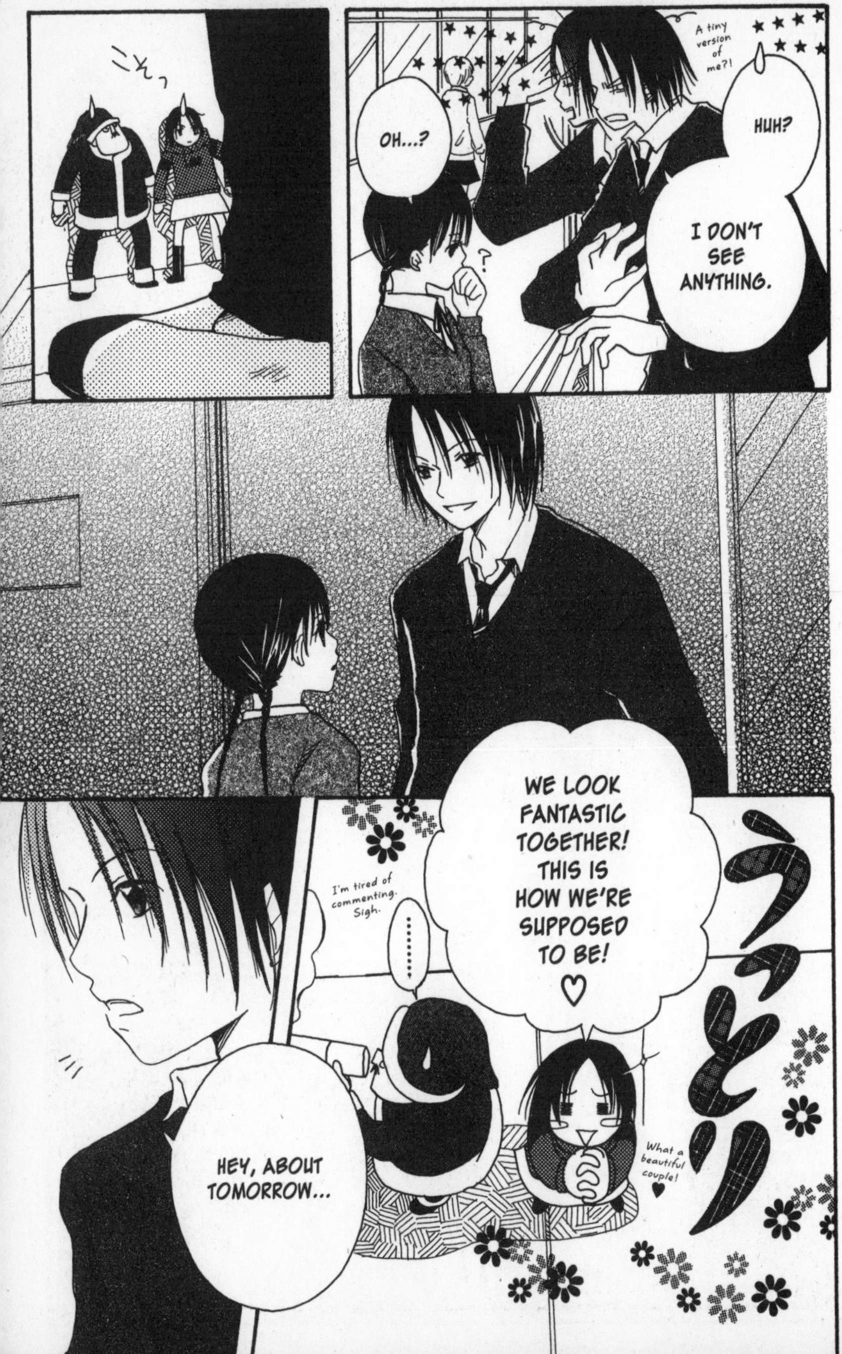

HUH?
A tiny version of me?!
I DON'T SEE ANYTHING.
OH...?
こそっ
うっとり
WE LOOK FANTASTIC TOGETHER! THIS IS HOW WE'RE SUPPOSED TO BE! ♡
What a beautiful couple! ♥
......
I'm tired of commenting. Sigh.
HEY, ABOUT TOMORROW...

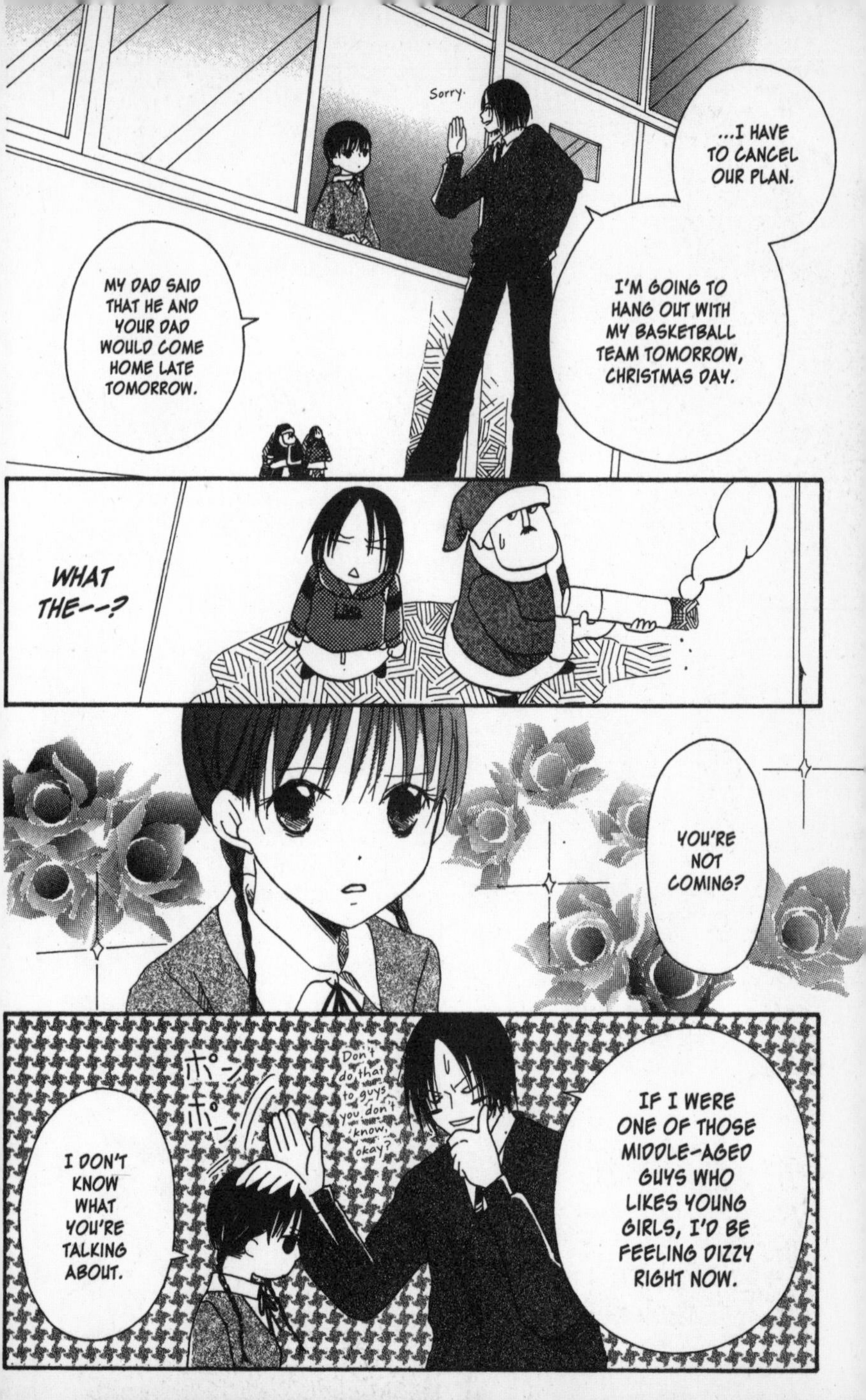
...I HAVE TO CANCEL OUR PLAN.
Sorry.
I'M GOING TO HANG OUT WITH MY BASKETBALL TEAM TOMORROW, CHRISTMAS DAY.
MY DAD SAID THAT HE AND YOUR DAD WOULD COME HOME LATE TOMORROW.
WHAT THE--?
YOU'RE NOT COMING?
IF I WERE ONE OF THOSE MIDDLE-AGED GUYS WHO LIKES YOUNG GIRLS, I'D BE FEELING DIZZY RIGHT NOW.
Don't do that to guys you don't know, okay?
ポンポン
I DON'T KNOW WHAT YOU'RE TALKING ABOUT.

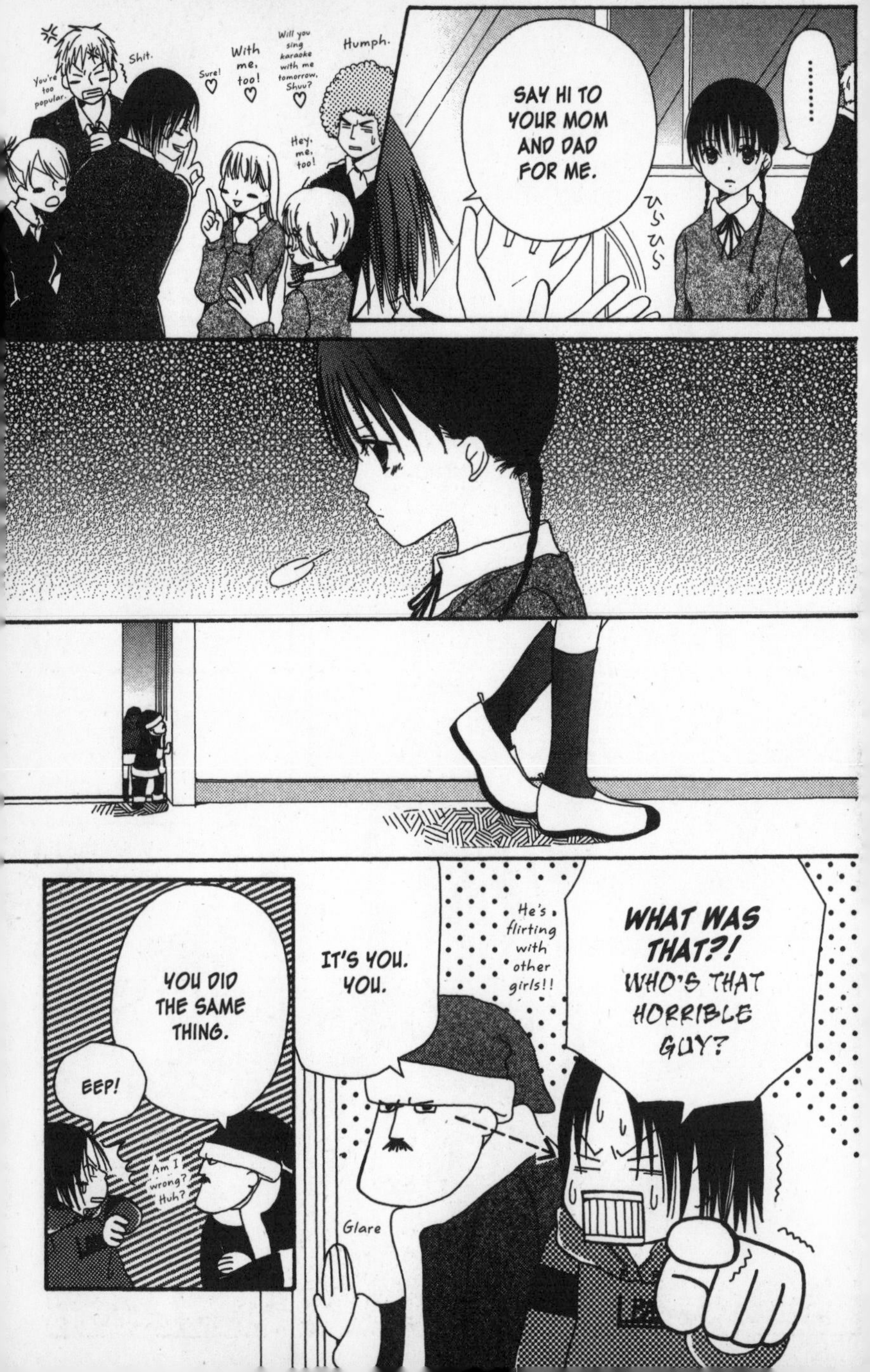
SAY HI TO YOUR MOM AND DAD FOR ME.
......
ひらひら
Humph.
Will you sing karaoke with me tomorrow, Shuu?
Hey, me, too!
With me, too!
Sure!
Shit.
You're too popular.
WHAT WAS THAT?! WHO'S THAT HORRIBLE GUY?
He's flirting with other girls!!
IT'S YOU. YOU.
Glare
YOU DID THE SAME THING.
EEP!
Am I wrong? Huh?

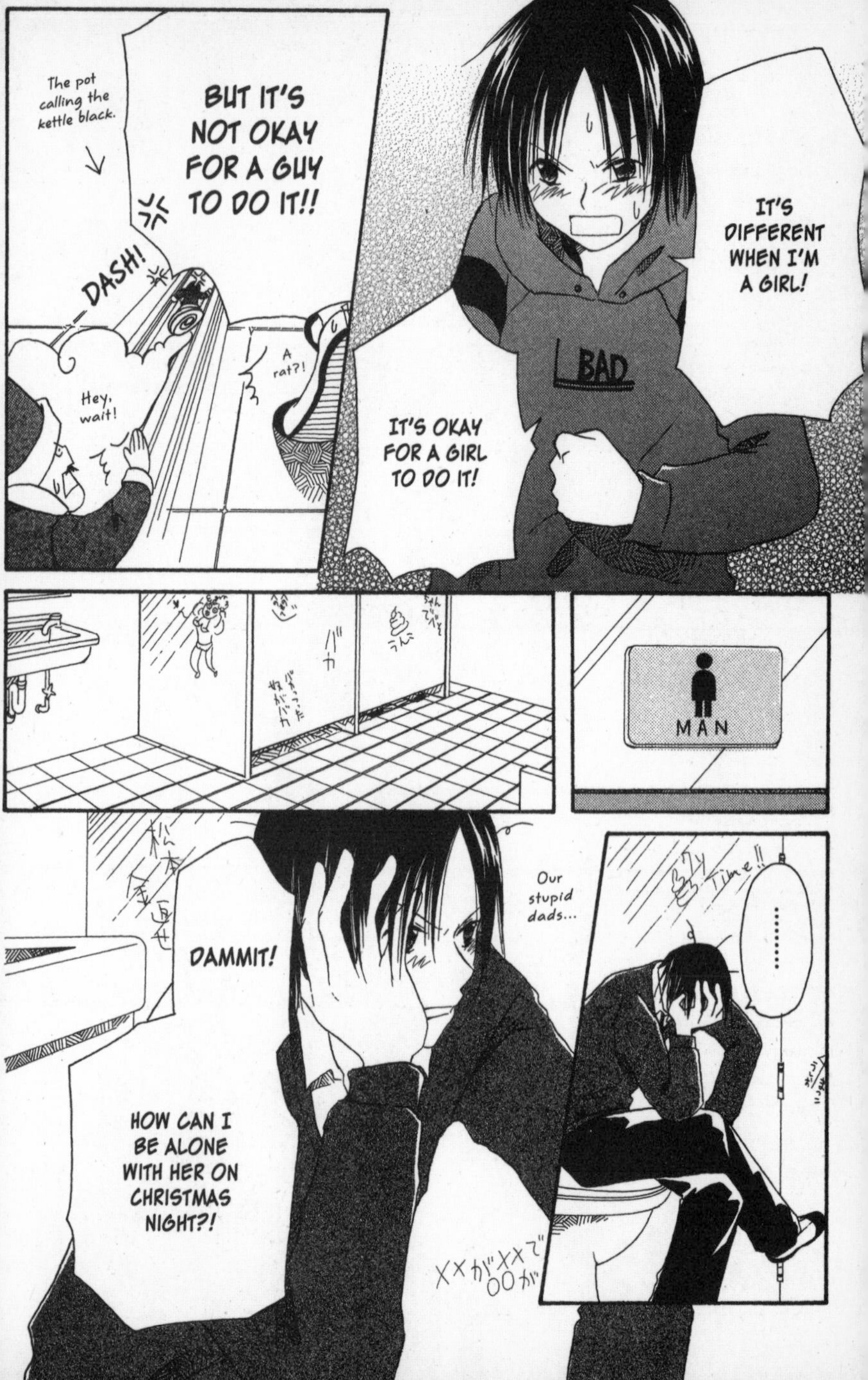
IT'S DIFFERENT WHEN I'M A GIRL!
IT'S OKAY FOR A GIRL TO DO IT!
BUT IT'S NOT OKAY FOR A GUY TO DO IT!!
The pot calling the kettle black.
DASH!
A rat?!
Hey, wait!
MAN
Our stupid dads...
Time!!
......
DAMMIT!
HOW CAN I BE ALONE WITH HER ON CHRISTMAS NIGHT?!
××が××で○○が

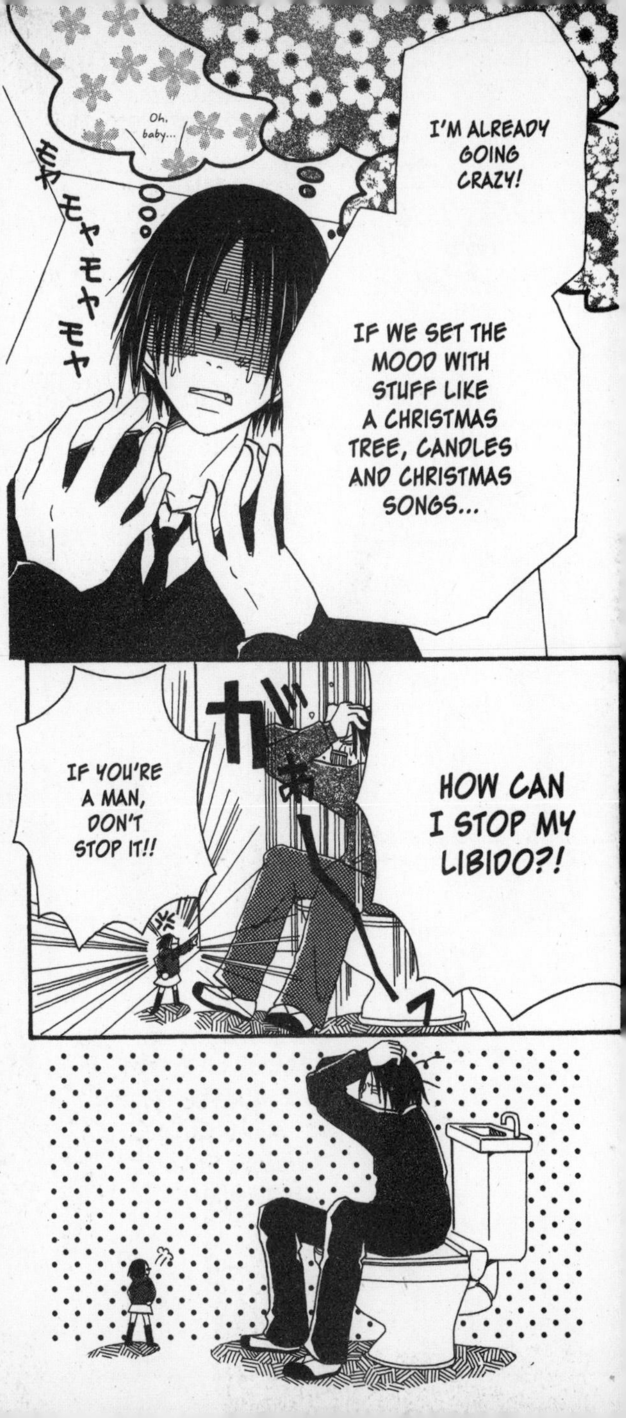
I'M ALREADY GOING CRAZY!
IF WE SET THE MOOD WITH STUFF LIKE A CHRISTMAS TREE, CANDLES AND CHRISTMAS SONGS...
Oh, baby...
モヤモヤモヤモヤ
HOW CAN I STOP MY LIBIDO?!
IF YOU'RE A MAN, DON'T STOP IT!!

☆ 5 ☆

I made the last column sound final, but there's one more.

"Parallel to the World"

I'm personally very fond of this story. Santa, a middle-aged man!! I love middle-aged men and I got to draw him a lot!!!

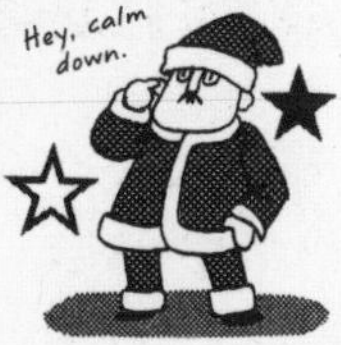
Hey, calm down.

I'm satisfied with Shuu and Takao's characters, I think. Most of all, it took very little time for me to correct the story! It's most memorable that my editor said, "you're like a different person." And I enjoyed drawing trees. (What am I talking about?)

End.

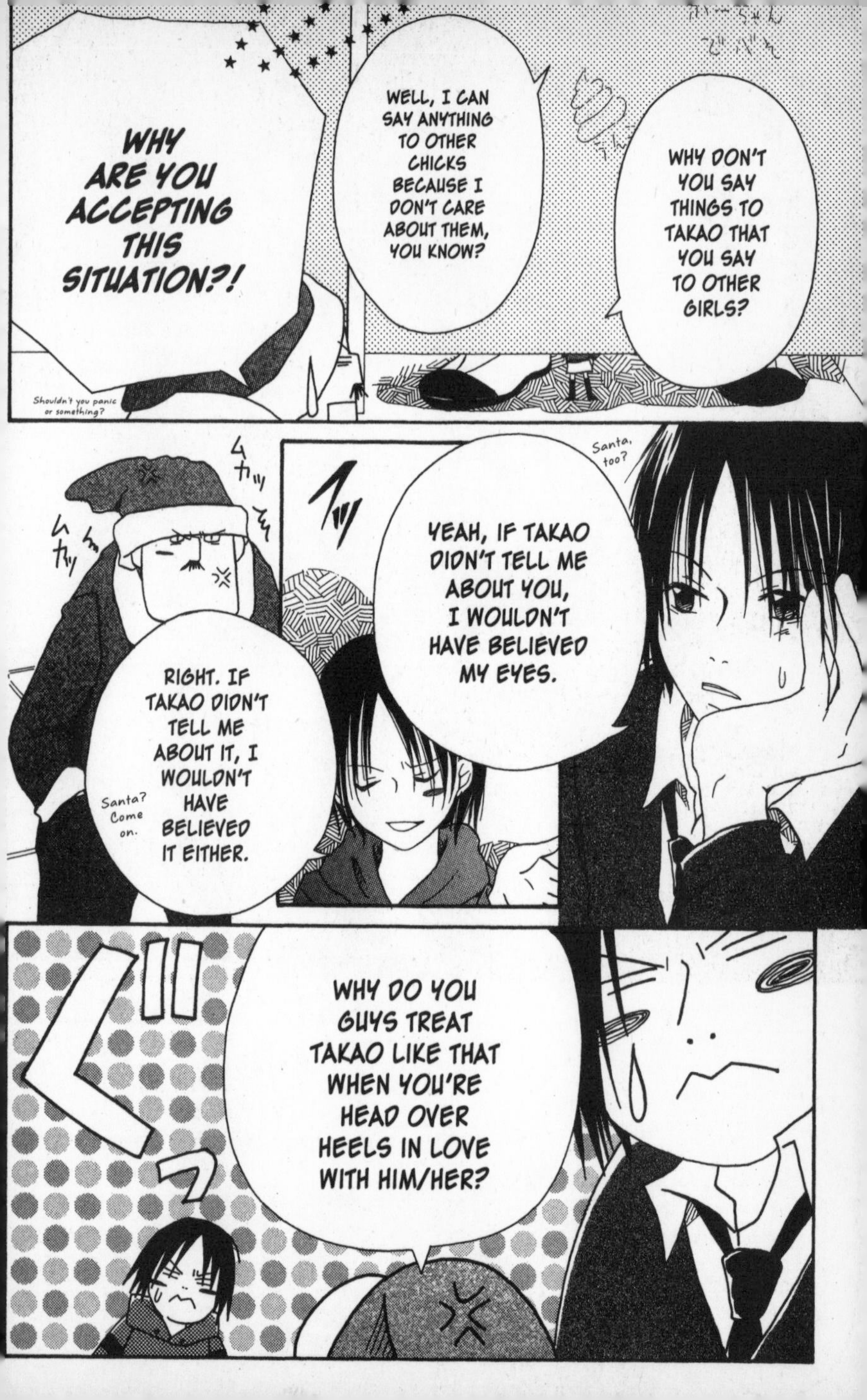
WHY DON'T YOU SAY THINGS TO TAKAO THAT YOU SAY TO OTHER GIRLS?
WELL, I CAN SAY ANYTHING TO OTHER CHICKS BECAUSE I DON'T CARE ABOUT THEM, YOU KNOW?
WHY ARE YOU ACCEPTING THIS SITUATION?!
Shouldn't you panic or something?
Santa, too?
YEAH, IF TAKAO DIDN'T TELL ME ABOUT YOU, I WOULDN'T HAVE BELIEVED MY EYES.
RIGHT. IF TAKAO DIDN'T TELL ME ABOUT IT, I WOULDN'T HAVE BELIEVED IT EITHER.
Santa? Come on.
WHY DO YOU GUYS TREAT TAKAO LIKE THAT WHEN YOU'RE HEAD OVER HEELS IN LOVE WITH HIM/HER?

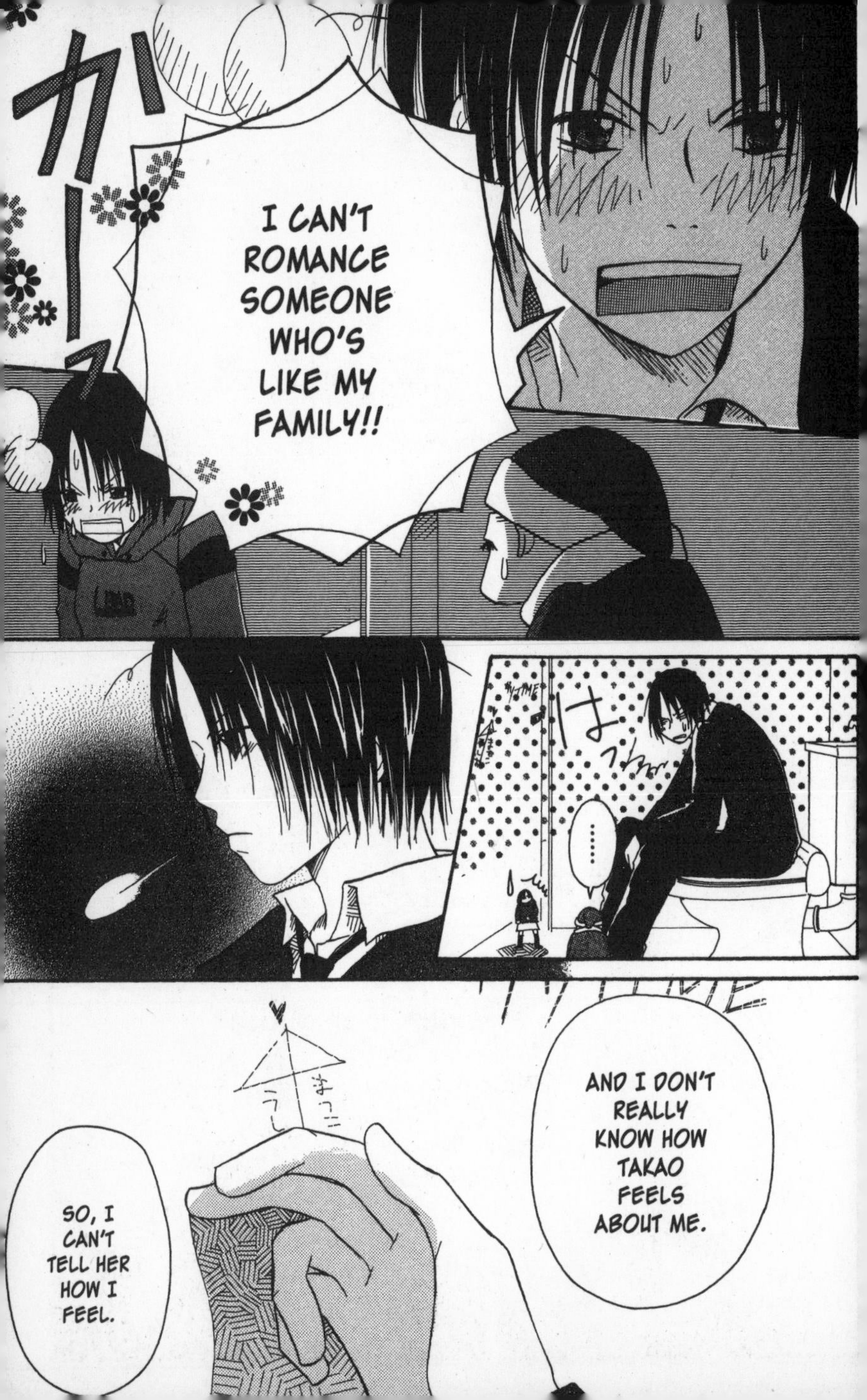
I CAN'T ROMANCE SOMEONE WHO'S LIKE MY FAMILY!!
......
AND I DON'T REALLY KNOW HOW TAKAO FEELS ABOUT ME.
SO, I CAN'T TELL HER HOW I FEEL.

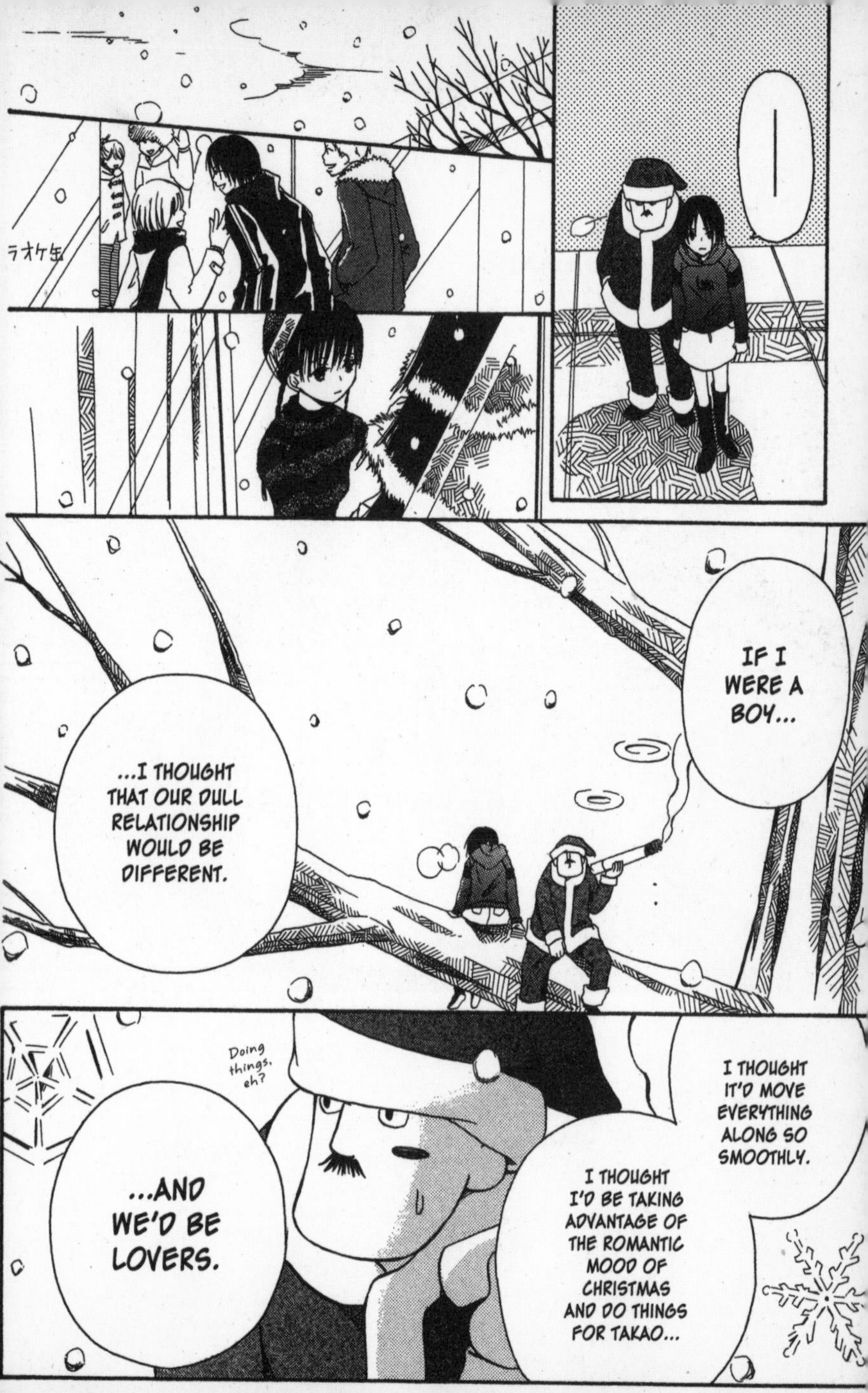
IF I WERE A BOY...
...I THOUGHT THAT OUR DULL RELATIONSHIP WOULD BE DIFFERENT.
I THOUGHT IT'D MOVE EVERYTHING ALONG SO SMOOTHLY.
I THOUGHT I'D BE TAKING ADVANTAGE OF THE ROMANTIC MOOD OF CHRISTMAS AND DO THINGS FOR TAKAO...
Doing things, eh?
...AND WE'D BE LOVERS.

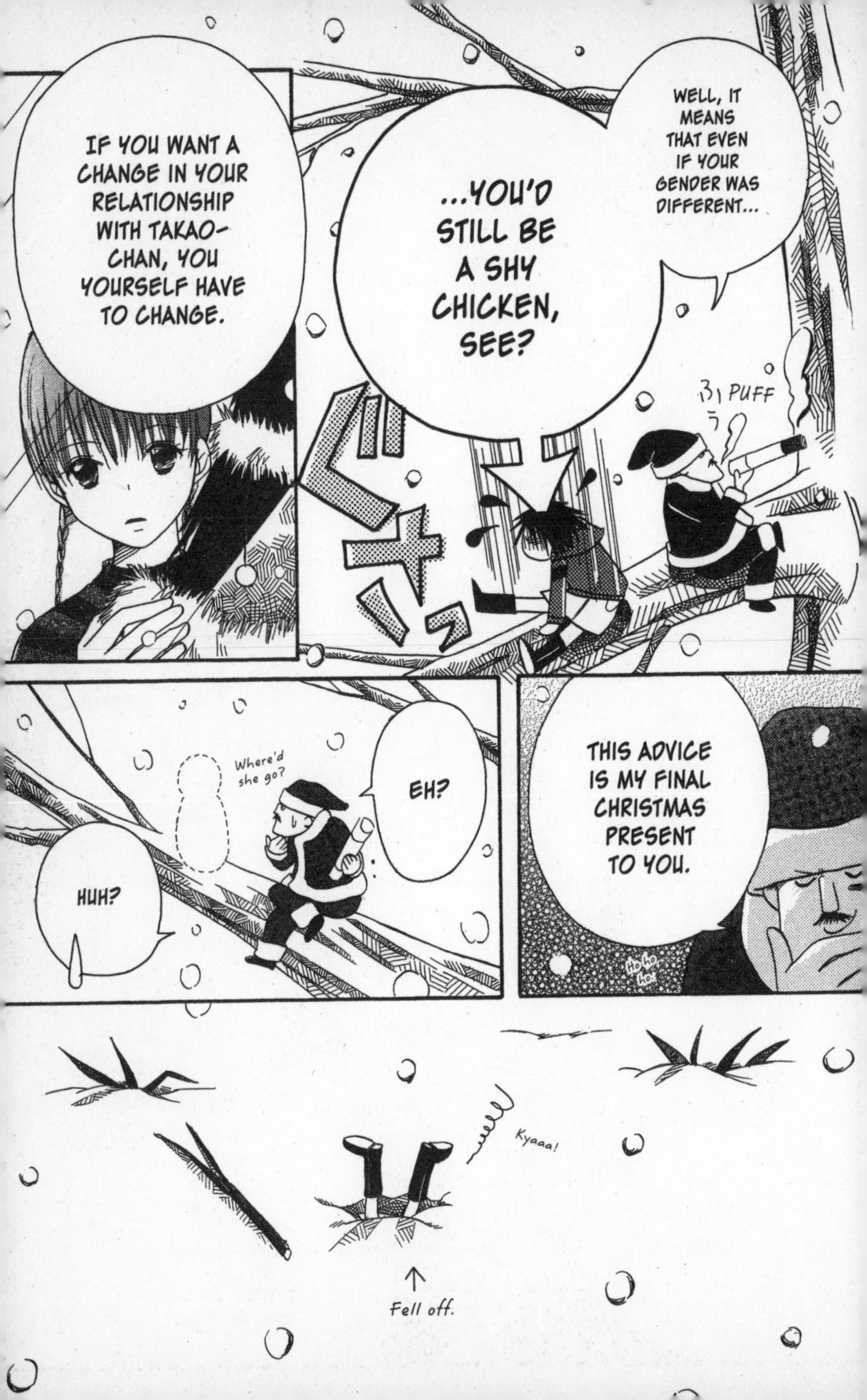
WELL, IT MEANS THAT EVEN IF YOUR GENDER WAS DIFFERENT...
...YOU'D STILL BE A SHY CHICKEN, SEE?
PUFF
IF YOU WANT A CHANGE IN YOUR RELATIONSHIP WITH TAKAO-CHAN, YOU YOURSELF HAVE TO CHANGE.
THIS ADVICE IS MY FINAL CHRISTMAS PRESENT TO YOU.
Ho ho ho.
EH?
Where'd she go?
HUH?
Kyaaa!
Fell off.

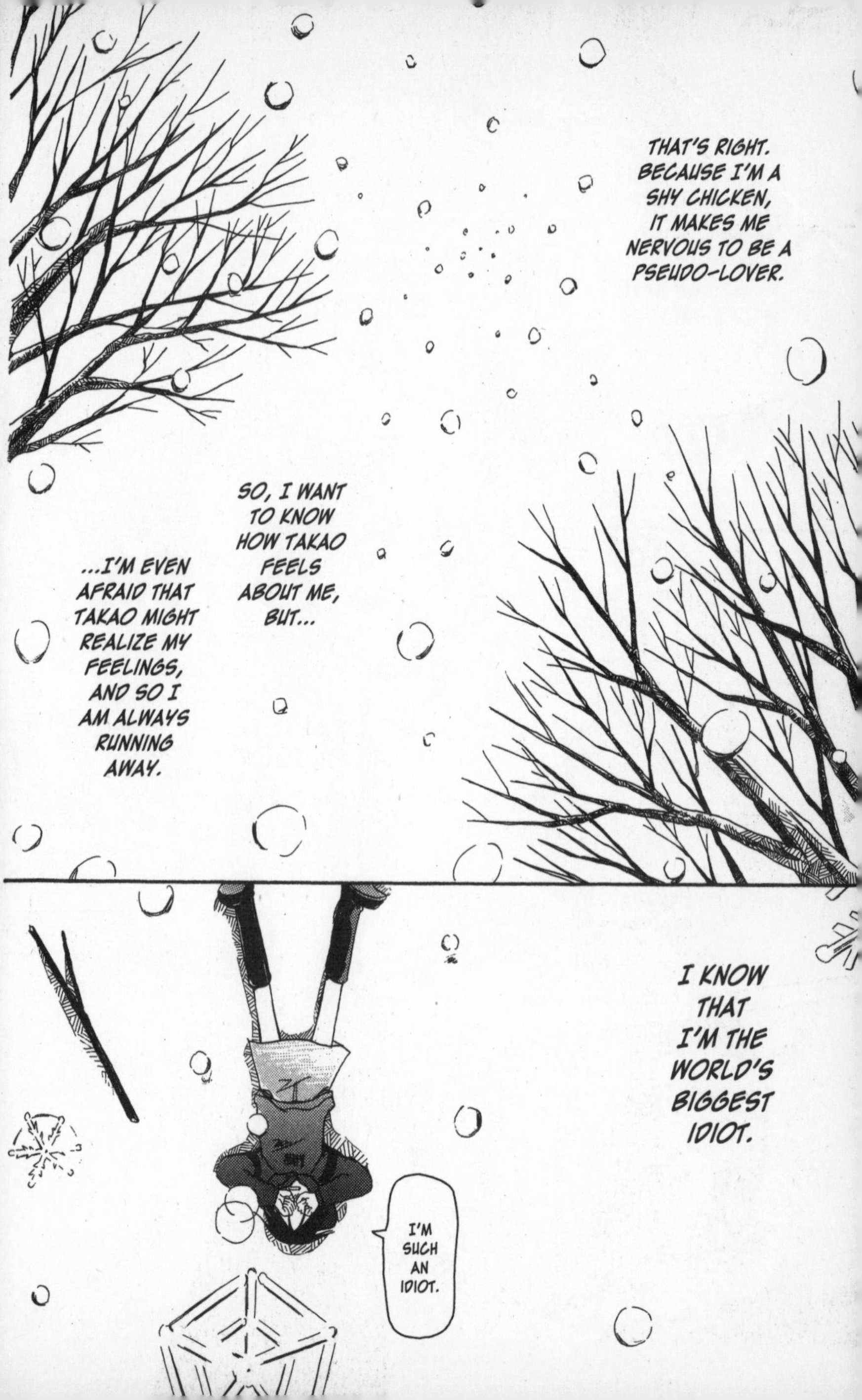
THAT'S RIGHT. BECAUSE I'M A SHY CHICKEN, IT MAKES ME NERVOUS TO BE A PSEUDO-LOVER.
SO, I WANT TO KNOW HOW TAKAO FEELS ABOUT ME, BUT...
...I'M EVEN AFRAID THAT TAKAO MIGHT REALIZE MY FEELINGS, AND SO I AM ALWAYS RUNNING AWAY.
I KNOW THAT I'M THE WORLD'S BIGGEST IDIOT.
I'M SUCH AN IDIOT.

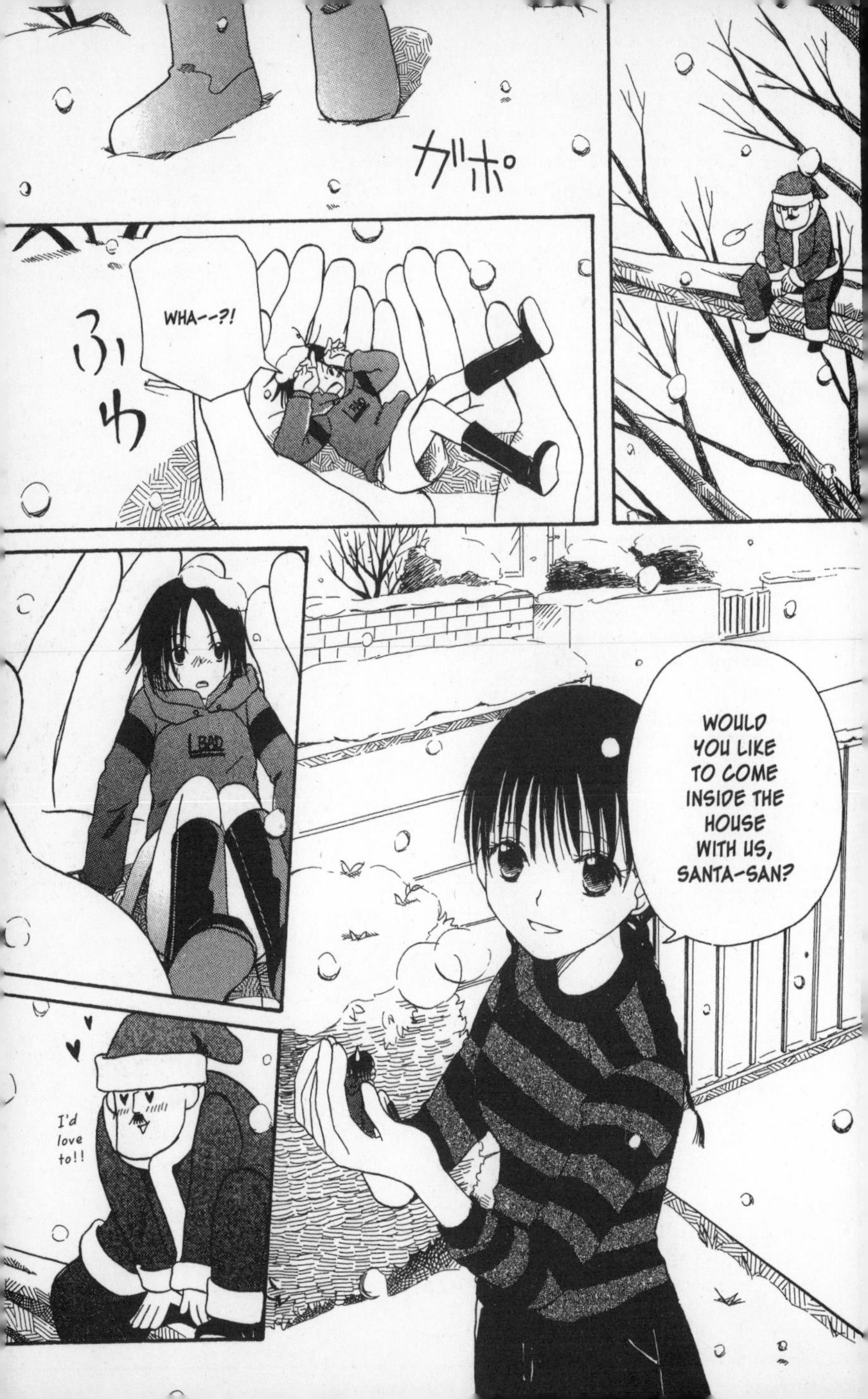
ガポ
WHA--?!
ふわ
WOULD YOU LIKE TO COME INSIDE THE HOUSE WITH US, SANTA-SAN?
I'd love to!!

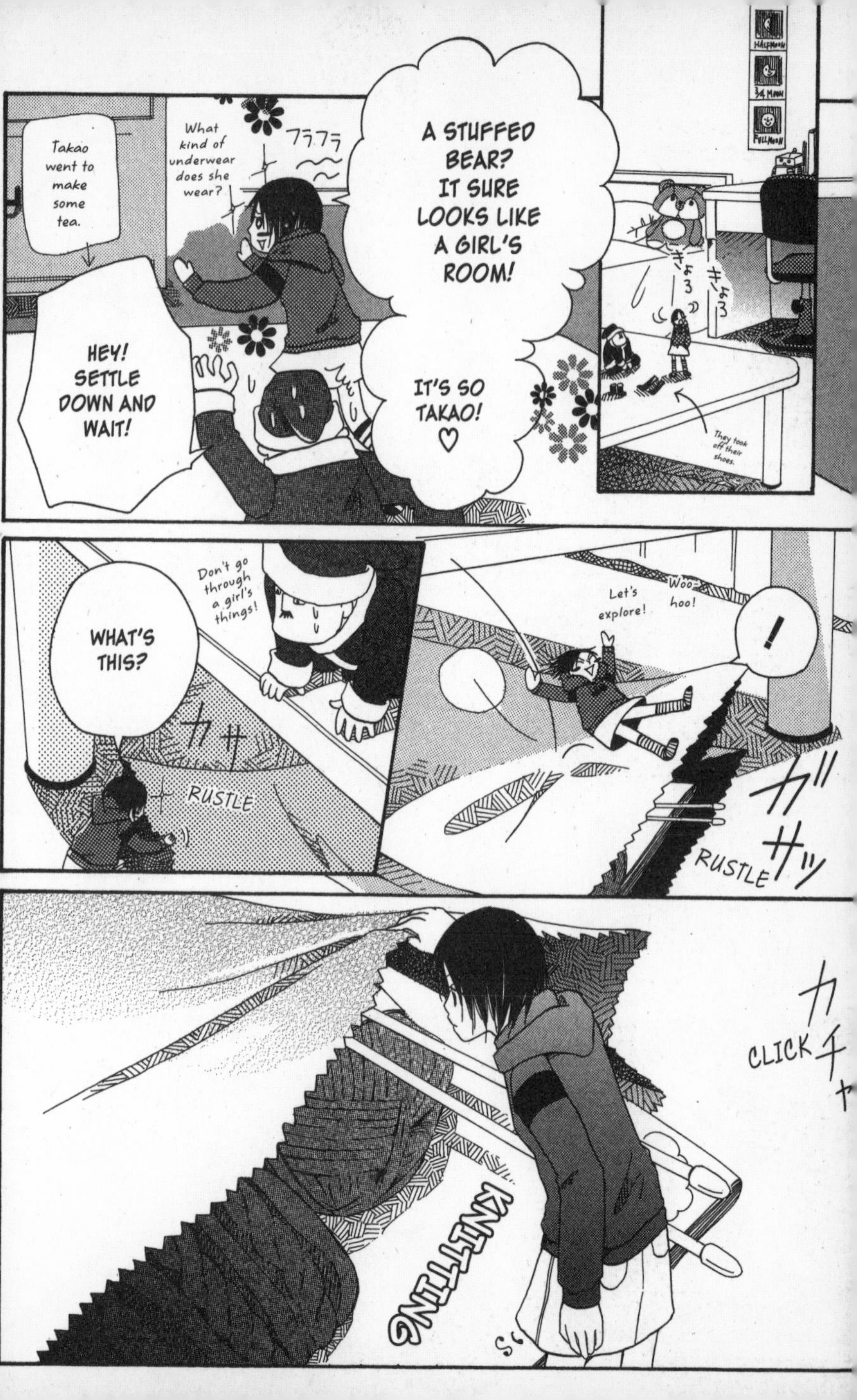

きょろきょろ
They took off their shoes.
A STUFFED BEAR? IT SURE LOOKS LIKE A GIRL'S ROOM!
IT'S SO TAKAO! ♡
フラフラ
What kind of underwear does she wear?
Takao went to make some tea.
HEY! SETTLE DOWN AND WAIT!
!
Woo-hoo!
Let's explore!
ガサッ
RUSTLE
Don't go through a girl's things!
WHAT'S THIS?
カサ
RUSTLE
カチャ
CLICK
KNITTING

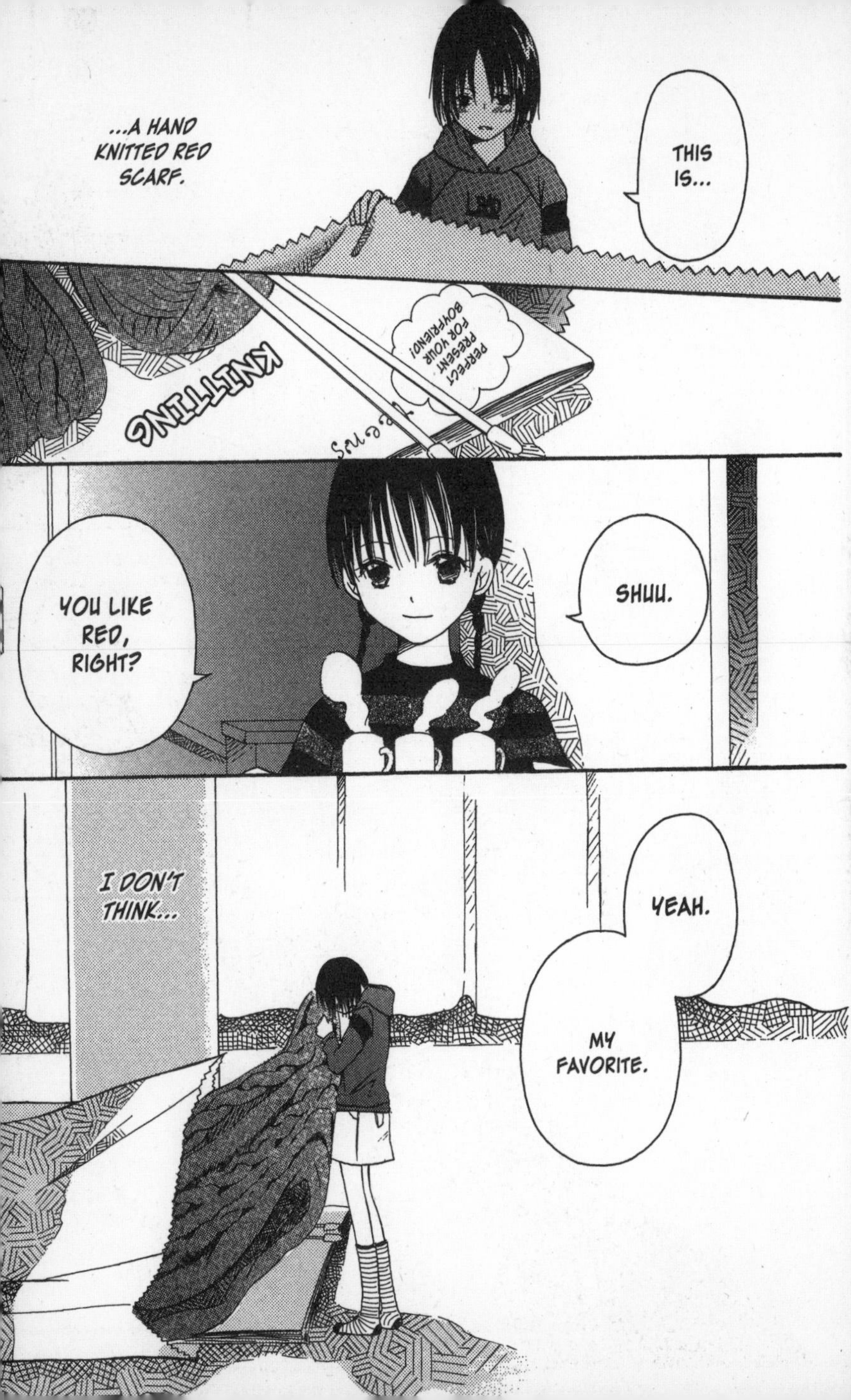
THIS IS...
...A HAND KNITTED RED SCARF.
PERFECT PRESENT FOR YOUR BOYFRIEND!
KNITTING
SHUU.
YOU LIKE RED, RIGHT?
YEAH.
MY FAVORITE.
I DON'T THINK...

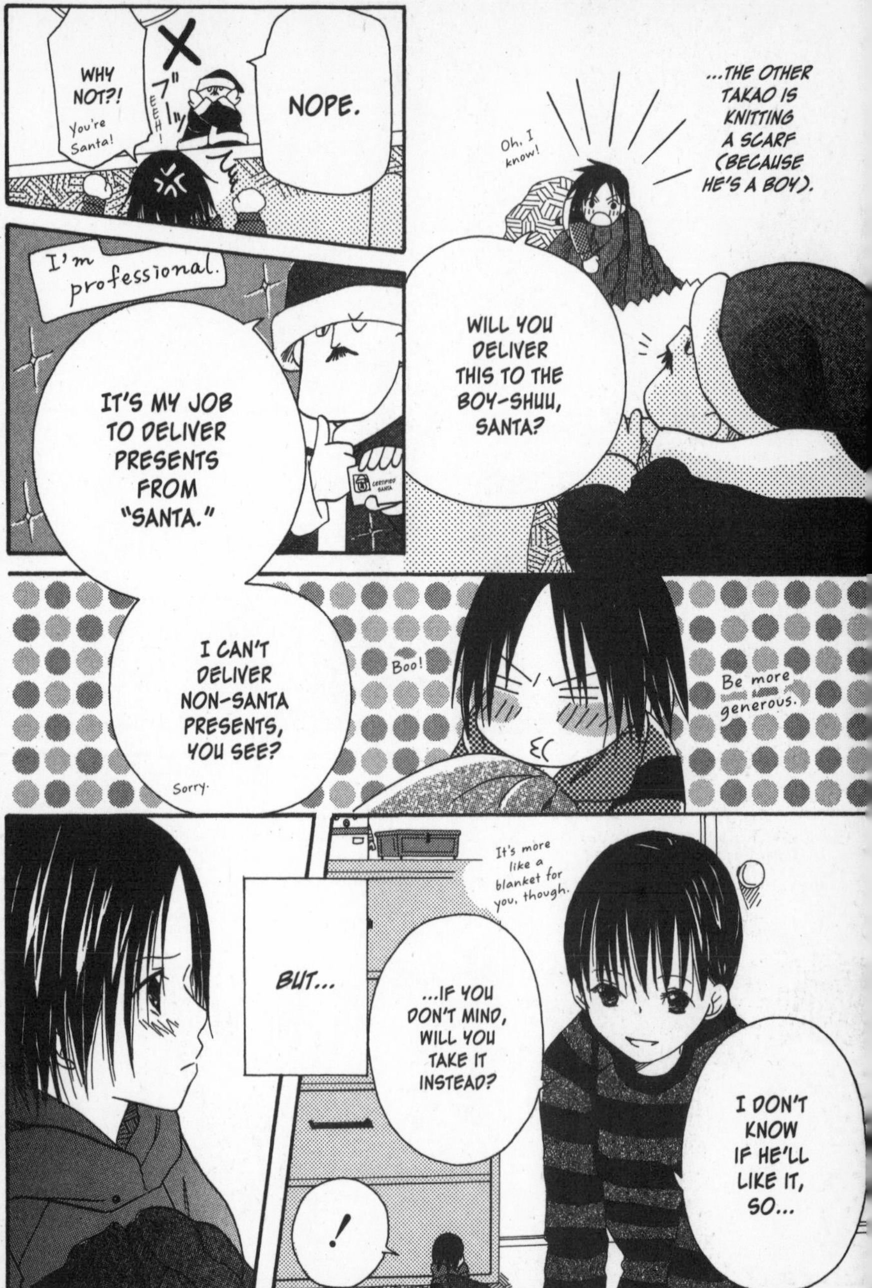
...THE OTHER TAKAO IS KNITTING A SCARF (BECAUSE HE'S A BOY).
Oh, I know!
NOPE.
EEEH!
WHY NOT?!
You're Santa!
WILL YOU DELIVER THIS TO THE BOY-SHUU, SANTA?
I'm professional.
IT'S MY JOB TO DELIVER PRESENTS FROM "SANTA."
CERTIFIED SANTA
I CAN'T DELIVER NON-SANTA PRESENTS, YOU SEE?
Sorry.
Be more generous.
Boo!
It's more like a blanket for you, though.
I DON'T KNOW IF HE'LL LIKE IT, SO...
...IF YOU DON'T MIND, WILL YOU TAKE IT INSTEAD?
BUT...
!

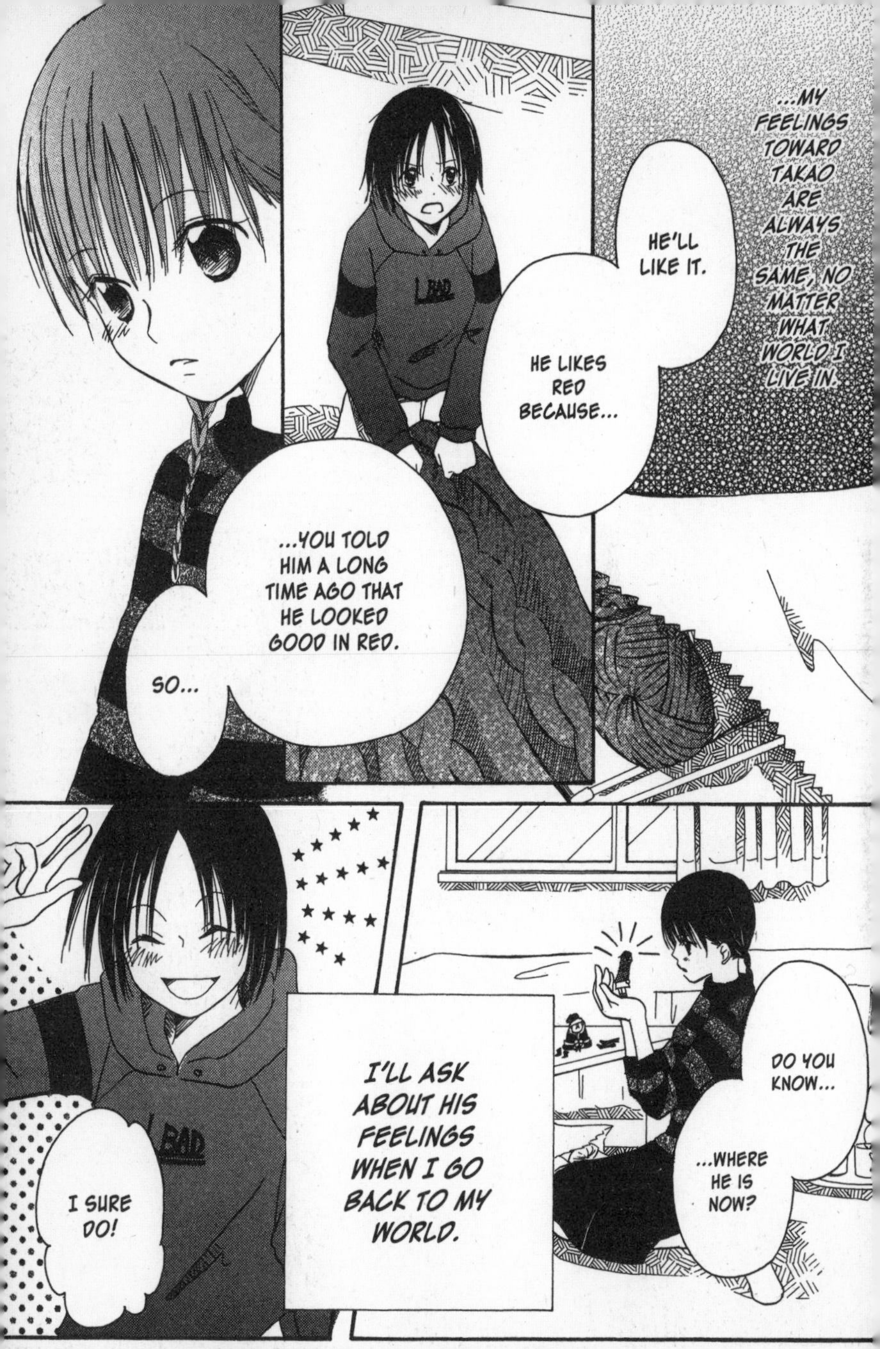
...MY FEELINGS TOWARD TAKAO ARE ALWAYS THE SAME, NO MATTER WHAT WORLD I LIVE IN.
HE'LL LIKE IT.
HE LIKES RED BECAUSE...
...YOU TOLD HIM A LONG TIME AGO THAT HE LOOKED GOOD IN RED.
SO...
DO YOU KNOW...
...WHERE HE IS NOW?
I SURE DO!
I'LL ASK ABOUT HIS FEELINGS WHEN I GO BACK TO MY WORLD.

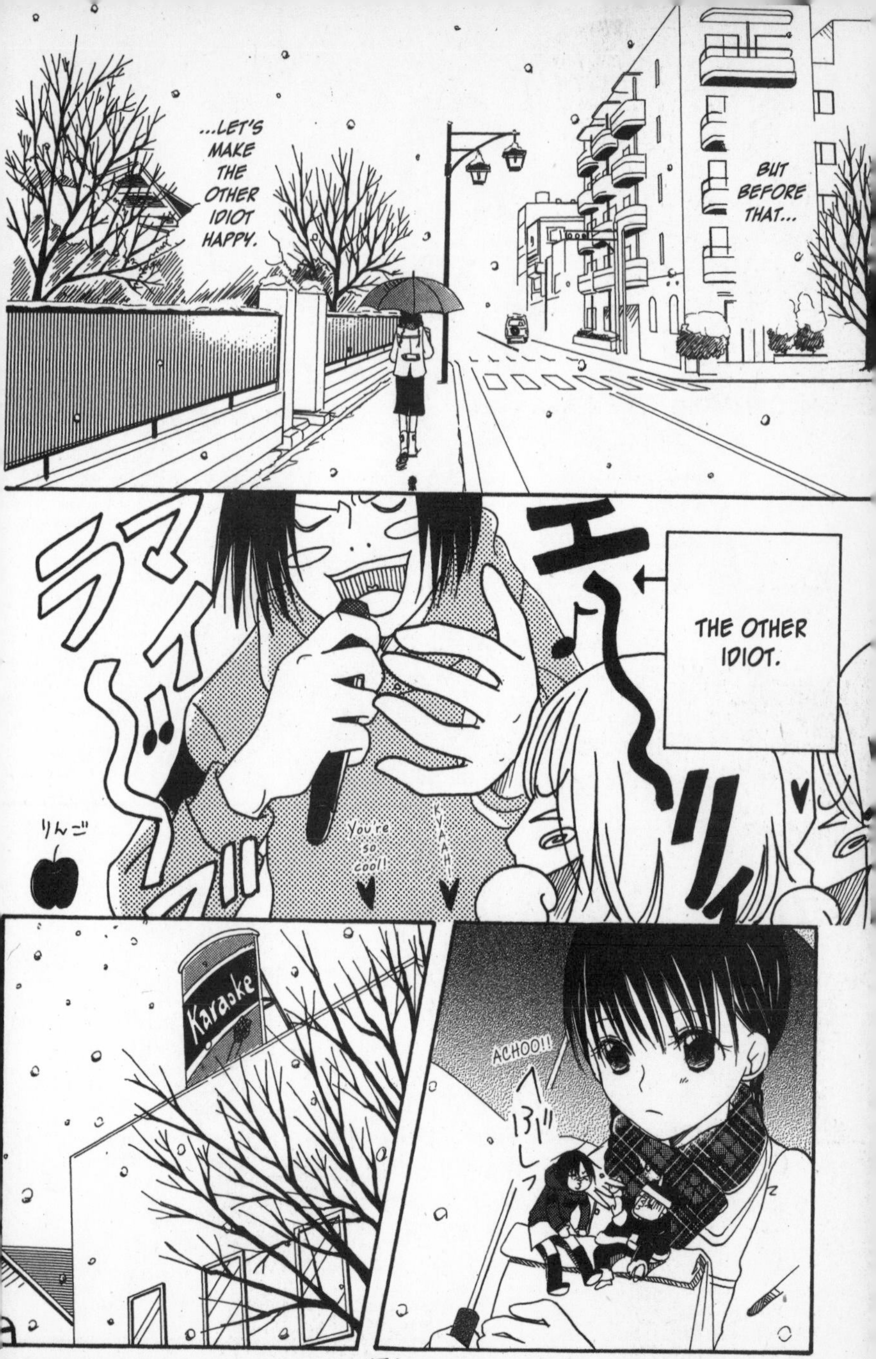
BUT BEFORE THAT...
...LET'S MAKE THE OTHER IDIOT HAPPY.
THE OTHER IDIOT.
KYAAAH!
You're so cool!
りんご
ACHOO!!
Karaoke

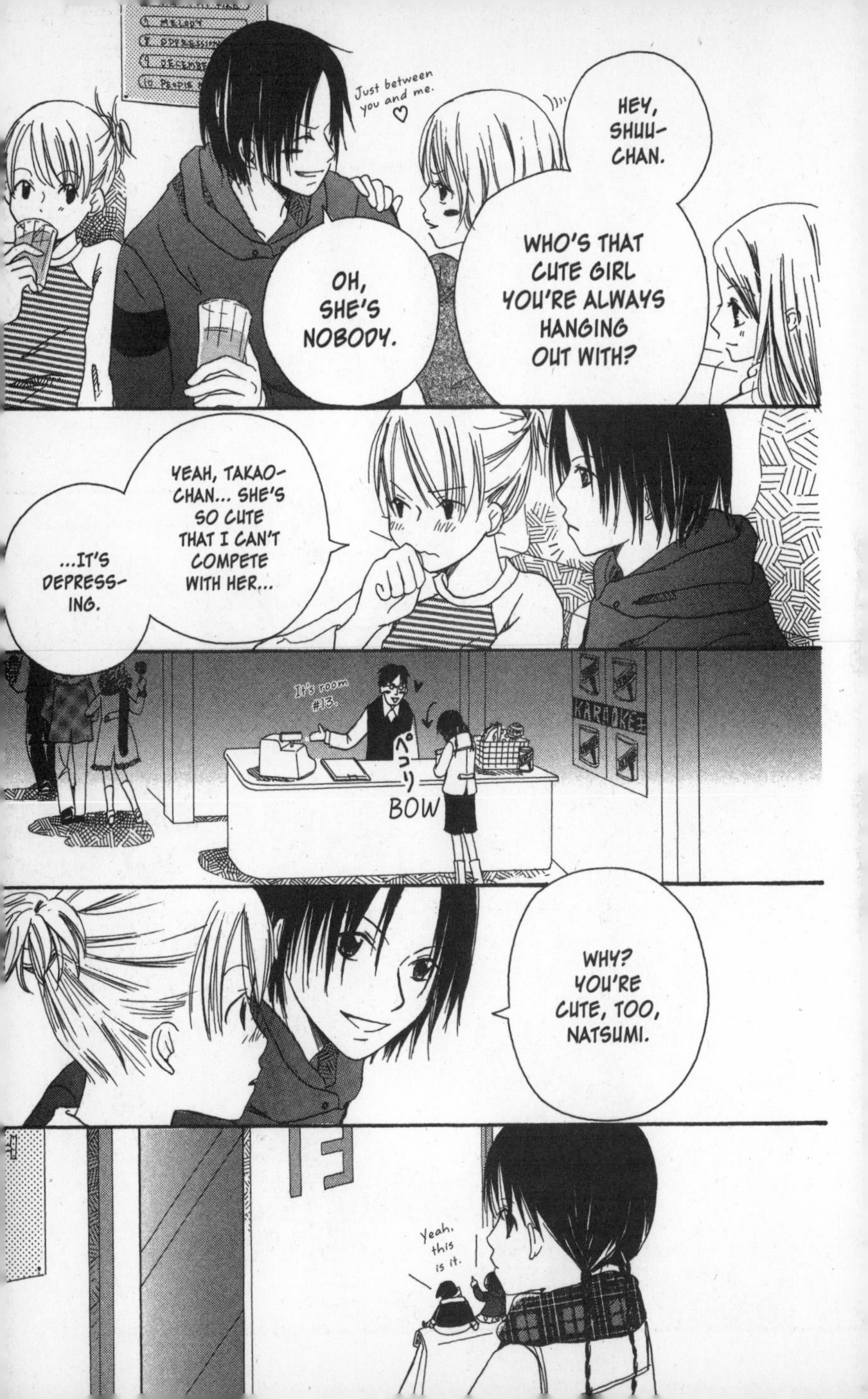
HEY, SHUU-CHAN.
WHO'S THAT CUTE GIRL YOU'RE ALWAYS HANGING OUT WITH?
Just between you and me. ♡
OH, SHE'S NOBODY.
YEAH, TAKAO-CHAN... SHE'S SO CUTE THAT I CAN'T COMPETE WITH HER...
...IT'S DEPRESS-ING.
KARAOKE
It's room #13.
ペコリ
BOW
WHY? YOU'RE CUTE, TOO, NATSUMI.
Yeah, this is it.

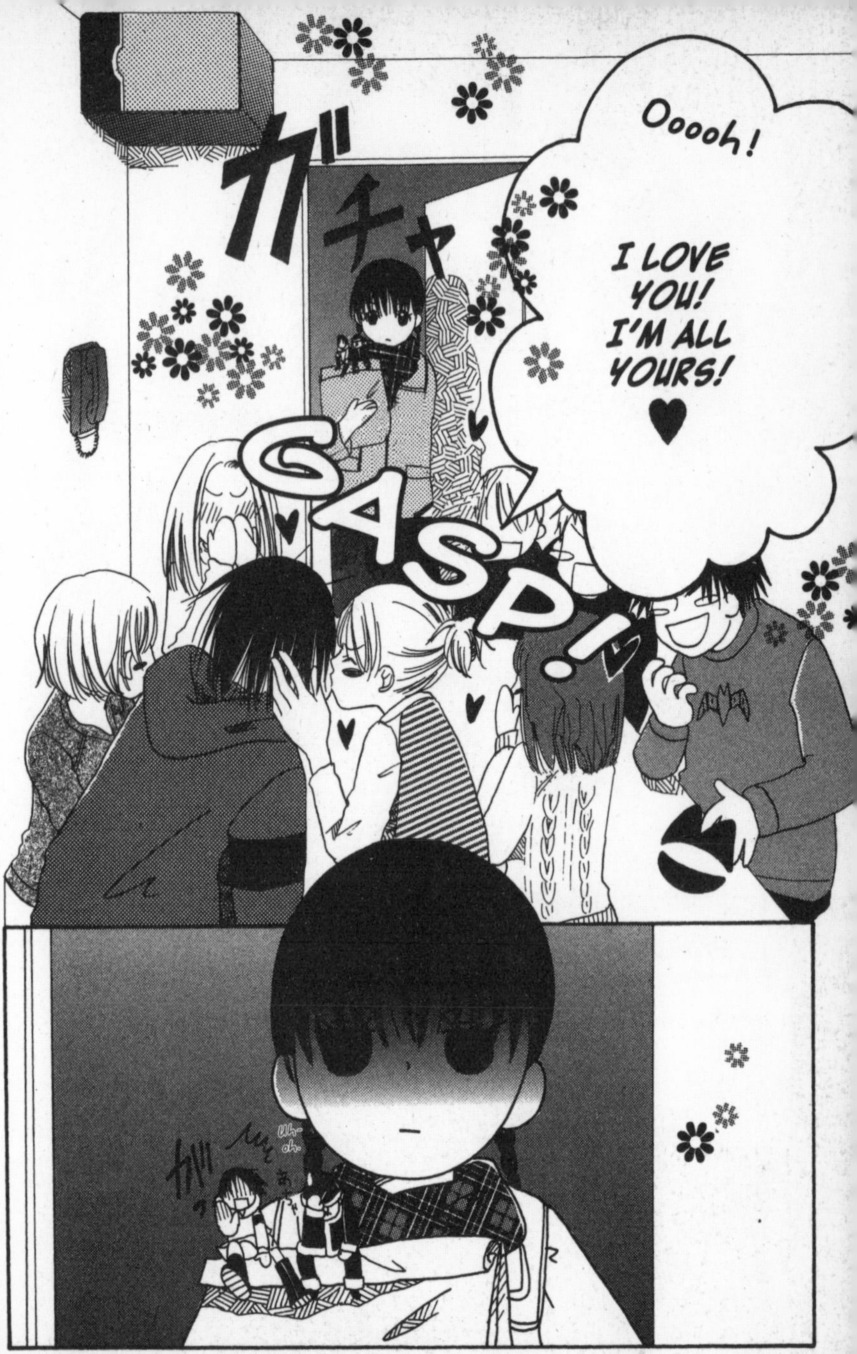
Ooooh!
I LOVE YOU! I'M ALL YOURS! ♥
ガチャ
GASP!
Uh-oh.

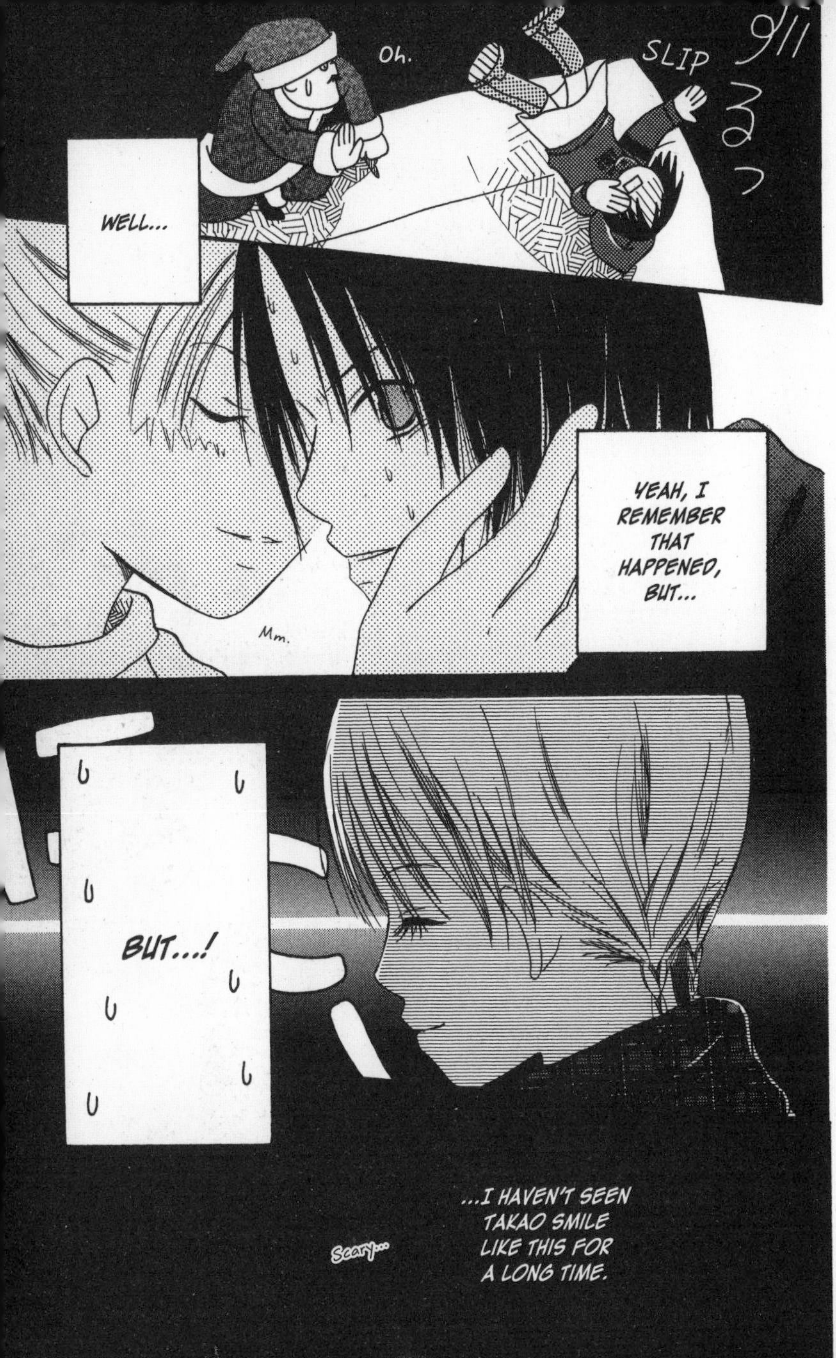
SLIP
Oh.
WELL...
YEAH, I REMEMBER THAT HAPPENED, BUT...
Mm.
BUT...!
...I HAVEN'T SEEN TAKAO SMILE LIKE THIS FOR A LONG TIME.
Scary...

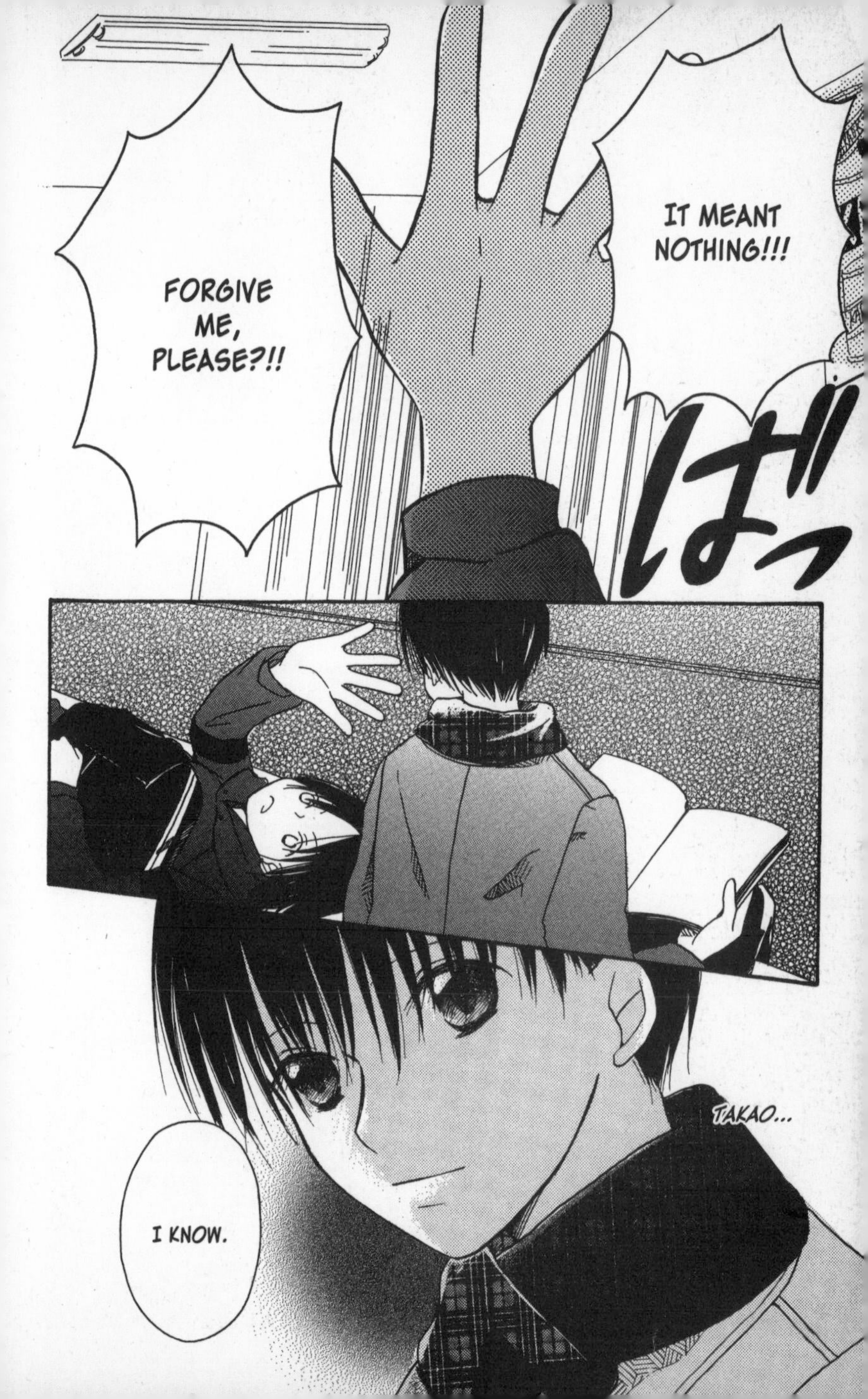
IT MEANT NOTHING!!!
FORGIVE ME, PLEASE?!!
ばっ
TAKAO...
I KNOW.

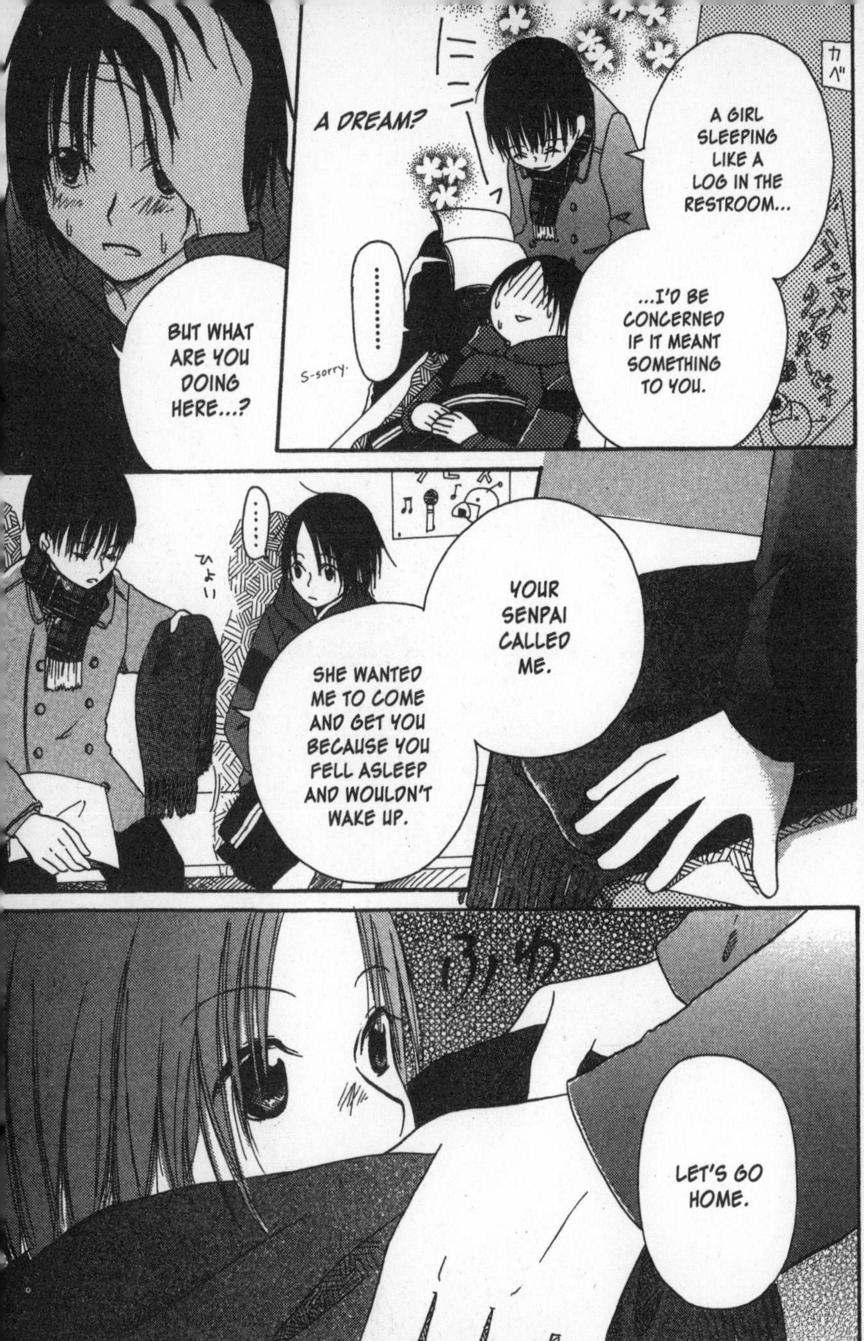
カベ
A GIRL SLEEPING LIKE A LOG IN THE RESTROOM...
A DREAM?
...I'D BE CONCERNED IF IT MEANT SOMETHING TO YOU.
......
S-sorry.
BUT WHAT ARE YOU DOING HERE...?
YOUR SENPAI CALLED ME.
SHE WANTED ME TO COME AND GET YOU BECAUSE YOU FELL ASLEEP AND WOULDN'T WAKE UP.
......
ひょい
ふわ
LET'S GO HOME.

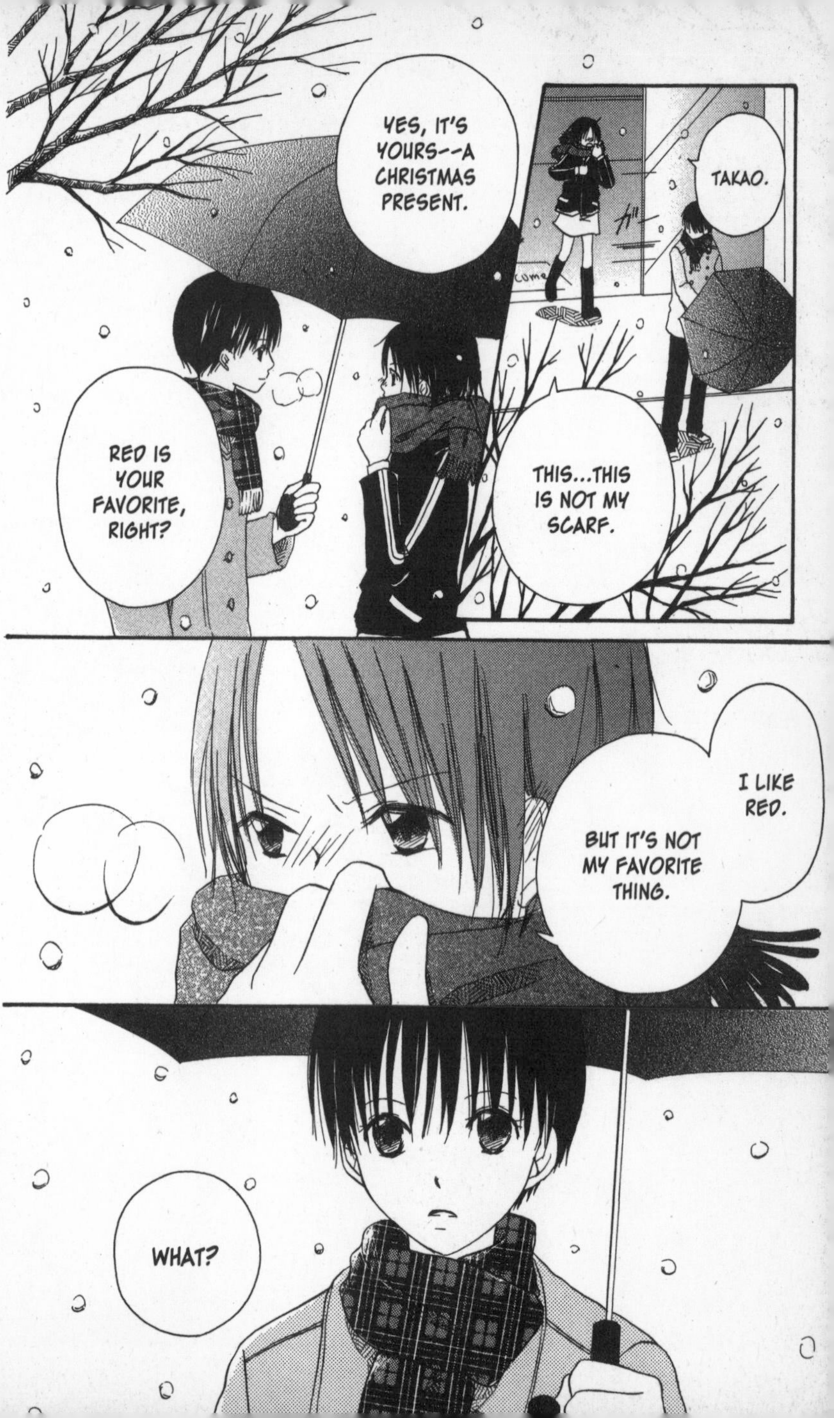
TAKAO.
THIS...THIS IS NOT MY SCARF.
YES, IT'S YOURS--A CHRISTMAS PRESENT.
RED IS YOUR FAVORITE, RIGHT?
I LIKE RED.
BUT IT'S NOT MY FAVORITE THING.
WHAT?

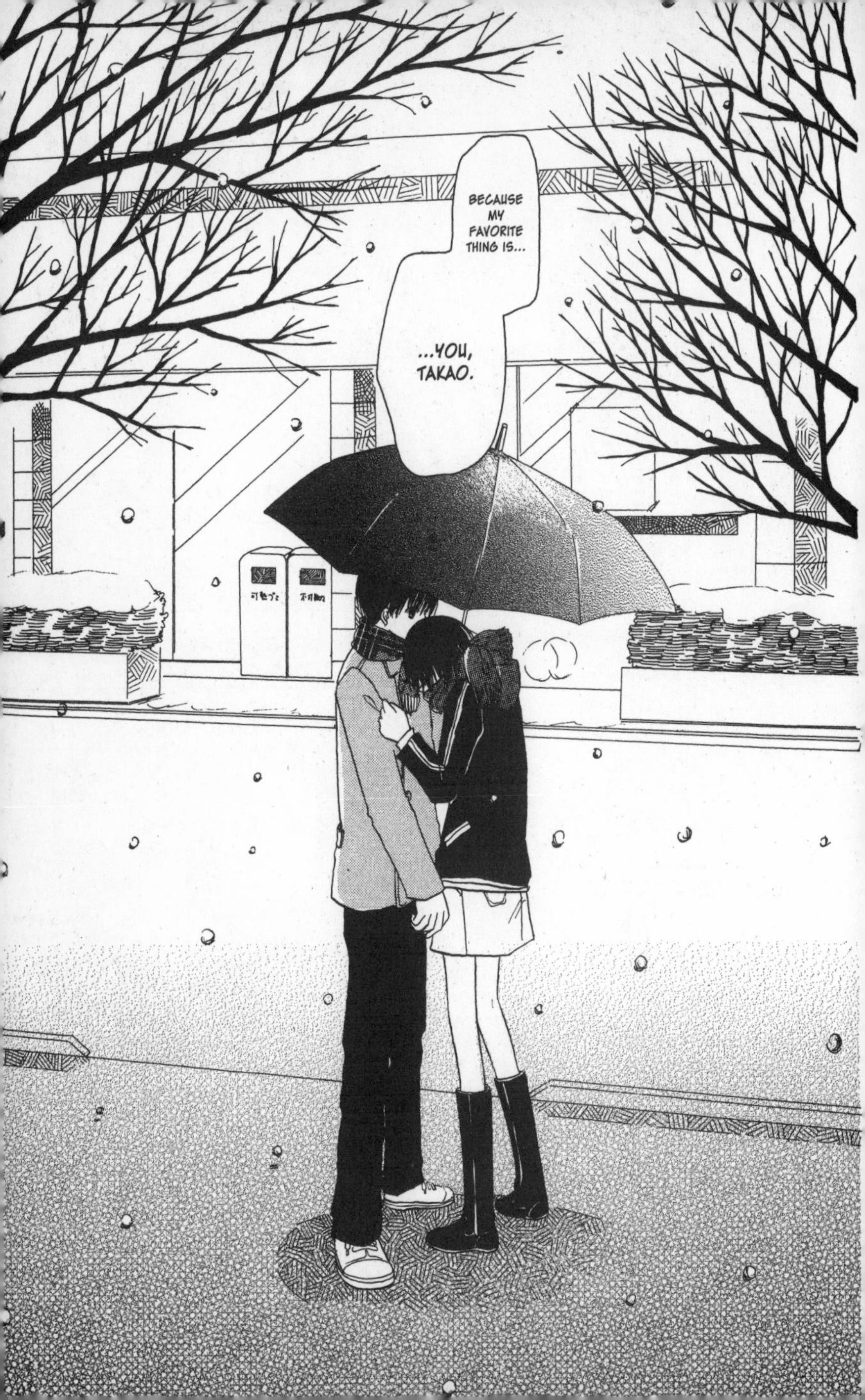
BECAUSE MY FAVORITE THING IS...
...YOU, TAKAO.

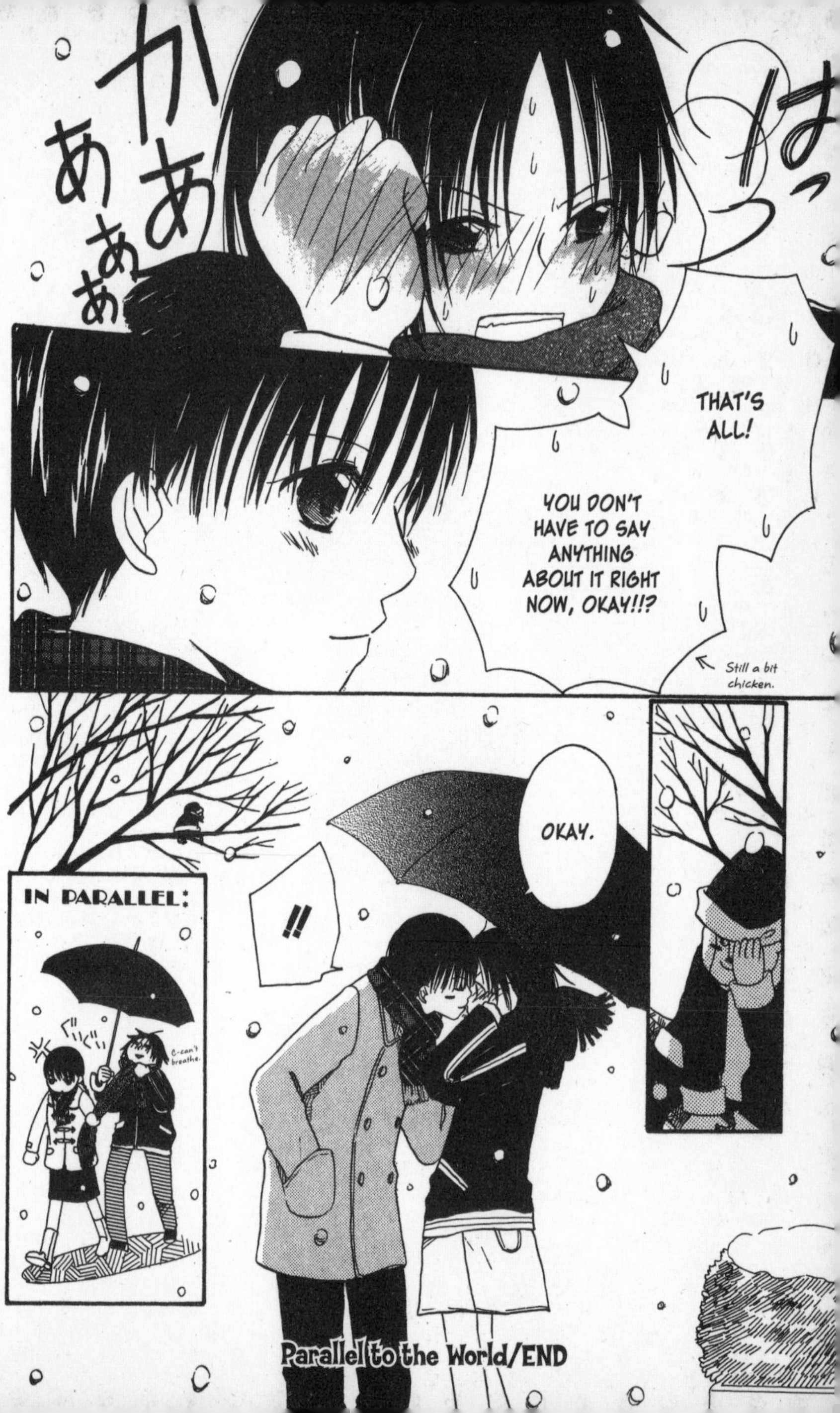
はっ
かああああ
THAT'S ALL!
YOU DON'T HAVE TO SAY ANYTHING ABOUT IT RIGHT NOW, OKAY!!?
Still a bit chicken.
OKAY.
!!
IN PARALLEL:
ぐいぐい
C-can't breathe.

Parallel to the World/END

Bonus Page

PLEASE READ IT IF YOU HAVE SOME FREE TIME.

Good job, everyone. It's almost the end of this manga. I wrote things I wanted in the columns, so I'll make some "bonus manga" after this page. It's a children's version of *Me & My Brothers*. To be honest, it was really easy to draw children. I was relaxed about the story, too, because it's a "bonus." I had fun. Well, thank you so much for staying with me this far!!!

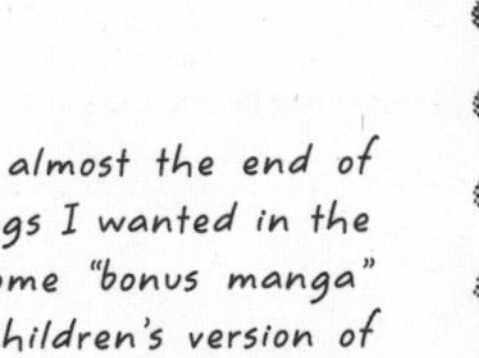

Announcement like a sales call.

If you'd like to send me comments about my book, here's the address:
Hyun Joo Kim
TOKYOPOP
5900 Wilshire Blvd #2000
Los Angeles, CA 90036

Hari Tokeino

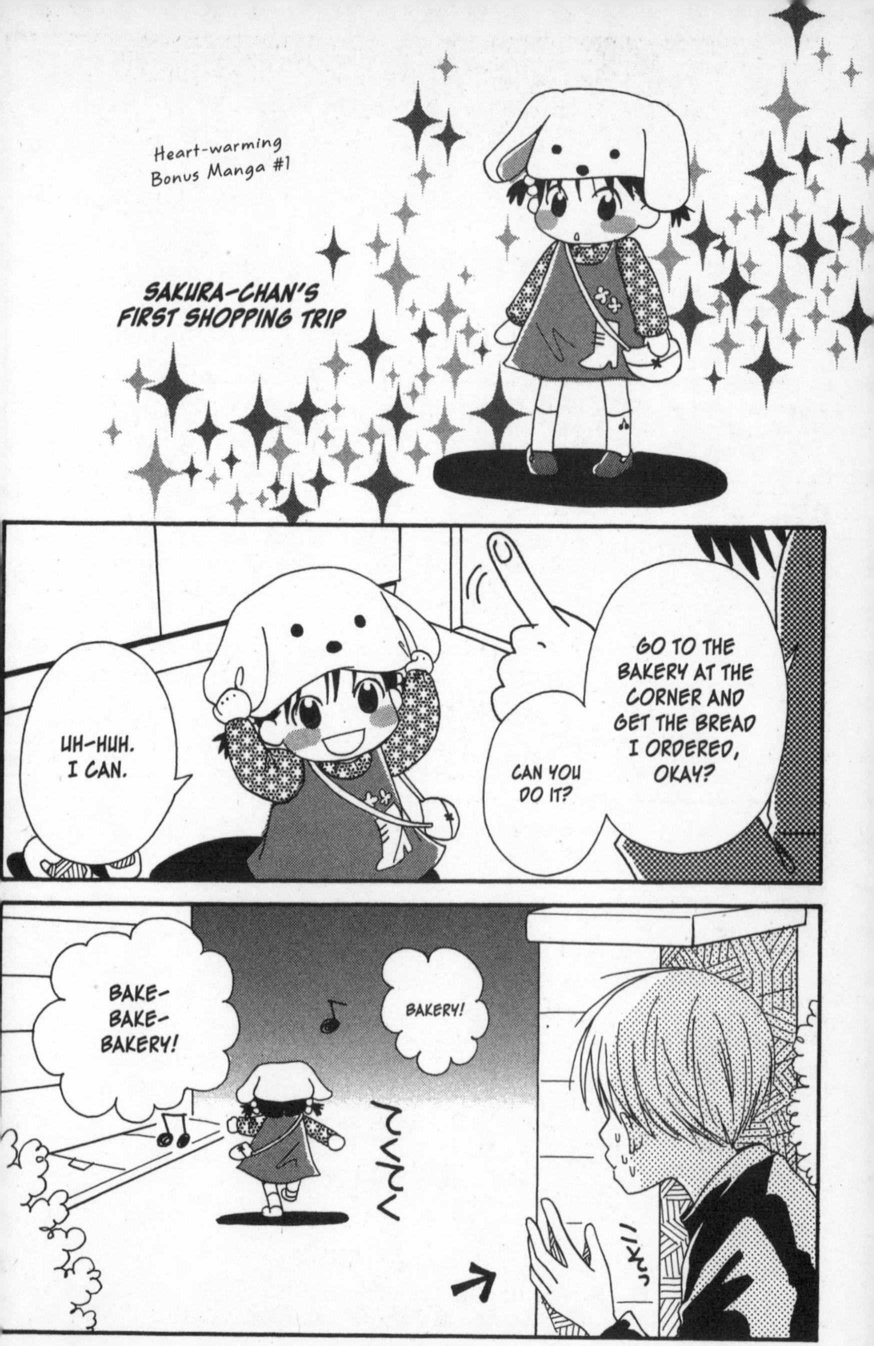
Heart-warming Bonus Manga #1
SAKURA-CHAN'S FIRST SHOPPING TRIP
GO TO THE BAKERY AT THE CORNER AND GET THE BREAD I ORDERED, OKAY?
CAN YOU DO IT?
UH-HUH. I CAN.
こそっ
てくてく
BAKERY!
BAKE-BAKE-BAKERY!

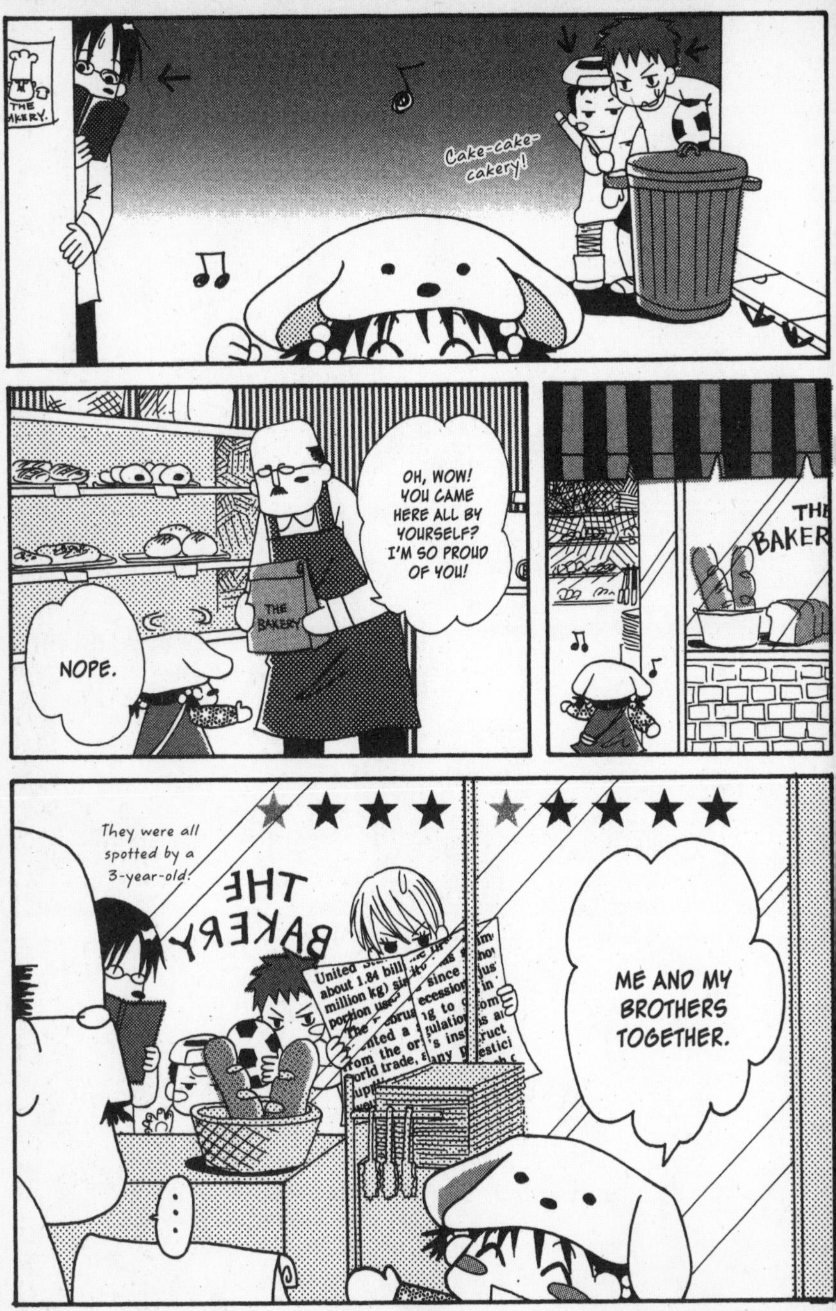
THE BAKERY.
Cake-cake-cakery!
THE BAKER
OH, WOW! YOU CAME HERE ALL BY YOURSELF? I'M SO PROUD OF YOU!
THE BAKERY
NOPE.
ME AND MY BROTHERS TOGETHER.
THE BAKERY
They were all spotted by a 3-year-old!
...

END

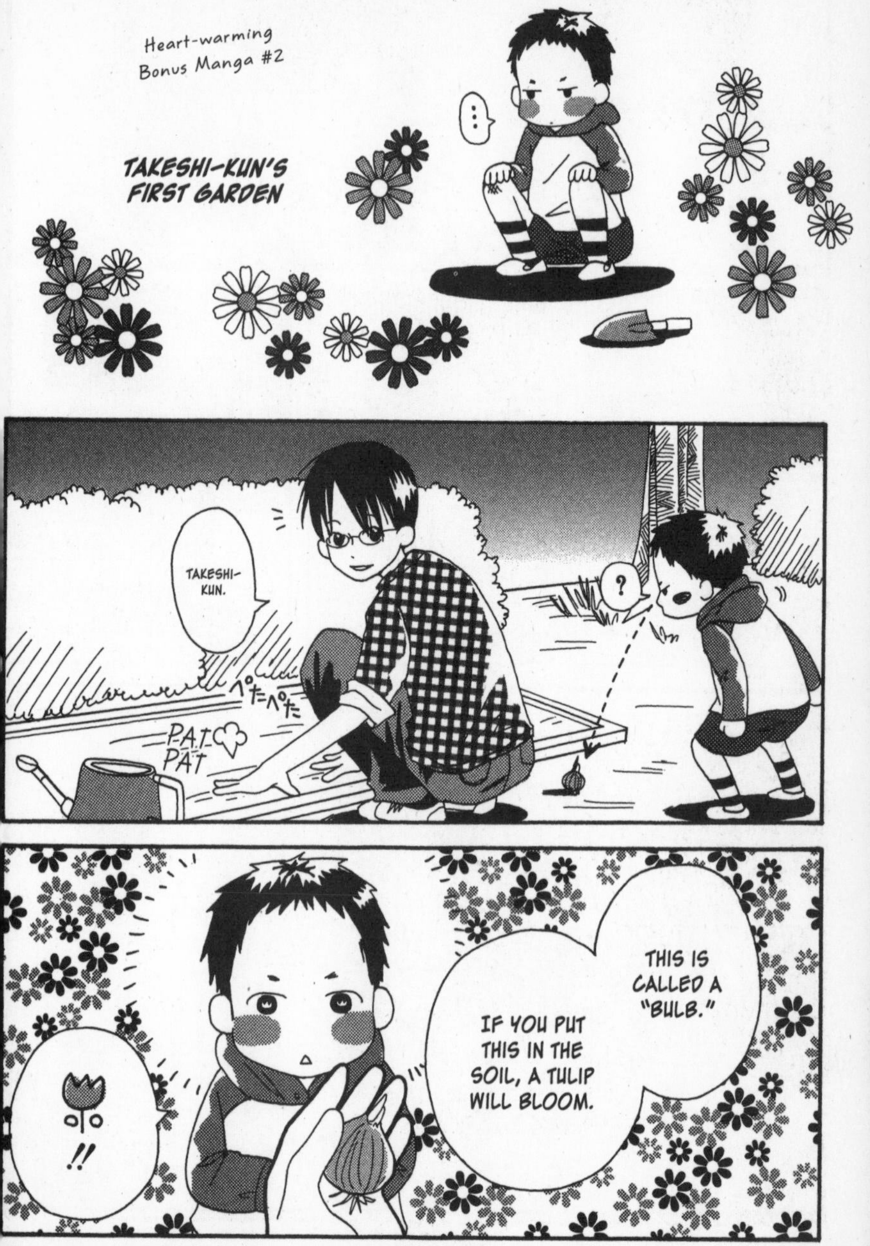
Heart-warming
Bonus Manga #2
TAKESHI-KUN'S FIRST GARDEN
…
TAKESHI-KUN.
ぺたぺた
PAT PAT
?
THIS IS CALLED A "BULB."
IF YOU PUT THIS IN THE SOIL, A TULIP WILL BLOOM.
!!

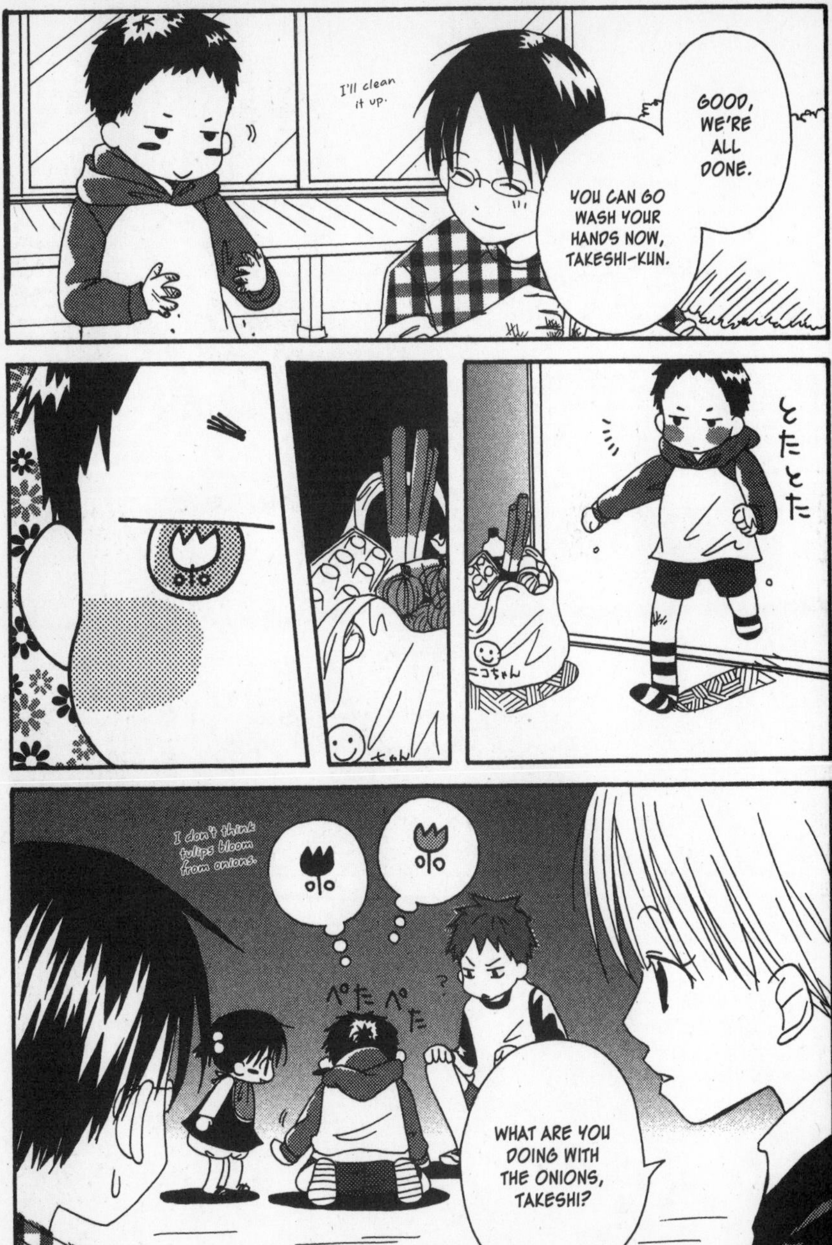
GOOD, WE'RE ALL DONE.
YOU CAN GO WASH YOUR HANDS NOW, TAKESHI-KUN.
I'll clean it up.
とたとた
ニコちゃん
WHAT ARE YOU DOING WITH THE ONIONS, TAKESHI?
ぺたぺた
?
I don't think tulips bloom from onions.

END

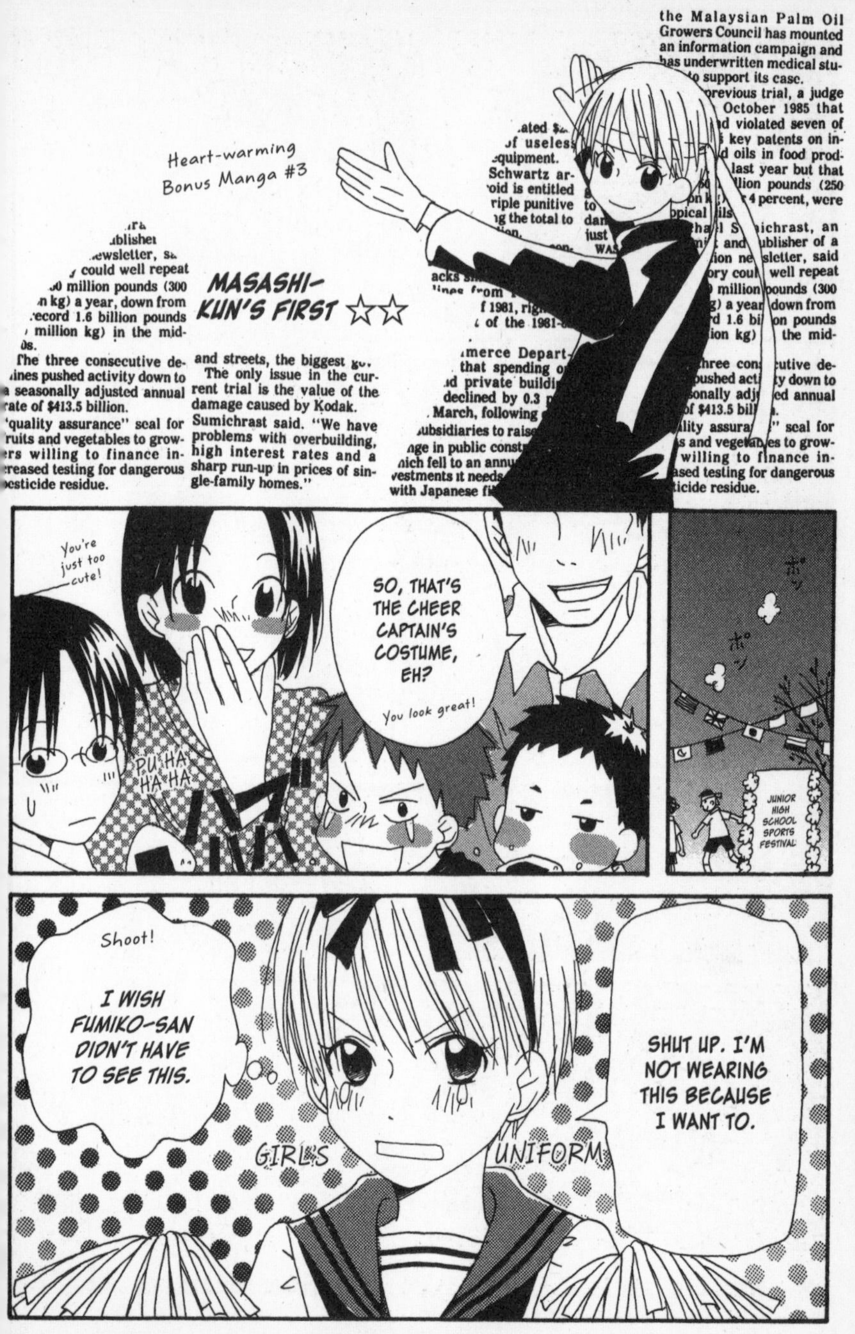
Heart-warming Bonus Manga #3
MASASHI-KUN'S FIRST ☆☆
JUNIOR HIGH SCHOOL SPORTS FESTIVAL
SO, THAT'S THE CHEER CAPTAIN'S COSTUME, EH?
You look great!
You're just too cute!
PU HA HA HA
SHUT UP. I'M NOT WEARING THIS BECAUSE I WANT TO.
GIRL'S UNIFORM
Shoot!
I WISH FUMIKO-SAN DIDN'T HAVE TO SEE THIS.

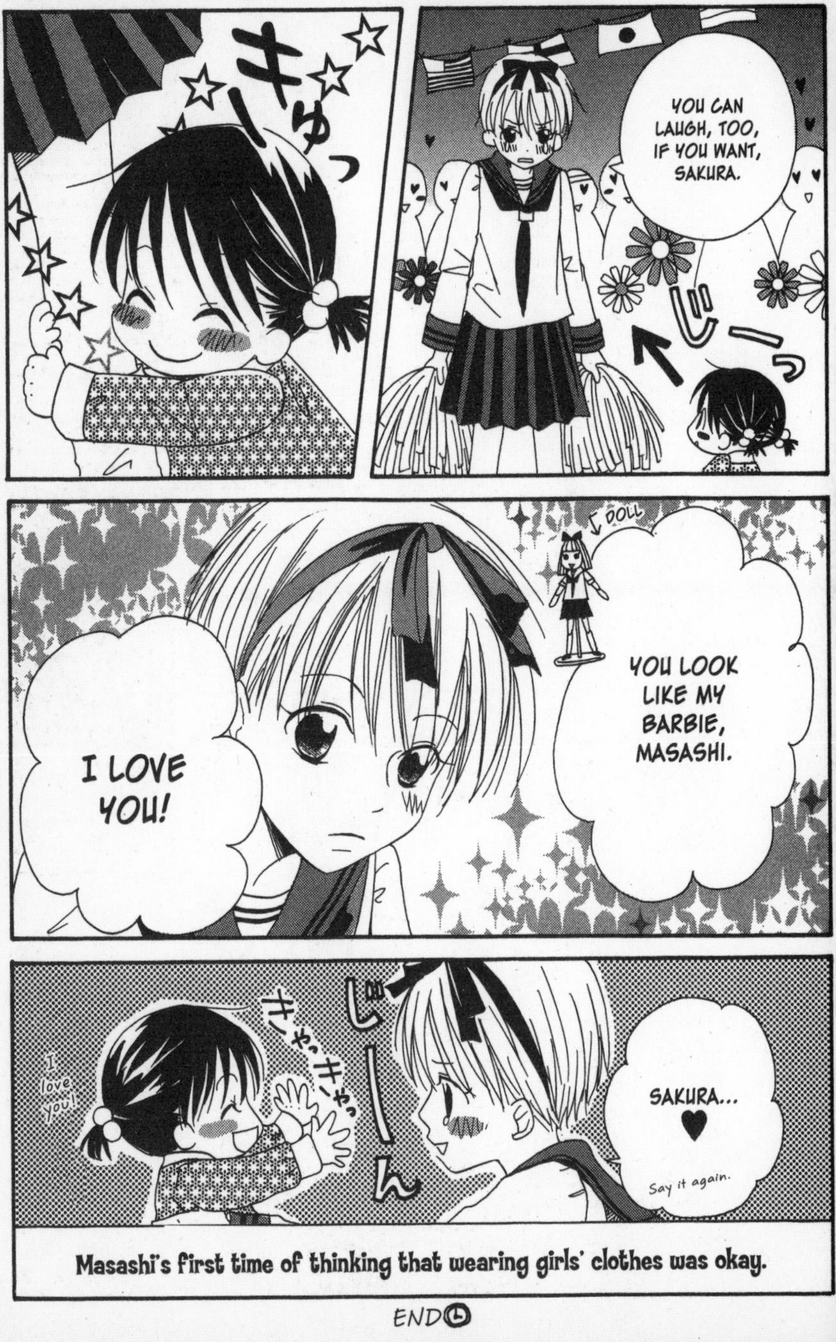
YOU CAN LAUGH, TOO, IF YOU WANT, SAKURA.
じーっ
きゅっ
DOLL
YOU LOOK LIKE MY BARBIE, MASASHI.
I LOVE YOU!
SAKURA... ♥
Say it again.
じーん
きゃっきゃっ
I love you!
Masashi's first time of thinking that wearing girls' clothes was okay.
END

THANKS !!

CHITOCHAN.
EBIKO.
MASAMICHAN.
MIRAIKO. (MISOKO)
YONECHAN. (→ABC)

&

MY FAMILY. (RELATIVE.)

&

MY FRIENDS.

&

KONDOUSAMA.

&

YOU!!

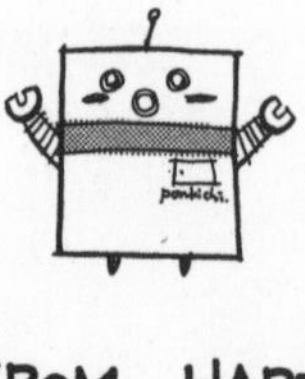
ponkichi.

FROM HARI. 针.

Now please enjoy this

Fruits Basket ™

Volume 17 preview

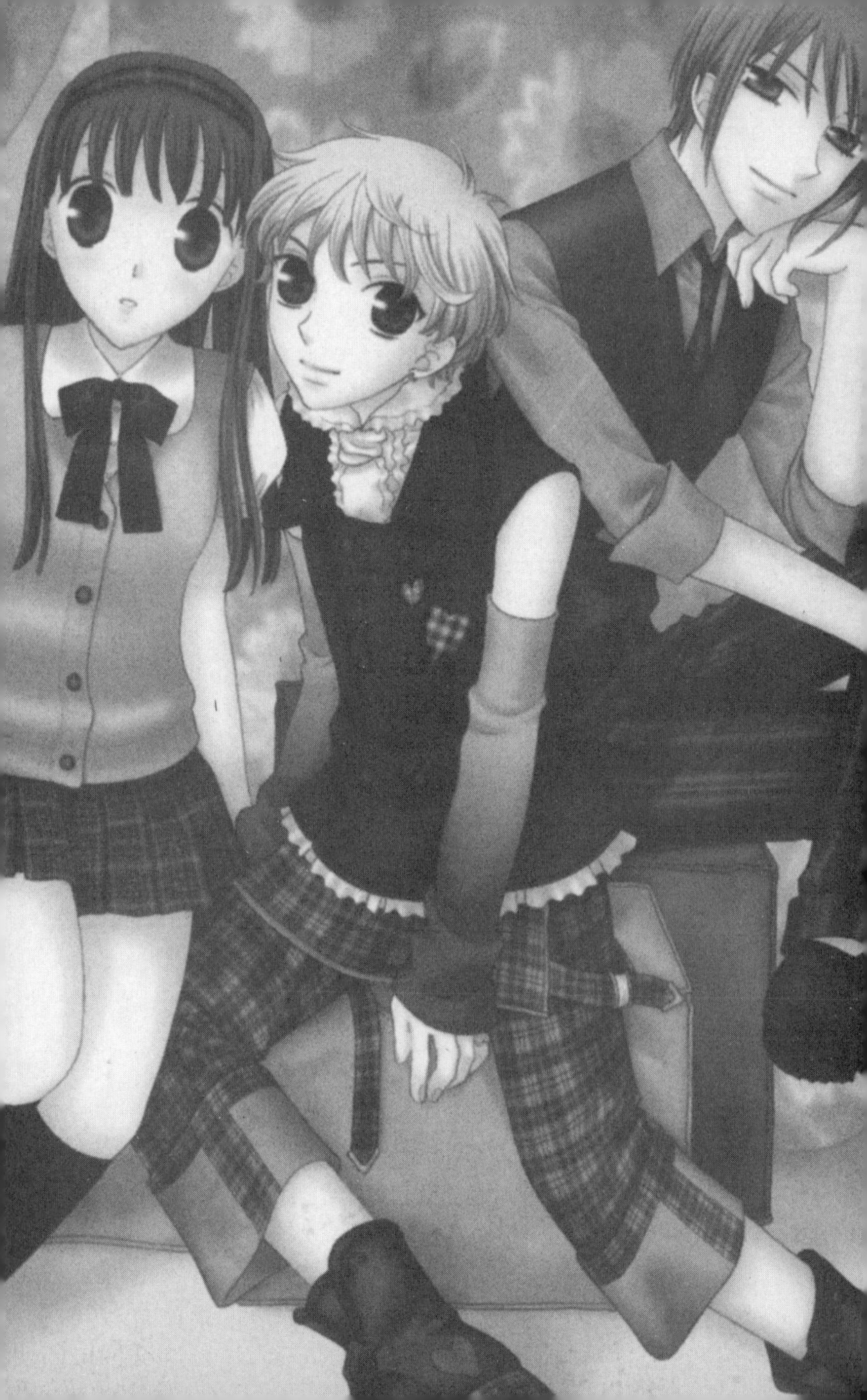

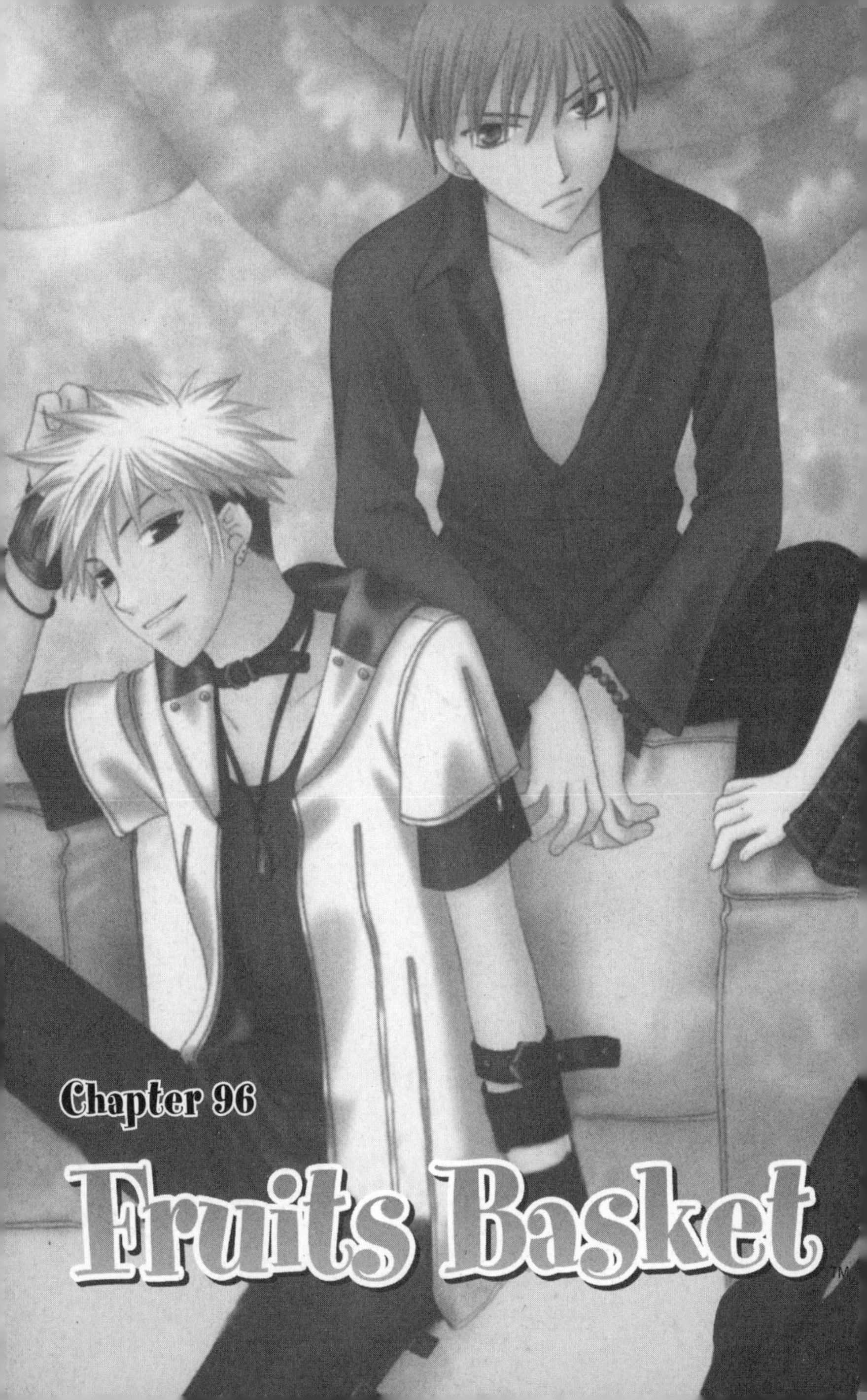
Chapter 96
Fruits Basket™

Filler Sketch

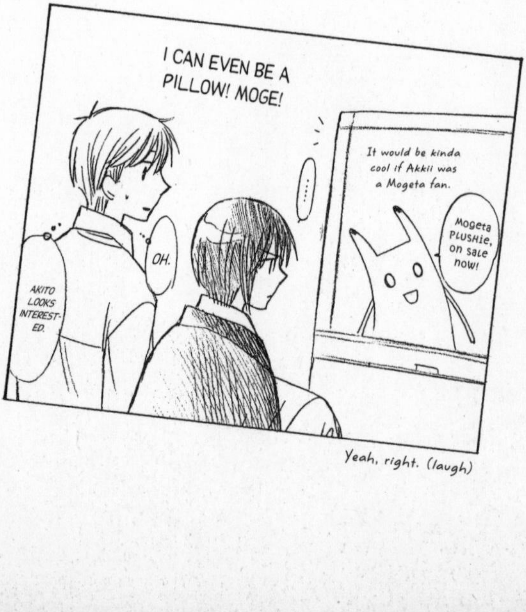
It would be kinda cool if Akkii was a Mogeta fan.
Mogeta PLUSHIE, on sale now!
I CAN EVEN BE A PILLOW! MOGE!
......
OH.
AKITO LOOKS INTEREST-ED.

Yeah, right. (laugh)

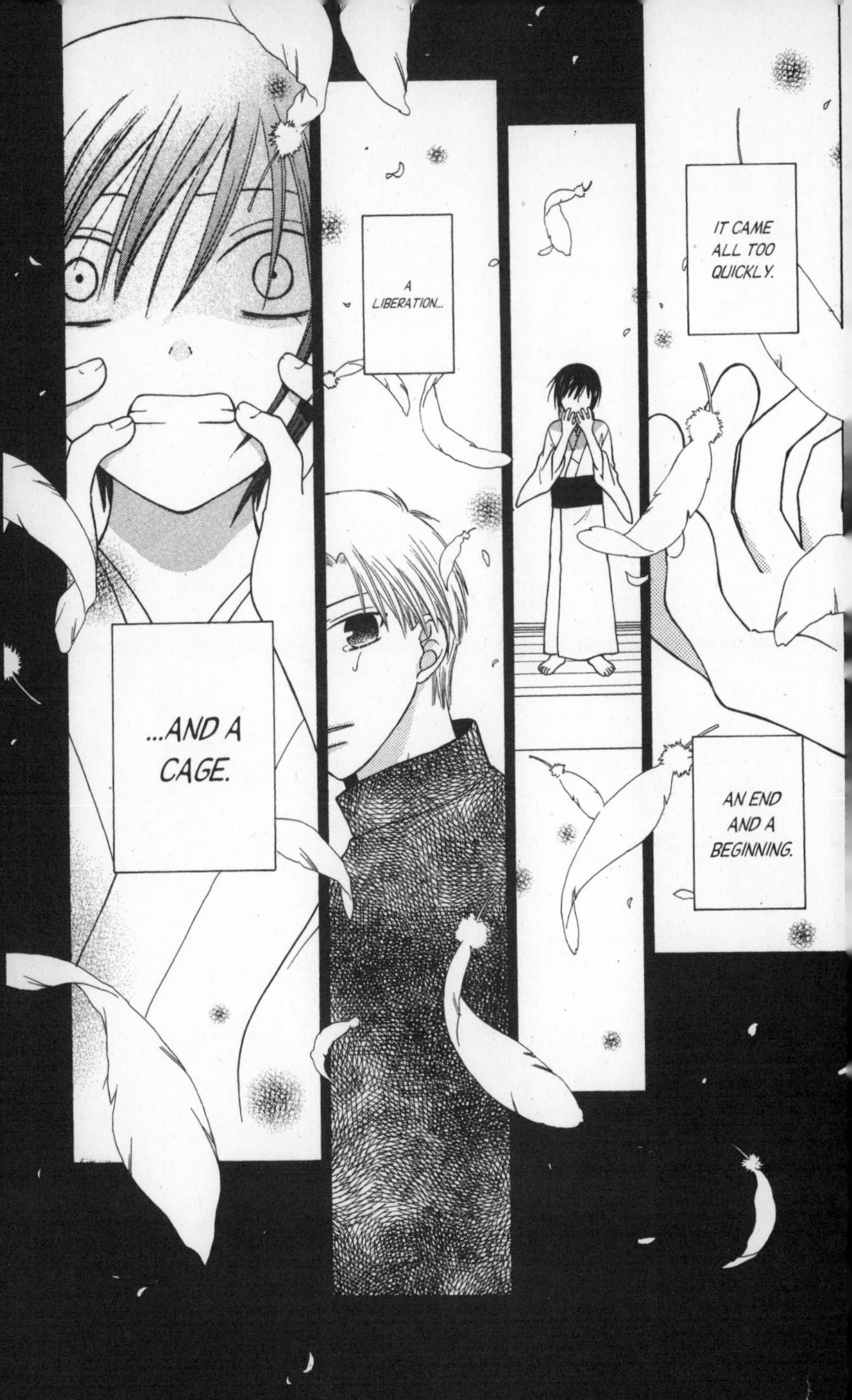
IT CAME ALL TOO QUICKLY.
AN END AND A BEGINNING.
A LIBERATION...
...AND A CAGE.

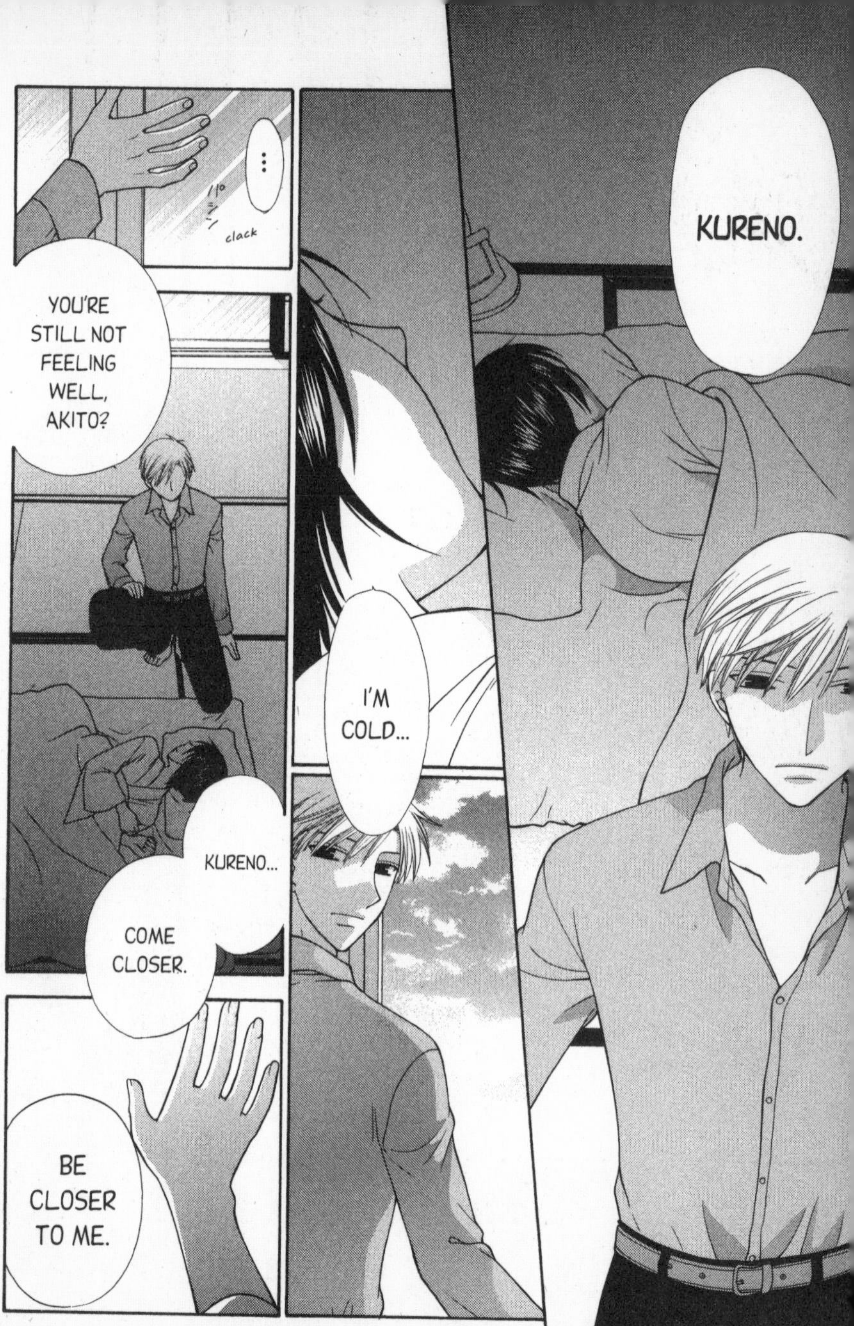
KURENO.
I'M COLD...
KURENO...
COME CLOSER.
...
clack
YOU'RE STILL NOT FEELING WELL, AKITO?
BE CLOSER TO ME.

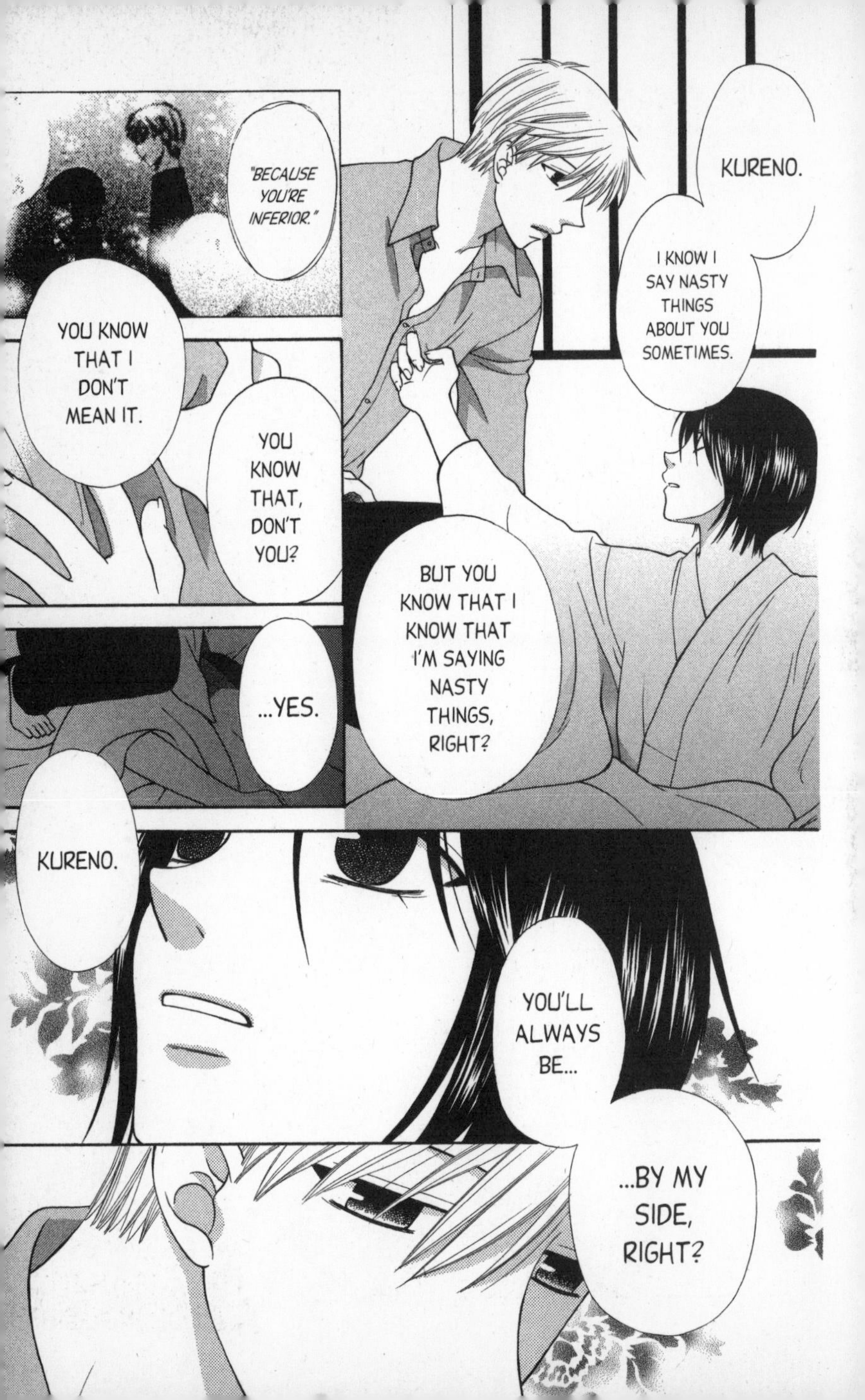
KURENO.
I KNOW I SAY NASTY THINGS ABOUT YOU SOMETIMES.
BUT YOU KNOW THAT I KNOW THAT I'M SAYING NASTY THINGS, RIGHT?
"BECAUSE YOU'RE INFERIOR."
YOU KNOW THAT, DON'T YOU?
YOU KNOW THAT I DON'T MEAN IT.
...YES.
KURENO.
YOU'LL ALWAYS BE...
...BY MY SIDE, RIGHT?

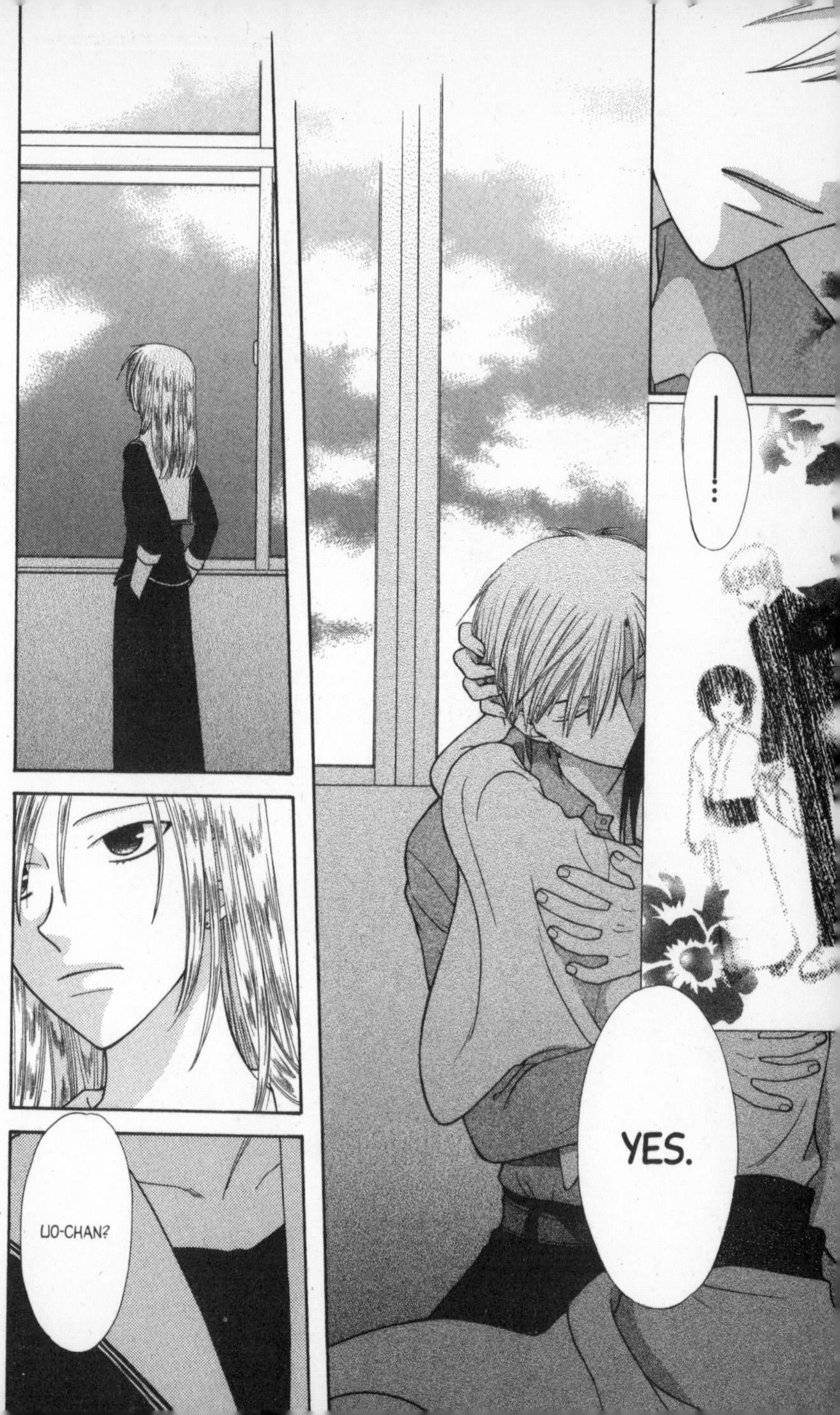
!...
YES.
UO-CHAN?

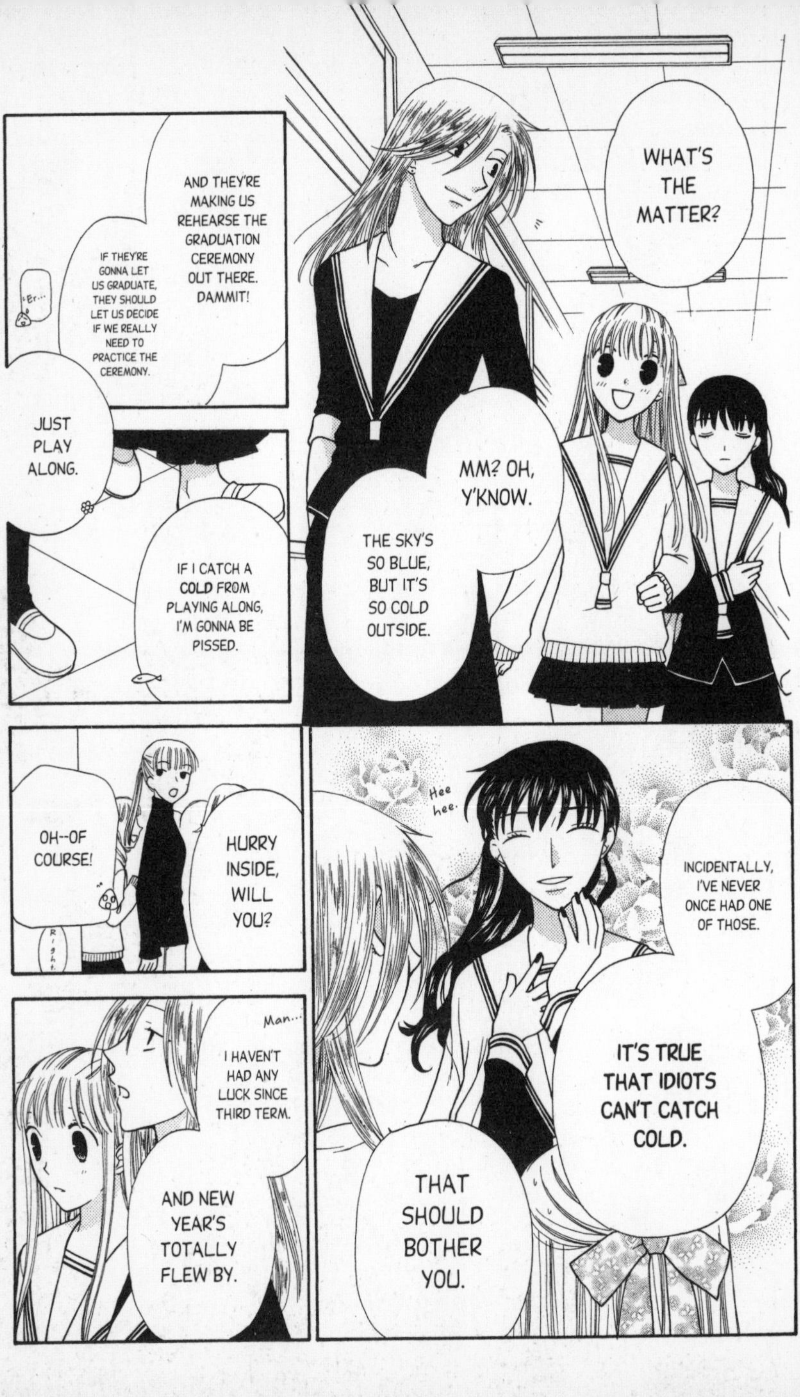
WHAT'S THE MATTER?
MM? OH, Y'KNOW.
THE SKY'S SO BLUE, BUT IT'S SO COLD OUTSIDE.
AND THEY'RE MAKING US REHEARSE THE GRADUATION CEREMONY OUT THERE. DAMMIT!
IF THEY'RE GONNA LET US GRADUATE, THEY SHOULD LET US DECIDE IF WE REALLY NEED TO PRACTICE THE CEREMONY.
Er...
JUST PLAY ALONG.
IF I CATCH A COLD FROM PLAYING ALONG, I'M GONNA BE PISSED.
Hee hee.
INCIDENTALLY, I'VE NEVER ONCE HAD ONE OF THOSE.
IT'S TRUE THAT IDIOTS CAN'T CATCH COLD.
THAT SHOULD BOTHER YOU.
HURRY INSIDE, WILL YOU?
OH--OF COURSE!
Right.
Man...
I HAVEN'T HAD ANY LUCK SINCE THIRD TERM.
AND NEW YEAR'S TOTALLY FLEW BY.

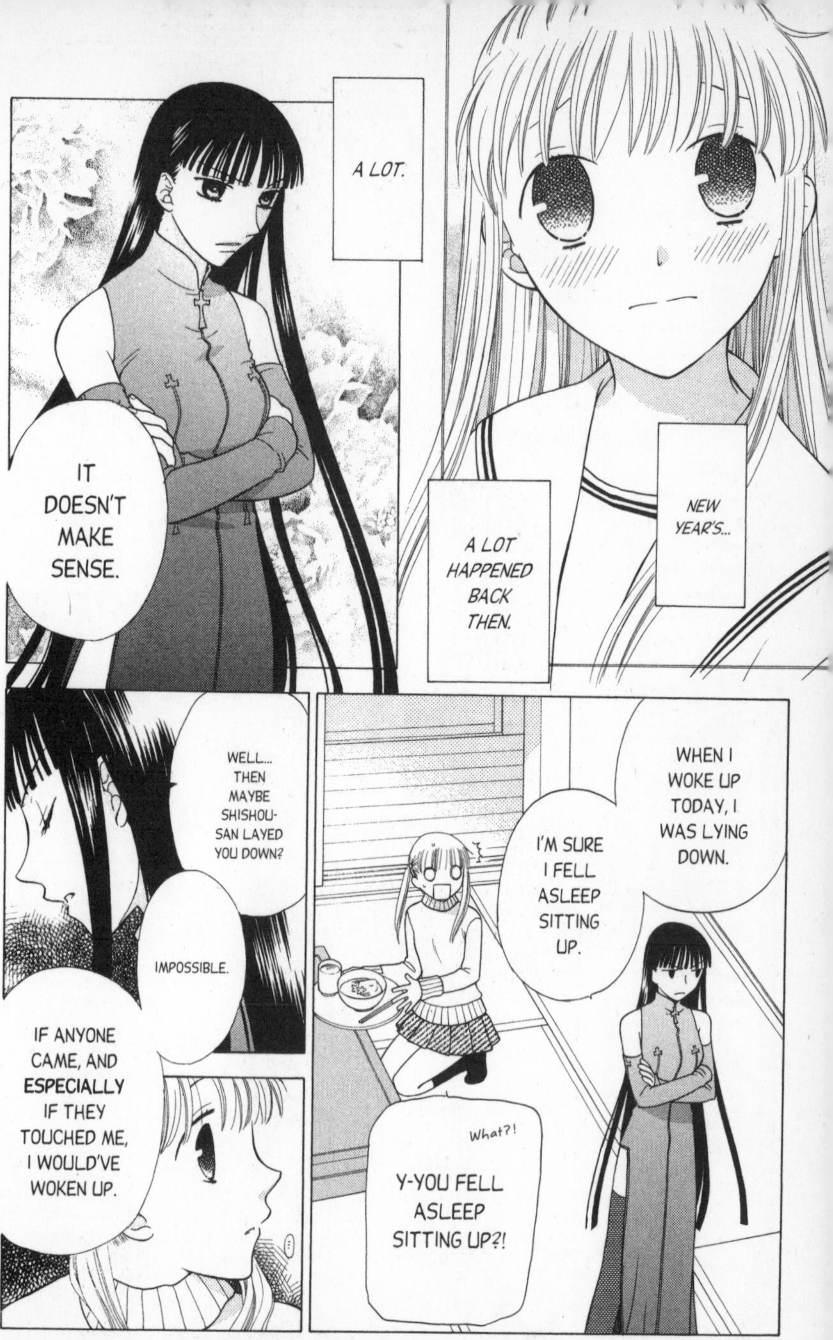
NEW YEAR'S...
A LOT HAPPENED BACK THEN.
A LOT.
IT DOESN'T MAKE SENSE.
WHEN I WOKE UP TODAY, I WAS LYING DOWN.
I'M SURE I FELL ASLEEP SITTING UP.
What?!
Y-YOU FELL ASLEEP SITTING UP?!
WELL... THEN MAYBE SHISHOU-SAN LAYED YOU DOWN?
IMPOSSIBLE.
IF ANYONE CAME, AND **ESPECIALLY** IF THEY TOUCHED ME, I WOULD'VE WOKEN UP.
...

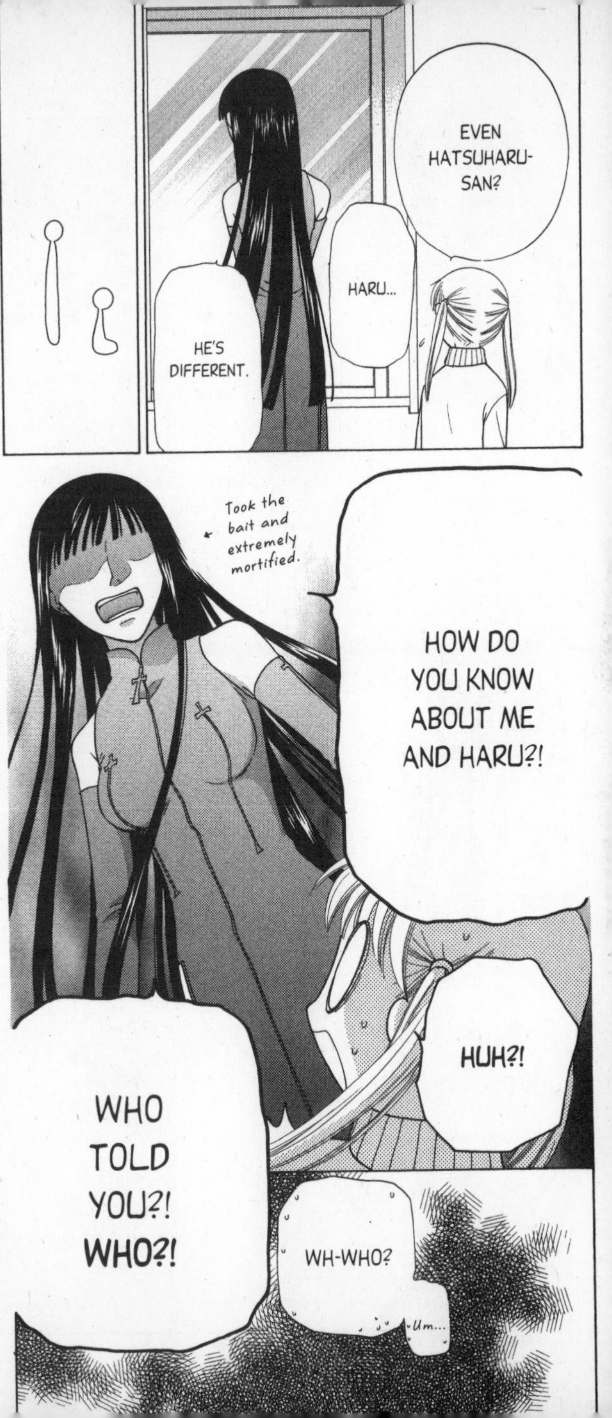
EVEN HATSUHARU-SAN?
HARU...
HE'S DIFFERENT.
HOW DO YOU KNOW ABOUT ME AND HARU?!
Took the bait and extremely mortified.
HUH?!
WHO TOLD YOU?! WHO?!
WH-WHO?
Um...

Fruits Basket 17

Pleased to meet you and hello. This is Takaya, presenting Volume 17. The cover is Hana-chan!

...Somehow it's been no time at all. I feel like time's passing by very quickly these days; I don't know if it's because I'm pushing forward or if it's because of my age. There are a lot of games on sale that I want to play, too, but I don't have the time, so I feel like they're piling up...

There may be people who think, "If you're not going to play it now, buy it later!" but I want to have it on hand. (How can I say what I mean here?) So that someday, when I have time, I can start playing. I wonder if anyone can understand that feeling (laugh).

Well then, please enjoy Furuba 17!

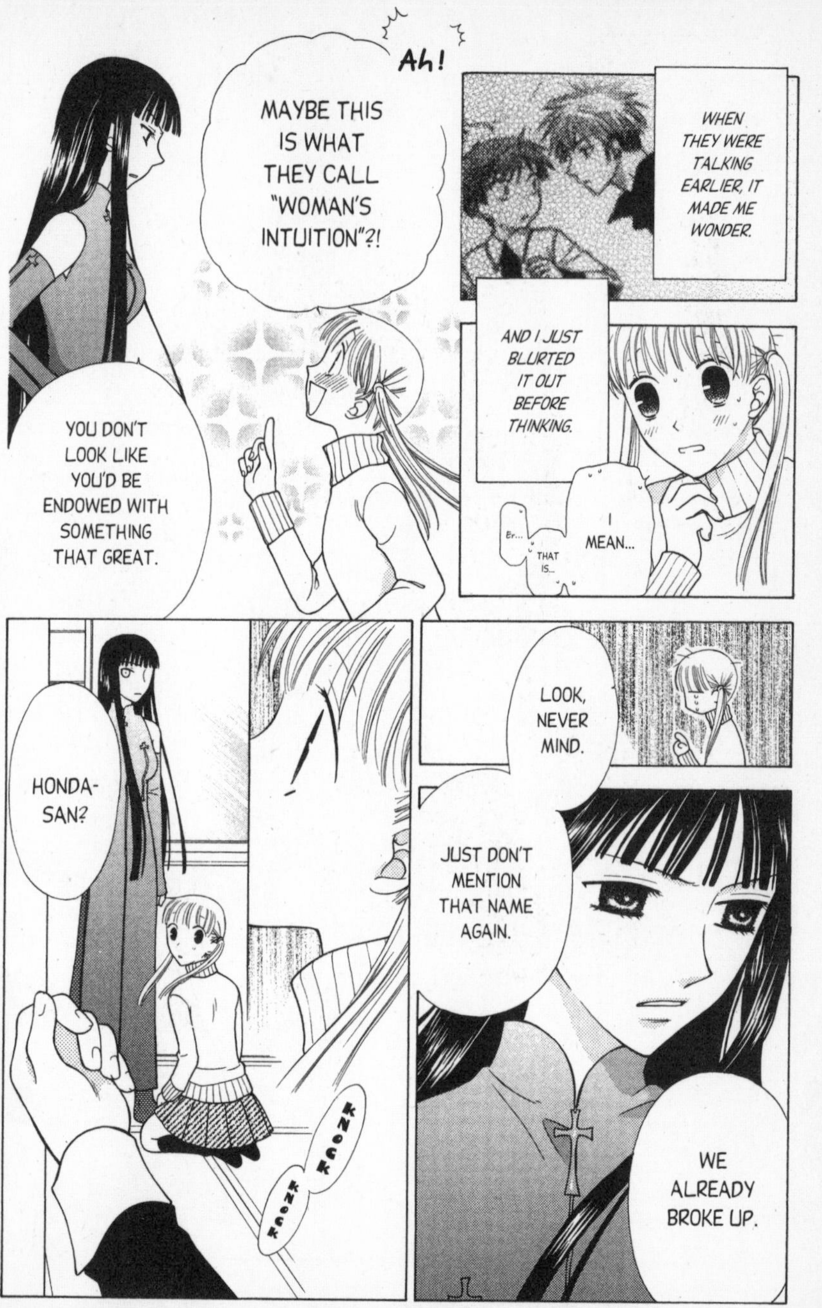
WHEN THEY WERE TALKING EARLIER, IT MADE ME WONDER.
AND I JUST BLURTED IT OUT BEFORE THINKING.
I MEAN...
Er... THAT IS...
Ah!
MAYBE THIS IS WHAT THEY CALL "WOMAN'S INTUITION"?!
YOU DON'T LOOK LIKE YOU'D BE ENDOWED WITH SOMETHING THAT GREAT.
LOOK, NEVER MIND.
JUST DON'T MENTION THAT NAME AGAIN.
WE ALREADY BROKE UP.
HONDA-SAN?
KNOCK
KNOCK

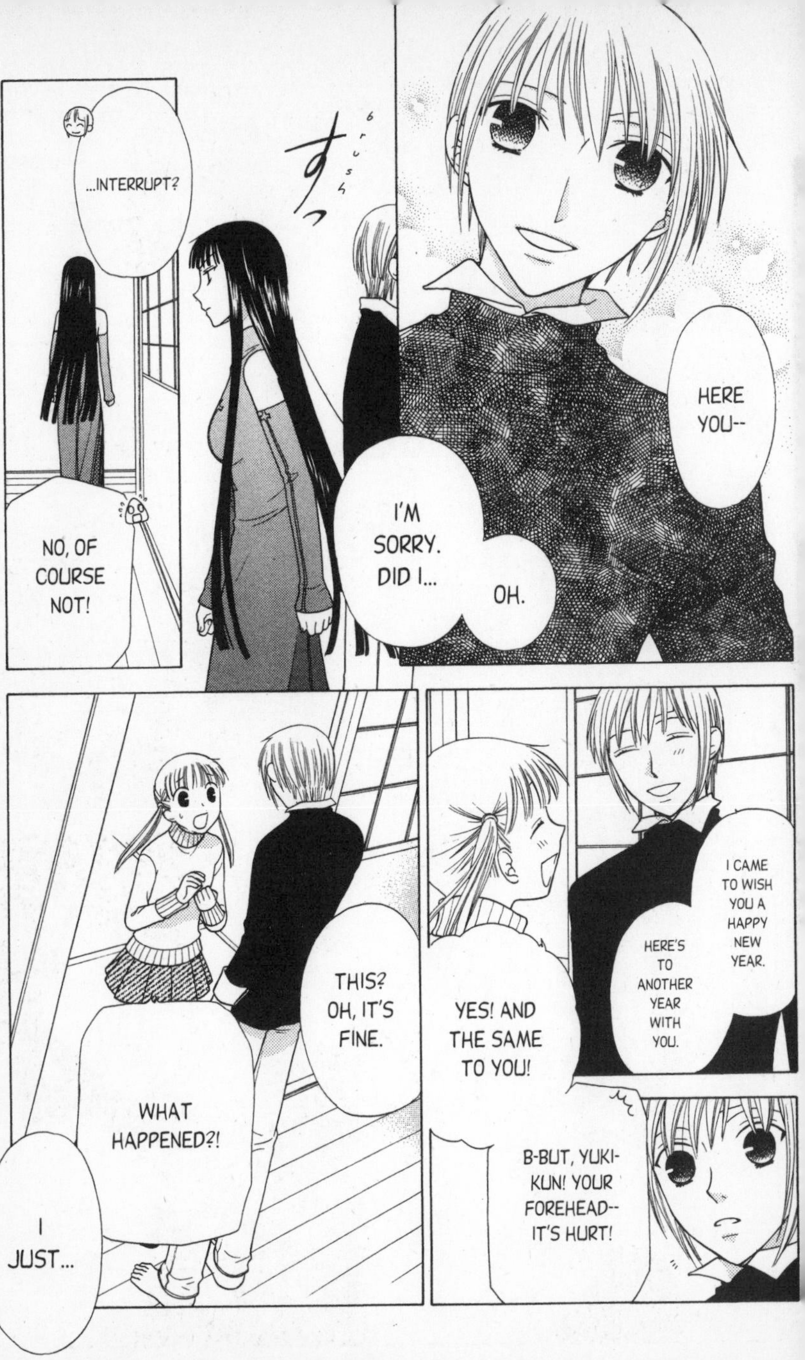
HERE YOU--
OH.
I'M SORRY. DID I...
brush
...INTERRUPT?
NO, OF COURSE NOT!
I CAME TO WISH YOU A HAPPY NEW YEAR.
HERE'S TO ANOTHER YEAR WITH YOU.
YES! AND THE SAME TO YOU!
B-BUT, YUKI-KUN! YOUR FOREHEAD-- IT'S HURT!
THIS? OH, IT'S FINE.
WHAT HAPPENED?!
I JUST...

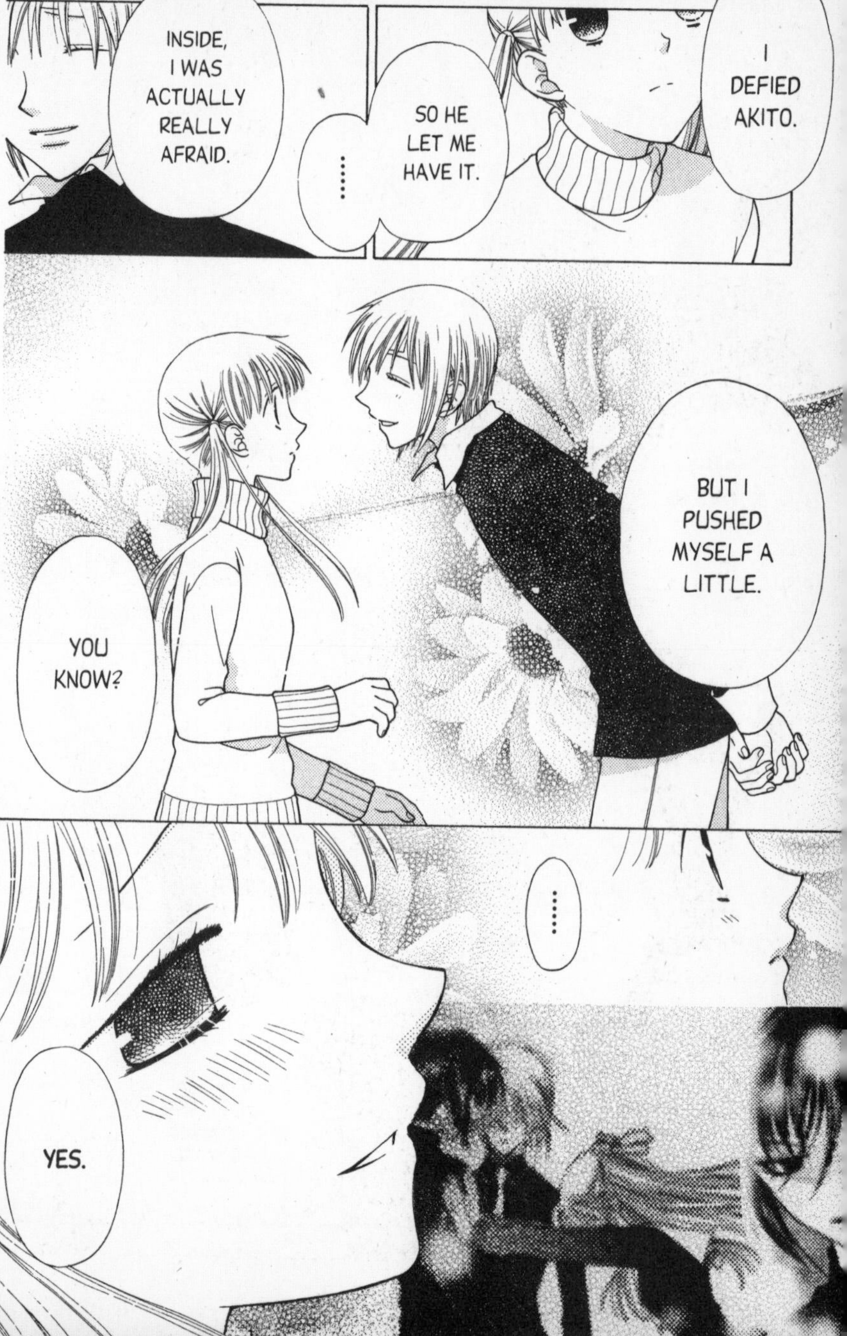
I DEFIED AKITO.
SO HE LET ME HAVE IT.
......
INSIDE, I WAS ACTUALLY REALLY AFRAID.
BUT I PUSHED MYSELF A LITTLE.
YOU KNOW?
......
YES.

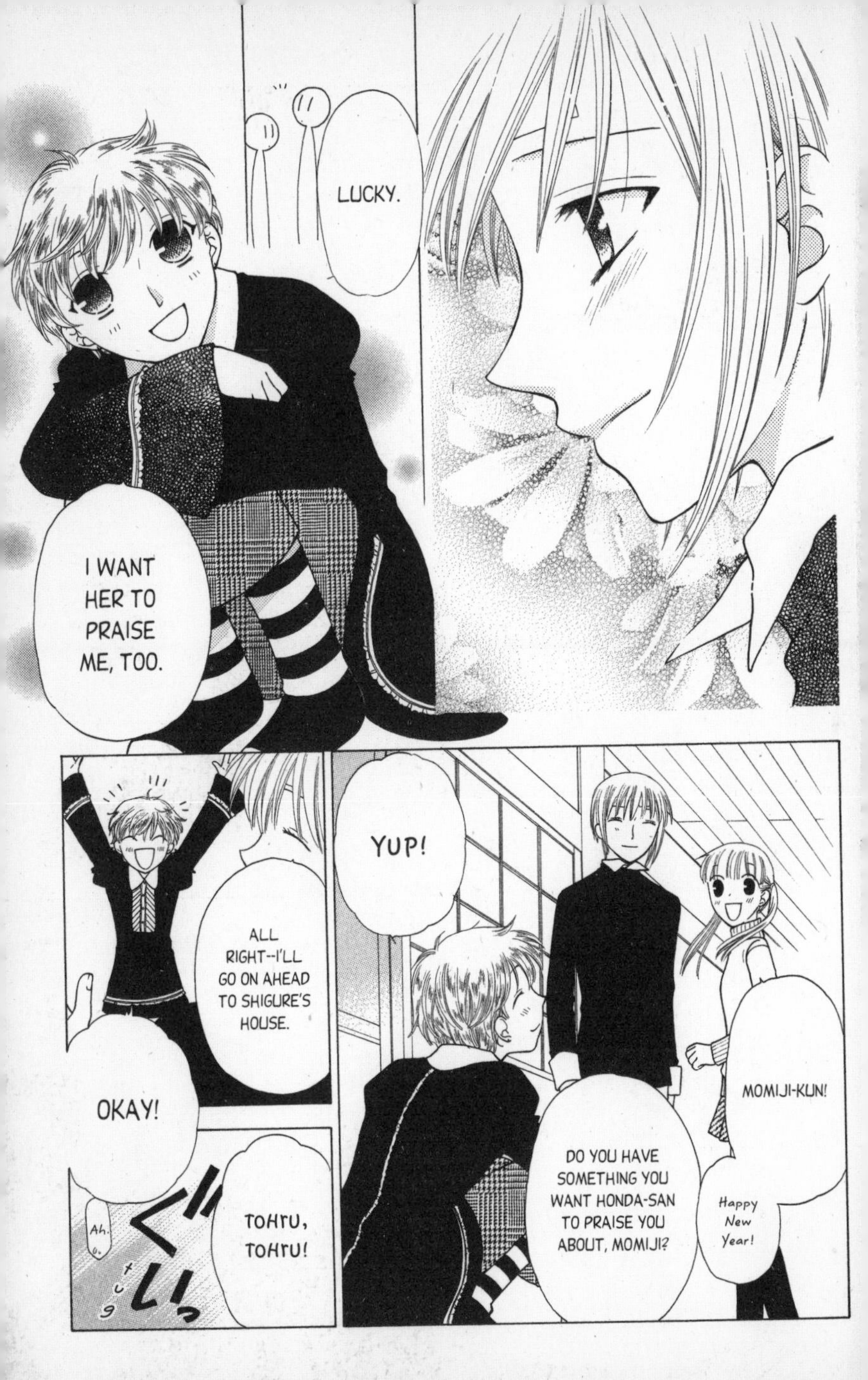
LUCKY.
I WANT HER TO PRAISE ME, TOO.
MOMIJI-KUN!
Happy New Year!
DO YOU HAVE SOMETHING YOU WANT HONDA-SAN TO PRAISE YOU ABOUT, MOMIJI?
YUP!
ALL RIGHT--I'LL GO ON AHEAD TO SHIGURE'S HOUSE.
OKAY!
TOHRU, TOHRU!
tug
Ah.

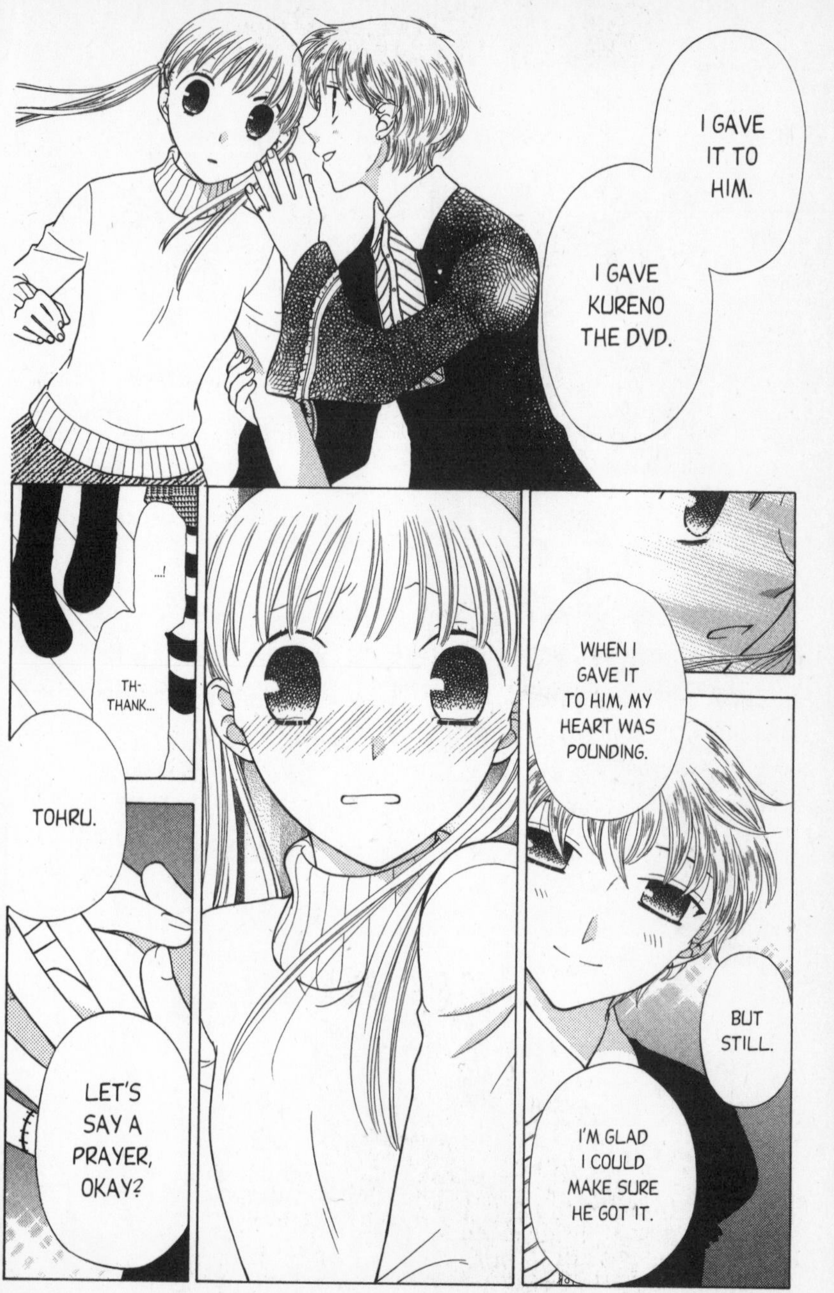
I GAVE IT TO HIM.
I GAVE KURENO THE DVD.
WHEN I GAVE IT TO HIM, MY HEART WAS POUNDING.
BUT STILL.
I'M GLAD I COULD MAKE SURE HE GOT IT.
...!
TH- THANK...
TOHRU.
LET'S SAY A PRAYER, OKAY?

Next Time On...

COME BACK FOR ANOTHER FUN AND CRAZY VISIT
TO THE MIYASHITA HOUSEHOLD AS SAKURA MARKS
OFF YEAR NUMBER ONE WITH HER NEWLY FOUND
BROTHERS! AN IMPORTANT FAMILY EVENT IS
COMING UP-- MASASHI'S BIRTHDAY! HOW WILL
SAKURA CELEBRATE THIS WACKY, FEMININE,
WACKILY FEMININE BROTHER'S SPECIAL DAY?

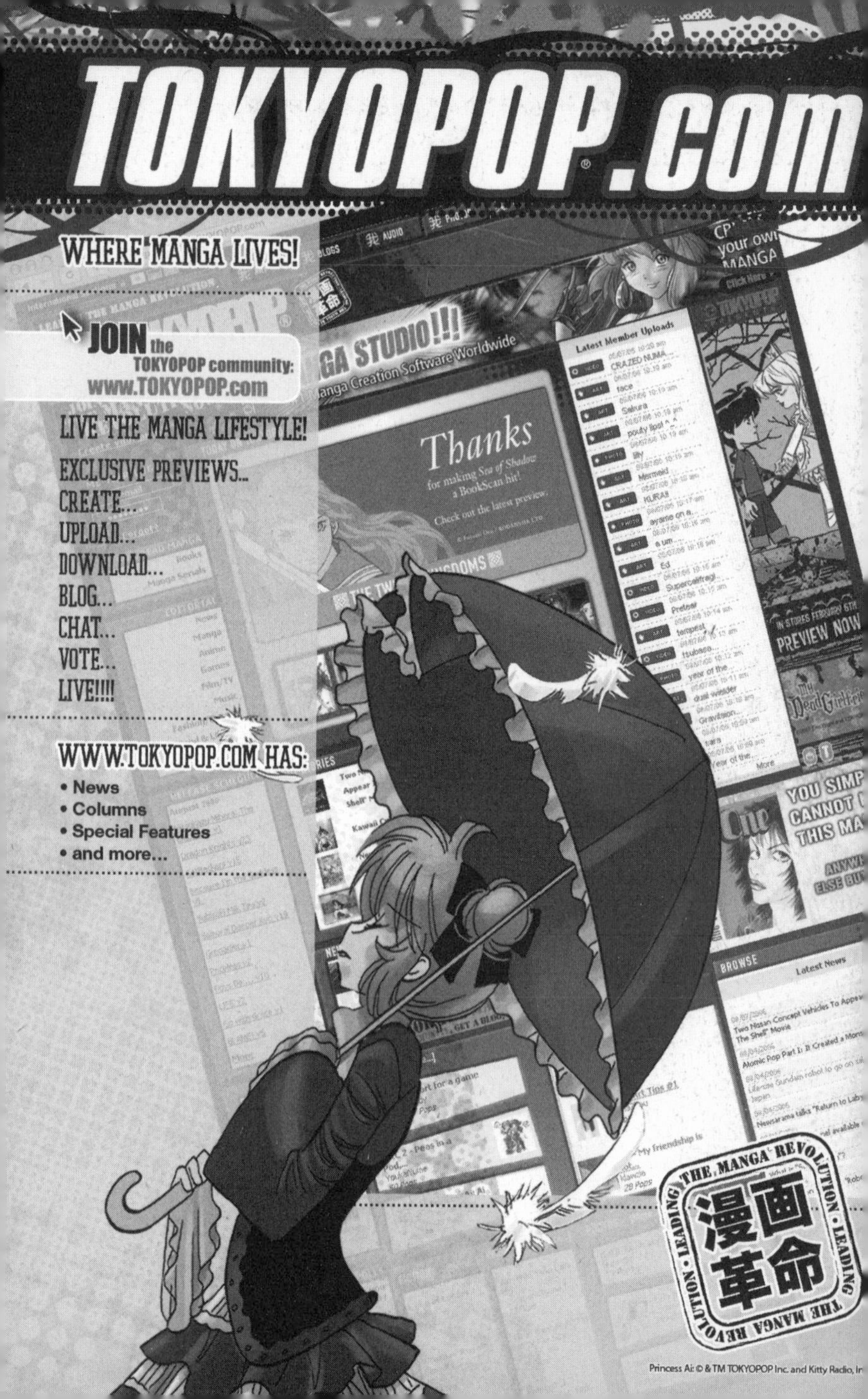
TOKYOPOP®.com
WHERE MANGA LIVES!
JOIN the TOKYOPOP community: www.TOKYOPOP.com
LIVE THE MANGA LIFESTYLE!
EXCLUSIVE PREVIEWS...
CREATE...
UPLOAD...
DOWNLOAD...
BLOG...
CHAT...
VOTE...
LIVE!!!!
WWW.TOKYOPOP.COM HAS:
• News
• Columns
• Special Features
• and more...
THE MANGA REVOLUTION • LEADING • THE MANGA REVOLUTION • LEADING
漫画革命
Princess Ai: © & TM TOKYOPOP Inc. and Kitty Radio, In

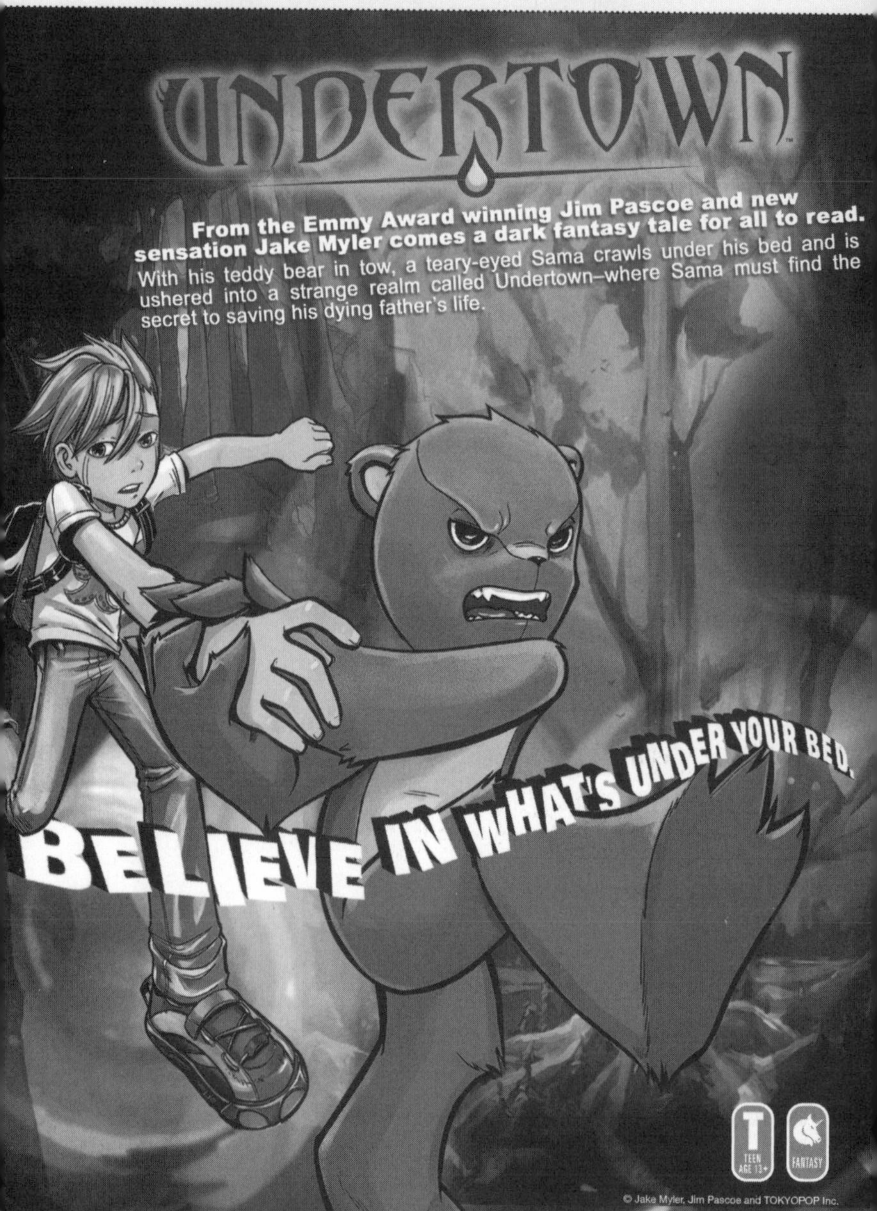
UNDERTOWN
From the Emmy Award winning Jim Pascoe and new sensation Jake Myler comes a dark fantasy tale for all to read.
With his teddy bear in tow, a teary-eyed Sama crawls under his bed and is ushered into a strange realm called Undertown–where Sama must find the secret to saving his dying father's life.
BELIEVE IN WHAT'S UNDER YOUR BED.
T TEEN AGE 13+
FANTASY
© Jake Myler, Jim Pascoe and TOKYOPOP Inc.

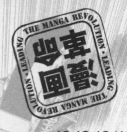

STOP!

This is the back of the book. You wouldn't want to spoil a great ending!

This book is printed "manga-style," in the authentic Japanese right-to-left format. Since none of the artwork has been flipped or altered, readers get to experience the story just as the creator intended. You've been asking for it, so TOKYOPOP® delivered: authentic, hot-off-the-press, and far more fun!

DIRECTIONS

1
2
3
4
5
6
7
8
9
10

If this is your first time reading manga-style, here's a quick guide to help you understand how it works.

It's easy... just start in the top right panel and follow the numbers. Have fun, and look for more 100% authentic manga from TOKYOPOP®!

THE MANGA REVOLUTION • LEADING THE MANGA REVOLUTION • LEADING 漫画革命

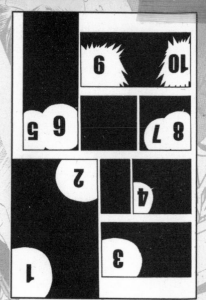